Genealogies of Conflict

Ran Greenstein

Class, Identity, and State in Palestine/Israel and South Africa

Wesleyan University Press

Published by
University Press of New England
Hanover and London

Wesleyan University Press
Published by University Press of New England, Hanover, NH 03755
© 1995 by Ran Greenstein
All rights reserved
Printed in the United States of America   5 4 3 2 1
CIP data appear at the end of the book

Contents

	Preface	vii
1	The Comparative Setting	1
2	Analytical Framework	12
3	Land, Labor, and Territorial Expansion	27
	Palestine/Israel	27
	South Africa	47
	Comparison and Conclusions	65
4	Identity Formation and Political Conflict	71
	Palestine/Israel	72
	South Africa	90
	Comparison and Conclusions	115
5	Development, Dependency, and Dispossession	124
	Palestine/Israel	124
	South Africa	157
	Comparison and Conclusions	189
	Appendix: The Politics of Sources	195
6	Nationalism, State, and the Struggle for Power	199
	Palestine/Israel	199
	South Africa	231
	Comparison and Conclusions	259

7	Historical and Theoretical Implications	263
	Bibliography	276
	Index	294

Preface

No scholarly work on highly charged political issues can itself avoid being implicated in controversy. It would be impossible to write about any aspect of Israeli/Palestinian and South African histories, let alone compare the two, without becoming involved in debates over basic issues of facts, figures, sources, and interpretations. This book is no exception. The mere suggestion that Israel and South Africa can be meaningfully compared, regardless of the focus and goals of the comparison, is highly contentious in the Israeli context, as it conflicts sharply with the self-image of most Israeli Jews, scholars and academics included. It is no wonder, then, that no comparative study of this nature has been undertaken from a mainstream Israeli position, and the few critical attempts to embark on such a project have met with strong public-academic condemnation. Not surprisingly, Palestinian Arabs are more open to the topic and, indeed, have used the comparison quite extensively as a political tool in the international arena. Serious scholarly attempts to explore the value and meaning of the comparison from a historical perspective have been rare, however.

The situation in South Africa is somewhat different. The notion that the two conflict situations exhibit many similarities is widespread, but it has been put to rather different political uses. The apartheid government in the past, and the Conservative Party and other right-wing forces in the present, have used the Israeli example to argue for white or Afrikaner right to national self-determination. The international recognition of Israel (in its pre-1967 boundaries) as a Jewish state has moved certain white South African forces to claim similar legitimacy for their own political projects. So much so in fact, that in late 1993 Alon Leal, then Israeli ambassador to South Africa, publicly requested the right-wing Afrikaner Volksfront to stop using the Israeli case to justify their own racially and ethnically exclusionary cause. On the other side of the political spectrum, identification with the Palestinian struggle has been common among the South African liberation movements, though the latter have never needed to bolster their cause by drawing on this analogy.

How does the present study stand in relation to this controversy? Although not following an explicit political agenda, I am aware that the comparison itself, and the historical interpretations offered here, might lend themselves to political use and abuse. This is inevitable since knowledge cannot be evaluated and deployed independently of the power relations within which it is produced and consumed.

My main concern in this respect is not to reject political involvement but, rather, to establish the merits of this study as a scholarly project that has managed to give due consideration to the many differing and contradictory positions advanced in relation to the conflicts discussed here. That the outcome is not politically neutral has little to do with conscious bias in the selection of facts and figures; rather, it stems from a belief that there is no contradiction between scholarly objectivity in the identification and evaluation of relevant data on the one hand, and adopting positions with regard to politically and morally controversial issues on the other.

It would be useful, therefore, to set out the political context within which this project has been carried out. When I began working on a draft for the first chapter in late 1988, the political situation in both countries looked rather bleak. The high expectations generated by the popular uprisings in the black townships of South Africa and the refugee camps and towns of the occupied West Bank and the Gaza Strip had dissipated as those uprisings degenerated into a seemingly endless cycle of bloodshed and repression. By the time the last chapter in what had meanwhile become a Ph.D. dissertation was concluded in December 1991, the situation had changed for the better. The November 1991 Middle East peace conference in Madrid and the launching of the Convention for a Democratic South Africa (CODESA) in Johannesburg in the following month both signified, despite their significant shortcomings, important steps forward.

At the time these lines are written, the transition to a democratic political system in South Africa has been completed at the national level, while the future of the agreements between the State of Israel and the Palestine Liberation Organization is still murky. Although the progress made in the former case is obviously more significant, there is room for cautious optimism in the latter as well, despite the numerous debilitating difficulties the process has encountered so far. Given the historical focus of the book, the changing political circumstances have had little direct impact on the theses advanced here.

However, as the divergent political dynamics within the two countries have become more distinct, my confidence has increased that the social dynamics of exclusion (in Palestine/Israel) and incorporation (in South Africa) identified in this work are not mere artifacts of my interpretive faculties. As mentioned earlier, this book originates in a Ph.D. dissertation in sociology, submitted to the University of Wisconsin-Madison in December 1991. Since then it has gone through substantial revision, both to incorporate new material and to cover several issues in greater detail and a more nuanced manner.

As is usual for projects of this nature, the work could not have been completed without the help and support provided by a number of people during its various stages. In addition, the financial help of the Graduate School of the University of Wisconsin, the Jennings Randolph Program of the United States Institute of Peace, and the Research Authority of Haifa University is gratefully acknowledged. Sammy Smooha of Haifa University has supported my academic work from its inception and made a crucial contribution to the task of formulating the questions underlying the project. His visit to Madison in 1988, and the many years before and since in which we have worked together, were essential to my thinking on the topic. Esmail Bagheri-Najmi provided support, peer pressure, and intellectual stimulation as a friend and a fellow graduate student. More than anyone else he has helped me tackle the theoretical issues involved in the project and significantly shaped my analytical approach.

I would also like to thank fellow graduate students Saraswati Sunindyo and Nalinee Tantuvanit for their support. My dissertation supervisor, Erik Olin Wright, offered extensive and valuable comments on the dissertation manuscript during its development. Gay Seidman provided essential help in getting me introduced to South Africa and has commented most usefully on successive drafts of the dissertation. During my stay in Madison I also benefited from discussions with Richard Lachmann, Gerry Marwell, Richard Ralston, and Herbert Hill. My frequent visits to South Africa were made fruitful by discussions with Carolyn Hamilton, Leslie Witz, and Mona Younis. My parents, Hava and Moshe, have shared the burden and joy of helping me complete my studies and I wish to express my gratitude to them. Above all, I would like to acknowledge the consistent support, useful insights, and emotional sustenance provided by Anriette Esterhuysen, to whom this work is dedicated.

Johannesburg   R.G.
March 1995

Genealogies of Conflict

1 | The Comparative Setting

Five years ago, a collection of essays titled *The Elusive Search for Peace* (Giliomee and Gagiano 1990) sought to demonstrate the intractable nature of political conflict in three of the most persistent conflict situations on earth: South Africa, Israel, and Northern Ireland. All three have since undergone striking changes in the nature of the political conflicts that shape and frame their ongoing development. This is particularly true for South Africa and Palestine/Israel—the two societies on which this study focuses. South Africa's interim constitution of December 1993, a product of over three years of negotiations, paved the way for the April 1994 general elections and the inauguration of the first democratically elected government in the country's history. Somewhat less dramatically, the September 1993 mutual recognition agreement between the State of Israel and the Palestine Liberation Organization, and the beginning of a phased Israeli withdrawal from the occupied territories of the West Bank and Gaza Strip, signal a new era of interaction between the two adversaries. In both cases, conflicts that have long been seen as having no solution seem closer than ever to a peaceful resolution.

These changes are particularly remarkable in view of the fact that only a few years ago political conflict in these two areas reached unprecedented levels of violence and acrimony. In the late 1980s the Palestinian uprising in the occupied territories was characterized by massive grassroots mobilization and opposition to military rule, and it encountered equally massive and violent repression by the Israeli occupation forces. In a similar manner, the struggle of the South African masses against racial oppression had intensified since the mid-1980s, leading to the death and detention of thousands of activists and ordinary people alike. In both societies a change in the nature of conflict became evident with the direct intervention of popular forces in the political process. Armed clashes between states and cross-border raids against external enemies receded in importance, and the increasingly explosive internal arena rose to political prominence.

There are obvious similarities in these responses by members of the subordinate groups in both Palestine/Israel and South Africa, but the groups have adopted different attitudes toward the solutions to the conflicts. The growing awareness of the inevitability and desirability of the political incorporation of all South African citizens in a unified nonracial system, as demanded all along by antiapartheid forces, has led to the demise of the apartheid regime and the coming into being of the new South Africa. In contrast, significant segments of the Israeli and Palestinian populations have recognized the principles of national self-determination, making the eventual partition of the territory between them and the formation of two separate states likely developments.

These current events have, as their immediate background, a relatively brief history. The political moves taken since February 1990 by the South African government and the major liberation organizations—the African National Congress and its allies—toward a negotiated settlement were based on an understanding that a viable solution must be based on integrative principles. Most parties to the South African conflict, as well as world public opinion, have come to share this perception. Radical forces on both sides of the racial divide, largely marginalized since the 1994 elections, do not pose a serious challenge to the notion that the South African state should incorporate all its citizens on an equal basis. The only exception is the extraparliamentary white right-wing, organized in the Conservative Party and the Afrikaner Volksfront, though even they do not call for an exclusively white South Africa, or part thereof, and satisfy themselves with a quest for an autonomous homeland that would retain cultural distinctness within the larger South African framework.

At the same time that South African forces were moving in the direction of political incorporation, Palestinians and Israelis were moving in a very different direction. The declaration of independence for the State of Palestine by the Palestine National Council in November 1988, the mutual recognition agreement with Israel, and the implementation of self-rule in the occupied territories in 1994 have set in motion processes of separation. Their culmination in the form of political independence is not preordained, however, although the majority of Palestinian Arabs, together with a substantial proportion of Israeli Jews, and virtually the entire international community, have expressed support for a solution based on the principle of separation of Jews from Arabs in the form of two independent states. Most opponents of such a two-state solution, and in particular those who are religiously motivated, do not offer an integrative alternative but advocate instead an exclusionary setup in which one group or the other is to be eliminated from the scene.

Posing the Question

Why two apparently similar conflict situations, bringing to mind images of unarmed militant youth fighting for liberation against heavily armed occupation forces, should call for such different solutions is the crucial question considered in this work. I argue that the nature of the recently negotiated solutions reflects a fundamental divergence in the locus of political conflict, manifested in various ways throughout the modern history of the two countries. Whereas in Palestine/Israel conflict has been defined as a process that primarily involves struggles between two external entities, in South Africa it has been defined as an internal struggle that takes place within a single political framework. This distinction has little to do with geography per se, but rather with the terms in which political actors in the two countries have come to perceive their situation.

A comparative historical study of the formative historical processes of class, identity, and state in Palestine/Israel and South Africa can provide insights into the emergence and evolution of the conflicts that have shaped the histories of these countries from their inception. By focusing on specific combinations of general historical factors in each of these cases, we can account for their similarities as well as their unique characteristics. The comparison can help us identify features particular to each case as well as those of more general relevance.

In principle, any society can be compared to any other society. Palestine/Israel and South Africa have several features in common that make the comparison particularly interesting. Both societies came into being in the course of conflict between indigenous people and settler immigrants. The process of settlement took place in the context of the overall expansion of European political and economic domination of the rest of the world, though in different historical periods. The majority of settlers, especially in Palestine/Israel, did not come from the ranks of the principal colonizing power—the British Empire. Before independence, then, both Palestine/Israel and South Africa could be seen as instances of what Scott Atran (1989) terms a "surrogate colonization" process. This should not be taken to mean that Zionist settlement before 1948, the State of Israel since then, and indeed twentieth-century South Africa exhibit all the features of classical European colonialism. Their similarities to other colonial projects, however, especially with regard to relations with indigenous people, are substantial enough to justify looking at their formative processes as part of the overall historical process of colonization of the non-European world.

In contrast to most other cases of colonial settlement, indigenous people in Palestine/Israel and South Africa have never ceased to pose a fundamental challenge to settler domination. Indigenous people in other colonies were largely exterminated, as happened in the Caribbean, North America, and Australia, or they merged to varying degrees with settlers, as in Central and South America. In other places, European powers took over Asian and African territories but later withdrew without leaving behind permanent settler populations. Only in a few places, most notably the two cases discussed here, is the conflict continuing as intensely as ever, and the originating violence, which always marks the founding of new states and nations, "remains at once excessive and powerless, insufficient in its result, lost in its own contradiction. It cannot manage to have itself forgotten, as in the case of states founded on a genocide or a quasi-extermination. Here, the violence of the origin must repeat itself indefinitely and act out its rightfulness in a legislative apparatus whose monstrosity fails to pay back" (Derrida 1987: 18). While these words refer specifically to South Africa, they capture equally well the essence of the Israeli-Palestinian conflict.

The colonial analogy allows us to place the conflicts in a specific historical context, though it is not meant to serve an explanatory function in itself. It is not offered as a theoretical model, nor is colonialism regarded here as a type of society with its distinct laws of motion. In this sense, I distance myself from conceptions that define colonialism as a social formation characterized by a clash between total opposites, which by definition cannot share any common ground among themselves (Fanon 1963; Balandier 1966; Memmi 1967; Sartre 1976). While typologies that identify specific models of colonialism (plantation, occupation, exploitation) offer a more elaborate picture, they share the assumption that colonialism is a special type of society, governed by a logic distinct from that of "normal" societies.

These common views take for granted in an uncritical manner existing colonial categories, rather than looking at them as having been constructed in a historical process of formation of interests, identities, and organizations. I maintain, in contrast, that colonizers and colonized have frequently come to share such cultural characteristics as religion and language; their political institutions have varied enormously in the extent to which they have accommodated indigenous people's participation in the exercise of power; their class structures have not necessarily reflected a rigid dichotomy. In short, colonial categories should not be seen as immutable, pitting two irreconcilable groups against each other, but as "problematic, contested, and changing . . . [since] the otherness of the colonized person was neither inherent nor stable; his or her difference had to be defined and maintained; social boundaries that were at one point clear would not necessarily remain so" (Cooper and Stoler 1989: 609–10).

Colonial models are neither sufficiently historical nor properly analytical. Their largely ahistorical nature is manifested in a general inability to account for the variety and changes in the nature, dynamics, and internal relations in colonial societies in terms of preconceived models. Thus both South Africa and Israel are commonly classified as settler colonial states. The two societies, however, have followed divergent historical courses, rendering the model useless as a predictive tool of their trajectories.

From an analytical point of view, colonial models are flawed in that they do not present clear positions with regard to the operation of theoretical concepts. They do not tell us if and how colonial societies differ from noncolonial societies (whatever definition one adopts for these categories) in the ways class, identity, and state manifest themselves, or in the patterns of interaction between these forces. In other words, they do not establish any *specific social-theoretical dynamics*—as distinct from historical descriptions—unique to colonialism that might serve to distinguish it analytically from other types of societies. As an alternative, a strategy of dealing with the multiplicity of colonial and postcolonial structures should involve a two-track approach: (1) study them in their historical specificity without imposing artificial boundaries between vaguely defined classes of cases (such as "mixed colonies"); (2) examine them by deploying general analytical concepts rather than by using idiosyncratic models (colonialism of a special type, deviant colonialism) that might serve as useful political labels but are not very helpful otherwise. The extension of this research strategy to the comparative field should not present special difficulties. The greater attention to the analytical dimension in comparative studies comes to some extent at the expense of historical specificity, but this could be justified in light of the potential rewards of stimulating research and making a contribution to theoretical elaboration.

Survey of Literature

A comparative study of the formation of conflict in the two societies offers a unique perspective from which to explore the various historical and theoretical issues raised in the context of settlement and resistance. Similarity does not mean identity, however, and pointing to certain common practices and structures should not imply that other, no less important, differences do not exist. Ethnic and racial conflicts are widespread phenomena and are not limited to South Africa and Palestine/Israel. And yet conflicts in these two places have consistently drawn extensive worldwide attention and have been frequently singled out by various bodies as, perhaps, the last major cases of colonial-type situations (Stevens and Elmessiri 1976: 183–214). In particular, military and economic relations between South Africa and Israel have been a controversial topic since the early 1970s. This issue led to a series of resolutions by international forums condemning Israel and demanding that it desist from and terminate all collaboration with South Africa. Several studies published in the last two decades seek to document the nature of these relations and assess their significance (Stevens and Elmessiri 1976; Chazan 1983; Adams 1984; Beit Hallahmi 1987; Hunter 1987; Joseph 1988). Only a few of these studies deal with the basic issue of concern here—the extent to which the two societies have historically developed in similar ways. Cooperation and similarity should not be confused, and they need to be analyzed separately. Extensive commercial and military cooperation do not indicate any necessary structural similarity between two societies, and political regimes of an identical nature do not always collaborate with each other. A growing body of literature confronts the question of similarity by examining South Africa and Palestine/Israel from a comparative perspective that seeks to describe and account for the many resemblances as well as the substantial differences between their patterns of national and political conflicts (Jabbour 1970; Farsoun 1976; Greenberg 1980; Houbert 1985; Chazan 1988; Smooha 1988; Adam 1989–90; Giliomee and Gagiano 1990; Ryan and Will 1990; Van den Berghe 1990; Younis 1995).

While many of these studies offer valuable insights into the dynamics of conflict in the two societies (the work of Younis stands out in particular, and I have greatly benefited from Smooha's work—the first to have raised many of the issues addressed here), they generally suffer from two problems. The first is their ahistorical nature. They rarely engage in an in-depth historical analysis of the development of the socioeconomic, identity, and political systems in question, nor do they explore alternative historical courses that have been open at various points in time. The Israeli-Palestinian and the South African conflicts are products of long and complex historical processes. It is possible to discover general themes that run throughout their history, as attempted here, but one must be sensitive to variations on these themes, evaluate optional courses of development, and observe the specific manner in which they have been expressed in different periods. Most of the studies mentioned above deal only with the end result of the process, that is, these societies as they exist today. We need, however, to go beyond contemporary events to explore the formative processes that gave rise to present conditions and made them intelligible.

A second problem with the literature is its general lack of engagement with theoretical issues (Greenberg 1980 is a notable exception). Most of the studies remain at the descriptive level without elaborating on the relevance of the comparison to theory in areas such as race and class, economic dependency and development, identity and state. This absence makes it difficult to evaluate the contribution of such work to theoretical disciplines. In the present study I attempt to fill some of the historical and theoretical gaps evident in the literature. (For a critique of the comparative field in the South African context see Greenstein 1994.)

A Comparative-Historical Method

A major difficulty in overcoming the limitations of previous work is the lack of synchronization between the two cases. Comparative studies of South Africa and the United States (Fredrickson 1981; Lamar and Thompson, 1981; Cell 1982) and the United States and Brazil (Degler 1971), to take a few examples, benefit from a close correspondence in terms of historical time between processes of conquest, slavery, emancipation, and segregation. To demonstrate this temporal dimension, Colin Bundy (1990) offers a "thumbnail sketch" of United States history that can serve equally well as an outline of South African history. Doing the same for Palestinian/Israeli and South African histories would require such a great deal of manipulation as to make the exercise meaningless. A possible solution to this problem is to make time itself—the world-historical context—an element of the explanatory framework and thus take a step toward bridging the gap separating the study of history from sociology (Braudel 1980).

I combine in this study the two classical comparative research strategies identified by J. S. Mill and use them in a loose manner as a general guide rather than as strict experimental designs. The method of agreement poses the following question: given the substantial historical differences in timing, background factors, and nature of the conflicting parties, what makes the similarity between Palestine/Israel and South Africa so obvious to numerous political organizations, governments, scholars, and media? The answer to this question would focus on the similarity in the basic setting of territorial and political struggles between indigenous people and settlers in both situations. The method of difference takes these resemblances as a starting point and proceeds to pose another question: given the similarity of the conflicts, how can we account for the different solutions currently being implemented? The answer would focus on the different materials out of which the formative processes of class, identity, and state were fashioned in the two cases and use these to explain the differences between exclusionary (Palestine/Israel) and incorporationist (South Africa) historical dynamics.

In stating the overall goal of this study I am inclined toward the latter of the two comparative historical research strategies identified by Theda Skocpol, the first of which attempts "to discover casual regularities that account for specifically defined historical processes or outcomes, and explore alternative hypotheses to achieve that end," while the second uses "concepts to develop what might best be called meaningful historical interpretations" (1984: 362). The latter strategy is similar to what Charles Tilly (1984) terms the individualizing, as opposed to the universalizing, approach in comparative investigation. My first goal, then, is to contribute to the understanding of the origins and development of political conflicts in Palestine/Israel and South Africa. I use the comparative framework to highlight features frequently obscured when these societies are studied in isolation, distinguishing between more general and more specific factors that operate in each case.

My second goal is to address theoretical debates on the operation of class, identity (nation, race, ethnicity), and state formation processes and their role in political conflicts. It is through the use of analytical concepts in the study of historically concrete cases that we can advance theoretical knowledge. The conclusions of this comparative study would be particularly relevant to the analysis of those societies, mostly in Africa and the Americas, that came into being as a result of the twin processes of European colonial expansion and the formation of the world capitalist system since the fifteenth century (thus covering much of the same ground as Fredrickson 1988).

Sources

A project of this nature requires the assimilation and reinterpretation of numerous, widely disparate, historical studies as well as primary documentary evidence. It is essential, however, to engage in a synthetic endeavor in order to compensate for the excessive specificity (from the point of view of a sociologist) characteristic of much historical work. As Janet Abu-Lughod puts it, "in the historians' matrix, constituted vertically by time, horizontally by space, and third dimensionally by focus, there are only a few specialists situated at each of the thousands of unique intersections; there they dig long and deep . . . their work is the basis on which all generalists must depend. And yet the cost of such concentration is often a loss of peripheral vision" (Abu-Lughod 1989: ix).

Even with a broad nonspecialist agenda, it proved impossible to cover the entire historical development of the two societies. Major issues such as the Great Trek, the Anglo-Boer War, and the relations between labor and revisionist Zionism are discussed briefly or not at all. Though undoubtedly important, these and many other topics had to be left out to prevent the book from growing to unmanageable proportions. My choices of topics were not arbitrary, though one could possibly undertake a similar project and focus on different questions. In this sense, this work is not meant to be exhaustive. In addition, the large gaps that exist in historical research, primarily with regard to issues of identity, made the discussion somewhat fragmentary at times. My main concern has been to build a solid, historically grounded skeleton, fit to tackle the question of concern here—the exclusionary and incorporationist dynamics generated by political conflicts. Further research could proceed from this basis and put more flesh, so to speak, on the existing structure.

I use primary and secondary sources as raw material, going back and forth between historical narrative and theoretical reflection of an explicit as well as implicit nature. In fact, empirical evidence and abstract conceptualization are inseparable, one rather useless without the other. As E. P. Thompson argues in his essay "The Peculiarities of the English,"

a model is a metaphor of historical process. It indicates not only the significant parts of this process but the way in which they are interrelated and the way in which they change. In one sense, history remains irreducible; it remains all that happened. In another sense, history does not become history until there is a model: at the moment at which the most elementary notion of causation, process, or cultural patterning, intrudes, then some model is assumed. It may well be better than this should be made explicit. But the moment at which a model is made explicit it begins to petrify into axioms . . . at the best . . . we must expect a delicate equilibrium between the synthesizing and the empiric modes, a quarrel between the model and actuality. This is the creative quarrel at the heart of cognition. (Thompson 1978: 77–78).

Periodization

Periodization is always a problem when one deals with historical processes that stretch over a long time span. To facilitate the discussion, I have divided the historical narrative into two parts, starting with the early period of encounter and settlement. In the case of Palestine/Israel, the narrative begins in the nineteenth century and concludes with World War I. In the case of South Africa, it begins in the immediate precolonial period and concludes just before the social transformations that accompanied the mineral discoveries of the late nineteenth century. In both places this period allowed settlers to establish a basis for future expansion—more securely in South Africa than in Palestine—and created the setting for critical struggles over political and economic domination in subsequent periods. From there, I proceed to deal with the ensuing period of political and economic consolidation, concluding in both places in 1948 with the establishment of the State of Israel and the launching of the apartheid era in South Africa. The principal features of political relations in both cases were set in place during that time, and the differences between the courses of the conflicts had become well entrenched by the end of the period.

Subsequent developments during the third period, from 1948 to the present, have further refined the trends in evidence by the end of the second. In this work, however, I discuss only the first two periods as they provide the essential background for understanding later events. The task of extending the historical analysis into the post-1948 period is best left for another study for reasons of time and space (but see Younis 1995 for a discussion of this latter period).

Historical Outcomes

By the end of the period discussed in this work, the operation of class, identity, and state formation processes in Palestine/Israel had led to an exclusionary outcome—the partition of the country, the establishment of the State of Israel, and the creation of the Palestinian refugee population. In preceding decades a distinct Jewish society was established and achieved a large degree of autonomy, though not complete independence, from indigenous Arab society. The same was true for Palestinian-Arab society, which was less dependent on its Jewish counterpart to begin with. Ideological and political-institutional processes brought about the coexistence of two autonomous communities with limited overlapping affiliations and alliances between them. The ground for an exclusionary outcome was prepared, though the exact shape of the outcome was determined by the relative military strength of the opposing sides and the regional and international support they managed to mobilize.

In South Africa, the outcome of the formative historical processes was more complex. Industrialization and urbanization processes resulted in a growing incorporation of indigenous people into white-dominated economic structures in the course of the twentieth century. Economic integration created an arena for struggle over the terms of ideological and political incorporation of people of various backgrounds in state structures. The call of the white supremacist National Party for the implementation of apartheid was one response to that reality. It was an attempt by a section of the settler community to maintain the presence and role of indigenous people in the economic domain, without allowing it to extend into the social and political domains. African political movements as well as white liberals called for accelerated integration in all spheres. The victory of the apartheid forces in 1948 resulted in a slowing down, and sometimes even a reversal, of incorporationist tendencies, but not in their complete halt.

Recent Developments

In both places the post-1948 period saw a further elaboration of the earlier processes. A section of the Palestinian-Arab people residing within Israeli boundaries was incorporated into Jewish-controlled economic, social, and political structures. However, about 85 percent of the Palestinians found themselves residing outside of Israel. Consequently, the main arena of Palestinian political activity remained beyond the boundaries of the Israeli state in geographical, institutional, and ideological senses. The occupation of the West Bank and Gaza Strip in 1967 did not result in the integration of their inhabitants. Economic incorporation has taken significant steps forward, but without any parallel move in the spheres of identity and state.

The "green line" has emerged as a social and legal divide between the Jewish and Arab parts of Palestine/Israel, firmly in place today despite twenty-eight years of consistent attempts by successive Israeli governments to erase it. The line has been reintroduced whenever political circumstances have called for a clear distinction between Israel proper and the occupied territories (as demonstrated by the blanket curfews imposed on the territories in times of acute political tensions, as was the case during the Gulf War of 1991 and the frequent closures of the last two years). The dominant tendency is still that of exclusion. Whether through a partition of the territory into two independent entities or through the "transfer" of one group elsewhere, the majority of Israeli Jews and Palestinian Arabs favor separatist arrangements. A two-state solution, seen by many interested parties as the way out of the conflict, would, if implemented, grant international legitimacy to the exclusionary dynamics that have been operating all along.

In South Africa, the erosion of apartheid since the early 1980s is testimony to the strength of the preexisting incorporationist tendencies which managed to survive and overcome decades of state planning and the implementation of segregationist policies enforced by massive political repression. By the 1980s, the South African state started relaxing its exclusionary policies. The 1983 constitution and the tricameral Parliament, the abolition of the Pass Laws in 1986 and of the Separate Amenities Act in 1990, the scrapping of the Land, Group Areas, and Population Registration Acts in 1991, the adoption of an interim constitution in 1993, and the elections of April 1994 are all steps taken in a new/old incorporationist direction, culminating with the incorporation of all citizens on a nonracial basis.

The strength of the historical dynamics of exclusion (Palestine/Israel) versus incorporation (South Africa) can also be seen by the fate of the attempts to reverse them: a failure to *erase* boundaries between Israel and the occupied territories, and thus block the prospects of partition, in the former case; a failure to permanently *erect* artificial boundaries between South Africa and the Bantustans, and thus permanently partition the country into ethnic homelands, in the latter case.

In neither of the two countries do solutions to the conflicts promise to proceed smoothly. Forces with high stakes in maintaining relations of domination have attempted to subvert any movement to dismantle the old order. This applies in particular to Jewish settlers in the Palestinian occupied territories; the resistance of the white and black beneficiaries of apartheid, organized before the 1994 elections in the misnamed Freedom Alliance, has virtually collapsed by now. Although these forces represent a minority in both cases, their disruptive potential should not be underestimated. It is implausible, though, that they would be able to block the process of change. Peacefully or violently, the historical dynamics of exclusion in Palestine/Israel and incorporation in South Africa are likely to continue to assert themselves in coming years.

2 | Analytical Framework

The basic argument of this work is that an understanding of the dynamics of political conflicts can be gained by studying the effects of the interconnected processes of class, identity, and state formation. The choice of the three processes was determined in large part by utilitarian considerations such as the availability of numerous historical studies and sources that focus on these issues and provide the necessary raw materials for a comparative inquiry. It is not meant as a rigorous theoretical statement of the importance of some factors relative to others. At the abstract theoretical level one cannot assume the primacy of any of these processes. Ethnicity, race, nation, gender, class, state, demography, and ecology are all basic organizing principles of human social activity. Each of them may acquire greater or lesser importance depending on the phenomena to be explained, the historically specific conditions under which they operate, the goals of the investigation, and their potential for opening new avenues of exploration. The selection of some of these factors in any concrete inquiry is of necessity arbitrary, at least to some extent, if only for reasons of time and space that limit the reach of any particular study and make theoretical choices inevitable. It may be possible to specify historically contingent conditions under which some factors play a more prominent role than others, but the principal task of historical studies is to establish the concrete ways in which social processes interact over time and indicate the likelihood of certain configurations with general theoretical implications. In this we can attempt to bypass, without actually overcoming, "the inherent disciplinary resistance of history to self-conscious theorizing" (Hunt 1990: 96).

Class, identity, and state respectively correspond, though they are not identical, to the classical distinction between the economic, political, and ideological spheres, which dates back to Karl Marx and Max Weber, the "founding fathers" of historical sociology. From the perspective adopted here, however, economy is not to be equated with class, ideology with identity, and politics with state. Each of the above spheres is itself shaped by class, identity, and state factors, the weight of which often shifts. We should avoid conflating two distinct issues here: the objects of historical inquiry on the one hand, and the theoretical perspectives used in analyzing them on the other. One could choose, say, the sphere of economic relations as a substantive area of investigation and analyze it from nonclass theoretical approaches which focus on identity, state, and gender. In a similar manner, one can study ideology within a class-analytic framework, dismissing identity as a theoretical factor. Many attempts have been made to address the relations of these factors, with varying results. In the following sections I discuss several of these approaches in a critical manner.

George Fredrickson constructs a comparative framework for the analysis of colonialism and racism. He regards class, race, and political power as equally independent explanatory factors, but leans toward granting the ideological dimension of race a primary role: "Racial attitudes arising from original or primal patterns of colonization became social and cultural norms for the dominant groups—ways of determining status and identity as well as rationalizations of direct economic interests"; consequently, "the status implications of the primal hierarchies outlived the material conditions of their genesis and inhibited the developments of the pure class situations that orthodox Marxists would expect to arise" (1988: 223).

Another approach that recognizes the multiplicity of causal factors is the pluralist perspective on race and ethnicity. Without denying the importance of class relations or of beliefs and attitudes, pluralists focus on the political dimension as the starting point for the study of multicultural societies: "Typically, the plural society is constituted by differential incorporation in the political structure, an unequal participation of the racial, ethnic or religious groups, prescribed by law or operative de facto" (Kuper 1980: 243). Once a system of domination is established, "there develops, over the years, an elaboration of [economic and cultural] social relations between the races on the basis of the original differential [political] incorporation" (255).

Orthodox Marxism relegated politics and ideology to the realm of the superstructure that was determined by its material base. In recent decades, numerous attempts to go beyond crude economic determinism and give larger weight to the relative autonomy of ideology and politics within a class analytic framework have been made. Erik Wright (1982) calls for incorporating "the political" in the very definition of class structures and modes of production, rather than treating it as an external and subordinate factor. In a similar vein, Harold Wolpe (1986) argues that classes are constituted through economic, political, and ideological processes in the sphere of production, making race an important factor in the shaping of class struggle under specific conditions (Burawoy 1985 and Miles 1987 present similar positions). These formulations represent a move toward more flexible versions of Marxism. They do not go far enough, however, in breaking out of the conceptual fetters imposed by class determinism as they retain the mode of production as the framework within which all other social processes take place.

The difficulty Marxists face in moving further is expressed by John Solomos, who maintains that "the fundamental problem with abandoning the relative autonomy model is that of avoiding the trap of simple pluralism, which sees 'race' and class relationships as completely separate. This is why it seems to me that it is important to insist on the complexity of 'determination in the last instance,' while accepting that there is some form of determination of racism by other social relations" (1986: 105). It is argued here, though, in contrast to even the more nuanced versions of the relative autonomy thesis, that the historical processes by which class structures, collective identities, and state institutions are formed are interrelated and should not be reduced one to another or arranged in accordance with any hierarchical principles.

A useful way of looking at the relationship between different analytical factors is conveyed in Philip Cohen's attempt to deal with the manifold representations of material realities through the (material) territory and (discursive) map metaphor, regarding the two as clearly interdependent though "their relation is not fixed and does not belong to some a priori principle of correspondence. Territory is not a *tabula rasa* of sense impressions awaiting the imprint of false consciousness; map does not model or reflect 'external reality.' Indeed, there are many ideological phenomena which cannot be located at either level, but are produced solely through particular forms of interaction between them. Their paradigm, perhaps appropriately, is the mirage. Neither a pure hallucination, nor a pure environmental effect, the mirage is produced at the intersection between certain climatic conditions in the desert and a certain movement of desire on the part of thirsty travellers" (Cohen 1988: 56). This approach suggests that no hierarchical relationship between analytical factors can or should be established. It thus joins the call for the development of a particular, local, regional knowledge that is "an autonomous, non-centralised kind of theoretical production, one that is to say whose validity is not dependent on the approval of the established régimes of thought" (Foucault 1980: 81). Configurations of class, identity, and state are historically specific; they are not fixed and rigid, nor are they entirely random: "Just to say that everything is contingent, then, is an assertion that would only make sense for an inhabitant of Mars. . . . [Social agents] are therefore never in the position of the absolute chooser who, faced with the contingency of all possible courses of action, would have no reason to choose. On the contrary, what we always find is a limited and given situation in which objectivity is *partially* constituted and also *partially* threatened; and in which the boundaries between the contingent and the necessary are constantly displaced" (Laclau 1990: 27; italics in the original). Analytical constructions do not have a lawlike validity, then. They can, however, provide useful guidelines for investigating the conditions of possibility for the emergence and elaboration of racial and political orders. In this sense, one can combine broad but diffuse theoretical concerns with concrete historical inquiries so that they illuminate and enrich one another without subordinating one to the other (West 1987; Hunt 1990).

The Object of Inquiry

The central axis of my comparison between Palestine/Israel and South Africa is the extent to which exclusionary and incorporationist dynamics became dominant in the material practices and political discourses that governed their conflicts in the period discussed here. I argue that the three processes of class, identity, and state formation led to an overall stronger exclusionary trend in Palestine/Israel, expressed in the formation of two distinct societies, as compared to a stronger incorporationist trend in South Africa, expressed in the formation of one internally differentiated and highly inegalitarian society. The task of the historical analysis is to explain why this turned out to be the case. Two notes of caution are in order before proceeding further.

First, whereas exclusion has a quite conventional meaning of a movement toward the restriction of access to social, economic, identity, and political institutions and structures, the term "incorporation" has a specific meaning here. It refers to a movement toward institutional inclusion *but not necessarily on an egalitarian basis*. Notions of incorporation are frequently associated with equality. However, different forms of class relations such as slavery, indentured labor, and wage labor are considered here as instances of economic incorporation because members of different groups inhabit the same institutions, though within radically different work settings and hierarchies. Economic exclusion consists of the preservation or creation of independent economic sectors within the same boundaries, each with its own internal stratification, or the establishment of independent political entities with no integration of labor markets between them. In this respect, white-dominated societies in South Africa developed a large degree of dependence on black labor. Jewish society in Palestine/Israel was considerably less dependent on Arab labor. This difference had important effects on the course of the respective conflicts, as is explored in the following chapters.

Second, I refer to trends. These are not linear tendencies, inexorably working their way toward a predetermined future, but rather outcomes of specific historical processes that could have turned out differently had other circumstances prevailed. Palestine/Israel and South Africa show evidence of other trends, working in opposite and contradictory directions, which were quite strong at times but not strong enough to offset the overall direction taken by their conflicts. Discussion of trends should be seen, then, in relative rather than absolute terms.

In more general terms, the issue addressed here is the ways in which people create social boundaries in the process of constructing their collective identities, defining their class interests, and organizing as parties to political conflicts. Within this broad area I focus on the factors that affect the extent to which racial and ethnic relations are defined by various parties in mutually exclusive or inclusive terms (as integrated or segregated, separate but equal, separate and unequal, etc.) in the spheres of economic organization, group identification, and political institutions.

In the historical sections of this work, chapters 3–6, I deploy three analytical factors to account for the divergent historical courses taken by the two conflicts in question. These factors are: (1) the world-historical context within which relations of confrontation and cooperation developed; (2) the capacities of indigenous people to respond to and shape the process of group encounter and conflict; and (3) the strategies adopted by settler and colonial forces in pursuit of their interests.

Analytical Factors

World-Historical Context

The concept of the world-historical context refers to the overall setting, which exists independently of the phenomena discussed here and has an effect on the unfolding of formative processes as well as their interrelationships. It is of particular importance when applied to comparative studies of intergroup encounters of a roughly similar nature, though undertaken in different periods. Such encounters can have dissimilar outcomes if they take place in different historical contexts.

To take a few examples, colonial settlement in the early era of commercial capitalism differed substantially from a comparable project unleashed in the later era of industrial capitalism. Political clashes between settlers and indigenous people developed in different ways, depending on whether they took place in the sixteenth century, before the emergence of a strong and centralized international state system, or in the nineteenth century, after the consolidation of such a system in Europe and its extension to other parts of the world. The nature and degree of incorporation at the level of identity varied enormously, depending on the prior appearance of nationalism as a major historical force in the last two centuries. Any theoretical conclusions we might reach would thus have to be historicized, that is to say, qualified in light of the temporal context.

Indigenous Capacities

Frequently, studies of colonial processes are presented from the perspectives of dominant groups. This does not mean that scholars identify with the goals and visions of such groups, but rather that they tend to regard them as the most significant actors in the making of the colonial world. This bias can and should be corrected by giving due consideration to the organization and activities of non-dominant actors which are generally no less critical to the analysis. Disregard for what James Scott (1990) calls hidden transcripts is a problem that plagues much of the comparative work on South Africa, and it affects almost all the studies mentioned in chapter 1, which mostly deal with the interests, strategies, concerns, and visions of colonial and settler forces as the only factors relevant to the development of conflicts. This attitude tends to replicate, in the analysis, the marginalization of indigenous people, and relegates the latter to the status of "people without history" (Wolf 1982). The role of indigenous structures is essential to the analysis of historical developments, however.

In focusing on the role of indigenous structures, I make no claims to speak for indigenous people (or any other group for that matter), nor am I arguing that indigenous sources are more valuable to the analysis or that indigenous scholars offer more correct interpretations of past events. Rather, the concept of indigenous capacities is deployed here analytically to refer to the characteristics of indigenous structures that affect the differential capacity of people to organize at the levels of economy, identity, and state and to use their modes of organization to sustain and open up avenues of independent existence and development outside the control of colonial and settler forces.

A historical inquiry that addresses this dimension should help us account for the ways in which the unfolding of colonial processes and their outcomes were shaped by factors other than those on which scholarly study has focused so far—colonial interests and settler strategies. It is important, at the same time, not to confuse history *from the bottom up* with history *of the bottom* (Kaye 1984: 228; italics in the original). The social history school in general, and its followers in South Africa in particular, have offered innovative views of political conflicts and transformations by attempting to incorporate the role of subaltern and indigenous actors into the analysis. We should be careful, however, not to romanticize the struggles and achievements of those who found themselves, at least temporarily, at the losing end of history (Fox-Genovese and Genovese 1983: 179–212). The actions and reactions of all sides to the conflicts deserve thorough consideration.

Colonial and Settler Strategies

Colonial and settler strategies have been extensively studied elsewhere and therefore do not require much discussion here (for typologies of colonial formations based on this factor see Fieldhouse 1966; Fredrickson 1988: 216–235). Colonial and settler forces defined in the course of conflicts their material and ideological interests. They devised strategies in order to realize such interests, frequently clashing among themselves in the process. No study of colonial processes, comparative or otherwise, could possibly proceed without taking these strategies into consideration. At the same time, they should not be dealt with solely in their own terms, as having existed prior to and independently of the colonial process itself. Rather than positing them as the primary explanatory factor, we need to outline and account for the ways in which they were shaped by the world-historical context and by indigenous capacities.

Demography

A major factor frequently used in the analysis of racial and colonial situations is, of course, demography (see, for example, Fredrickson 1981). While all of the processes discussed so far were influenced by demographic realities, demography should not be regarded as an independent factor, at least not in the period preceding the consolidation of international boundaries. Rather, it was itself shaped by other formative processes. A few examples illustrate this point. If South Africa has had a black majority in its population, it is because of the expansionist nature of European settlement in the country. If Europeans had been confined to the area of original settlement—the southwestern Cape, which could support a dense settlement of hundreds of thousands—they would have been a majority there. They moved beyond the Cape because of the inadequate supplies of capital and labor needed to establish the Dutch intensive family-labor farm as the basis for settlement. In other words, the availability of capital, labor, and land resources determined demographic factors rather than the other way around.

Similarly, Jews are a majority in Israel today because a specific territory was targeted for settlement by the Zionist movement, and hundreds of thousands of Palestinian-Arabs were evicted to other Arab territories during the War of 1947–48. This fitted the plans of the Zionist movement to maintain a solid majority in the population and clear the way for massive Jewish immigration into the country. The drive toward these goals was due to the exclusionary nature of the identities and political institutions established in the pre-1948 period. The relative proportion of settlers and indigenous people in the population today appears thus as an *effect* of the formative processes and not their *cause*. Once demographic realities are firmly in place they have their own impact, of course, but they do not operate on their own and have no effect independently of the other social processes.

Historical Processes

The three historical processes dealt with in this work are (1) class structure formation—the establishment of land and labor relations between and within different groups, and the changes these went through over time; (2) identity formation—the emergence, development, and consolidation of racial, national, and ethnic identities; and (3) state formation—the construction of political institutions and the ways in which they came to exercise authority over disparate territories and inhabitants. In the following sections I raise several theoretical issues that guide the concrete historical discussion in later chapters.

Class Structure Formation

Within the overall context of formation of class structures, this study primarily deals with control over land and labor resources. Several factors need be taken into account: (a) *The background to the settlement process*: precolonial social forms and in particular indigenous land tenure and patterns of class differentiation; the nature of settler populations—sources of personnel and capital, their class divisions and interests; (b) *processes of economic development*: incorporation into the world system; changes in land tenure; industrialization and urbanization; and (c) *the changing class structure*: the transformation in class relations as a result of operation of the previous two factors; the nature of class relations formed between members of different groups and the extent to which systems of racial and ethnic stratification developed.

Several perspectives analyze class relations within the specific historical context of European colonial expansion. A common way of theorizing the contact between widely disparate societies and economic systems is modernization theory—a cluster of approaches that emphasize the distinction between the traditional and the modern (or some other similar dichotomy) as the key to understanding the nature of economic, social, and political developments. More specifically, this perspective regards the spread of European hegemony over the rest of the world as having led to the transformation of stagnant traditional societies under the impact of modern and dynamic values, methods of organization, and technology. European patterns of development served as a model to be followed by non-Western societies: "The Western model of modernization exhibits certain components and sequences whose relevance is global . . . [and it] reappears in virtually all modernizing societies on all continents of the world, regardless of variations in race, color, creed" (Lerner 1958: 46). Change is a process of convergence between different societies, and "it is therefore only a slight exaggeration to say that all contemporary societies are more or less modern" (Parsons 1977: 229).

The orthodox Marxist approach is, in a way, a variant of modernization theory. The *Communist Manifesto* asserts that "the bourgeoisie . . . compels all nations, on pain of extinction, to adopt the bourgeois mode of production; it compels them to introduce what it calls civilization into their midst, i.e., to become bourgeois themselves. In one word, it creates a world after its own image" (Marx 1977: 225). Another formulation repeats the same idea that "the country that is more developed industrially only shows to the less developed, the image of its own future" (416). In other writings Marx put stronger emphasis on the distorting effects of colonial domination, but he continued to maintain that the destruction of indigenous societies in the colonies was necessary for further progress, and that imperial powers were an unconscious tool of history in facilitating social revolution in Asia. (For a modern version of this approach, see Warren 1980.)

What modernization and (some) Marxist theories have in common, despite the use of very different concepts and value judgments to describe the process, is the assumption that the source of economic change is external. Colonialism has had the effect of pushing traditional, undeveloped, precapitalist societies to adopt modern, capitalist forms of economic organization. This process is seen as progressive, whether in its own right or as a necessary step toward further social transformations.

The dominance of modernization approaches has been increasingly challenged since the 1960s. Its most forceful critique came in the form of dependency, world-system, and articulation of modes of production theories. Common to all of the above is the rejection of notions of convergence and of the progressive elimination of the distinct characteristics of non-Western economic systems. Dependency theory asserts the opposite, in fact. Tradition and underdevelopment are *results* of modernization processes rather than their starting points: "Even a modest acquaintance with history shows that underdevelopment is not original or traditional and that neither the past nor the present of the underdeveloped countries resembles in any important respect the past of the now developed countries. . . . Contemporary underdevelopment is in large part the historical product of past and continuing economic and other relations between the satellite underdeveloped and the now developed metropolitan countries" (Frank 1969: 4).

From this perspective, then, colonialism incorporated non-European societies into an economic world system in a dependent position, as suppliers of raw materials and cheap labor and as markets for goods produced by the dominant elements in the system. The capitalist world economy is based on a transfer of surplus from the periphery to the core, thereby making the relationship highly profitable for the latter and disastrous for the former. The goal of the core is not to transform the periphery in its own image, but to maintain it in its subordinate role. What seem to be traditional structures (serfdom, coercive agriculture) are either new forms emerging from the incorporation into the world system (Wallerstein 1974) or old forms that were retained in a new context because they served capitalist interests in that way: "Far from banishing pre-capitalist forms, it [the capitalist world economy] not only coexists with them but buttresses them, and even on occasions devilishly conjures them up *ex nihilo*" (Foster-Carter 1978: 51).

Despite the obvious differences between the perspectives presented thus far, they all treat precolonial social forces as passive objects, totally overwhelmed by the colonial invasion and the transformations brought about in its aftermath. Whether they regard these processes in a positive or negative vein, modernization, dependency, and world-system perspectives emphasize the European impact and its ability to impose visions and designs on the rest of the world.

A different focus is presented by Steven Stern in a thorough critique of the world-system perspective. He argues for an analytical framework based on the need to take seriously three motors of development: "the European world-system, popular strategies of resistance and survival within the periphery and the mercantile and elite interests joined to . . . [local] 'centers of gravity'. It is in the contradictory interplay between these three grand motors, and in the divisions and contradictions internal to each of them, that we will find keys to a deeper understanding of the structures, changes, and driving forces of colonial economic life" (Stern 1988: 871). This approach directs our attention to class divisions and conflicts not only between colonizers and colonized (or core and periphery), but also within these categories. It serves to bring the role of popular and indigenous forces back into the picture. Having said that, it is obvious that the capacity of indigenous people to resist encroachment on their land and labor power, to take advantage of newly opened opportunities, and to participate in new economic orders on an equal footing has varied tremendously. Precolonial social differentiation, prior exposure to the operation of market forces, and the adaptability of their political institutions have all affected local responses to the economic challenges posed by colonial forces.

Patterns of class interaction can be seen, then, as outcomes of conflicts between various segments of settler and indigenous populations over terms of incorporation (or lack thereof) in the domains of land and labor. These patterns should not simply be considered results of conscious strategies pursued by colonial powers (and settlers), though those were important of course. The historical chapters of this work analyze the evolution of class relations from a perspective that seeks to account for divergent social dynamics in terms of material interests and organizational capacities of all sides, dominant and nondominant alike. The comparative study should allow us to evaluate the conditions which give rise to different constellations of class relations in the context of settlement and resistance.

The nature of the politico-economic project pursued by settlers determined the ways they defined their interests with regard to indigenous people's land and labor. In confronting this project, indigenous people in societies that had had prior experience of settled agriculture and production for the market were able to defend themselves from incorporation into a subordinate class position. Furthermore, certain segments within these societies could benefit from the opening of new economic opportunities. The ability of local elements to gain (or retain) independent access to capital and land resources allowed them to develop their economic autonomy. Internal class differentiation and incorporation into the world system on terms not defined by settler interests created a space for separate economic development. Different historical trajectories have thus been shaped in a process of interaction between the class interests and capacities of imperial, settler, and indigenous forces.

Identity Formation

Of particular importance in analyzing identity formation is the extent to which the formative processes of group identities (that is, the ways in which people define themselves as belonging to larger collectives perceived in various group terms such as nation, race, ethnicity, and religion) shape the nature of conflicts and are shaped, in turn, by them. The existence of parties to conflicts as cohesive and self-conscious groups cannot be taken for granted. Collective identities are contingent in nature; they emerge and decline under specific historical circumstances in a process that frequently involves struggles over definitions of terms. The issues of concern here are as follows: (a) *pre-encounter group identities*—the identities prevalent among different indigenous and settler forces before the colonial encounter; (b) *the process of group formation*—the extent to which people managed to overcome internal divisions on various grounds and construct coherent group identities; and (c) *blueprints*—the manner in which the unfolding of conflict was affected by the existence, or lack thereof, of conscious designs formulated by members of groups with regard to the society they want to build and the ways to get there.

Parties to conflicts attempt to overcome internal obstacles to the construction of a common identity among their members. The more successful groups in this respect gain an advantage over their opponents. Furthermore, they frequently use their power to make it more difficult for others to bridge over their own divisions in the framework of a divide and rule strategy. At the same time, the experience of living together within the same structures can result in the construction of new identities or the reinforcement of unifying old elements. The degree of cohesion of identities is not easy to detect. It is less obvious than other material or institutional realities since it has a larger hidden and unarticulated dimension. Nevertheless, we can attempt to deduce beliefs and attitudes from the analysis of activities, alliances, and forms of organization. In addition, social phenomena which do not clearly belong to the realm of "ideas," such as relations across the color line, the emergence of mixed populations, linguistic heritage, and church membership, can be indicative of the workings of group formation.

One instance of identity, of great importance in the context of this work, which emerges and takes shape as part of a political process, is nationalism. Nations (as well as ethnic and racial groups) have not existed from time immemorial in their present form, nor have they sprung into existence out of nowhere. They come into being as the culmination of a formative process in which they become a focus of identification for people who share common descent, or at least a belief in such an origin. Identity is a construct, and it exists in the mind of people as a subjective experience, not as an objective reality existing "out there." Nation, thus, "is an imagined political community and imagined as both inherently limited and sovereign. . . . In fact, all communities larger than primordial villages of face-to-face contact (and perhaps even these) are imagined" (Anderson 1983: 15).

National consciousness and nationalist movements are historically new phenomena in much of the world, and their existence is not obvious. As Ernest Gellner argues, "nationalism tends to treat itself as a manifest and self-evident principle, accessible as such to all men, and violated only through some perverse blindness, when in fact it owes its plausibility and compelling nature only to a very special set of circumstances, which do indeed obtain now, but which were alien to most of humanity and history" (Gellner 1983: 125). The need of nationalists to construct a credible common identity can be seen as a process of creating and maintaining ethnic and national boundaries which reflect group attitudes based on myths, symbols, and means of communication, rather than mere geographical or physical divisions, although the latter are also crucially important (Armstrong 1982).

As part of the process of creating boundaries, and thereby constructing viable symbolic communities, nationalists usually advance reasons and justifications for engaging in such a project of identity formation. Of particular interest are legitimations used by leaders and members of a group to account for their right to exist and prosper in specific times and places. Anthony Smith (1984) lists six essential myths that play an important role in every national movement and that can be used as a framework for the study of variations in the way nationalism is expressed. His categories could be grouped into myths of origin (time, place, and ancestry), which are set in remotest times, and myths of political developments, more historical in nature, which deal with the rise, decline, and regeneration of the group.

Much nationalist mythology is a conscious creation by intellectuals who take it upon themselves to construct a viable identity for their own group. This process frequently involves the "invention of tradition" (Hobsbawm and Ranger 1983)—the use of new cultural elements that are disguised, for purposes of legitimation, as old and traditional artifacts. A variation on this theme, particularly important in the African context, is the "creation of tribalism" (Vail 1989)—the existence of tribal identities not as relics from precolonial times but as new institutions created during the colonial period. This process has often been initiated by outsiders such as missionaries, colonial administrators, and social scientists, sometimes in collaboration with local elements. The obvious manipulative aspects of these phenomena, emphasized by the literature discussed earlier, should not lead us to conclude that the people, in whose name and for whose supposed benefit these identities are constructed, are passive in this process. Their active intervention in the form of constructing their own traditions of group consciousness, and of setting limits on, accepting, or rejecting externally induced identities, plays a vital role. A fruitful approach to the study of the formation of identities should consider all contributions to the process, by external and internal elites as well as by the masses.

The principles presented above can serve as organizing tools in analyzing identity formation. We should look at it as a process rather than as a fixed inventory of elements that always exhibit themselves in the same way. Specific movements draw upon different symbolic repertoires in order to enhance cohesion and solidify a sense of common destiny. The success of some identity projects, but not others, depends on the plausibility of their constructions in the eyes of their potential constituents, and their ability to mobilize mass support behind them. The existence of objective linguistic, religious, and other preconditions for such movements facilitates their task.

In addition to nation, race and ethnicity also function as principles of organization of collective identity. All these are not mutually exclusive principles but rather partially overlapping and partially competing foci of identity formation. In a manner similar to the concept of nation itself, race can be seen as "an unstable and 'decentered' complex of social meanings constantly being transformed by political struggle" (Omi and Winant 1986: 68). The concept of racial formation as used by these writers outlines a strategy of investigation, similar to the one pursued here, of showing "how the widely disparate circumstances of individual and group racial identities, and of the racial institutions and social practices with which these identities are intertwined, are formed and transformed over time . . . through political contestation over racial meanings" (69).

The process of identity formation shapes the overall direction of conflicts. Exclusionary and incorporationist outcomes are affected by struggles between and within groups. The varying capacities of groups (or segments thereof) to build clear and mutually exclusive identities depend on their prior historical experience. If such identities had already been in existence, or in a process of being formed, in the precolonial period, the prospect of exclusionary developments in subsequent periods became more likely. In contrast, in situations in which no rigid boundaries between groups had been formed, more space existed for the construction of comprehensive identities later on.

State Formation

The third process, the formation of political institutions, is discussed with a focus on the following factors: (a) *the nature of precolonial political realities*—the scale and bases of organization of the political structures of indigenous people; (b) *indigenous resistance*—indigenous people's political and military capacities, including the ability to resist settler expansion; and (c) *imperial and settler control*—the consequences of the modes of organization of settlers and their relations to larger colonial or imperial projects.

State formation is a process of extension of centralized rule over geographically disparate areas, previously independent or autonomous, and the concomitant establishment of administrative institutions for the governing of these territories and their inhabitants. A variant of this is the carving of new states out of larger political units. These processes consist of military and political struggles over territorial control and legitimacy. The formation of state institutions and the consolidation of their territorially bound authority have an internal dimension, focused on the elimination of alternative power centers (ending a situation of "multiple sovereignties" as Charles Tilly puts it), and an external dimension, focused on interstate relations and international legitimacy.

The orientation of nondominant groups toward state power is a key element of these processes. They may seek to incorporate themselves within established structures on an equal basis, to destroy existing structures and create entirely new ones, or to adopt intermediate strategies. Choices made in this respect, even when they take place outside of the state apparatus proper, greatly affect the locus of the entire political process.

An important dimension of state formation, particularly relevant in the context of this work, is the expansion of European domination over much of the rest of the world. This movement transformed the nature, scale, and capacities of state structures in Asian, African, and American territories. It led to the creation of new states where none had existed and to the modification of political organization in existing states that became incorporated into larger transnational networks. Even states that had never been colonized (such as Thailand, Persia, and the Ottoman Empire) underwent adaptation to the new political environment. State formation in peripheral regions, then, should be analyzed in terms of its own dymanics as well as in the framework of a European-centered process.

The importance of the study of political developments in the context of the international system of states has been emphasized by Theda Skocpol (1979). A key ingredient of colonial expansion, seen in this context, is the violent encounter between political systems based on widely different forms of organization. The occupation of new territories, and the imposition of administrative control over them, presented new dilemmas for which the European experience offered no ready-made solutions. The extension of rule over hostile and culturally alien populations, spread out over large territories in remote areas, had to be tackled by using innovative methods of control.

One of the aspects of colonial rule particularly relevant here is the relations established between expanding empires and local elites. A provocative thesis dealing with the non-European foundations of colonialism claims that "the financial sinew, the military and administrative muscle of imperialism was drawn through the mediation of indigenous elites from the invaded countries themselves." The central mechanism of this development was expressed in "meshing the incoming processes of European expansion into indigenous social politics and in achieving some kind of evolving equilibrium between the two" (Robinson 1972: 120). One does not need to assume that the entire colonial project was driven by these factors to realize that the strength of collaborative mechanisms greatly affected the development of the colonial state and its postcolonial successors.

The compatibility of the political interests of indigenous and external forces usually varied with the power of settlers relative to empires. In places where there was a substantial body of settlers of European origin, the potential for conflict between them and the colonial authorities was ever present. This was especially the case when the colonizing power was not the mother country of the settlers. Policies toward the "Native Question" were a particular source of clashes among colonizers. The various social and political forces involved in settlement processes (missionaries, imperial authorities, local officials, traders, and landlords) formulated their interests in different ways. The drive for territorial expansion served some of these interests, while others benefited from alternative arrangements based on treaties and indirect rule over indigenous populations. Indigenous elites had their own interests in collaborating with or resisting colonial forces. Their own processes of state formation were frequently entangled with colonial expansion and led to clashes as well as to cooperation. The relative strengths of the various contenders for power played a major role in affecting the results.

An important element accompanying the process of state formation from its beginnings is popular resistance. The quantity and quality of resources allocated for the pacification of indigenous peoples were a function of their capacity and determination to maintain or regain their independence. Their military and organizational capacities were determined, in turn, by the internal cohesion of their political institutions, the openness of the colonial political system, independent access to advanced military technology, and the ability to forge alliances and take advantage of conflicts among their opponents. Similar factors affected the ability of empires and settlers to formulate and achieve their own political goals.

In cases in which indigenous political organization was fragmentary in nature, factional fighting resulted in greater openness to colonial intervention. In a similar manner, when settlers were split among themselves, or entered a conflict with the colonizing power, more space for politics of collaboration was created. In such cases parties struggling for power tended not to phrase their conflicts in mutually exclusive terms. In contrast, when internally coherent parties faced each other in a struggle over resources, the conflict was usually constructed in zero-sum terms. The higher the degree of internal consolidation of parties to the conflict, the less likely it was to lead to incorporationist politics or to interpenetration of political processes among the different groups.

These analytical reflections provide a framework for discussing the formative historical processes outlined earlier in the chapter, beginning with class structure formation during the early period of settlement.

3 | Land, Labor, and Territorial Expansion

The first part of this chapter deals with economic development, land regime, labor relations, and their effects on political conflict in Palestine/Israel, seen in the historical context of the late Ottoman Middle East. The second part does the same for the territories that became part of South Africa in the precolonial and early colonial periods. In the third part I compare the two countries. My main argument is that precolonial social and economic structures shaped the ways in which indigenous societies met the challenges posed by the arrival of European immigrants in possession of different technologies and modes of organization.[1] Further, I argue that indigenous capacities not merely determined the responses of indigenous people to the strategies pursued by settlers but also affected the formulation of these very strategies and the ability of settlers to implement their policies. Overall, the clashes between various indigenous and settler forces resulted in a larger degree of economic incorporation between the different groups in South Africa as compared to Palestine/Israel.

Palestine/Israel

The Middle Eastern Context

For four hundred years, between 1517 and 1917, Palestine was part of the Ottoman Empire and was ruled from the capital of Istanbul (Constantinople). Its economic development in that period should be seen in the context of the social and economic relations in the empire as a whole, and in particular in its Syrian provinces—Bilad al-Sham (present-day Syria, Lebanon, Palestine/Israel, and Jor-

---

1. While the term "precolonial" has a straightforward meaning in South Africa, it is ambiguous in Palestine/Israel. In this latter case indigenous people were not subject to settler economic and political domination before 1948. I do use it to refer to the pre-1882 period, however, in order to focus attention on developments among indigenous people that took place prior to any impact of Zionist settlement.

dan). The last century of Ottoman rule was a period of increasing vulnerability to European pressure, leading to various attempts to reform the empire's administrative and political structures, known as the Tanzimat reforms. These state-sponsored changes were accompanied by an underlying transformation of socioeconomic conditions. The process of change formed the background to the economic encounter between Jews and Arabs in Palestine in the late Ottoman period, and later on during the British mandatory rule.

A most important factor affecting economic conditions in the Ottoman Empire in the nineteenth century was the growing impact of the European economy. Extensive trade relations with European countries had been a feature of economic realities in the various territories of the Middle East for centuries (Abu-Lughod 1989). The period following the industrial revolution in Europe was different, however. For the first time commercial exchange took the form of a division of labor in which the empire exported food and raw materials and imported capital and machine-manufactured products. This trend was not limited to the Middle East, of course, and was found in many other non-European countries, later known collectively as the Third World.

Economic transformations resulting from integration into the world economy led to the expansion of agricultural production and export of cash crops, a change from communal or tribal to private ownership of land, a decline of handicrafts in a process of deindustrialization, and an increase in internal inequalities. (For an unfavorable comparison between the impact of these processes on the Middle East and its effect on India and Japan, see Issawi 1970.) All the major regions of the Middle East were affected by this process, though not to the same extent. Differences in demographic conditions, geography, natural resources, and political centralization resulted in various degrees of involvement with the world economy, with Egypt and the western provinces of the Ottoman Empire leading the way (Keddie 1981).

The issue of economic transformation in the Middle East has been approached from different theoretical directions. Writing in the spirit of modernization theory, Bonne (1955) regards the process of capitalist penetration as the only force capable of shaking traditional Middle Eastern society from its lethargy, stagnation, and the acquiescence of its population to living in miserable conditions. Political reforms, combined with a process of secularization, began undermining the centuries-old feudal socioeconomic structures but encountered numerous obstacles of social and cultural nature in the process. Among these were "the absence of a healthy sense of acquisitiveness in the make-up of the Oriental peasant" (Bonne 1955: 383) and the overall lack of a positive sense of freedom, initiative, and social change. The way forward for the region, from this perspective, lies in the combination of Western knowledge, entrepreneurship, and scientific skills, on the one hand, and Oriental human and natural resources on the other (394–415).

A similar picture is presented by Hershlag (1964), who portrays the meeting between East and West as a clash between the traditional immobility of Oriental institutions and the modern Western conceptions of economic administration and social structure. The resistance of traditional elements to this Western onslaught was expressed, among other things, by anti-Zionist campaigns led by conservative and feudal elites. These social strata felt threatened by Westernization since they derived their power from obsolete religious and authoritarian social hierarchies undermined by this process. The power of this conservative resistance delays and distorts the development of the Middle East along modern lines.

The enthusiasm for the benefits of increased contact with Western institutions expressed by modernization theorists is not shared by Smilianskaya (1966), who argues that the introduction of market relations led to dislocations in the feudal economy of Syria, Lebanon, and Palestine in the mid-nineteenth century. The penetration of foreign capital and the influx of machine-made goods (especially textiles) caused the collapse of local craft production and the decline of urban population in old manufacturing centers such as Damascus and Aleppo. The growing commercialization of agriculture led to an intensified exploitation of the peasantry by landlords who combined feudal and capitalist methods of surplus extraction. As a result of these processes, the general conditions of subsistence in these regions became worse for the majority of the population.

Basing themselves on this analysis, a group of writers has recently applied the world-system perspective to the study of the economic history of the Ottoman Empire. They see the incorporation into the capitalist world economy as a process of peripheralization in which the traditional unity of state and society dissolved under the impact of foreign trade. Though nominally independent, the Ottoman state lost its ability to control its economy and was largely powerless to stop the disintegration of its internal cohesion. Various coastal regions within the empire formed stronger economic relations with the European centers of trade and industry than with their own hinterland. Technological advances in transportation, communication, and production speeded up the breakdown of the empire as a meaningful economic unit. Far from promoting order and progress, capitalist expansion led to widespread disruptions and loss of sovereignty (Islamoglu-Inan 1987; Pamuk 1988).

Despite their differences, these perspectives share an attitude of playing down indigenous people's capacities. Contrary to the impression they create, however, indigenous economic structures proved adaptable to the realities created as a result of European economic expansion. The traditional sector was less stagnant and incapable of meeting economic challenges, and therefore less in need of being replaced, than modernization theorists would have us believe; nor did it become totally dominated by the European capitalist economy, as adherents of the world system perspective argue. What actually transpired was a complex process in which elements in the "traditional" sector, primarily middle and rich peasants, urban merchants, and landowners, adapted and took advantage of new commercial opportunities at the same time that poor peasants suffered from increasing internal inequalities, growing debt burdens, and loss of land. The effects of "modernization," then, were far from uniform and cannot be adequately grasped by any one-sided approach.

Late Ottoman Palestine

Against this background, the question of most concern here is what effects these general processes had in the specific case of late Ottoman Palestine.[2] The modern Zionist-inspired Jewish settlement of Palestine began in the early 1880s with the first *aliyah* (immigration wave). This wave consisted of thousands of Jews, mostly from eastern Europe, who moved to Palestine to settle on the land or find a place for themselves in an urban area. The origins of the economic transformation of the country, however, precede this immigration by several decades, or even a century according to one account. (Doumani 1992 traces the roots of the process back to the eighteenth century.) Economic change was not an outcome of the presence of Jewish immigrants, though they contributed to it.

According to Shamir (1986), the period of Egyptian rule (1831–40) saw the first significant opening toward the West and the beginning of integration into the international economic system. The most important elements in the process were the extension of the cultivated area due to increased security in the countryside; growing adjustment of agricultural production to market demand; extension of local, regional, and international trade; and improvements in the means of transportation and communication. Both internal and external factors were operating at the time. The Egyptians were an indigenous regional power aiming at the reorganization, mobilization, and development of local societal resources, but they needed European support and thus opened the way to further and more thorough foreign involvement. Other accounts give different dates for the beginning of the process of change. Schölch (1982) considers the period following the Crimean War (1856–82) as more important in laying the foundations for accelerated economic development, with the earlier periods of Egyptian rule and the first Tanzimat period (1839–56) as a background for it. Gilbar (1986) suggests 1865 as a starting point.

Be that as it may, the new period in the economic history of Palestine had opened well before any impact of the Zionist settlement project was felt. The contention of modernization theorists that economic stagnation and neglect reigned in the pre-Zionist period, and the arguments of followers of world-system and dependency perspectives who regard the Jewish-Arab conflict as a clash between capitalist and noncapitalist sectors (Asad 1975) are faulty, then. While economic change in Palestine was not a purely endogenous process, it originated and was further promoted by noncolonial and nonsettler forces. This state of affairs sharply contrasted with the situation in southern Africa in which capitalist relations were introduced in the course of the colonial process. The prior extensive

2. Since an administrative or political unit of Palestine did not exist before 1918, when used in earlier contexts the term "Palestine" refers to the autonomous *sanjak* (district) of Jerusalem and the *sanjaks* of Nablus and Acre, which formed a part of the *vilayet* (province) of Beirut.

contact of Palestine with the world economy, as compared to the meager exposure of southern Africa in the precolonial period, had a significant impact on the future economic history of the respective societies, as is explored later in the chapter.

Of the main forces responsible for initiating the process of social and economic transformation, one important element was the government, beginning with the reforms introduced by the Egyptian authorities in the 1830s and continuing with the Tanzimat (directed from the center) and the activities of the provincial administration of Jerusalem. There was no direct intervention in the economy in the form of state-sponsored industrialization, but the authorities acted to facilitate development in various ways: through increasing security and granting protection from nomad incursions, thereby opening the coastal areas and the plains to permanent settlement and cultivation; by breaking the power and resistance of local notables in the mountainous regions and thus putting an end to destructive local feuds; by improving roads and port facilities (though to an insufficient degree); by reorganizing the tax and land registration systems in order to encourage investment in production; and by improving the position of non-Muslim minorities and giving the local population some say in the administration (Gerber 1985; Shamir 1986).

Foreign powers also played an important role in the country in that period, either directly through trade and initiative in the areas of sea and land transportation (establishing regular shipping services for freight and passengers, investing in railroad construction), communications, and banking services, or indirectly through diplomatic and missionary activities (increasing tourism, pilgrimages, consular protection of minorities, construction, health, and education). In fact, the European intervention is widely seen as the crucial factor in this process of change. We must keep in mind, though, that the bearers of the process were mostly local actors—landlords, farmers, and merchants; Muslims and Christians alike (Agmon 1986; Gilbar 1986). Gross (1976) divides these innovative capitalist elements into two subgroups: indigenous capitalists including Arabs, Levantines (of Greek and Italian origin), and local Jews; and new foreign entrepreneurs, mostly German and Jewish immigrants. The first group was larger, though less innovative. The second group was smaller but influential because of their modern approach to business organization. The two sectors competed with each other, but also collaborated in some areas, especially in the fast growing field of citrus cultivation and exports.

In striking a balance between different views of the sources of change, Gross argues that "it should be emphasized that the local population, even the rural one, was capable of responding to incentives and of imitating and absorbing innovations. Without external factors the economy would not have changed much in that period, but without the 'internal' responsive factors the growth which took place would not have occurred" (Gross 1976: 138). An even stronger emphasis on the role of internal factors is provided by Doumani, who claims that "some aspects of 'modernity' surfaced long before they were 'initiated' by outside stimuli, while 'traditional' modes of organization survived much longer than is usually admitted." He further argues that local structures, which were connected by flexible and dynamic networks, "interacted with externally imposed changes and filtered them into the rhythms of everyday life" (Doumani 1992: 23). Whatever the exact weight of internal and external dynamics, it is clear from the above that we have to fully incorporate indigenous capacities and processes in any account of economic transformation.

Perhaps the most crucial area of economic transformation in late nineteenth- and early twentieth-century Palestine was the land tenure system, especially important because life in the country at the time was dominated by agriculture. For most of the Ottoman period, until the late nineteenth century, private property in land was virtually nonexistent. The state held nominal title to most agricultural land, which was classified as *miri* (state-owned). Corresponding to this type of tenure was the *iltizam* (tax-farming) system, which was widely used as a form of extraction from peasants. Agricultural surplus was divided between the state and the *multazim* (tax-farmer), who usually came from the ranks of the rural notable class. Taxes were imposed on the village as a unit rather than on individual families, and they were mostly paid in kind. There was no interference in the production process by forces external to the village. (See Granott 1952 and Baer 1971 for surveys of agrarian relations in the Middle East in general and Palestine in particular.) A common form of landholding widespread in the plains and valleys, and to a much lesser extent in the hilly regions, was the *mushaʿ*. Consisting of communal land periodically redistributed among all village families, it was a form of equalizing the burden of fiscal exactions (by the state, local strongmen, nomads), which were especially heavy in the accessible and poorly defended coastal regions. The mountainous communities could better resist external predators and had less need for the *mushaʿ* arrangement (Firestone 1981).

This state of affairs began to change in the second half of the nineteenth century under the impact of the commercialization of the economy—a product of the integration into the European world system. Three major developments in the Middle East at the time were the emergence of private ownership of agricultural land and the gradual abolition of the *iltizam* system, the formation of large landed estates, and the dissolution of the village community (Baer 1983). The Ottoman land law of 1858 established for the first time legal title to the land, thus making the creation of large private estates possible through the purchase of previously uncultivated land (Gerber 1987: 67–73). This process occurred in the plains and coastal areas of Palestine, where increasing physical security, growing local and European demand for foodstuffs, and the availability of land encouraged the urban and commercial elites to buy land in large quantities in order to grow cash crops for export. Many villagers from the mountain areas and nomadic tribesmen also settled in these areas to take advantage of the newly opened opportunities. In the central hilly regions of the country, small-scale landholding was much more common, and a large number of peasants acquired individual title to their land.

Peasants there maintained a stronger and more independent position in relation to the state and large landlords, and the family farm remained the dominant form of land tenure (Gerber 1985: 199–222).

The second half of the nineteenth century witnessed a steady rise in the volume of production for the market. The most important commodities were cereals (wheat, barley, durrah), oranges, sesame seeds, olive oil, and soap. These products were exported primarily to Egypt and Anatolia, but also and increasingly so to Europe (especially Britain and France). Imports consisted mainly of processed foods: sugar, tea, coffee, tobacco, rice; raw materials: timber, iron, kerosene; and machine-made goods: textiles and hardware. The latter came mostly from European countries, either directly or through Ottoman and Egyptian ports. The overall balance of payments was positive until the turn of the twentieth century (Schölch 1982; Gilbar 1986).

Industry remained largely undeveloped, and its share in exports was small, though in addition to soap some other modest industries such as manufacturing of religious artifacts and souvenirs developed. Even the influx of German and Jewish immigrants who brought with them capital, industrial skills, and more advanced technology did little to change the composition of trade. Until the beginning of the First World War in 1914, the situation remained largely the same, with the exception of the growth of the wine and spirits industry in the new Jewish agricultural colonies.

Most of the growth in agriculture, then, could be attributed to large- and small-scale local initiative in extending the cultivated area and responding to market opportunities. Technological innovations in production and large investments of capital did not play a major role in this process except for the citrus-growing sector. Most of the production for the market was carried out by small family units, even when the land was nominally held by large landlords. The latter, Palestinian and foreign (Arab) alike, mostly were absentee landlords who collected rent from peasant cultivators without being involved directly in productive activities. The contribution of foreigners and immigrants was more considerable in the development of services: roads, mail, banking, and insurance (Buheiry 1981; Reilly 1981; Agmon 1986; Gilbar 1986). Local entrepreneurs adapted to changing circumstances without following a model established by immigrants. Indigenous people proved capable of absorbing externally induced stimuli without undermining themselves in the process.

This pattern of trade relations did not mean that the country became peripheralized, despite increasing integration into the world economy. Diversification of agricultural production for local and international markets prevented excessive dependence on one dominant crop, as was the case for cotton in Egypt and, to a lesser extent, silk in Lebanon. Consequently, there were no serious crises owing to sharp market fluctuations. Local crafts and industries were not wiped out, and the severe urban dislocations identified by Smilianskaya (1966) for the case of Syria were not repeated in Palestine. The urban economy was not particularly dependent on manufacture to begin with, and the effects of cheap mass-produced European goods were mixed. Their importation did initially lead to a decline in local textile production, but there remained sufficient market outlets for indigenous producers. Very cheap labor, imported raw materials (cotton yarn), and sensitivity to local customs and tastes allowed weavers and spinners to survive and even expand their production, especially in the southern part of the country. The regional markets for soap and olive oil also were, for the most part, unaffected by foreign competition (Schölch 1982).

The image presented by the world-system perspective—of peripheral countries overwhelmed by massive invasion of industrial goods—does not reflect the economic realities in nineteenth-century Palestine, then. The country as a whole enjoyed greater prosperity, though only a small part of the profits from increased trade benefited the immediate producers. The real beneficiaries were merchants, middlemen, big landowners, tax farmers, and the state itself, which increased the tax burden on the peasants. These developments resulted in growing capital and income inequalities in Palestinian-Arab society, and an increasing social differentiation in villages between those who profited from the economic changes by accumulating land and orienting production to the market, and those who were crushed under heavy tax impositions, lost their land, and were forced to rely on off-farm occupations (Owen 1981: 173–79; Smith 1984: 18–37; Stein 1984: 16–34).

The formation of a rural labor force settled on the land and rooted in village life, through the operation of these processes, proved of great consequence in later periods. In the late nineteenth century, when Jewish settlers needed additional agricultural laborers to survive economically, they had to look no farther than the neighboring villages, in which surplus labor was already available. The enormously destructive operation of economic coercion, forcing relatively undifferentiated indigenous societies into meeting the labor demands of settlers in South Africa and elsewhere, was not replicated in Palestine. Although the Zionist settlement project eventually proved destructive to indigenous society, the exclusionary form taken by the settlement process was directly related to the capacity of indigenous society to avoid the prior processes of fragmentation, subordination, and incorporation of labor characteristic of colonial settlement in other parts of the world. This issue is further explored in subsequent chapters.

The Old Jewish Community

The economic position of the Jewish population before the beginning of Zionist immigration into Palestine was changing as well. Throughout most of the nineteenth century the Jewish community was concentrated in the four holy cities of Jerusalem, Hebron, Safed, and Tiberias and maintained its religious and institutional autonomy. It was integrated into the socioeconomic structure of the country as a whole and did not form a foreign enclave devoid of ties with the local economy. This is particularly true of the Sephardi community,[3] whose members were Ottoman subjects. They had lived in the country for centuries and were the only ones officially recognized by the government as Jews. Ashkenazi Jews began forming their own communities much later, at the beginning of the nineteenth century.[4]

The most important source of income for Ashkenazim was the *halukkah* (distribution) system, which channeled contributions and donations collected from Jewish communities all over Europe to the Jews of Palestine. The Sephardim also benefited from this system, but to a lesser extent, and they were not as dependent on it. The money was distributed through the *kolelim*—community organizations representing groups of Jews from different regions and religious backgrounds. While the majority of the Ashkenazi population were dependent to some extent on *halukkah* money for survival, the Sephardim allocated money only to students and scholars of religious law, thus forcing the rest to find other means of subsistence. The small number of people who worked on a regular basis were engaged in various occupations, including craft production (carpenters, tailors, shoemakers) and small-scale trade, serving the needs of the limited local market. According to some estimates, about 80 to 90 percent of the total Jewish population needed some kind of community support in order to survive (Gat 1974: 34–39).

This state of affairs began to change toward the latter part of the nineteenth century, together with the growing impact of the European economy. Increased demand for more sophisticated goods and services, encouraged by the rise in eastern European immigration, led to larger involvement in modern economic activities. Both Sephardi and Ashkenazi entrepreneurs were active in import and export agencies, construction, real estate, banking, and hotels. Their economic role did not differ much from that of the wealthy Arab merchants and urban bourgeoisie; they took advantage of the new commercial opportunities, just like members of all other groups (Bartal 1976).

An important development that started in the 1870s and continued throughout the rest of the Ottoman period was the quest for the "productivization" of the Jewish community—a term used by those who believed a society based largely on alms, donations, and welfare was unhealthy and doomed to decay. Various earlier attempts made by Jewish and non-Jewish philanthropists to settle poor Jews on the land and employ them in production were not particularly successful. More lasting results were achieved with the settlement of west Jerusalem (outside the walled city), and the establishment of agricultural colonies, most notably Petah Tiqvah in 1878. While these steps were modest in comparison to the massive transformations that would affect Palestine in the twentieth century, they demonstrate that

---

3. Sephardi literally means "Spanish." It refers to Jews who were exiled from Spain in 1492 and continued to speak Judeo-Spanish or Ladino in their new locations around the Mediterranean.

4. Ashkenazi literally means "German." It refers to European Jews who spoke Yiddish, a German-Jewish dialect.

well before the rise of Zionism a process of change involving large numbers of people had started from within. It seems that the common view in Israeli traditional historiography—seeing the pre-1882 Jewish community as stagnant and corrupt—is exaggerated, to say the least, if not outright false.[5] (See Herzog 1987 and Halper 1991 for a focus on the dynamic nature of the old community.)

We can reach the same conclusions about the Jewish population of Palestine that we reached about the Arab population. Both communities were undergoing a process of gradual change under the impact of contact with Europe and their own internal dynamics. There were no major clashes between the communities as a result of these limited economic changes, since they were not in direct competition *as groups* (though, obviously, members of any community may have competed with members of other communities *as individuals*). There was a major ecological difference between Jews and Arabs, though; whereas the former were virtually all urban, the latter were mostly rural. Jews did not take direct part in agricultural production, though a few were involved in marketing produce. Overall, the Jewish community did not enter hierarchical or exploitative economic relations with Arabs.

The Zionist Settlement Process

The "prehistory" of the Palestinian-Israeli conflict, then, was a period of relatively peaceful coexistence between the different religious and ethnic groups. This situation went through important changes with the establishment of Jewish settlement movements in eastern Europe, putting forward the goal of an independent Jewish commonwealth (or state) in Palestine/Israel. Only then does the history of the conflict proper begin. The increase in anti-Semitic incidents in the Russian Empire, coupled with economic dislocations and growing demographic pressure in the last quarter of the nineteenth century, led to the largest Jewish population movement in modern history. Most of those affected by this process (about three million people until the outbreak of the First World War) moved west, to North America and some to South America. Only a few, around 2 percent of the total number of immigrants, moved to Palestine during the same period. This was the beginning of the new Jewish community, a segment of the Jewish population of Palestine different in its character, organization, and goals from the older segments. It did not include all those who immigrated to Palestine at that time as many were integrated into the existing socioeconomic and communal structures, and its boundaries were sometimes fluid, but its members increasingly consolidated a distinct identity.

The most important characteristic of the new Jewish community which set it apart from the old one was its strong emphasis on agricultural settlement. There had been several prior attempts at settlement in rural areas by members of the

---

5. This view in its academic version has gone through major revisions since 1980 but is still common in political circles and among the general public.

pre-1882 Jewish community, but these were not successful and were abandoned soon after they started (Bartal 1983: 224–32; Avitsur 1971). The new wave of settlement, in contrast, resulted in the establishment of more than forty viable villages and towns by 1914 (a list of all settlements, area, population, and principal crops appears in Ruppin 1918: 29–31). Thus the Jewish community (or a segment thereof) entered for the first time into direct contact with the Palestinian-Arab inhabitants of the countryside who were the majority of the population. Individual Jews had all kinds of commercial dealings with peasants before, but the circumstances were changing. A large and growing group of Jews established a presence in regions that had been practically off-limits for them until then because of unstable security conditions. Furthermore, the encounter between settlers and peasants pushed issues of land and labor to the fore. The resulting conflicts signaled the beginning of a century-long political struggle over the future of the country.

As mentioned earlier, wealthy Palestinians invested in large pieces of land in the wake of security improvements in the countryside and the opening of commercial opportunities in agriculture. Many of these landowners were primarily interested in easy and quick gains from their new acquisitions, and were more than willing to sell it away for a handsome profit. Granott (1952: 78–84) goes so far as to claim that Arab capitalists bought land anticipating an increase in its value as a result of the growing Jewish demand. Whether that was indeed the case, with the beginning of an influx of Jewish immigrants into the country in the last two decades of the nineteenth century, indigenous landlords with large holdings and Jewish settlers shared an interest in such transactions.

Much of the land purchased by the Jewish settlement movements (the Palestine Jewish Colonization Association, the Palestine Land Development Company, and the Jewish National Fund, alongside other private individuals and groups) was in regions dominated by large landed property—the coastal areas and the plains. These parts of the country were less densely populated, and the soil was seen as more suitable for cereal and citrus cultivation, the supposed mainstay of the new settler economy. Only in the 1930s, after the reservoir of large estates ready to be sold had been exhausted, did Zionist organizations turn to purchasing land from small owners (Porath 1977: 80–87). In the early period of 1878–1914, 50 percent of the land was bought from large Palestinian and Arab absentee landowners and another 37 percent from other sources (the Ottoman government, Christian churches, foreign companies, and wealthy businessmen). Only 12.5 percent was purchased from peasant cultivators (Granott 1952: 275–78). Khalidi (1988: 225), using Arab sources, quotes similar figures for 60 percent of land purchased at that period: 58 percent of it was from non-Palestinian absentee landlords, 36 percent from Palestinian absentees, and only 6 percent from local landlords and fellahin (peasants).

Granott regards these figures as indicative of a progressive development, a breakup of big and inefficient units: "The transfer of the land for Jewish settlement purposes always involved a fundamental change in the character of the ownership; large and medium stretches of land were for the most part replaced by small holdings. This brought about an important change in the economic sphere also—an increase in production through more intensive and improved cultivation of the soil and a considerable growth of the number of [Jewish] peasants and of the population in general" (1952: 275). This view is not surprising, coming as it does from a leading official of the Jewish National Fund, who played an important role in efforts to acquire land for Jewish settlement. Unfortunately, Granott deals only with legal ownership and conveniently ignores production. Contrary to the impression one gets from his presentation, large-scale landholding usually went hand in hand with small-scale cultivation. In other words, land transfers from Arabs to Jews did *not* mean a more egalitarian land tenure system. Absentee property, prior to its sale, was usually cultivated by tenants and agricultural laborers whose livelihood was dependent on access to land, access subsequently denied as a result of the transfer. Most of them must have found it difficult to share Granott's enthusiasm for the progressive nature of this transformation in agrarian relations.

Conflicts over Land

The rights of tenants quickly became a bone of contention between the old indigenous cultivators and the new settler owners. It provided the background for most of the security problems that faced the Jewish colonies as soon as they were established. Some people were conscious of the problems involved in land purchases early on. Shmuel Hirsch analyzed an attack on Petah Tiqvah in 1886 and argued that the refusal to acknowledge customary tenant rights made the colonists appear as robbers in the eyes of the fellahin (*Ha-Melitz*, 7/5/1886, in Eliav 1981: 113–15). According to Moshe Smilansky (a leading figure of the first *aliyah* settlements), "the new settlers bought land from large landowners who had acquired their land, for the most part, through robbery and infringement of rights. The peasant, whose land was robbed . . . will never forget it nor forgive," and "the memory of his land and the feeling of revenge will pass from father to son. And the claim is for the land itself" (*Ha-Aretz*, 12/30/1949, in Assaf 1970: 11). The Ottoman government was responsible for selling off land confiscated from peasants who defaulted on their debts. The result was increasing tensions between colonists and local villagers. Even before the beginning of the first *aliyah*, the agricultural school of Mikveh Israel entered into a conflict with the peasants of neighboring Yazur on whose land it was built in 1870 (Cohen 1970: 56–57).

Another typical conflict involved the settlement of Metullah, whose lands were bought in 1895 from a Lebanese landowner. Until then, about six hundred Druze tenants lived and worked the land there, but the officials of the settlement agency, accompanied by Ottoman soldiers, forced the cultivators to evacuate and move to neighboring villages. As a result, for years after, the former inhabitants continued to raid the newly established colony. Metullah spent more than any other Jewish settlement on security. Only in 1904 was the case settled by paying compensation to the tenant families (Be'eri 1985: 83–84). In this incident the Ottoman state intervened in support of the legal landowners, the settlers. In addition, the colonists frequently enjoyed the assistance of European consuls whenever clashes with peasants occurred, because most colonists kept their foreign nationality and were entitled to diplomatic protection.

The Metullah events inspired a landmark discussion of the implications of the Zionist strategy of land purchases. An 1907 article, "The Hidden Question," published in the Russian-based *Ha-Shiloah* magazine, argued that "the tenant fellah is not a guest on the leased land but a permanent resident. . . . It is customary that when the property changes hands the tenants remain as they are, but when we buy such land we totally remove from it the previous cultivators." This is problematic since "unless we want to deceive ourselves deliberately, we have to admit that we have thrown poor people out of their miserable lodgings and taken away their sustenance. . . . [The fellah] continues to look upon the land as his birthright, temporarily usurped by foreigners" (Epstein 1907: 194; for a discussion of this article and the responses to it, see Cohen 1970: 66–69; Be'eri 1985: 123–26; Gorny 1985: 48–51, 56–59).

In addition to the root problem of land dispossession, tensions and hostilities occurred over various other issues such as use of water resources, grazing rights, demarcation of boundaries, money matters, defense of the settlements, property violations, and blood vengeance (detailed descriptions appear in Assaf 1970: 9–39; Cohen 1970: 45–61; Yaari 1974; Mandel 1976: 34–40; Kayyali 1979: 16–24; Ro'i 1981; Be'eri 1985: 35–84; Khalidi 1988). The German Templars, who established several agricultural colonies in Palestine around the same time as the first *aliyah*, encountered similar problems of hostile relations with neighboring Arab villages (Carmel 1973: 180–97). Both groups of settlers were outsiders to the country and its customs in the eyes of indigenous people, and many of their conflicts had to do with misunderstandings resulting from language difficulties and cultural differences. There was a major difference between them, however. The Germans, a tiny, idiosyncratic minority in their country of origin, did not become a significant force. This was not the case with Jewish immigrants, whose movement, despite encompassing a minority of Jews, was backed by the human, financial, and moral strategic reserves of the Jewish people in Europe.

The Labor Issue

The struggle over land has been central to the conflict ever since the days of the first *aliyah*. Soon after the first settlers arrived in Palestine in 1882, another crucial issue emerged: the role indigenous Arab labor was to play in the life of the new Jewish community. The original Zionist vision of Bilu, Hibat Zion, and other organizations saw the return to the land and the establishment of autonomous rural communities employing their own labor as the core of the program of regenerating the Jewish people in their ancient homeland. They quickly realized, though, that Palestine was different from what they had imagined. This forced some radical changes in the way they managed their affairs and pursued the goal of working the land on their own. Commitment to the cause could not compensate for harsh economic realities.

Their initial plan was to concentrate on subsistence crops in a way similar to the indigenous peasants, but using more advanced technology and forms of organization that would allow them a higher standard of living. They grew grains (primarily wheat and barley) and other food crops with the goal of constructing a viable community on the basis of production for their own needs (Giladi 1983). Needs, however, are to a large extent culturally and historically determined rather than objectively given. What may have been considered by Arab peasants as enough for survival did not necessarily satisfy the settlers' self-defined needs. As the head of the Colonization Department of the Zionist Organization put it, "the [immigrant] Jew wants to remain a civilized man in Palestine. He does not want to descend again to the same level of civilization which Europe has left behind a century ago and which still exists only in the Orient. . . . This contradiction, that the Jew in Palestine wants to remain civilized while competing economically with the majority of the population who do not have the needs of civilized people, is the root of all the difficulties with which the agricultural settlement has had to struggle" (Ruppin 1925: 2–3).

The difficulties facing settlers included new and unfamiliar conditions, cultural isolation, insecurity, health problems (especially malaria), hot climate, hard labor, and lack of public services. With all these, the most important threat to the foundation of the enterprise was economic: their income was not as high as expected. The settlements were not self-sufficient, and their Jewish sponsors back in Russia did not raise enough money to provide for their needs. Thus they went bankrupt within the first year of operation (Aaronsohn 1983). Shortly thereafter most of the settlements became clients of the French Jewish Baron Edmund de Rothschild, who assumed the role of patron of the new *moshavot* (Jewish agricultural communities) from 1883 to 1900. Some settlements did not become as financially indebted to him as others, and in a few cases were not indebted at all. However, the enormous sums of money, technical help, and personal interest Rothschild invested in the settlement project made him, without doubt, the most important factor in the economic development of the Jewish agricultural sector for years to come.

The crisis of the settler subsistence farm, coupled with outside intervention, led to a change of direction in agricultural activities with far-reaching consequences: "Instead of the traditional multi-crop farm based on grains, Rothschild decided to invest in modern, mono-culture farming. This was a revolutionary idea that changed the face of settlement in Palestine for a whole generation" (Aaronsohn 1983: 248). It resulted in the adoption of a mode of farming based on fruit tree plantations and citrus orchards. In the beginning the farmers worked as tenants, the nominal ownership of the land having been taken away from them, but later they were given back practical ownership and themselves started employing agricultural wage-labor on a large scale. They produced primarily for export and became dependent on the prices paid for their crops on the European market. Their food supply came from the indigenous market to which the surplus left after the Arab family-labor farm provided for its own subsistence needs was directed. The new strategy adopted by settlers required massive investments of capital and heavy subsidies until the farmers got on their feet. The major crops were grapes, almonds, olives, and oranges, but they experimented with tobacco, mulberry trees for silk worms, and peaches. The experiments were accompanied by technological innovations and some industrial development for processing crops, primarily wine cellars in Rishon le-Tzion and Zikhron Yaakov (Giladi 1983).

In 1900 Rothschild transferred his Palestine assets to the Jewish Colonization Association, another philanthropic organization which stressed Jewish agricultural settlement in Palestine and elsewhere. The association made an effort to give the farmers back their autonomy and wean them from dependence on foreign subsidies. The old *moshavot* became efficient and self-managing, basing themselves on Arab wage-labor. The new settlements established after 1900 attempted a system of mixed farming which did not require large capital investments and was mostly based on self-labor. By the end of the Ottoman period these settlements had not yet established a secure basis and continued to rely on external subsidies. As Arthur Ruppin put it: "As a matter of fact, grain cultivation in Palestine is less profitable for the European immigrant than orchards and, moreover, the Jew seems to have a greater aptitude for the care of trees than for grain cultivation. In any case, the excellence of the tree plantations in the Jewish colonies is admitted without a dissenting voice. They are generally considered models, whereas grain cultivation and animal husbandry as practiced by the Jews leave much to be desired, and have not as yet proved unquestionably profitable" (Ruppin 1918: 28). Despite the advances the settlers made in supplying their own needs, they continued to spend a considerable part of their income on basic foods obtained from Arab producers. The goal of viable and self-sufficient Jewish agricultural economy was yet to be achieved.

The development of the *moshavot* is important not only in its own right, as the foundation for the new community, but also in its implications for Jewish-Arab relations. With the change to orchard cultivation, the settlers started employing indigenous labor on a large scale. In many cases the number of Arab families working in Jewish settlements, or leasing land from them, exceeded the number of Jewish colonists. As early as 1878, when the first Jewish farmer of Petah Tiqvah begin ploughing his land, twelve Arab laborers were working at his side. A survey of the same place in 1892 discovered that about half the farmers leased out all of their land to Arabs, and other farmers also employed Arab laborers on their land to a lesser extent (Be'eri 1985: 79–82). The marketplace of the settlement was described in 1910 as a place in which "the buyers are Jewish, the vendors Arab" (S.

Dayan, quoted in Yaari 1974: 937). In Rishon le-Tzion a few dozen settler families employed hundreds of Arab families in fieldwork and in services. In 1911 Zikhron Yaakov was described as "a Jewish colony, the majority of whose inhabitants are Arabs who were born there, and its marketplace full of Arab vendors" (quoted in Assaf 1970: 28).

Leading Zionist activists were concerned by what they described as partial Arabization of the colonies. In 1915 Ruppin estimated that there were about two to three times as many Arab laborers as Jewish ones in the settlements of Judaea. In Lower Galilee their proportion was smaller, but in Upper Galilee most of the Jewish-owned land was leased to Arab tenants (Ruppin 1918: 29). There are no accurate statistics on the extent of Arab employment in the *moshavot*, and it varied between places and seasons, but it was clearly widespread and was the major source of labor power throughout the period. Significantly, neighboring Arabs were employed not only in agricultural activities but in construction, security, and personal services as well. Their presence in a large number of settlements was strongly felt. This state of affairs generated much resentment among Zionist activists, who saw it as a mockery of the underlying rationale of the settlement project.

Without underestimating the difficulties settlers encountered in the form of raids, attacks on person and property, and harassment by some government officials, it is safe to say that even at that earlier stage they began to exercise some measure of economic power over (some) indigenous people. Settlers in the *moshavot* began to form an economic elite, making a living off the labor of others. However, their small numbers and limited territorial spread prevented them from having a significant effect on indigenous society as a whole. The vast majority of peasants still had little if any contact with settlers. The settlers did have an impact on their immediate environment, however, the neighboring Arab villages and Bedouin settlements. The establishment of labor relations between settlers and peasants added a new and different dimension to intercommunal relations, reflected in the changing attitudes of many settlers toward their indigenous workers and tenants. Feelings of fear and of being under siege by an alien and hostile population frequently gave way to expressions of dominance, superiority, and contempt, commonly found among ruling agrarian elites the world over. Settler political power was very limited, but their mental attitude quickly adjusted to their new economic situation.

In a widely quoted article published in 1891, "The Truth from Eretz Israel," the Zionist thinker Ahad Ha-Am exposed the problems he saw in the relations between Jewish farmers and their Arab laborers in the *moshavot*. He believed that the Arab population, including the peasants, benefited economically from the Jewish settlements in their midst. Despite that, he regarded the settlers' attitudes as harmful and dangerous to the long-term prospects for Jewish presence in the country; he warned that in the event "the life of our people in Palestine develops so far that they push out the inhabitants of the country on a small or on a large scale, then the latter would not easily yield their places" (Ahad Ha-Am 1930: 28).

Ahad Ha-Am was worried in particular about the effects of the manner in which the farmers treated their workers. They were behaving like people "who were slaves in their country of exile, and suddenly find themselves with unlimited freedom, a wild freedom which can only be found in a country such as Turkey.[6] This sudden change has inspired in their hearts a tendency to despotism, as always happens with the slave who becomes a master, and they treat the Arabs with hostility and cruelty, unjustly trespass their boundaries, shamelessly beat them without good reason, and even boast of having done so" (1930: 40). This relationship between settlers and indigenous people had both an intensifying and a mitigating effect on intercommunal conflict. Maltreatment of the Arab workers by Jewish farmers caused anger and resentment among the former. These feelings were probably compounded by the farmers' foreign origins. At the same time, the initial hostility of many Arabs toward the settlers whose land purchases caused the eviction of tenants was moderated as time passed and the situation became normalized. With the development of the orchard farm as the economic foundation of many *moshavot*, the establishment of Jewish settlements no longer necessarily meant the displacement of former occupants, since these were frequently able to lease back part of the land or gain employment in the settlements.

Against this background Khalidi claims that "the pragmatic and unideological settlers of the first Aliyah were thus in effect treating the fellahin little differently than had their former Arab landlords, disappropriating but in most cases not fully dispossessing them. This changed definitively with the second Aliyah early in the twentieth century, when the idea of the 'conquest of labor' meaning replacing Arab workers with Jewish ones took hold, and a new, exclusivist form of colonization began" (Khalidi 1988: 215). The idea that the second *aliyah* transformed the pattern of the national conflict is common among supporters and opponents of the Zionist project alike. Assaf describes the tensions and fights between settlers and peasants as prepolitical and unrelated to political relations between Arabs and Jews as national groups (as opposed to individuals). Only the founding of the Zionist movement in 1897, and the second *aliyah*, which began in 1904, introduced an explicit political element (Assaf 1970: 37–44). Along the same line, Mandel argues that before 1908 there existed "a rough pattern of initial resentment, suppressed or open hostility, giving way in time to acceptance of the situation and generally good day-to-day relations" (Mandel 1976: 38).

Jewish (Hebrew) Labor

The second *aliyah* (1904–14) introduced a new dimension into the conflict, but its effects were not felt so strongly until the end of the period. During that time, labor became an important issue in Jewish-Arab relations. The second immigration wave from eastern Europe brought with it thousands of people with limited means who were looking for jobs. The Arab-owned economy was virtually off-

---

6. This is an interesting twist from the notion of Oriental Despotism.

limits for them: there was no demand for their expensive, as compared to their local competitors', labor. They were therefore restricted to Jewish-owned enterprises. The employment of Arab workers in the *moshavot*'s expanding orchard economy was clearly beneficial for the farmers, but it increasingly clashed with the needs of the newly arrived immigrants who rejected the prevailing system of Arab labor on both principled and practical grounds. They saw it as conflicting with the goals of the productivization of the Jewish people and the construction of a self-sufficient Jewish society in Palestine. On a more immediate level, employment of Arabs limited the opportunities for newcomers to find jobs that would enable them to establish a permanent basis in the country. Most migrants were dependent on the limited local labor market for survival. Thus the question of Jewish labor—the exclusive or considerable employment of Jewish workers in Jewish enterprises—became a source of conflict within the Jewish community, and to some extent between it and Arab laborers.

The farmers chose to employ Arabs in agriculture, construction, and services for several reasons: they were more productive because they were used to the conditions of hard labor in the fields; they were cheaper because, still rooted in their own land as tenants, they were capable of providing part of their living through the subsistence sector; and they were more easily disciplined because they lacked a tradition of organized resistance to labor exploitation. In contrast, Jewish workers were less experienced and less adapted to the climate and the harsh demands of agricultural labor; they were more expensive to hire since they were used to higher standards of living and had to satisfy all their needs from wages; and they were difficult to discipline. In the words of a contemporary of the second *aliyah*: "You cannot insult a Jew[ish worker], it is difficult to scold him, he hardly submits to authority and he costs a lot of money" (quoted in Assaf 1970: 45).

The farmers' interest in lowering their costs dictated a preference for Arabs rather than Jews as a major source of labor, especially since an indigenous village-based labor force had already come into being independent of the settlement process. There was thus no need to interfere in costly and potentially dangerous ways with the indigenous rural economy; it generated labor surplus on its own. And indeed, in all of the large orchard-based *moshavot*, Arabs became the majority in the labor force. Appeals to nationalist principles and Jewish solidarity which were not backed up by material incentives did not prove convincing to employers. The Zionist movement was too weak politically, and its resources too meager, to be able to coerce farmers into compliance with Zionist imperatives or to compensate them for financial losses incurred because of higher labor costs. As a result, Jewish labor policies were not implemented on a significant scale.

The issue of Jewish labor has been analyzed in terms of split labor market theory, an approach that focuses on struggles between (Jewish farmer) capitalists and "expensive" (Jewish immigrant) workers over the employment of "cheap" (indigenous Arab) workers. (Bonacich 1979 provides the general theory; Shafir 1989: 45–90 applies it to this case.) It is obvious that the material interests of

Jewish immigrants played a role in the formulation of Jewish labor policies, as Shafir argues, but we have to go beyond mere economic concerns in analyzing labor strategies. The conflict over the employment of indigenous workers took place in a context of colonization and settlement. Incoming workers were those who sought to bar local workers from being employed, rather than the other way around, as in cases in the United States and western Europe which informed the original theory. This reversal of roles calls for a radical modification of the theory. The Jewish immigrants were not defending an established class position. Rather they were attempting to *form* a class not yet in existence and to guarantee access to the labor market to a group of people defined in *national* rather than *class* terms.

As a result of this unusual setup, the conflicts that took place in the Jewish community over the employment of Arab labor were framed as part of a national debate over settlement strategies and the manner in which a "complete" Jewish class society could be formed in the country. Conflicts between Jewish farmers and workers were meaningless outside of this political context. Split labor market theory as applied to Palestine/Israel deals with labor market strategies, without accounting for the presence of Jewish immigrants on the scene and the prior structuration of class organization on national grounds. Settled Jewish workers organized to promote further immigration and acted to reserve jobs not just for themselves but with a view to a future mass influx of European Jews. That workers should even contemplate policies likely to intensify competition over scarce jobs (such as the encouragement of Jewish immigration from Europe and Yemen), and threaten their own positions in the process, cannot be adequately explained from within the market nexus itself.

Advocates of Jewish labor believed they were fighting a dangerous development seriously damaging to the settlement project in Palestine/Israel. They feared that the exploitation of Arabs for their labor would lead to the same development that "had already taken place in other countries, and which must take place by force of historical inevitability—the peasant will rise . . . and try to throw off the yoke of his oppressors . . . when the day of settling accounts comes, the Arab worker will direct his rage first of all against his Jewish employers" (a 1907 editorial in *Ha-Poel Ha-Tzair* magazine, in Be'eri 1985: 113). In a similar way, David Ben-Gurion argued in 1910 against the danger of combining class and national confrontation: "Like all workers, the Arab worker hates his oppressor and exploiter. In addition to the class contradiction *there is in this case a national difference between workers and farmers*; hatred thus takes the form of national hatred and, furthermore, *the national factor predominates over the class factor*, and a fierce hatred of Jews is aroused among the masses of Arab workers" (quoted in Gorny 1985: 80, italics in the original).

The national factor also predominated over the class factor in the thinking of labor activists, including Ben-Gurion himself, whose socialism had a clear nationalist rationale. The theoretical justification for their approach was based on the argument that international class solidarity (to which many of the Zionist labor activists were committed in principle) could not be actively expressed as long as the specific national interests of Jewish workers were not addressed (as articulated in Ben-Zvi 1962a). Rhetoric celebrating socialist solidarity notwithstanding, the relatively peaceful coexistence between the *moshavot* and neighboring Arab villages gradually gave way to growing distance and segregation between the national communities as a result of the rising influence of labor Zionism. The campaign for Jewish labor did not result in any immediate changes in the structure of production and employment, but it did eventually lead to the adoption of a colonization strategy which gave preference for the self-employment of Jewish settlers in small agricultural communities. It was the beginning of a growing geographical and economic separation between the national communities.

In hindsight we now realize how important Jewish labor policies were. However, in the last decade of Ottoman rule it was far from obvious that the Zionist labor movement would play a major role in the future. The campaign for barring Arab labor from Jewish-owned farms was largely unsuccessful, though it did contribute to increasing tensions in the country, especially when it involved the security of the *moshavot*. Some clashes occurred over the employment of Arabs by Zionist institutions, but these took place mostly among Jews without directly involving the Arab side. Of more long-term significance was the revival of a pattern of settlement sponsored by the Zionist Organization which resulted in the dispossession of tenants from land bought by the Jewish National Fund. As the Jerusalem Palestinian political activist Ruhi Bey al-Khalidi complained in an interview he gave in 1909 to the Hebrew newspaper *Ha-Tzevi*, Jews could enter the country as individuals, "but to establish Jewish colonies is another question. The Jews have the financial capacity. They will be able to buy many tracts of land, and displace the Arab farmers from their land and their fathers' heritage" (quoted in Mandel 1976: 77).

The exclusionary settlement strategy encountered a "largely mute process of resistance" (Khalidi 1988: 228) by affected peasants, whose cause was taken up and given political expression by the urban Arab elite. The latter articulated peasant-related grievances in their anti-Zionist discourse, but continued to focus on their own more immediate concerns, which had little to do with rural class relations: the rise of Zionism and its political designs on the country, and the emergence of Arab nationalism and the growing sense of the imminent demise of the Ottoman Empire, which made the future of the country an increasingly urgent concern (Mandel 1976: 223–31). In that sense, Palestinian activist Najib Nassar's alarm, put in general national rather than specific class terms, over the establishment of (Jewish) societies "for the purchase of our country and for its colonization" (*al-Karmil*, 3/27/1909, in Muslih 1988: 80) was typical of Palestinian-Arab agitation in that period.

With the outbreak of the world war in 1914, and the British takeover of the country in 1917–18, a new era opened, bringing major changes in intercommunal relations in general and land and labor relations in particular. The British period leading to the partition of the country in 1948 is analyzed in chapters 5 and 6.

Conclusions

Late Ottoman Palestine saw the launching of the Zionist settlement project. The unfolding of land and labor relations between Jewish settlers and indigenous Arabs took place in the historical context of the expansion of the European-dominated world system into the Middle East. Indigenous society had already begun its transformation through integration into regional and international markets, legalization of private property in land, internal social differentiation, a gradual spread of capitalist relations in the countryside, and the generation of a rural labor surplus. These processes made Jewish settlement possible by transforming land and labor into commodities. At the same time, these changes rendered the direct impact of the Zionist project on indigenous society rather slight. Settlers did not need to disrupt, fragment, and subordinate indigenous people, as was done in numerous colonial territories, in order to gain access to land and labor. Endogenous processes of differentiation, in conjunction with externally induced stimuli, made the requirements (especially land) for settlement available on the market. Indigenous capacities thus critically shaped the contours of the settlement process.

Market relations affected the interaction between settlers and indigenous people but did not govern it. Jewish settlement was largely motivated by nationalist and religious sentiments rather than by a search for profits, as was the case in most other colonial enterprises. In addition to the contribution indigenous capacities made to the shaping of settlement processes, the latter were also affected by internal conflicts among settlers over the role material factors should play in the project. The Zionist labor movement was in favor of an exclusionary pattern of settlement that would be based on Jewish employment. They did not succeed in having their policies implemented, but they managed to plant the seeds of a new strategy of economic and political segregation that proved to be of great significance in later years.

South Africa

The Southern African Setting

The economic history of South Africa presents a more fragmented and complex picture than that of Palestine. South Africa came into being as a unitary political system as a result of a long history of interaction and conflict between various indigenous and settler states and societies. Processes of migration, settlement, conquest, and incorporation had been going on in the region for centuries, before and independent of the arrival of white settlers in the territory. Even after the founding of the Union of South Africa in 1910, important economic and social differences remained between the various regions of the country. It goes without saying, then, that when we deal with earlier periods we cannot assume uniformity in the economic developments that took place in the different territories later to become incorporated into modern South Africa. What Marks and Atmore say about South Africa in the nineteenth century is definitely true for earlier periods: "The political, social and economic structures of South Africa were, in large measure, regionally differentiated, and although all areas were ultimately affected albeit unevenly by the penetration of mercantile capital from the coast, processes set in train in one part of the region in the early nineteenth century were only in evidence much later in another" (Marks and Atmore 1980: 4). This implies the need to treat economic transformations and their effects on political conflicts in a historically differentiated manner. By the same token, we must not lose sight of the overall picture of the gradually emerging social formation coming into existence. We start by looking at the background of the colonial encounter in southern Africa.

The indigenous inhabitants of southern Africa are usually classified into two groups with distinct modes of socioeconomic organization: the Khoisan, who practiced hunting, gathering, and pastoralism and were concentrated in the southwest, and the more sedentary Bantu-speaking farmers, who practiced pastoralism and agriculture and occupied the territories to the east and north of the Khoisan. The distinctions between the two types of societies do not present a clear dichotomy, and there were various intermediate groups between them. The Khoisan could be further divided into the various societies of the Khoikhoi, who specialized in pastoralism, and the San, who focused on hunting-gathering activities, though the distinctions between the two are controversial (Elphick 1977: 3–10). They are commonly conflated and referred to jointly as the Khoisan, thus giving less weight to their internal differences. I follow this practice here except where the case clearly requires a separate treatment. At any rate, these people were the inhabitants of the Cape peninsula in the seventeenth century, and the first to encounter the merchants and settlers of the Dutch East India Company.

The central economic asset for the Khoisan, around which their societies were organized, was livestock. They did not practice agriculture but made a living from hunting, gathering, and herding. The weight of these different economic activities changed according to ecological circumstances: climate, rain, pastures, epidemics, and predation. Pastoralism, more so than cultivation, was subject to violent fluctuations in its prospects as the most important economic activity. As a result, the boundaries between hunting and herding communities were not rigid. In prosperous times hunters could join the ranks of the more established pastoralists as herdsmen and shepherds, or even acquire cattle themselves. In less fortunate times, people who lost their cattle became hunters and foragers. This movement between the pastoral and the hunter-gatherer states of existence was a constant feature of precolonial society (Elphick 1977: 23–42).

Land, Labor, Territorial Expansion | 49

The Khoisan did not have property in land though they privately owned cattle and sheep, used primarily as sources of dairy products and to a lesser extent as meat. Property inequalities between rich individuals and tribes led to the emergence of relations of clientage—a form of sharecropping, in a nonagricultural setting, whereby the more wealthy rented their cattle to the poor in return for a part of the product (newborn calves and milk). Their societies were not completely self-sufficient. Some limited trade connections with other groups were established, largely consisting of exchanging livestock for iron and copper. Surplus labor and market activities were not as common as they were among indigenous Palestinians, and their role in overall societal activities was minor. They are mentioned here, to give a comprehensive understanding of the dynamics of the Khoisan economy; in later periods, acquaintance with these forms of economic relations proved significant for the interactions between indigenous people and settlers (Elphick 1977: 43–68).

Ownership of cattle and control over labor were the central elements of the socioeconomic organization of other indigenous societies in the region, those practicing sedentary agriculture and belonging to the so-called Iron Age. Concepts such as primitive communist, lineage, and tributary modes of production have been advanced by scholars in debates over categorizing different precolonial societies (see, for example, Hall 1987). The exact terms are not as important here as the identification of the mechanisms of economic and political domination and their implications for the capacity of the indigenous people to respond to, take advantage of, and resist European expansion. In an attempt to analyze the characteristics common to all indigenous societies of the region, Guy claims that "it was the continuous acquisition, creation, control, and appropriation of labour power which was the dynamic social principle upon which South African pre-capitalist societies were founded. This labour power was realised by men, through the exchange of cattle for the productive and reproductive capacities of women" (Guy 1987: 22). The dominant group of married men and homestead heads controlled access to cattle and its products (meat, milk, leather) and appropriated the subsistence necessities produced by women, children, and young men. The differences between more and less wealthy men, or between chiefs and commoners, were less important than the gender and age divisions within the household which resulted in placing all older married men at the top of the social hierarchy.

Other writers, dealing with specific precolonial societies, put greater emphasis on struggles over possession of cattle—the main form of property—between chiefs and commoners. Peires (1981b), in his history of the Xhosa people, acknowledges the primacy of subsistence production within the homestead, but minimizes the extent of exploitation of women, seeing them instead as being controlled but not deprived of the products of their labor. He also stresses the chiefs' nominal ownership of land as an element of political and economic stratification. He argues, though, that despite payment of tribute and judicial fines to the Xhosa chiefs, their power over commoners and the differences in wealth among them were limited. Other forms of inequality such as cattle clientage, similar to that of the Khoisan, existed but did not create a permanent class of laborers (27–44). Trade relations in cattle, metals, beads, skins, and ivory with other indigenous societies existed but were not of much economic importance: "The goods obtained in these exchanges were utilised not as consumption or capital goods, but as cattle equivalents or as direct means for the acquisition of more cattle. Consequently, exchange did not lead to the internal diversification of the economy" (98).

The coexistence of and tensions between the subsistence-based economy centered on individual homestead units, and the larger units of which they formed a part and within which they were incorporated were a common feature of all societies of the Bantu-speaking people. (See the collection of articles in Marks and Atmore 1980 and in Peires 1981a.) The degree to which chiefs were able to exercise their authority over and exact tribute from commoners varied among the different groups. Generally speaking, the northern Nguni (Zulu, Swazi) were more centralized than their southern neighbors (Xhosa, Mpondo, and others).

In choosing between those analyses that regard gender and age as the crucial principles of stratification, and those that direct attention to the class differences between chiefs and commoners, the former approach seems more appropriate as a general picture of precolonial realities. However, since the end of the eighteenth century there was a marked increase in internal inequalities, in part as a result of the opening of international trade routes, without negating the principles of equal adult male access to land. What Marks argues with regard to the nineteenth-century Zulu state may have been applicable to other cases as well: "There were of course incipient cleavages within this society, if not fully fledged class divisions: between men and women, between elders and juniors, and between the aristocracy, the Zulu royal family, the subordinate chiefs, and the commoners" (Marks 1986: 24).

This summary description of social stratification among the Zulu people in the precolonial period reflects the situation in other African (but not Khoisan) indigenous societies, with some variations. (See Bonner 1983 for a discussion of the Swazi; Beinart 1982 for the Mpondo; Delius 1983 for the Pedi; Shillington 1985 for the southern Tswana.) The most important elements were communal landholding, the homestead as the basic unit of production, sex and age as the bases for the division of labor, occasional relations of clientage between more and less wealthy individuals, and the beginning of surplus extraction by the emerging states. Indigenous South Africans, especially the Khoisan, differed from Palestinians in that they had minimal exposure to the operation of market forces, little contact with the world economy, and a less differentiated social structure. These factors affected the ways different groups responded to the intrusion of new economic and political elements.

The Cape Settlement

The first European outpost in South Africa was established by the Dutch East India Company in 1652 to serve as a supply and refreshment station for Company ships going between Holland and the East Indies (parts of present-day Indonesia). The board of directors hoped that this step would help organize what had been only sporadic trade with indigenous people and that a regular supply of fresh water, meat, and vegetables would be guaranteed its crews. The Company did not intend at that time, or at any other subsequent time, to found a permanent colony on the Cape. It was not interested in building a costly and unmanageable empire. The western Cape was more fertile and hospitable than other parts of southern Africa, but its prospects as a commercial enterprise were in no way similar to the bounties of the spice-producing Asian territories. In fact, the Cape station never managed to sustain itself; it was run at a loss throughout its existence (Ross 1989; Schutte 1989). However, precisely because the Company was unwilling to invest any resources beyond what was necessary for its commercial purposes it was also prevented from arresting the eventual process of white settlers' territorial and political expansion.

Discussing the economic foundations of racial conflict in South Africa during the Company period (until the end of the eighteenth century) requires looking at two sets of relations: (1) that between the Europeans and the indigenous populations of the area of initial settlement—the Khoisan, and (2) those between the Company and the white settlers, on the one hand, and their Asian and African slaves on the other. Both sets were affected by the relations between the settlers and the colonial administration. Since the beginning of European settlement in South Africa, race relations presented a complex picture with multiple elements coexisting within each of the groups rather than a dichotomous black-white division. The interests and concerns of the Company were not identical to those of settlers, and indeed they often clashed. Indigenous and other subordinate groups were equally heterogenous, as they came from different places, played different economic roles, and enjoyed (or suffered from) different legal privileges and liabilities. The plurality of interests was much more pronounced than that of the equivalent parties in Palestine/Israel, although the latter case itself showed a degree of internal diversity.

The Khoisan: Initial Encounters

The initial relations between Company officials and the Khoisan involved exchange of European copper, iron, and tobacco for indigenous sheep and cattle. The Dutch were dependent on indigenous people for their supplies, and they wanted to ensure peaceful and regular contacts with them as external partners and not as internal subordinates. Company directives mandated that the Khoisan were not to be enslaved or conquered, and were to be treated as a free and sovereign people. The principle that guided the Company was to minimize involvement as much as possible. Reality on the ground soon became far less idyllic. Elphick and Malherbe (1989) describe the process through which the Khoisan lost their political and economic independence and were gradually transformed into landless and cattleless laborers on white-owned farms.

Internal divisions among indigenous clans and tribes, a consequent lack of a unified leadership, and the rapid decline of their vast herds and flocks as a result of increased European demands all combined to disrupt the normal ecological cycle and economic viability of the Khoisan. As in precolonial times, those who lost their cattle resorted to working for others, Europeans in this case. Since the early stages of white settlement some Khoisan worked in the colony in a variety of jobs. This was especially the case with the peninsular Khoisan (in the vicinity of Cape Town), who felt the impact of colonization most directly and immediately. The rapid loss of cattle and sheep through unfavorable terms of trade with the Company forced many others to look for jobs on white-owned farms. These people usually settled on farms together with their families and livestock, although they lived separate from the farmers. Their principal occupations were shepherd and herder, but they also engaged in other kinds of agricultural tasks. In exchange for their labor they were paid in food, housing, and tobacco. Occasionally they were also paid with lambs and calves, but usually not in sufficient quantities to enable them to regenerate their stock and return to pastoralism. Their loss of economic independence prevented them from rebuilding an effective leadership, as that was traditionally based on access to cattle as a reward to followers. Thus their ability to resist military and economic pressures had already been undermined by 1713, when a catastrophic epidemic gave the coup de grâce to their independent political and economic existence (Elphick 1977).

Formation of a Slave Society

The demographic decline of the Khoisan in the western Cape made imported slaves the major source of labor for the Company and for the freeburghers (independent settlers). Slaves had been used by the Company in its Asian domains, before the establishment of the Cape station, in plantation work, construction, and domestic service; the practice was continued in the new settlement. European perceptions of the indigenous population as uncivilized nomadic savages and therefore unreliable for any task other than their customary herding activities facilitated the spread of slavery. Within a few years of the establishment of the colony, the Company went on slaving expeditions to West Africa, Madagascar, and East Africa, while Asian slaves were sent on Company ships en route from the East Indies to Europe (Armstrong and Worden 1989).

Only a small and decreasing proportion of the slaves worked directly for the Company. The vast majority were owned by urban and rural freeburghers. In addition to slaves, the Company used the labor of Chinese and Javanese convicts exiled to Cape Town. The number of slaves owned by the Company itself was not large, never exceeding one thousand. This figure reflects the limited nature of the Company's activities, which involved managing the port and performing related construction work. Primarily a commercial enterprise, the Company did not engage in production and only supervised the marketing of agricultural commodities from the interior. Company slaves were employed as general laborers, skilled artisans, domestics, and overseers of other slaves. Their role in the economic life of Cape Town was considerable, though for the colony as a whole they were of less importance. The slaves who were employed on white-owned farms played a more important role. They were indispensable for agricultural production, and without them the economic nature of the colony would have been very different.

The initial plan of the Company was to develop small-scale farms engaged in intensive agriculture in order to satisfy its needs for food supplies. It was, however, unwilling to invest the capital necessary for that purpose or to pay the freeburghers enough for their products to make intensive cultivation worth their while. These economic circumstances, combined with the lack of adequate tools, seeds, draft animals, and labor, undermined the basis for the growth of a labor-intensive family farm. Instead, there emerged two main types of settler agricultural activities. The first one, located primarily in the western Cape, involved enterprises focused on food production for the local and international markets, especially wheat and wine. The second was a mixture of cattle farming with self-sufficient agriculture. Both types used coercive mechanisms to ensure a supply of cheap labor—slaves in the former case, Khoisan in the latter.

The adoption of extensive agricultural settlement patterns, the consequent territorial expansion, and the emergence of racial stratification were not inevitable processes. A different strategy pursued by the Company, such as investing capital in agriculture and encouraging European immigration, could have made intensive agriculture viable and therefore obviated further expansion beyond the Cape peninsula (Guelke 1989). Such policies could have resulted in making settlers more similar to their North American contemporaries. This did not turn out to be the case, however (Lamar and Thompson 1981: 14–40). South Africa had no intrinsic economic value to the Company except for its strategic location. Its economic attractions were minimal. The Company was not engaged in a state- or empire-formation project and was run on a strict costs and benefits logic. There was little reason for the Company to engage in economic experiments or to actively attempt to replicate Dutch farming patterns as long as its needs could be satisfied by other, cheaper, arrangements.

Settlers faced different economic opportunities and constraints than did the Company. Only a minority of them had enough capital or credit to become arable farmers and to operate a business based on cash crops produced with slave labor. Those who could not afford such an endeavor moved into the interior and became *trekboers* (pastoralist stockfarmers). For these people, the interior's "free" land and its potential reservoir of Khoisan labor offered the opportunity for independence without much initial capital.[7] As long as the *trekboers* could survive without working for others, intensive agriculture based on white labor could not be made the foundation of the settler economy.

Putting the labor calculus in economic terms, Neumark remarks that "there was no virtue in farming more intensively if the returns on the expended capital and labor were inadequate. It was not out of human weakness that the colonists obeyed the economic principle demanding an extensive use of the abundant factor, land, relative to the scarce factors, capital and labor" (Neumark 1957: 18). Under these circumstances, various forms of coerced labor were the most profitable solution for all white forces. The legitimacy of this course was founded on the view that land not used for agricultural cultivation was there for the taking, a view backed up by superior military power.

Similar economic and ideological calculations affected slavery. As Baron van Imhoff, governor-general of the East Indies, argued in 1741, the existence of slavery doomed the prospects of intensive farming: "I believe it would have been for the better had we, when the colony was founded, commenced with Europeans and brought them hither in such numbers that hunger and want would have forced them to work. But having imported slaves, every common or ordinary European becomes a gentleman and prefers to be served than to serve" (*Reports of Chavonnes and His Council and Van Imhoff at the Cape* [1918], in Fredrickson 1981: 67). The same logic was spelled out later in the century by W. S. van Ryneveld of the Council of Policy at Cape Town: "There is no man in the world who works without being incited to it by some motives. These consist either in ambition or in necessity . . . it follows that as long as there are in this country those resources to get subsistence in an easier manner, no [white] farmer will by way of preference devote himself to such a really toilsome and hard labour as our tillage, and especially our culture of grain . . . when a young [white] peasant marries and sees an opportunity of obtaining land fit for breeding cattle, by which he may get his livelihood, he would act like a fool by leaving that, and hiring himself out to his fellow peasant, in order there, along with the slaves, by a continual labour, to earn scarcely as much as only food and clothing for himself" (reply to Governor Macartney's questionnaire, 11/29/1797, in Du Toit and Giliomee 1983: 48).

The role of unfree labor in the social structure of the Cape is best seen in the context of the development of market-oriented agriculture. For most of the first two hundred years of Cape settlement, its products did not penetrate European markets. There was little demand for grains, meat, and wines from overseas as these were grown in abundance on European soil. Agricultural production at the

---

7. The land was free in the sense of not being occupied by a permanently settled indigenous population which could effectively prevent settler expansion and make takeover relatively costly.

Cape responded to the demands of other customers, principally those of passing ships, the urban market of Cape Town, and the European communities in other tropical regions. Commercial production was the norm all over the colony, though the areas closer to the main (and for a long time the sole) market outlet, Cape Town, were the leading sectors in this respect. Even in remote areas of the interior at least some form of production for the market took place in order to satisfy farmers' needs for cash to buy weapons and other products such as sugar, coffee, tobacco, and garments (Ross 1986, 1989a). Although the process of commercialization was not so complete as to prevent the continuation of pockets of white subsistence agriculture into the twentieth century, market demands have always had an impact on land and labor relations in South Africa.

Slave ownership was widespread among white farmers to a degree rarely seen in other slave societies. It was particularly common in the Cape district (the agricultural hinterland of Cape Town), where it was virtually universal for most of the eighteenth century. The more distant districts of Stellenbosch, Drakenstein, and Swellendam had smaller proportions of slave ownership. Even there, in the later part of the eighteenth century about 70 percent of farmers in Stellenbosch and Drakenstein had at least one slave, and in Swellendam about 50 percent owned slaves. The prevalence of pastoral farming in the more remote areas to the north and east of Cape Town was the main reason for this state of affairs. The *trekboers* of the interior, compared with the settled farmers of the southwest, had less use for slaves and could not afford them anyway. By the time slavery was abolished in 1834, a majority of the slaves (almost 70 percent) were found in the districts near Cape Town. Relatively few (16 percent) were in the eastern pastoral districts of Graaf-Reinet, Uitenhage, Albany, and Somerset. They lived mostly in relatively small units, the plantation-type slavery of the New World remaining rare in South Africa (Armstrong and Worden 1989: 129–36).

White farmers at the Cape used labor intensively, though they possessed land on an extensive scale. Work was varied, and slaves were employed in different jobs depending on the season. They sowed, ploughed, harvested, and threshed wheat and other grains. They planted, pruned and cut vines, picked grapes, and pressed them to make wine. These activities involved concentrated efforts in certain times of the year. Other year-round tasks included keeping livestock, collecting wood, driving wagons, and doing domestic labor. More prosperous farmers bought a large number of slaves to cover their needs during the peak periods and hired some of them out to work in the city or on other farms during less demanding periods. Farmers who could not afford a permanent slave labor force hired slaves from more wealthy owners on a temporary basis. Others hired Khoisan for limited periods without giving them permanent employment. Overall, wine farmers tended to rely exclusively on their own slaves, while grain farmers used hired labor more frequently (Worden 1985: 19–28). Slaves were subjected to brutal exploitation by their masters. The system of slavery was repressive and necessitated tight control and harsh disciplinary measures, which triggered acts of resistance by defiant slaves (Ross 1983).

The Khoisan: Further Incorporation

The other major subordinate group in Dutch South Africa, the Khoisan, shared with slaves a history of labor exploitation, but differed from them in that they maintained a stronger, if tenuous, link with the means of production—land and cattle. Slaves had no claim to the land, being foreigners brought to South Africa against their will. They had already been dispossessed by the time they arrived in the new country. The Khoisan and other indigenous peoples experienced an active process of dispossession as a group, a process that led to a gradual loss of land and cattle and to incorporation in colonial society as farmhands, herders, and shepherds. There were regional variations in this process, and the economic role of the Khoisan was particularly important on the frontiers. There they entered into relations of exchange, clientage, and conflict with white settlers, most of whom were pastoral farmers like themselves.

The demographic decline of the peninsular Khoisan of the Cape by the early eighteenth century moved the main arena of interaction between settlers and indigenous people farther inland. The main actors on the European side were the settler-farmers themselves rather than the Company whose power was largely limited to the Cape district. The *trekboers* were not as strongly linked to the market as the farmers, though they were not self-sufficient. The main economic assets on the frontier were herds and flocks. Animal products such as meat, hides, butter, and soap provided much needed cash income which was used to buy guns and other commodities (Neumark 1957; Ross 1986; for a different view that puts less emphasis on the role of the market see Giliomee 1981). The Khoisan were an ideal labor force for the settlers because of their experience with seminomadic pastoralism, livestock keeping, and labor clientage. Although the Khoisan were nominally free and could not be enslaved according to Company policy, this did not prevent settlers from coercing them into working on farms and imposing restrictions on their movements—the beginnings of the Pass system—and their right to own land and property.

The Khoisan milked cows, slaughtered cattle and sheep for meat, treated skins and hides, made leather products and butter and soap from animal fat, and also worked as domestics, drivers, shepherds, and herders for the colonists. They were paid in tobacco, food, beads, knives, clothing, and less often, breeding animals (Elphick and Malherbe 1989). The Khoisan kept their own livestock alongside the farmers' and had access to grazing land. Thus they were not transformed into full-fledged wage laborers. Their partially autonomous economic basis allowed them a limited maneuverability, as their dependence on the farmers for survival was not complete. This, combined with low wages, made it difficult for the colonists to recruit and keep the Khoisan labor force on the farms and caused concern for their ability to survive without an effective labor-repressive system to discipline the "Hottentots" (Khoisan), whom they saw as preferring "to spend their time in laziness and idleness, to suffer want and poverty, than to be employed for this [agricultural] work" (W. S. van Ryneveld writing in 1805, in Du Toit and Giliomee 1983: 52). Indenturing Khoisan children and thereby forcing their families to stay on the farm was seen as the way to deal with the "Hottentot who [when he] is freed from service, and who may therefore come and go as he pleases, is never inclined to work, much less to learning a trade . . . the very prospect is difficult for them to envisage" (letter from R. J. van der Riet of Stellenbosch in 1810, in Du Toit and Giliomee 1983: 54).

African Farmers: Frontier Encounters

Toward the end of Dutch East India Company rule in South Africa, a new factor was introduced into the complex picture of land and labor relations in the Cape Colony: the relatively densely populated African agricultural settlements to the east of the areas of white colonization. These communities proved a more serious obstacle to further expansion than the Khoisan ever were, and the result was fierce competition for land, cattle, water, and grazing rights. European settlers did not have the power to remove indigenous peoples from their way as did settlers in North America, and in any event they wanted to acquire land as well as to exploit indigenous labor. At the same time, they were not ready to assimilate indigenous Africans into their own society as the latter had previously done with the Khoisan: "Indeed, extensive subsistence farming practiced by a small white settler population dictated the incorporation of large numbers of black workers into their society. These Africans formed a client and later a laboring caste; their descendants did not become Afrikaners" (Giliomee 1981: 77). African farmers, for their part, did not treat Europeans differently than they treated other indigenous groups. They traded and formed alliances with them, and occasionally entered into relations of cattle clientage with wealthy settlers, just as they did among themselves (Peires 1981b).

In previous preencounter centuries, settlers and indigenous Africans had expanded their territory by focusing on cattle herding and practicing extensive land use. When they began to meet in the 1760s and 1770s, a frontier zone was opened. The concept of the frontier has been used to describe a situation in which two previously distinct societies meet and coexist within the same territory, without an overriding legitimate political authority recognized by both sides (Lamar and Thompson 1981). The Zuurveld, the eastern part of the newly established colonial district of Graaf-Reinet, thus became an arena for frontier conflict. In between the two expansionist forces stood the Khoisan, whose weak political organization disintegrated under pressure from all sides. Looking for security, the Khoisan frequently entered relations of patronage and clientage with both African chiefs and white settlers, and entered into shifting alliances with some of them against others. The Khoisan were often allowed to keep their herds and to settle with their families on settler farms and thus became the chief source of farm labor (Giliomee 1989a).

From their first encounters, indigenous Africans and colonists entered economic relations, usually in violation of Company policies. The Company insisted on monopolizing all trade between the colony and outside forces, but its capacity to enforce the ban on unauthorized commerce was limited. Its reluctance to pursue a state formation project made its disciplinary power ineffective, especially on the remote frontiers. In addition to trade, a steady trickle of laborers entered the colony from the 1770s on. These were employed in the same capacity as the Khoisan: men tended herds, and women performed domestic labor and garden work. Because of labor shortages on white-owned farms, settlers employed them regardless of the prohibitions against it.

This new addition to the laboring classes of the colony could not, however, replace the slaves and the Khoisan as the bases of the white settlers' agriculture and stock farming. Those Africans who hired themselves out to white farmers, or settled on farms as labor tenants, were a small proportion of their own people and of nonwhite workers on settlers' farms. As long as most Africans continued to enjoy access to the means of production—cattle and land—they had no reason to look for employment and assume a subordinate role in the colonial economy. This was especially true given the low wages and harsh treatment awaiting them on the farms (Peires 1981b).

The labor situation on the frontier became more orderly with Ordinance 49, issued by the colonial government in 1828, which made the temporary employment of African labor legal by allowing settlers "to procure such number of useful labourers from the Frontier Tribes as the Colonists may be desirous of engaging and it may be safe and prudent to admit" (quoted in Peires 1989: 486). For a long time after that, however, Africans in the labor force remained relatively few in number because they had alternative means of survival. In the Graaf-Reinet district in 1853, for example, there were 768 African workers, as compared to 5,265 coloreds, who were the descendants of the emancipated Khoisan and slaves (Smith 1976: 184–89). As A. Stockenstrom predicted in 1827, "it were irrational to suppose that as long as the interior is in a state of peace, and space plenty, that the good savage [meaning African] will abandon his liberty for the bondage we 'invite' him to" (quoted in Du Toit and Giliomee 1983: 69).

Cape Liberalism: Economic Dimensions

The end of Company rule in 1795 and the establishment of a British administration in 1806 set in motion changes in labor market policies. The liberal capitalist worldview dominant in Britain at the time maintained that free buying and selling of labor at the market was a more efficient way of dealing with the growing labor shortages. The new rulers gradually moved toward reduction of overt legal coercion and extension of the role of market forces. This did not lead to the elimination of labor repression altogether. A variety of formal and informal control mechanisms remained in place even after the abolition of slavery and indenture. The dominant actors in an economic system based for more than 150 years on coerced labor were reluctant to adjust to new rules. Nevertheless, some changes did take place. Ordinances 49 and 50 of 1828 removed legal restrictions imposed on the Khoisan by the Hottentot Code of 1809 and other regulations. The Khoisan could hold legal title to land, their children could not be forcibly apprenticed on white farms, and they no longer needed passes for traveling. The change in policy was aimed at dealing with grievances in a manner that would encourage Khoisan to become obedient wage laborers. The process of dispossession seemed to have gone so far as to leave them no option but to work in the service of whites, with no need for a racially specific legal coercive apparatus.

Economic liberalism, combined with a growing humanitarian sentiment in Britain fueled by the activities of missionary societies in the colonies, contributed to the elaboration of a new spirit at the Cape which affected labor relations. Officials came to regard existing restrictions on the free movement of laborers, such as slavery, pass laws, or indenture, as obstacles to the spread of "civilization" and "progress" in South Africa. The latter consisted in the adoption of a Christian way of life, residence in a fixed place, production of cash crops, the acquisition of a work ethic of hard labor, and a desire for material improvement. From the British point of view, Khoisan and Africans in particular, but also white pastoral farmers, were lacking in these attributes. The abolition of obsolete social relations was seen as necessary for making the country more civilized, economically viable, and competitive in international markets (Atmore and Marks 1974; Newton-King 1980).

This new logic was spelled out by one of the main advocates of free labor: "Make the coloured population in your colony free . . . permit the natives to choose their own masters—secure to them, inviolate from the grasp of colonial violence, the right which God and nature have given them to their offspring— allow them to bring their labour to a free market, and the farmers will no longer have occasion to complain of a want of servants" (Rev. Dr. J. Philip writing in 1828, in Newton-King 1980: 198). The colonial desire to increase labor supplies on the frontier combined with other forces to push for liberal reform. Another element that facilitated the campaign to abolish legal racial discrimination was the missionaries. They appealed to public opinion at home (Britain) to protect indigenous people from overt restrictions and abuse, and generally acted as an influential antislavery lobby (Comaroff 1989). In addition, the British hoped that addressing Khoisan grievances would lead to the formation of a political alliance between colonial forces and Khoisan against Africans, thus improving security conditions on the frontier.

The effects of the legislation on the status of the Khoisan were not very significant. Legal equality did not translate into better economic position or even better working conditions. The British wanted to remove obsolete barriers to the free operation of market forces and institute a system of wage labor, but they had no intention of undermining the basis for colonial prosperity—the availability of nonwhite cheap labor power (Elphick and Malherbe 1989). The abolition of slavery (emancipation in 1834, followed by four years of apprenticeship ending in 1838) was another step in the same direction. Most slaves remained on farms as laborers for lack of better options (Armstrong and Worden 1989).

In the cases of both Khoisan and slaves, legal restrictions were lifted, but the living conditions of subordinate groups remained largely unchanged. The loss of independent access to the means of production, primarily land, left the free people of color with little choice other than to continue selling their labor to white farmers and urban burghers. Nevertheless, employers reacted by demanding that the government enact vagrancy laws to prevent dislocations in production: "The whole Colony loudly calls for certain Rules, or Legal enactments, whereby idle persons, thieves, and vagabonds [meaning unemployed free people of color], are prevented from living upon the hard earnings of the laborious [meaning white farmers], and are then consequently indirectly compelled to seek for service, and for work, in accordance with the principle of the present Poor Laws in England" (editorial in *De Zuid-Afrikaan*, 5/3/1839, in Du Toit and Giliomee 1983: 75).

The government did not take long to respond to settler demands. It did not intervene on behalf of the freed slaves, believing that "the most desirable result would be that they would be induced to work for wages as free labourers. Whatever tends to counteract that object seems . . . unadvisable, with a view to the interests of all classes" (British Secretary of State for the Colonies Lord Glenelg, November 1837, in Rayner 1986: 320). It goes without saying that Lord Glenelg had in mind the interests of *white* classes rather than the interests of the population as a whole. The Masters and Servants Ordinance of 1841, and the 1856 Masters and Servants Act adopted by the new self-governing parliament of the Cape Colony, served to tie farm workers to the land. Penalties for breach of contract, desertion, and insubordination were imposed on laborers. By that time white South Africa had become firmly committed to a racial division of labor by which white masters survived and prospered at the expense of brown servants. The settlers could not envision economic life without subordinate indigenous labor.

The Emergence of Indigenous Peasant Production

From the 1830s onward, settlers, followed by British troops, moved into new regions to the north and east of the Cape Colony. This migration was confronted by indigenous populations in the territories that became known as Natal, Transvaal, and Orange Free State. Some contact, primarily limited trade relations, had been established before the arrival of a large number of Europeans into these regions. It was during the second half of the nineteenth century, however, that the process of European conquest and the incorporation of indigenous people into the white-dominated economy took significant steps forward. The last two decades of the century were decisive in this respect, though major developments had taken place before that.

In the Cape Colony itself, some members of the largest indigenous group, the Xhosa, moved from trading in cattle with settlers and the government to producing crops for the market. They grew grains—corn, sorghum, barley, and oats to be consumed by colonists and passing ships—and with their income purchased finished textile products (Peires 1981b: 102–3). Thus a new social class was born—the indigenous peasantry. First appearing in the eastern Cape and later spreading to other territories, this group provided, at least for a while, an alternative model of economic relations, one not based on outright exploitation and dispossession.

Previous attempts by British administrators and missionaries to create a viable class of small agricultural producers among the nonwhite population had been unsuccessful because they always faced strong opposition from white farmers. In the case of the eastern Cape, sheep farmers led the way in campaigning against allowing indigenous people to play any economic role other than that of worker on a white-owned farm. The Kat River Settlement, which allocated land to the descendants of the Khoisan and slaves, and enabled them to live in relative independence from whites, was condemned by the colonists as detrimental to their interests. Successful export-oriented wool production required large investments of capital and an adequate supply of land and labor. From this perspective, then, landholding by nonwhites was seen by farmers and investors in wool production as an irrational use of resources. The desire to channel these assets to "productive" commercial purposes led to a growing pressure on the government to abolish the Kat Settlement, which it eventually did (Kirk 1980).

It is important to introduce here a distinction within the white population between land- and labor-greedy farmers on the one hand, and missionaries and merchants on the other. The latter played a role in mitigating pressures for the total expropriation of indigenous people. Evangelical work in the southern African context stood for the promotion of "civilization," social order, hard work, and loyalty to the government, all of which could best be achieved by helping the indigenous population change "the old kraal into a decent village—the old kaross into substantial European clothing—idleness into industry, ignorance into intelligence, selfishness into benevolence and heathenism into Christianity" (Rev. J. J. Freeman, *A Tour in South Africa* [1851], in Trapido 1980: 249). Commercial entrepreneurs benefited as well from the promotion of "civilized" indigenous peasants as producers of commodities for the market and consumers of finished products. Government administrators were interested in fostering less costly peaceful relations on the frontier, and they also encouraged the tendency to form free peasant communities (Trapido 1980). Thus, a contested terrain was formed in which different colonial models competed over the appropriate ways of managing relations with indigenous people. These models were variously articulated by the

British administration (state colonialism), by white farmers (settler colonialism), and by missionaries (civilizing colonialism) (Comaroff 1989).

Whereas settler colonialism was based on the complete economic and political subjugation of indigenous people, Cape liberalism—associated with but not identical to civilizing colonialism—promoted the incorporation of indigenous people who qualified as respectable members of the community by being self-supporting agricultural producers rather than servants of white masters. While these indigenous peasants were always a minority among their people, their numbers grew substantially with the spread of missionary influence and the weakening of traditional religious authority. They were first found on the eastern Cape in the 1830s among refugees from the Mfecane Wars of Natal and the interior. The dislocation of these refugees, known as the Mfengu, facilitated the adoption of innovative social and political forms. The period 1840–70 saw the spread of peasant production among other groups in the region. Working on reserves, missions, and white-held lands as tenants, these peasants marketed a surplus of grains and vegetables and also engaged in sheep farming and wool production using new advanced techniques (Bundy 1979: 29–64). Their ability to take advantage of market opportunities enabled them to survive without selling their labor, except in poor years. Their commercial success was directly related to white complaints of labor shortages: "The scarcity of labour . . . has been to a great extent caused by the last two fruitful seasons, the abundance of food in Kaffraria [Ciskei] having induced most of the natives to leave this district [Bedford]. . . . The wants of the natives in their present state are so few, that they are easily supplied, and like most men, white or black, they will not work when they have no want" (civil commissioner for Bedford, in *Blue Book for the Cape Colony* [1868], in Bundy 1979: 56).

Similar developments, with a time lag, took place in the more remote (from white population centers) territories of the Transkei. Access to desirable European commodities such as guns, ammunition, blankets, and household utensils necessitated a redirection of production toward external markets: grains, tobacco, wool, pigs, and poultry were sold to traders. Only much later, when the incorporation of the territory into South Africa had been completed did these developments lead to the emergence of the same kind of peasantry as in the eastern Cape (Beinart 1982: 22–30).

African cultivators, like their Palestinian counterparts, were neither the proverbial stagnant farmers inhabiting the universe to which they were assigned by modernization theory nor the passive victims of conquest and expropriation by an all-powerful white entity as portrayed by the world-system perspective. Whenever possible they used market opportunities to improve their material conditions, exploiting in the process internal conflicts of interests among whites caused by economic (different class segments), political (settlers and colonial officials), and ideological (missionaries and white supremacists) factors. The major difference between indigenous people in the two countries, however, was that Africans were exposed to the operation of the market much later in the settlement process than

Palestinians. The latter were actually the ones to have initiated the processes of integration into the world economy and the commercialization of production, and were less dependent than the former on colonial forces for initiating and sustaining commercial activities.

Slater (1980) relates the degree to which white farmers managed to control the economic destiny of Africans to two factors: the availability (to the latter) of alternative means of subsistence, and the relative physical force of both sides. Natal and other areas far from the Cape Colony, long the center of white power, proved more problematic for the settlers, who were few in number and not strong enough to compel indigenous people to meet their demands for labor. The desire on the part of the Natal Africans to accumulate resources, including European goods, could be satisfied through trade in ivory and agricultural surplus in maize, milk, vegetables, and fruit. Under these conditions, the subordination of the indigenous population seemed a costly and wasteful enterprise.

This state of affairs led white farmers to fight other white interest groups that supported and benefited from Africans having access to means of subsistence. Missionaries and government officials formulated policies that would confine indigenous people to locations in which "the whole of the native population in the district and gradually those beyond it, will become consumers of imported articles and producers of articles for export, and after a time with a judicious system of taxation will defray the expenses of their own establishments and furnish an excess to the treasury of the district" (report of the Location Commission, 1847, in Slater 1980: 157). In addition, individual speculators and land companies permitted Africans to live on their land as rent-paying tenants and thus practice "Kafir farming" and stock rearing. Not only could indigenous people maintain access to the means of production in that way, but many of them actually managed to buy land from the absentee landholders. The *kholwa* (African Christian converts) in particular showed their ability to compete successfully with white settlers in all spheres of economic activity, as long as no political restrictions prevented them from doing so (Etherington 1985).

When in the 1850s Natal entrepreneurs began establishing sugarcane plantations and processing plants, they could not rely on the availability of local African labor. The ability of indigenous people to survive without having to sell their labor forced white commercial interests to entice workers from other African territories and from overseas. African migrant workers from the north and, primarily, Indian contract laborers indentured for five years, performed the major part of labor services. Local workers were also employed on a seasonal basis on short-term contracts (Richardson 1985). Indians became especially important in Natal, where they took up other productive activities as soon as their indenture ended (Brain 1985).

The extent to which those developments affected the independent Zulu kingdom, bordering on colonial Natal, is debatable. Guy (1979) maintains that the impact was marginal. The Zulu people showed minimal interest in the white colony, rejecting any attempt to enlist their labor in the service of white masters and restricting their contact to limited trade relations. Colenbrander (1989), on the other hand, estimates that the commercial penetration of the Zulu kingdom was much more extensive and had started to transform production relations even before conquest and annexation. In any event, Africans in Natal itself continued to resist expropriation and maintained a large degree of economic autonomy, even after they had already been politically incorporated into the colonial state. Long exposure to European trade pressures and even loss of political independence did not necessarily mean immediate subordination to the economic demands of white settlers. Through subsistence and market-oriented production, indigenous people succeeded in avoiding, or at least delaying, the impending threat of proletarianization.

During the same period (the 1840s to the 1870s) white settlers of the Transvaal faced similar difficulties in extracting labor services from Africans. The latter were reluctant to work for wages, except when they were paid with guns and ammunition—scarce and expensive commodities not easily given up by whites. Whenever indigenous people could not acquire guns through the exchange of cattle and the marketing of agricultural surplus, they resorted to selling their labor for a limited period of time. Working for local white farmers was not a very attractive proposition, however, and many young Africans from the eastern Transvaal, for example, preferred to migrate to places in the Cape Colony that offered higher wages (Delius 1983: 62–82). The inability of settlers to arrange for a stable and secure pool of indigenous workers pushed them to try other means of coercion, which is how the *inboekselings* became a source of forced labor. These were African children captured in battle or kidnapped and raised as domestic servants. Upon growing up, many of them became *oorlams*, that is, loyal Christians acculturated to, but not assimilated into, settler society. These sources of labor allowed white farmers to overcome some of their labor recruitment problems, but sporadic coercion was a substitute for the failure to submit indigenous people to systematic land and labor control (Delius and Trapido 1983).

Internal divisions among whites existed not only between different colonial models (as Comaroff 1989 shows) but also among settlers themselves. Large landholders, farmers, and businessmen, in contrast to smaller settler "family farms," could coexist with indigenous peasant communities without serious problems. In places where this was the dominant pattern of land and labor relations, as in the northeastern Orange Free State, the two were complementary: "African tenant households could cultivate the land and graze their stock in return for the labour services of the younger males without too much harassment. If the land was extensive and the African communities large, labour could be provided for the white farmer without unduly interrupting the productive cycle in the peasant economy. A crucial factor was the capacity of the black community to accumulate stock without pressures being brought to bear on them by a white landlord anxious to use his grazing veld for his own purposes" (Keegan 1986b: 229).

Pressures on the state to squeeze out African peasants were mostly exerted by small-scale settler farmers who saw indigenous access to land and cattle as directly competing with their own needs. Thus the major factor in land and labor relations was the extent to which the interests of various settler and indigenous forces could be reconciled. The emergence of indigenous peasantry all over South Africa reflected a convergence of interests between African cultivators and white merchants, land speculators, and large landholders. Politically and ideologically this "alliance" also served white colonial state and religious interests. The extension of white settlement into Natal and the interior did not mean, therefore, an extension of the land and labor relations that had developed in the Cape Colony among settlers, Khoisan, and slaves. As long as South Africa remained a preindustrial society, settler economic domination outside the Cape territories proved difficult to create and maintain.

Conclusions

The early period of colonial settlement in South Africa saw the establishment of hierarchical labor relations in the western Cape between European masters and their African and Asian slaves and servants. Settler territorial expansion extended these relations toward the northern and eastern Cape, incorporating in the process significant sections of the fragmented societies of the Khoisan. The process of expansion began to encounter serious difficulties when, in the early nineteenth century, settlers began to confront the more stable and organized farming and herding African communities of the eastern Cape and the interior.

From that time onward, the territorial extension of European settlement no longer entailed the relatively uncomplicated subordination of indigenous people. Settlers managed to establish their presence in new areas and assert a degree of economic control, but their ability to secure domination there was much lower than in the Cape. A new arena of struggle over land and labor thus opened, covering vast territories and involving a large number of indigenous people whose resistance enabled some of them to incorporate themselves into capitalist economic structures not only as laborers but also as independent producers and consumers.

Comparison and Conclusions

The World-Historical Context

The different world-historical contexts within which settlement processes in South African and Palestine/Israel unfolded had important consequences for the direction of their respective developments. The seventeenth and eighteenth centuries, the initial era of colonization in South Africa, were a period in which the world economic system was disjointed, forming an arena for competition, collaboration, and conflict among the many actors—states, trading companies, and settlers—involved in creating a new world order. The degree of coherence of interests of the various forces taking part in the colonial project varied enormously in time and space. No single strategy of expansion, settlement, and exploitation of indigenous land and labor resources was followed by colonial forces, and the outcome of these processes ranged from outright extermination to collaboration between European traders and indigenous elites for the mutual benefit of both. Capitalist relations were not clearly consolidated on a world scale, and they operated in a historical environment which facilitated the rise of multiple configurations of imperial, mercantile, settler, and indigenous sets of interests.

The late nineteenth century, in contrast, the period in which the Jewish settlement project in Palestine/Israel was launched, had already seen the emergence of industrial capitalism as a major force in the world economy. European colonial expansion followed a coherent road of acquisition of Asian and African territories and their conversion into suppliers of raw materials and consumers of finished goods. The world economic system had been consolidated under British dominance, which served as a guide for other European powers. The enormous diversity in material and political interests among imperial, settler, and indigenous forces which had existed in earlier periods was reduced, giving rise to a more clear configuration of colonial agendas and strategies.

The varying world-historical contexts of colonial encounters in the two countries created terrains on which land and labor relations between indigenous people and settlers unfolded. The overall societal dynamics in the early historical period, that affecting South Africa, was more open and fluid than that of the later period affecting Palestine/Israel. This does not mean that colonial South African social structures were more egalitarian than those of Palestine/Israel; in fact, the exact opposite was the case. What it does mean is that the early historical context was more conducive for the operation of a variety of incorporative and frequently coercive mechanisms, consisting of trade, slavery, tenancy, indentured labor, sharecropping, and wage labor. The later historical context, on the other hand, created more room for the operation of exclusionary processes because it tended to bring about encounters and conflicts between more clearly formed and internally consolidated forces. The world-historical context did *not* determine the precise nature of interaction between settlers and indigenous peoples, but it did encourage particular patterns of collaboration and conflict specific to each case.

Indigenous Capacities

Analyzing indigenous capacities means giving adequate consideration to the ways in which precolonial structures affected the ability of indigenous people to engage in economic activities and initiatives without losing their independence in the process of production. The extent of economic incorporation or exclusion of indigenous people varied across time and space, and there was no uniformity in their responses to colonial challenges. Overall, Palestinian Arabs could form and pursue their economic interests independent of settler control to a larger extent than could indigenous Africans. I discuss here the origins of these differential capacities and their effects on the land and labor relations developed in the aftermath of the initial colonial encounter.

The general level of economic development as measured by productive technology, diversification of production, and integration into the world market was higher in nineteenth-century Palestine than in seventeenth- to nineteenth-century South Africa. The starting points for settlement processes in the two countries were thus quite different. Indigenous Palestinians lived for the most part in densely settled villages and towns, and engaged in subsistence and (local) market-oriented agricultural cultivation. The weight of production for regional and European markets grew substantially in the nineteenth century. The arrival of European immigrants toward the end of the century further increased the economic weight of export-oriented agriculture. However, indigenous people were the ones who initiated the processes of commercialization of production, creation of large landholding units, and spread of sharecropping and tenancy relations between landlords and peasants, primarily in the coastal areas.

In South Africa, in contrast, the precolonial Khoisan people of the Cape peninsula did not engage in agriculture, were seminomadic, and lived in small-scale communities based on hunting, gathering, and pastoralism in sparsely populated areas. Trade connections with outsiders were minimal; the Khoisan had practically no contact with the world market. Other indigenous Africans who lived in eastern and northern territories were different in that respect. They practiced mixed farming, were relatively settled, lived in larger and more stable units, and maintained more extensive trade relations than the Khoisan did. Like them, however, they were subsistence-oriented and did not produce for the (hardly existing) markets.

How did these different backgrounds to colonial settlement affect the land and labor relations which developed between indigenous people and settlers? Palestinians in the pre-Zionist period had had much more intensive contacts with regional and international markets, experienced greater exposure to the world economy, and had already started to transform their economy along capitalist lines. As a result, the economic disruption caused by the arrival of settlers in Palestine was minimal. A substantial minority of indigenous businessmen and well-off peasants responded to world market demands in a way that increased their material welfare and enhanced their capacity to maintain their autonomy, increase their numbers, and extend their settlement of the land. The Khoisan, in contrast, had no such history of dealing with market forces in the precolonial period. Their tenuous links to the land and consequent vulnerability to ecological pressures made it difficult for them to establish a sustainable economic base from which to meet foreign economic challenges. This was not the case with other indigenous Africans whose denser settlement patterns, stronger communal hold on the land, and agricultural production created a larger capacity for autonomous development. The lack of prior exposure to the transformative power of capitalism, however, resulted in a limited ability on the part of Africans to withstand external economic pressures.

As a result of these factors, Khoisan societies at the Cape could not effectively maintain economic independence when faced with colonial pressures on land and livestock. Those left without such resources were forced into employment by the Dutch East India Company or free settlers. The abundance of land not previously used for agriculture and the existence of sources of potentially cheap labor in the form of the Khoisan encouraged settlers to use their coercive power to expropriate land and force indigenous people into labor. The outcome was the rise of an expansionist settler society based on the acquisition of large landholdings on which various forms of unfree labor were practiced.

In Palestine, in contrast, indigenous peasants were too entrenched in their position and too dense in their settlement patterns to be significantly affected by the small if steady stream of European settlers into the country. The Palestinians were less vulnerable than the Africans and less easily alienated from the means of production, by virtue of their firmer attachment to the land and greater exposure to the new market orientation that had begun transforming agricultural production since the mid-nineteenth century. The disruption, dispossession, and incorporation of indigenous people into a subordinate position which took place in South Africa as a result of the settlers' quest for cheap labor were not replicated in the case of Palestine. There were many indigenous peasants without sufficient land who could use an additional source of outside employment; processes of primitive capitalist accumulation internal to Palestinian society had already generated a reservoir of labor supplies, the creation of which had nothing to do with Jewish settlement. The result of these differences between the two countries was that even when indigenous people were squeezed off the land in similar ways, they almost inevitably entered into settler service in South Africa, but not so in Palestine/Israel.

In conclusion, the isolation of precolonial southern Africa from the world economy and the relatively less differentiated indigenous social structures facilitated the incorporation of Africans in a subordinate position in the settler-dominated economy. The exposure to the capitalist world economy and the internal differentiation among indigenous Palestinians, expressed in the existence of a landholding and commercial elite alongside middle strata and landless peasants, led to the maintenance of a large degree of economic independence among Palestinian Arabs. The outcome was the creation of a "complete" indigenous structure that remained distinct from settler economy and society.

Settler Strategies

The Dutch East India Company (and its Portuguese, French, and British counterparts) sought to monopolize trade routes and ensure control over strategic sites along the road between Europe and the East Indies. The Company did not intend to establish a settlement colony at its Cape outpost, and had no interest in extending its control beyond Cape Town and its hinterland into regions with little economic and strategic value. Most of the expansion that did take place was not coordinated by any central authority but was the result of a movement of settlers who adopted extensive patterns of land and labor usage because of the reluctance of the Company to invest resources in developing a capitalized and labor-intensive agricultural economy. Settlers, just as the Company itself, evaluated economic options according to their profit-bearing potential. They did not arrive in South Africa as part of a political-ideological project and were not motivated by any grand design other than the need to survive while maintaining "civilized" standards of existence. Sparse indigenous settlement patterns made settler expansion easier, but not without having to resort to military power in order to coerce people off their land and into labor. Territorial expansion was relatively less problematic than the extraction of labor from indigenous societies. As a result of these processes, there emerged an expansionist settler society based on the incorporation of different elements within highly inegalitarian structures.

Jewish settlement in Palestine/Israel, on the other hand, was not a part of any European commercial enterprise and was not driven by the profit motive, though the latter exercised its influence once the project was under way. Settlers established small and intensive farming units rather than large-scale ranches or estates. Such farms were difficult to sustain on the basis of self-labor, and many settlers therefore turned to the employment of indigenous agricultural workers, relying on the supply of surplus labor in the neighboring Arab villages. The major constraint on expansion was the availability of land for settlement because there was no empty space in which they could freely settle; land had to be bought. This was never the case in South Africa, where settlers used force to occupy "unclaimed" (by European, not indigenous, standards) land. In Palestine, monetary compensation was offered to landowners, small and big, and that expense drove the costs of settlement upward to uneconomic levels. Without external subsidies the Zionist project would not have survived, Ruppin wrote in 1913, because "those enterprises in Palestine which are most profitable for the businessman are frequently of least benefit to our national task; and *vice-versa*, many enterprises which are unprofitable from a business point of view are of supreme national value" (Ruppin 1971: 47). It was impossible to create a self-sustaining Jewish society under these conditions. Land rather than labor became the major scarce factor of production for the settler economy in Palestine, whereas in South Africa the reverse was largely true.

Strategies of land and labor management were a major reason for the difference between the development of the respective conflicts. The purchase of land by settlers, and the consequent fate of the tenants working on it, became a contested issue in Palestine/Israel. Conflicting claims to the land were a constant source of tension. The use of indigenous labor, however, did not become a cause for conflict between the farmers of the *moshavot* and their indigenous workers and tenants. There was a collusion of interests among all of them, based on demand for and supply of labor, as determined by the marketplace. Tensions and clashes *did* result whenever the purchase of land was *not* followed by the employment of the actual producers and led, rather, to their eviction from the territory in question. The transfer of ownership became particularly problematic when it disrupted the preexisting patterns of labor relations—sharecropping and tenancy—not when it reinforced them. Exclusion rather than exploitation became a major grievance of indigenous people. Their incorporation into the economic structures erected by Zionist settlers was partial and deeply contested among Jews.

In South Africa, in contrast, both the dispossession of indigenous people from their land and the exploitation of their labor contributed to the emergence of conflict. The taking over of indigenous land did not usually lead to exclusion but rather to forced incorporation of indigenous people and slaves into the settler-dominated economy. Coercion into labor was a major source of conflict. The result was a more thorough incorporation of indigenous people into the economic structures of South Africa.

4 | Identity Formation and Political Conflict

Identity formation and state formation—two closely related processes—are the focus of my concern. The first—the formation of collective identities—is a process involving the creation and dismantling of external and internal (national, ethnic, racial, religious) boundaries. This process operates to create new groups, dissolve old ones, amalgamate old and new, and constantly modify the terms in which people define their individual identities in collective terms. In the cases of Palestine/Israel and South Africa, indigenous people and settlers possessed different raw materials out of which to assemble their sense of group identity. The relative permeability of boundaries in South Africa, in precolonial times as well as later on, can be contrasted with the more rigid ethno-religious dividing lines in Palestine/Israel, making incorporation more likely in the former case. Incorporation, or lack thereof, cannot be measured solely by explicit statements. The existence of "objective" foundations for a common identity, such as church membership or linguistic assimilation, can serve as evidence in evaluating these processes. The process of identity formation therefore consists of material-institutional as well as discursive practices.

In the sphere of state formation, I discuss the processes of construction of state and other political institutions and the extent to which these institutions came to encompass within their authority people of different origins and backgrounds. Precolonial political fragmentation was greater in the case of South Africa. The gradual territorial and institutional expansion of European rule, and the heterogeneous circumstances under which settlers encountered, fought, and cooperated with indigenous political organizations, facilitated the partial incorporation of indigenous Africans in colonial institutions. In comparison, the character of the Zionist movement as an ethnically exclusive Jewish political project, unlike European imperial projects in southern Africa which were motivated by mercantile and strategic factors, contributed to these outcomes. In addition, the solid indigenous foundations for coherent identity and state institutions found among Palestinian-

Arabs contrast with the fragmentary bases among precolonial indigenous South Africans. To a large extent, this variation in indigenous capacities in the two cases accounts for their divergent routes.

Palestine/Israel

The Ottoman Background

The rise of a nationalist movement among the Arabs in general, and among the Palestinian Arabs in particular, in the beginning of the twentieth century, took place against the background of the centuries-long Ottoman rule. The Ottoman Empire, which controlled the Middle East from the early sixteenth century to the end of the First World War, four hundred years later, was a society composed of many groups with diverse identities. Although commonly referred to by Europeans as "Turkish," it was in fact a multiethnic society. Its official language was indeed Turkish, though with heavy borrowing of script, vocabulary, and grammatical structures from Arabic and Persian. The house of Osman itself, the ruling dynasty for over six hundred years, was of tribal Turkish origins. Its most important legitimizing principle, however, was not national or ethnic but religious: "From its foundation until its fall the Ottoman Empire was a state dedicated to the advancement or defence of the power and faith of Islam. . . . for the Ottoman Turk, his empire, containing all the heartlands of early Islam, was Islam itself. In the Ottoman chronicles the territories of the Empire are referred to as 'the lands of Islam,' its sovereign as 'the Padişah of Islam,' its armies as 'the soldiers of Islam,' its religious head as 'the Şeyh of Islam'; its people thought of themselves first and foremost as Muslims" (Lewis 1968: 13).

The imperial administrative elite included people of diverse ethnic backgrounds united by adherence to Islam and loyalty to the Ottoman dynasty and state. In many cases non-Turks were given preference over Turks (and other Muslims) by the *devşirme* recruiting system, which enlisted boys of Christian origin (to be later converted to Islam) in the service of the state. Consequently this system opened the door to membership in such political and military elites of the empire as the Yeniçeri corps (Itzkowitz 1980: 49–54). The relatively open nature of the system can be gauged by the origins of 215 grand *vezirs* of the empire (the highest administrative post): Turks comprised the largest group, followed by significant numbers of Albanians, Bosnians, Georgians, Abkhazians, Greeks, Circassians, and others (Davison 1977: 35).

The period of territorial expansion of the empire, from its origins in 1280 to the peak of its territorial control in 1683, saw the incorporation into its boundaries of dozens of ethnic, national, and religious groups in Europe, Asia, and Africa. The gradual loss of territory since the late seventeenth century reduced that diversity, but up until its final dissolution in the aftermath of the First World War it remained a mosaic of numerous elements. The last population statistics for 1914 list twenty-two religious and ethno-religious groups which can be further subdivided on linguistic and tribal grounds (Karpat 1985: 170–89). The basic division in the empire for most of its history, however, was that between Muslim and non-Muslim subjects. Islam was the state religion, and Muslims were politically and militarily, but not necessarily economically, dominant. Ethnic and linguistic differences among various Islamic groups were considered less important than their common membership in the Islamic community. To a lesser extent, the same was true until the nineteenth century in regard to Christians. Official statistics before the 1881–82 census used religious categories for classifying Christians, without providing an ethnic breakdown. As for Muslims, they were never differentiated into their ethnonational components, such as Turks, Albanians, Kurds, and Arabs (Karpat 1985).

Religious diversity was handled by the state through the *millet* system—an administrative arrangement granting *millets* (religious communities) wide autonomy in managing internal affairs such as education, welfare, and family law. The main *millets* established in the 1450s were the Greek, Armenian, and Jewish, all with similar privileges and duties toward the state (Shaw 1976: 58–59, 151–53). In practice, however, these communities were internally divided, and their ways of functioning varied locally over time and place. (See Braude 1982 for a view that questions the antiquity and organization of the system.)

Until the nineteenth century there were remarkably few signs of strong Turkish (or other non-Christian) nationalist currents at work. Furthermore, even the terms "Turk" and "Arab" were not used by members of the urban elite, who referred to themselves as Osmanli (Ottoman subjects): "The term 'Turk' was used occasionally, but only to designate the ignorant nomad or peasant of Anatolia, often with a definite derogatory connotation, or else to distinguish between a Turkish-speaking Ottoman and those who spoke other languages" (Kushner 1977: 2). Likewise, "the word 'Arab' itself as a designation for the inhabitants of the Arab provinces of the Ottoman Empire rarely occurs in the books and documents of the period. It was reserved mainly for Bedouins of the desert and for all the non-town dwellers in the Near East" (Zeine 1966: 38).

This situation began to change in the second half of the nineteenth century. The gradual breakaway of various minorities, predominantly Christian in composition (Serbians, Greeks, Romanians, Bulgarians) from the empire, accompanied by European pressure to introduce reforms in the status of minorities, led to growing efforts to find nonreligious bases of identification with the state. The period of the Tanzimat reforms, 1839 through 1876, saw several attempts to create a common identity that would incorporate all religious and national groups on a new basis of equality before the law. *Osmanlilik* (Ottomanism) was expressed in the imperial proclamations of *Hatt-i Şerif* of Gülhane of 1839 and *Hatt-i Hümayun* of 1856, which abolished legal restrictions on non-Muslims and granted them full civil rights. This strategy did not prevent the process of dissolution of the empire from going forward, and by 1878 several groups had gained independence or at least a significant degree of autonomy (Karpat 1972).

The result was a strengthening of the Islamic character of the population, as large numbers of Christian subjects formed their own independent states and many Muslim immigrants from the Balkans and the Russian Empire (Circassians, Bosnians) moved into Ottoman territories (Karpat 1985: 60–77). The quest for a non-Islamic unifying identity was therefore abandoned, and during Sultan Abdülhamid II's rule (1876–1909) an alternative official ideology emerged known as *Islamjilik* or *Muslumanlik* (Islamism or pan-Islam). The state attempted to unite Muslims from within and without the empire in defense against the European political and cultural assaults that threatened to destroy it. At the same time, a contradictory trend began asserting itself in the form of Turkish nationalism. This tendency began as a cultural movement in the late nineteenth century, reached political maturity with the Young Turks Revolution of 1908, and became the dominant state ideology with the demise of the Ottoman dynasty and the foundation of republican Turkey in 1923 (Kushner 1977; Lewis 1968: 175–279).

The Rise of Arab Nationalism

What concerns us here is the effect of these developments on the rise of a specific Palestinian-Arab identity, embedded in general pan-Arab nationalism. Identity formation processes in the late Ottoman period operated against a background of multiple divisions on the basis of religion, denomination, region, and ecology. The people of Palestine had shared one very important common element, however, throughout the Ottoman period. With the exception of several minor variations in pronunciation, Arabic had been the unifying language of the country for many centuries. On the other hand, Arabic, with minor differences in dialect, had also been the language of neighboring territories, primarily Syria and Lebanon. The construction of a distinct Palestinian-Arab identity was hence also a process of differentiation from the more general Arab (and regional Syrian) identities.

Seen in conceptual terms, identity formation consists of a process of simultaneous creation and dismantling of boundaries of inclusion and exclusion. In the case of Palestinian-Arab national identity, a multilayered process was at work. Its first facet was the erection of a boundary between Arabs and Turks, thereby excluding Muslims who were not Arab (or Arabic-speaking) from the emergent identity. Concurrently, a breaking down of boundaries between Arabic-speaking Muslims and Christians took place, thereby incorporating members of both religions in the national community. The third aspect of the process required the creation of boundaries between Palestinian and non-Palestinian Arabs, thereby excluding those Arabic speakers not affiliated with the delimited territory of Palestine. The first two aspects of the process were indispensable to it and rather straightforward; without them no meaningful Arab national identity could have emerged. The third aspect was more ambiguous: the construction of a general pan-Arab identity continued even as a distinct Palestinian-Arab identity was being formed. Tensions between these two competing but not mutually exclusive foci of identity, in addition to the Islamic focus, have been an element of debate and struggle among Palestinian Arabs ever since.

The rise of pan-Arab nationalism in the Arab provinces of the Ottoman Empire was premised on two preceding cultural movements. The first one was the Nahdah, the renaissance and modernization of the Arabic language and the revival of the rich cultural legacy of the Arab past. This movement was led mostly by Christian intellectuals who emphasized the important elements they shared with the Muslim majority—the Arabic language and a sense of patriotism, that is love of the homeland (Antonius 1965: 35–60; Sharabi 1970: 53–65). The other movement was that of Islamic modernism, led by scholars who believed in the need to reform Islam and return it to its supposed pure and uncorrupted origins. The glorification of early Islam was, in essence, a call for the restoration of the central role of Arabs in Islamic affairs, as the Egyptian Muhammad 'Abduh advocated in 1887: "The Koran must be taken in its strictest aspects in accordance with the rules of the Arabic language, so as to respond to it as did the shepherds and camel-drivers to whom and in whose language the Koran descended. The Koran is close to its student when he knows the Arabic language, the practices of the Arabs in disputation, their history, and their customs in the days of the revelation, and knowledge of these is the most excellent way to understand it" (quoted in Dawn 1973: 135).

'Abduh's Syrian student Muhammad Rashid Rida further emphasized the crucial role of Arabs in the revival of Islam in an article published in 1898: "To be filled with passion for the history of the Arabs, to strive to revive their glory, is the same as working for Islamic union, which in the past was achieved only through the Arabs and which will not be regained in this century except through them" (quoted in Dawn 1973: 137). Two years later Rida went on to claim that "the greatest glory for the Moslem conquests belongs to the Arabs and . . . the religion grew and became great because of them. Their foundations are the most solid, their light is the clearest, they are in truth the best nation born into the world" (137; see also Hourani 1962: 130–92). The growing sense of urgency and need for revival, whether put in religious or national terms, were related to the economic and political processes discussed in the previous chapter. The military, economic, and cultural impact of European powers, primarily France and Britain, on the nineteenth-century Middle East created a sense of vulnerability among state officials and local intellectuals. Their calls for cultural revival were not merely responses to events such as the 1798 French invasion of Egypt or the 1838 British imposition of disadvantageous trade agreements on the Ottoman Empire, but they were formulated in the context of decline in indigenous power and prestige.

Reformist Islamic ideas were an important intellectual backdrop for the later rise of Arab nationalism, though they did not find much support among the masses of Arab denizens of the empire prior to the second decade of the twentieth century. This was not due to loyalty to the empire; discontent with the Ottomans was widespread in the second half of the nineteenth century, particularly in relation to the Tanzimat concessions to Christians which aroused the anger of many Muslims. Popular dissatisfaction on these grounds dissipated to a large extent during Abdülhamid II's rule, since "by giving the appearance of resisting the West and opposing modernization, by his displays of ostensible piety and respect for the shariʿa and men of religion, and finally by his consciously pan-Islamic policy, Abdülhamid seems to have succeeded in laying to rest the fears of conservative Muslims who had been shocked and outraged by the reforms and policies of his father, Sultan Abdülmecid. Abdülhamid thus neutralized any possible appeal dissidents may have made to the populace" (Khalidi 1977: 210).

As long as the prevailing religious boundaries incorporated all Muslims on an equal basis, most Arabs saw no need to replace these with national boundaries, which would have had the effect of dividing the community of believers and exposing it to the perceived danger of domination by local and foreign Christians. This situation began to change with the rise of a specific national-Turkish component in the ideological definition of the empire and the ensuing creation of new boundaries, which excluded Arabs from playing a significant role in state affairs.

The Young Turks (the Committee of Union and Progress) took power in a coup in 1908 and began pursuing a new policy of Turkification of all the various elements of the empire: "That the Committee have given up any idea of Ottomanizing all the non-Turkish elements by sympathetic and constitutional ways has long been manifest. To them 'Ottoman' evidently means 'Turk' and their present policy of 'Ottomanization' is one of pounding the non-Turkish elements in a Turkish mortar" (Lowther, the British ambassador to Istanbul, to the foreign secretary in 1910, in Zeine 1966: 87). The intensification of the Turkish character of the Ottoman state was bound to arouse Arab anger because it relegated them to an inferior status. The imposition of the Turkish language in government schools, courts, and administration in the Arab provinces caused resentment against the empire among all classes of society: "The antagonistic sentiment between Turk and Arab is beginning to permeate downwards to the lower classes; and will soon be no longer confined to the ulama, notables and grandees and official circles" (Devey, the British consul in Damascus, to Lowther, ambassador in Istanbul in 1910, in Khoury 1983: 122). The extent to which such feelings were widespread among the masses is unclear. The daily lives of most people, especially in the countryside, were hardly affected by these changes.

Incipient anti-Turkish sentiments were expressed in the formation of several associations that participated in the first Arab Congress held in Paris in June 1913. The resolutions adopted by the congress fell short of a separatist nationalist program, with their demands limited to a call for a reformed empire in which Arabs would have equal rights: "(1) Radical and urgent reforms are necessary in the Ottoman Empire; (2) the Ottoman Arabs should be able to exercise their political rights by effectively participating in the central administration of the Empire" (Zeine 1966: 161; my translation). More radical demands advocating separation and independence were raised by such secret associations as al-Jam'iyyah al-Qahtaniyyah, Jam'iyyat al-Umma al-'Arabiyya al-Fatat, and al-'Ahd, but these had limited influence and no more than a few hundred activists between them (Zeine 1966; Dawn 1973; see also Khalidi 1991 for a stronger emphasis on the broader cultural and political impact of Arabism—a predecessor of Arab nationalism proper).

Arab nationalism did not manage to shake significantly the hold of the empire on the minds (though perhaps not the hearts) of the prewar Arab population: "In the case of Arabism, it was not translated from an idea into a viable political instrument until just before the 1914 War. And though it was in ascendance, managing to attract and convert influential elements in Damascus in this period, it nevertheless remained a humble minority position in Damascus and elsewhere, unable to erode the loyalty of the dominant faction of the local political elite in Syria to Ottomanism" (Khoury 1983: 74).

Toward Palestinian-Arab Identity

The formation of a specific Palestinian-Arab national identity unfolded against the rise in Arab nationalism and in the historical context of religious and sectarian divisions. Lebanon and Syria in particular suffered from intense intercommunal hostilities: "They hate one another. The Sunnites excommunicate the Shiahs and both hate the Druzes; all detest the Ansariyyehs; the Maronites do not love anybody but themselves and are duly abhorred by all; the Greek orthodox abominate the Greek Catholics and the Latins, all despise the Jews" (I. Burton, *The Inner Life of Syria* [London, 1875], 105–106, in Maoz 1982: 92).

The situation in Palestine was similar but less openly violent: "Moslem boys do not generally play with Christians and even the Christian children are divided among themselves. Those belonging to the Greek church have their street games apart from those who belong to the Latin Church and they only unite to persecute the poor little Jews" (M. E. Rogers, *Domestic Life in Palestine* [London, 1866], 190, in Parfitt 1987: 186). In the Nablus riots of April 1856, one Christian was killed and several Christian houses and European consular agencies were attacked as a result of Muslim outrage over the Tanzimat policies promoting religious equality (Maoz 1968: 226–30). Such resentment against government policies was documented by James Finn, the British consul to Jerusalem, who reported in 1858 that local Arabs "speak of 'Abdu'l Mejeed el Khain" (the betrayer of trust) [and] detest and hate the Turks . . . due to difference of race and traditional remembrance of conquest . . . [and are] often heard to affirm that if they (the Arab-speaking population of Palestine) could but suppress their own dissensions, and unite under one leader, they were able to drive away the Turks from their presence with sticks and stones" (quoted in Maoz 1968: 246).

Anti-Ottoman feelings were obviously not motivated by a sense of nationalism—a common sentiment superseding religious loyalties. Palestine was a country of many groups with multiple and frequently conflicting identities. In the mid-nineteenth century the population was 85 percent Muslim, 11 percent Christians, and 4 percent Jewish. About half of the population resided in the independent district of Jerusalem, and the rest in the districts of Nablus and Acre (Schölch 1985). In addition to religious divisions, the people were split between various denominational, regional, and factional identities. These were expressed by skirmishes among different Christian denominations over control of the holy places (see chapters 1–3 in Finn 1878 for a detailed description of intra-Christian conflicts and the background to the 1856 Crimean War), fighting between political factions over control of territory and resources (Finn 1878, chap. 9; Hoexter 1973; Tamari 1982), and the attempts of the authorities to impose centralized control over the territory, especially the central hilly district and the desert.

The fragmented situation began to change toward the end of the nineteenth century. One aspect of the change was administrative. For most of the Ottoman period Palestine was not a coherent unit. It was usually divided between the provinces of Damascus and Sidon, though from time to time all of its districts were joined under the same administration. Despite the absence of a unified political framework, the Arabic name of the country, *Filastin*, and the Ottoman term, *Arazi-i Müqaddese* (the Holy land), helped sustain a notion of unity. (On administrative divisions see Ben-Zvi 1962b: 93–100; Cohen 1973: 119–78.) In addition, Jews, local Christians, and European powers maintained for centuries a religious interest in the land and emphasized its distinct identity and place in history. This approach was reflected in the area of jurisdiction of the Jerusalem Greek Orthodox patriarchate which extended over all of Palestine. The same was true, though in less explicit form, for the authority of the Muslim qadi of Jerusalem (Porath 1974: 4–16).

After several rearrangements of the *sanjaks* of Jerusalem, Nablus, and Acre in the nineteenth century, they were disconnected from Syria and Lebanon, and united in 1872 to form the province of Küdüs-i Şerif, incorporating all of Palestine. The unification lasted for only a few months, but until the First World War Jerusalem (south and central Palestine) maintained its central position as an independent district linked directly to the capital of Istanbul. The consequences were significant for the direction of identity and state formation processes: "The existence of the sanjak of Jerusalem for almost two generations as a separate entity from the other regions of Syria was of tremendous importance for the emergence of Palestine about fifty years later. It also did much to determine the character and future of Palestinian politics, and contributed to the emergence of Palestinian nationalism as distinct from Syrian-Arab nationalism" (Abu Manneh 1978: 25).

The creation of the independent district of Jerusalem was part of a general drive by the Ottomans to restructure the administration and strengthen centralized control. It was accompanied by concerted efforts to eliminate the operation of local power centers which limited the ability of the government to exercise its rule in the provinces. The rural sheikhs of the central mountain region and the tribal Bedouin chiefs were prime targets of the centralization campaign. Steps in that direction had already been taken in earlier periods of strong governors and in 1831–40 by the Egyptian occupation forces (Hofman 1975). The campaign continued later with the return of Ottoman rule and the institution of the Tanzimat (Maoz 1968). In the late 1850s the constant warfare between the political factions known as Qays and Yaman was brought to an end through decisive Ottoman military intervention in the Nablus area, and the dominant position of the cities (especially Jerusalem) and the urban notables over the countryside was established (Hoexter 1973; Baer 1983). Similar interventions in Hebron and Lower Galilee managed to further reduce the capacity of local rural leaders to challenge central rule, leading to the conclusion that after 1864, "the supremacy of Ottoman authority in Palestine was never again in doubt. The very term village shaykh seems to have disappeared, being largely replaced by muhtar, that is, a puppet of the Ottoman administration, completely subservient to the müdur, or governor of the nahiye [an administrative unit of several villages]" (Gerber 1985: 18).

Another challenge to centralization was posed by Bedouins. For centuries they dominated the plains, exacting tribute from villagers, robbing passengers, and resisting any attempt to restrict their activities and incorporate them into the political system. The better organization and more powerful firepower used by the authorities in the second half of the nineteenth century resulted in the reestablishment of Ottoman control over the plains and deserts. By the end of the century nomads had ceased to pose a danger. Jewish observers remarked at the time that "Turkish rule is becoming stronger and stronger. Slowly it restrains the wild shaykhs and it now levies taxes from the most rebellious tribes, and forces them to submit to the government" (H. Hissin in 1890, in Gerber 1985: 23). Similarly, with regard to the security situation on the roads: "There are still on the road the remains of the booths in which ten years ago guards were stationed to protect the road to Jerusalem. But now these guards are no more. For now even in the dark night there is no danger on the road" (M. Ussishkin in 1891, in Gerber 1985: 23). These assessments should be qualified in view of the fact that Ottoman control in the desert regions, particularly the Negev, continued to be very tenuous (Bailey 1980).

The imposition of strong administrative boundaries, the elimination of internal threats to the authority of the central government, and the establishment of urban dominance over the rural areas and the nomadic populations were all steps taken by the Ottomans to secure their position and ensure the compliance of the population. Another element in that policy was the creation of representative bodies that mediated between the government and the people. Despite the fact that these were not truly democratic structures elected by the population as a whole, their formation managed to foster the rise of a corporate identity common to all religious groups. The Mejlis-i Idare (Administrative Council) of the provinces, the municipalities of the big cities and towns, and the *nizami* (civil) courts were new bodies which included Muslims and Christians (sometimes also Jews) on an equal basis as representatives of the population. All Ottoman citizens meeting certain tax requirements were eligible to vote in the municipal elections, and many used this right as a bargaining point, as described by a contemporary Jewish observer: "The success of those wishing to be elected (be they of whatever religion), is much dependent on a general agreement between the various groups, and this general agreement, by the help of God, is now extant in our city for tens of years. One group elects so-and-so from the other group, so that the other group would vote for its candidate" (D. Yellin in 1898, in Gerber 1985: 116; for the general administrative setup see Gerber 1985: 93–159, and Muslih 1988: 11–45). These structures did not replace the communal religiously based solidarities, but they promoted for the first time an expression of the interests of citizens of different backgrounds.

The existence of organizational frameworks shared by members of different groups facilitated, though in itself did not guarantee, the growth of a common identity transcending sectarian loyalties. Another process contributing to the same results was the growth of Palestinian and Arab patriotism among Muslims and Christians alike. A significant development in that direction was the struggle of the Arabic-speaking Orthodox community against their Greek clergy. The religious definition of the *millets* in the Ottoman Empire became obsolete with the rise of nationalism in the European provinces. The Orthodox church was transformed in the eyes of many of its adherents into a Greek national body rather than a transnational religious organization. The struggle of Arab rank-and-file members, toward the end of the nineteenth century, to wrest control over patriarchal assets and affairs from the Greek hierarchy strengthened their secular Arab identity. Many Muslims identified with the attempt to assert national identity against the Ottoman-backed church (Hopewood 1975). This growing Arab consciousness, with a specific Palestinian dimension, was expressed by a leading spokesman of the Orthodox Arab community: "I am an Arab first of all, and I think it preferable that we should form a national party, to unite the sons of the fatherland [*watan*, meaning Palestine] regardless of religion and sects, to awaken the national feeling and infuse a new spirit" (Khalil al-Sakakini in 1914, in Kedourie 1958: 92).

The growing sense of a Palestinian-Arab territorial identity coexisted with cases of intercommunal violence, which occurred in conjunction with general religious tensions in the empire as a whole. Local Christians were perceived by many Muslims, and sometimes by the authorities as well, as allies of European enemies who posed a threat to Islam. Furthermore, religious distinctions became more acute and potentially explosive because of economic competition between the communities and the greater prosperity of Christians relative to Muslims. The tensions between Muslims and non-Muslims during the last decades of Ottoman rule were relatively less alarming in Palestine than elsewhere in the empire: "By and large, Palestine was spared the horrors and massacres that befell areas such as

Syria, Lebanon, Bulgaria and Anatolia. . . . What made the country relatively peaceful was the very strength of the non-Muslim community of Palestine, the interlocking of interests among the groups of all communities in sharing in the new economic growth, the strong foreign interests that were building up in the country, and the sensitivity with which the Ottomans were ruling it" (Kushner 1984: 204).

Arab Responses to Zionism

Against this background, the rise of Zionism in Europe became a crucial catalyst. One can only speculate what Palestinian-Arab identity would have looked like if a Jewish national movement had not emerged. Perhaps Palestinians would have continued to identify themselves with pan-Arab nationalism, with no specific identity of their own. Indeed the dominant Zionist position in that respect, expressed by such leaders as Golda Meir and Menahem Begin, is that a distinct Palestinian nationalism never did emerge. A contrary position is that, with the fragmentation of Arab nationalism, "it seems unlikely that the Palestinians would have abstained from establishing their own independent national movement, even if Zionism were absent from the scene. After all, the mighty British empire was there to divide, rule, and subjugate" (Muslih 1988: 215). Counterfactual arguments are difficult to pursue, but the evidence presented so far indicates that a specific Palestinian-Arab territorial identity had begun to emerge before, and independent of, Zionism and British rule. At the same time, the rise of one national movement (Zionism) regarding the country as its homeland clearly contributed to the formation of a distinct identity among those excluded from it. Palestinian Arabs had to confront the Jewish-Zionist project that targeted the territory to which they themselves laid claim.

The first expression of Arab protest against organized Jewish immigration was made on June 24, 1891, only nine years after the beginning of the first *aliyah* and six years before the foundation of the Zionist movement. Muslim and Christian notables sent a telegram from Jerusalem to Istanbul, demanding a stop to the immigration of Russian Jews into the country and their purchase of land (Mandel 1976: 39–40; Be'eri 1985: 76–78). It seems that already at that stage, and more so in following years, the notion that Jewish immigration posed a threat to the Arabs, not just the Palestinians, had started to spread among the population. In an article by Rashid Rida, writing in the Cairo newspaper *al-Manar* in 1898, Arabs were criticized for not uniting to face this danger: "Are you content for it to be reported in the newspapers of every country that . . . they [the Jews] can take possession of your country, establish colonies in it, and reduce its masters to hired laborers and its rich to poor men?" (quoted in Mandel 1976: 45).

A more massive political campaign against Zionism began in 1908 after the Young Turks coup and the beginning of publication of several Arabic newspapers and magazines in the country. The most prominent among these were the Haifa *al-Karmil* and the Jaffa *Filastin*, both edited by Christian Palestinians. From that time onward Zionism became the most important issue discussed in the Arabic press. These newspapers, and others inside and outside the country, were the major carriers of anti-Zionist sentiments, engaging in "a process of political education that verged on Palestinian patriotism and Arab nationalism, a process that posed Zionism as a threat to Palestine and to the larger Arab cause. Herein we have the embryo of Palestinian patriotism, because after 1909 the Palestinian Arabs increasingly became local patriots in the context of their opposition to Zionism" (Muslih 1988: 87).

As time passed, the need to organize as Palestinians rather than as Ottoman or Arab patriots was increasingly emphasized by the press and political activists. The different elements in the opposition to Jewish settlement were not mutually exclusive and, in the mind of most people, could coexist. An example is the work of Najib Nassar who in 1911 published a book about Zionism, calling the Arabs of Palestine "to rely upon ourselves and to stop expecting everything from the government. . . . Why do we, who have spent centuries suffering tragedy and misery, not become men and go on the way of freedom and live for our patrimony (*watan*) and for ourselves, so that we shall not invoke upon ourselves the curses of our ancestors and our sons by losing the country (*bilad*) which [our] ancestors acquired with their blood?" (quoted in Mandel 1976: 111–12). Even as he was writing that, however, Nassar was also speaking as an Ottoman, calling on fellow Ottomans to organize. Palestinian identity was consequently not seen as conflicting with wider loyalties to the ethnic group, state, or religion. It broke down the boundaries between Muslims and Christians in that respect.

More explicit references to Palestine (rather than the *sanjak* of Jerusalem, or Syria) as the homeland, *watan* or *bilad*, are contained in the name of the newspaper *Filastin*, and in an article by a prominent activist: "if this state of affairs continues . . . then the Zionists will gain mastery over our country, village by village, town by town; tomorrow the whole of Jerusalem will be sold and then Palestine in its entirety" ('Arif al-'Arif writing in *Filastin*, 1/25/1913, in Mandel 1976: 139–40; see also the evidence on the early activity of Amin al-Husayni, in Mattar 1988). This notion of Palestine reappeared six months later in a call, published in the same newspaper, to build a *sharika wataniyya filastiniyya* (a Palestinian patriotic company), which would buy land before Zionists do and be formed of notables from Jerusalem, Jaffa, Haifa, Gaza, and Nablus—cities that were part of three different *sanjaks* (published in *Filastin*, 7/12/1913 in Mandel 1976: 173–74; see also Kayyali 1979: 33–42).

Toward the conclusion of Ottoman rule, then, Muslim and Christian Palestinians had begun to develop an identity as a group consisting of the Arabic-speaking inhabitants of a specific territory within the general framework of the Ottoman Empire. Shared language, territory, and administrative structures facilitated these developments. This identity did not exclude feelings of solidarity with or belonging to other collectives—Ottoman, Arab, and Muslim. Whatever specific identity was created from the combination of such elements, it was clearly different from and opposed to any Jewish national, rather than religious, presence in Palestine. This became obvious to both groups on the eve of the World War. The Zionist leadership began to realize that "neither economic and cultural advantage [supposedly accruing to Arabs from Zionist activities] on the one hand nor Zionist initiative and attempts to establish friendly relations on the other were relevant to the position as it stood in 1914. . . . [Arab activists] made it abundantly clear that their plans left no room for both an Arab and a Jewish nationalist revival in one and the same place" (Ro'i 1968: 236).

The Jewish Community in Palestine/Israel

Palestinian nationalism-patriotism, encompassing Muslims and Christians, was open in principle to local Jews as well. The latter, however, did not affiliate with it and went instead through their own identity formation processes. Throughout the period, and indeed for many centuries before that, Palestine/Israel maintained its centrality for Judaism and for the Jewish people. Known in Hebrew as Eretz Israel (the Land of Israel), the country occupied a unique place in the religious and historical consciousness of Jews all over the world, despite the fact that only a tiny minority of Jews actually resided in the territory. The definition of the physical boundaries of the country had not been very precise, with the Bible and other sources presenting many varying opinions. There is no doubt, however, that the core of Eretz Israel in Jewish thought has always included the territories which were to become Palestine/Israel after the First World War, with Jerusalem as a geographical and spiritual center. Having said that, it would be wrong to regard Jewish nationalism as an ever-present notion waiting for the right time to express itself. Jewish perceptions of Palestinian realities and their political relationship to the country were shaped in a historical process that took place both inside and outside the country.

Up until the nineteenth century, the Jewish community in Palestine numbered no more than a few thousand people. Most of its members lived in the four holy towns of Jerusalem, Safed, Hebron, and Tiberias; only a few resided in other towns, and fewer still in the countryside. The dominant group among them, numerically and culturally, was of Sephardi origin. In fact, the Sephardim were the only ones officially recognized by the Ottoman government as Jews. The Jewish *millet* in the empire as a whole, and in Palestine in particular, was headed by the *haham bashi* (chief rabbi) who was a Sephardi Jew. A small number of Ashkenazi Jews began moving into Palestine at the end of the eighteenth century, largely for religious reasons. They settled in Safed and Jerusalem, and to a much smaller extent in other places. By the 1850s they had already formed a substantial group that posed a challenge to Sephardi hegemony. (For a general survey of Palestinian Jewry in Ottoman times, see Ben-Zvi 1962b; specific studies of the nineteenth-century Jewish community are Gat 1974; Parfitt 1987; Halper 1991.)

The growth of the Ashkenazi community brought about not only more ethnic and cultural diversity, but also more organizational fragmentation. The Ashkenazim created a network of religious and communal institutions, in competition with Sephardi-dominated structures, that collected donations and provided such services as burial and the ritual slaughter of animals (Kaniel 1976). In addition, they themselves were internally split into the Hasidim and their opponents, the Prushim. The former were divided, in turn, into sects, followers of different rabbinical dynasties. Other bases for divisions were country of origin and sometimes even a region within a country. Their common roots in Europe and the Yiddish language they all spoke did not prevent Ashkenazim from engaging in bitter factional fights over resources (primarily *halukkah* money), prestige, and political power vis-à-vis the other (Jewish) ethnic groups and the Ottoman authorities. In the 1870s there were sixteen separate and frequently competing *kolelim* (community organizations, representing Ashkenazi communities), increasing to twenty-four in 1900 and twenty-nine by the end of the period in 1914 (Friedman 1976; Eliav 1981).

The Sephardim, though internally less fragmented, also faced problems in maintaining organizational unity. For several centuries they controlled the communal affairs of all other groups. Following the Ashkenazi refusal to recognize Sephardi authority, other communities attempted to break away. The North Africans, the Yemenites, and the Georgians gradually managed to establish their autonomous religious-communal institutions, though not always with official Ottoman approval. They were still subject, however, to the authority of the *rishon le-tzion*, the Sephardi rabbi subordinated to the *haham bashi* in Istanbul (Barnai 1973; Druyan 1981).

Of particular relevance for this study are the struggles between the two largest communities, Sephardim and Ashkenazim, as these raised the issue of the relations of the Jewish community to the Ottoman authorities and to the Arab population. Ashkenazim, to a larger extent than any other Jewish community, were foreign nationals, whereas the Sephardim had been Ottoman citizens for centuries. The latter were also in much closer contact with their Arab neighbors, cultivating in some cases relations of friendship and business. Generally speaking, Sephardim were more integrated into Palestinian society; the Ashkenazi community, in contrast, maintained its estrangement from the locals, limiting interaction with them and with the government to a necessary minimum. With the establishment of European consulates in Jerusalem and the coastal towns beginning in 1839, most Ashkenazi Jews gained consular protection according to the centuries-old Capitulations Agreements between the empire and European powers. They could thus deal with government officials, and consequently with the other Jewish and non-Jewish communities, from a more comfortable position.

The growing economic and political involvement of the Ottoman Empire and Palestine with Europe, toward the second half of the nineteenth century, affected internal relations in the Jewish community. The Sephardim managed to retain their official status in the eyes of the authorities, but they started losing their numerically and culturally dominant position to the rising Ashkenazi community. The increasing safety of travel, more secure living conditions in the country, and protection provided by foreign consuls all combined to facilitate European-Jewish immigration into Palestine. As a result, Ashkenazim became a majority of the Jewish population in Jerusalem, and in Palestine as a whole, by 1880 or shortly thereafter. (Statistical figures for the nineteenth century are of questionable accuracy. The best data available are for Jerusalem. For various estimates, see Gat 1974: 19–20; Ben-Arieh 1976; Parfitt 1987: 33–38.) With the beginnings of European-based Jewish immigration and settlement movements, Ashkenazi numbers rapidly increased, reaching a clear numerical dominance.

Despite the heterogenous nature of the Jewish community in the Ottoman period, it maintained a sense of identity as a distinct group. The government, and their Muslim and Christian neighbors, regarded Jews as a separate community, united in their segregation, regardless of their internal divisions. Overall social interaction between members of different religious groups was limited, and even Arabic-speaking Jews did not consider themselves, nor were they considered by others, Arabs (Parfitt 1987: 180–223). In other words, Jews were seen not only as a religious group but as an ethnic or national group. These terms were not used as such by their contemporaries, but Jews obviously differed from others in more than just their religion. The Ashkenazi immigrants' influx into the country increased Jewish distance, as a group, from the emerging Palestinian-Arab identity. The Arab cultural and literary revival, and the forging of a Palestinian-Arab national identity based on the Arabic language, and common to Muslims and Christians, largely passed Jews by. In addition, a large number of Jews were unable to take part in the newly created municipal and representative structures because they were not Ottoman citizens. In fact, the majority of the Jewish population maintained their foreign citizenship until the First World War.

Even for Arabic-speaking Jews, Hebrew was the language of scripture and prayer, though rarely that of everyday life. Since the earliest times however, Hebrew served as a means of communication for Jews of different ethnic backgrounds. At home, most people continued to speak a variety of languages such as Ladino, Arabic, Yiddish, and Persian. The linguistic situation was mixed, and the sense of peoplehood did not depend on a shared day-to-day language. Adding to the sense of common Jewish identity were the Hebrew-language newspapers that began to be published in Jerusalem in the 1860s (Halevi 1976). There were also many incidents of cooperation in religious and spiritual affairs, but in Jerusalem these coexisted with continuous tensions and cultural differences (Kaniel 1976). In other towns, such as Jaffa, more cooperative relations among Jewish ethnic groups prevailed (Kark 1983).

At one point the leaders of the Sephardi community refused to confirm that the Ashkenazim were indeed Jews, their reason being their desire to maintain a monopoly on ritual slaughter of meat and thereby prevent Ashkenazim from forming their own communal institutions. In response, the Ashkenazim asserted that both groups were part of the same people, practiced the same religion, shared the same sacred language, and were for all intents and purposes similar, despite the fact they used different languages in their daily profane affairs (Kaniel 1973). There was never any serious doubt with regard to the historical accuracy of these assertions, and eventually the Ashkenazim were granted official recognition of their claims by the authorities.

The Rise of Zionism

The increasing immigration of Jews into Palestine after 1882 and the rise of the organized Zionist movement served to bring Jewish distinctness into sharper focus. The massive immigration wave, coming from the various provinces of the Russian and Austro-Hungarian empires, was triggered by deteriorating physical and economic conditions, the growing persecution of religious and ethnic minorities, and feelings of hopelessness in the face of popular and official anti-Semitism.

The reaction of the Jewish masses in eastern Europe can be roughly divided into three categories: (1) Some searched for individual solutions, the most popular one being immigration to the Americas; between 1881 and the early 1920s over two million Jews chose this option. (2) Some attempted to organize for change from within, usually as part of the socialist labor movement. This minority response was a substantial one. (3) Others embraced Jewish nationalism—attitudes and organizations emphasizing the ethnic (as opposed to the strictly religious) character of the Jewish people, and the need for a collective national solution to their problems. Zionism became the most prominent among these currents, though initially, it was the response of a small minority. It is significant in the context of this study that, among the three, adherents of the most exclusionary approach were those who moved to Palestine, which had a profoundly adverse effect on the prospects of a common Jewish-Arab identity.

Zionism as an organized world movement was founded in 1897, but it had many antecedents dating back to the 1830s and 1840s. In that earlier period, coinciding with the growing contacts of the Levant with Europe and the spread of commercial and diplomatic relations, the perception of Palestine in the West went through a change of focus. From an inaccessible, almost imaginary, "holy land" it became a real country open to tourism, pilgrimages, geographical expeditions, and systematic scientific surveys (Ben-Arieh 1970). This transformation of the concept of Palestine was first effected by Protestants, though it spread to other groups, including European Jews: "Romantic currents in literature and art as well as historical and archaeological research gave that material an exotic charm and strengthened certain images that were likely to bring out the connection between the Jewish people and its land: the glorious past that contrasts with the miserable present, and the oriental Jews who were seen as ancient tribes uncorrupted by Europeans (unlike the Jews of Poland and Germany). Trends in Protestantism, particularly the millenarians, combined with romantic elements to create a favorable attitude towards the Jewish past of Palestine and the possibility of renewed Jewish settlement there" (Ettinger and Bartal 1982: 201).

Sharing many of these cultural attitudes and influenced by the rise of nationalism in Europe, some Jewish intellectuals began redirecting Jewish energies away from religion proper and toward the national idea. They focused on the revival of Palestine as a historical homeland, so that Jews in Europe and elsewhere would have a territory of their own. In the mid-nineteenth century, the great historian Heinrich Graetz presented a concept of Judaism composed of three elements: "The Torah, the nation of Israel, and the Holy Land stand, one might say, in a mystical relationship to each other; they are inseparably united by an invisible bond" (in his *The Structure of Jewish History*, quoted in Avineri 1981: 28). Others, viewing Judaism from a similar perspective, began calling for the revival of Hebrew and the settlement of Palestine. Early proponents of these ideas, such as Hess, Alkalai, and Kalischer, worked from different ideological angles, but all shared the notion of Jews as a nation that must liberate itself through its own efforts. Jews were urged not to wait for divine intervention, but not to reject it should it offer itself: "The Redemption will begin with efforts by the Jews themselves; they must organize and unite, choose leaders, and leave the land of exile. . . . The organization of an international Jewish body is in itself the first step to the Redemption, for out of this organization there will come a fully authorized Assembly of Elders, and from the Elders, the Messiah, Son of Joseph, will appear" (Yehudah Alkalai, quoted in Avineri 1981: 51–2).

A more direct call to action, offering an analogy with other national movements, was made by Zwi Hirsch Kalischer, writing in 1862, who asked "why do the people of Italy and of other countries sacrifice their lives for the land of their fathers, while we, like men bereft of strength and courage, do nothing? . . . Let us take to heart the examples of the Italians, Poles and Hungarians, who laid down their lives and possessions in the struggle for national independence, while we, the children of Israel, who have the most glorious and holiest of lands as our inheritance, are spiritless and silent" (quoted in Avineri 1981: 52). These ideas, though formulated in Western and Central Europe, had little appeal to western European Jews who, although subject to much informal discrimination and popular anti-Semitism in the nineteenth century, managed to integrate themselves to a large extent into the fast-growing capitalist economies of such countries as Britain, France, and Germany.

Eastern European Jews, in contrast, faced a systematic threat to their economic position as well as to their national survival. Legal persecution and industrialization combined to undermine their traditional middlemen position as peddlers, small-scale merchants, and leaseholders in the Russian economy. They were residentially and occupationally segregated from non-Jews, for the most part, and largely unable to benefit from the advances of capitalism and industrialization: "Thus, while most Russian workers participated in the dynamic, rapidly expanding sectors of the economy, Jewish workers were fighting to maintain their hold on stagnant, dead-end, rapidly declining forms of production" (Peled 1989: 30). It is against this background that the rise of Zionism, as well as radical change-oriented socialist organizations such as the Bund, should be seen. These catered to the manifest needs of the impoverished Jewish masses of eastern Europe for economic and physical security, or frequently even sheer survival.

Zionism, more than any other response to the late nineteenth-century crisis of Jewish existence, emphasized the distinctness of Jewish experience. For centuries Jews had considered themselves "a people who dwell alone," but they did not organize to actually separate themselves from the non-Jewish populations among whom they lived, until the arrival of Zionism. Building on earlier notions of Jewish national identity, Zionism provided a reinterpretation of Jewish history. This new vision of the Jewish condition was not free from internal contradictions as it sought to combine three elements: the historical continuity of Jewish existence throughout the millennia of life in "exile," the need for a revolutionary change of this situation, and classical restoration—a return to the supposed glory and power of the ancient past (Almog 1987).

These general principles informed the action programs of a number of organizations created toward the end of the nineteenth century. The Bilu society, organizer of the first wave of immigrants, demanded "a Home in our country. It was given to us by the mercy of God, it is ours as registered in the archives of history." To that end they planned "to beg it of the Sultan himself, and if it be impossible to obtain this, to beg that at least we may be allowed to possess it as a state within a larger state; the internal administration to be ours, to have our civil and political rights, and to act with the Turkish Empire only in foreign affairs" (1882 manifesto of Bilu, quoted in Kaplan 1983: 3). The Basle Program adopted in 1897 by the first World Zionist Congress articulated the official goal of the movement: "a publicly recognized, legally secured homeland in Palestine. To achieve this goal, the Congress envisages the following methods: (1) By fostering the settlement of Palestine with farmers, laborers and artisans. (2) By organizing the whole of Jewry in suitable local and general bodies in accordance with the laws of their respective countries. (3) By strengthening the National Jewish feeling and National consciousness. (4) By taking preparatory steps to attain government consent which may be necessary to reach the aim of Zionism" (quoted in Kaplan 1983: 5).

The Restructuring of the Jewish Community

Practical steps taken by the movements included the creation of financial institutions (Jewish Colonial Trust, the Anglo-Palestine Bank), land companies (the Jewish National Fund), and settlement organizations (such as the Palestine Land Development Company). On a voluntary level, not officially controlled by the Zionist Organization but loosely affiliated with it, the new immigrant Jewish community in Palestine provided fertile ground for the development of diverse social, economic, and political organizations—workers' unions and parties, teachers' associations, municipal councils, farmers' cooperatives, and even a rudimentary military arm. Various attempts had been made since the beginning of the century to build countrywide representative structures to unite all segments of Jewish society, but without much success (Kollat 1975; Giladi and Shavit 1983). What is most significant, however, is that whether on a local or on a national level, these new structures represented Jews only. Arabs were not invited to join, nor did they show any interest in taking part in these activities since no sense of a common nationhood encompassed all the inhabitants of the country.

The move toward a unified Jewish cultural identity was more successful. The new, mostly Zionist, Jewish community was largely oriented toward the creation of a modern identity based on nationalism rather than religion. From that point of view the importance of a unifying national language became obvious. The revival of Hebrew as the living language of Jews in Palestine was a complex process, and it did not become the means of communication in the strongholds of the old Orthodox community. In fact, to this day a large number of Orthodox Ashkenazim avoid using Hebrew for profane purposes, except when necessary for dealing with outside elements. Hebrew became, however, the only language of instruction in the *moshavot* and the new urban communities. The educational system proved crucial in this respect and was conceived by Zionist activists as the major means for raising national consciousness. The stated objective of the first Hebrew Boys School, opened in Jaffa in 1892, was "to make Hebrew the vernacular in the school, to plant a love of the People and of the Land, and the concept of settlement of the country, in the hearts of its pupils, to unify the various ethnic groups, to give the children a knowledge of the Torah of Israel and a general education" (quoted in Kark 1983: 227). By the end of the Ottoman period, about 40 percent of the Jewish community spoke Hebrew as their sole or primary language, and many more used it on various occasions (Shavit 1983). The changing linguistic makeup of Jews in Palestine/Israel thus provided a solid basis for constituting a distinct national community.

Conclusions

The growing consolidation of a common identity *within* each community became detrimental to the prospects of constructing an identity shared *between* communities. That was particularly the case with Jewish identity formation. The crucial role of the European Jewish component in the process meant that most Jews arrived in Palestine after the 1880s with an already-formed sense of their identity. In fact, the exclusionary nature of that identity was the reason they moved into the country in the first place. Palestinian-Arab identity formation, rooted in territory and language, was potentially more inclusive. It might have included Arabic-speaking Jews, but that possibility became unlikely with the rise of Zionism as a major ideological and political force among Jews. Processes of identity and state formation in Palestine, then, led to a crystallization of two clearly demarcated and mutually exclusive groups with their own linguistic, ethnic, religious, and political identities. Politics of exclusion became the norm by design, in the case of the modern Jewish community, as well as by default, in the absence of a Jewish or Arab constituency for a comprehensive identity.

South Africa

In South Africa the processes of identity and state formation were more gradual and complex than in Palestine/Israel. A large number of people of diverse ethnic, linguistic, religious, and geographic backgrounds were drawn together over a period of centuries so that by the end of the 1870s South Africa had become a mosaic of groups, regions, and autonomous political entities. A large degree of territorial and cultural intermixture coexisted with distinct identities which were created and transformed in that same period. Only with the tighter integration of the country at the turn of the twentieth century did a coherent and unified sense of South Africa as a nation emerge among a large section of the population. Even before that, however, people of different origins began to share such political interests and cultural characteristics as language and religion to a much greater extent than was the case in Palestine/Israel, where Arabs and Jews formed distinct identities and political structures in ways that created very little space for institutional incorporation.

Precolonial Identity and State Structures

It is very difficult, if not impossible, to reconstruct the ethnic identities prevalent among the oldest indigenous people of southern Africa, the San and the Khoikhoi, in precolonial times. Original records of their beliefs about themselves and their identities do not exist. Projections into the past of conclusions derived from research about the contemporary San populations of Botswana and Namibia suffer from serious methodological problems (Wilmsen 1989). The desire of anthropologists to discover the primal human way of life, presumably undisturbed by contact with other, more modern groups, has led to the invention of a past of questionable authenticity. There is a major flaw in attempts to discover "origins," since in many cases the expansion of Bantu-speaking African farmers and European settlers in precolonial and early colonial times pushed indigenous groups out of their original areas which were rich with natural resources into marginal desert territories where they reside today (Thompson 1990: 5–15).

What we do know is largely derived from the contacts employees of the Dutch East India Company and other trade missions had with the indigenous populations of the Cape before and in the immediate aftermath of the establishment of Cape Town in 1652. The Dutch used various terms to refer to these people, but the two that became most common were Hottentot for the seminomadic pastoralists, and Bushman for those who had no livestock and were engaged in hunting and gathering activities. These terms acquired a clear derogatory connotation. The terminology commonly accepted today uses Khoikhoi (a self-designating term) for the former, San for the latter, and Khoisan as a comprehensive term for both categories taken together, a usage I follow here. Even this usage in not unproblematic, however. San was a derogatory term used by the Khoikhoi to refer to nomads whom they considered robbers and thieves. For this reason, Elphick (1985) prefers to refer to the latter in terms of their activity as hunters.

The different groups of Khoikhoi such as the Cape peninsulars, Namaqua and Korana, spoke closely related dialects and apparently maintained a notion of themselves as having common ancestry (Elphick 1985; but also see Ehret 1982 for a view which puts greater emphasis on their internal diversity). The San, in contrast, were split among numerous small groups that maintained little contact with one another, spoke different languages, and apparently had no sense of an overarching common identity. Their nomadic way of life and consequent isolation from each other acted as an obstacle to the crystallization of any large-scale territorial and political institutions. Their societies were relatively egalitarian in nature and did not support the creation of permanent hierarchical structures.

The Khoikhoi were organized in larger political units than were the San. The basic unit was the extended family in which kinship played an important organizing role. Beyond the family there existed two larger units: the clan (a number of related extended families) and the tribe (a number of clans), ruled respectively by a captain and a chief. All these categories were European conventions, frequently used by officials and scholars in an indiscriminate manner, and do not necessarily reflect indigenous people's usage. The boundaries of the effective political unit were not fixed. Some issues fell under the authority of the clan and others under tribal authority. Some tribes recognized the authority of other tribes and paid tribute to them, though usually without forming common political organizations. Intertribal conflicts over cattle, pastures, and women were common. Resulting hostilities and lack of internal unity had a significant impact on the ability of the Khoikhoi to respond effectively to European pressure: "Though the spread of Khoikhoi culture was extensive, Khoikhoi polities were small, exceedingly unstable, and apparently incapable of uniting for a prolonged period against a common enemy" (Elphick 1985: 68).

The San and Khoikhoi were geographically concentrated in the western parts of southern Africa, though they maintained substantial presence in other areas as well. To their east and north lived more settled and densely populated farming communities. Their residents spoke dialects which can be classified into two large language groups: the Nguni and the Sotho, both of which belong to the Bantu family of languages. Nguni-speaking people were spread along a coastal strip of about a thousand miles, from around present-day Port Elizabeth in the south to Maputo in the northeast. The Sotho-speaking people inhabited territories in the interior. These divisions were linguistic in nature and do not necessarily indicate either the existence of common ethnic or political identity within the groups or rigid cultural differences between them. (See Wright 1986 for the problematic nature of using these categories ahistorically.) Furthermore, although Khoisan languages are totally different from Bantu languages, there was a large measure of crossover between them as a result of prolonged contacts. This was especially true of the southern Nguni languages, such as Xhosa, which borrowed heavily from the Khoikhoi vocabulary and sound system (Harrinck 1969).

The political units of the Bantu-speaking people were not fixed in size, though usually larger and better organized than those of the Khoisan. The two most important elements in their sociopolitical organization were, on the one hand, "the principle of kinship centred on the clan and the homestead," and on the other, "the principle of state authority centred on the chief and the Great Place" (Peires 1981a: 5). Though Peires refers specifically to the Nguni-speaking people, similar conditions obtained among the Sotho-Tswana people as shown by Legassick (1969). The basic process affecting most of these societies in the precolonial period, extending into the period of colonial expansion, was the rise of the state principle into a more prominent position, though without eliminating the kinship principle. This was expressed in a period of intensified state formation in the whole region (Marks and Atmore 1980; Peires 1981a; Maylam 1986; Thompson 1990: 70–109).

The balance of forces between units based on kinship, such as the homestead, clan, or lineage, and units based on political allegiance, such as chiefdom or state, changed over time and was not the same for different groups and regions. The extent to which the increase in the power of chiefs or kings came at the expense of the power of homestead and clan heads in debatable. One position emphasizes the incompatibility of the two modes of organization since "once territorially-based structures of government are established there is no room for kinship-based authority located in descent groups" (Hammond-Tooke 1985: 312). A contrary point of view regards the two principles as mutually reinforcing since "chiefly power . . . was in fact based on massive, ingenious extensions and improvisations on the principles derived from the social laws of motion within the homestead," and therefore "the differences between chief and homestead-head were differences of degree and not differences in kind" (Guy 1987: 28–29). Guy's analysis seems more valid for earlier periods of state formation when the centralization of power was not very thorough, while Hammond-Tooke's approach might be more appropriate for later periods when state structures reached a higher degree of consolidation. In any event, all periods were characterized by a permanent unresolved tension between the two principles, neither of which ever achieved unchallenged primacy.

The crucial point here is that descent groups were politically incorporated in chiefdoms. While the latter frequently used kinship ideology to legitimize themselves, their territorial rule was not restricted to any particular descent group. They were therefore not tribal entities embodying a common culture. The boundaries of chiefdoms were fluid, and the authority of chiefs extended to all residents in a given area who accepted it, Khoisan included, regardless of their linguistic or cultural background. Membership was open to outsiders as long as they were willing to recognize the authority of the chief. (See Harrinck 1969 and Peires 1981b for a discussion of the Xhosa in the eastern Cape; Legassick 1969 for the Sotho-Tswana of the highveld; Delius 1983 for the Pedi of the Transvaal.) Attempts to read back into precolonial times such present-day ethnic categories as Zulu, Tswana, and Swazi are misleading. These identities emerged much later, as part of nineteenth-century processes of indigenous people's identity and state formation, which became implicated in the overall phase of European commercial and military penetration of southern Africa.

Generally speaking, chiefdoms were not authoritarian political structures in any modern sense of the word. The ability of chiefs to control commoners was limited, as the latter could move to other territories if they suffered harsh or unjust treatment. Chiefdoms were subject to a process of political segmentation through which descendants of chiefs and their followers split off to found new political structures. This could continue as long as free land (unoccupied or occupied by Khoisan who could be driven off) for settlement was available. The process of segmentation was spread over many generations, and it resulted in slow territorial expansion accompanied by growing political decentralization. Toward the end of the eighteenth century, and extending well into the nineteenth century, a reverse process of centralization of power began to take place in some parts of southern Africa, most notably among the northern Nguni-speaking people and the southern Sotho. Thus, many chiefdoms were consolidated into stronger territorial states competing for land and livestock resources and control over trade routes. (See Wright and Hamilton 1989 for the Zulu state; Bonner 1983 for the Swazi; Cobbing 1981 for the Ndebele; Delius 1983 for the Pedi; Wilson and Thompson 1969: 341–446 for the Sotho.)

The creation of state structures was accompanied by the emergence of new ethnic identities. Using real or imaginary common descent of the people who were incorporated within the new political structures, state elites attempted to forge identities that would facilitate the consolidation of centralized political structures. In the early nineteenth-century Zulu kingdom, for example, the state defined members of core chiefdoms in ethnic terms: "To foster the growth of a sense of corporate identity among them, they were encouraged by their Zulu rulers to regard themselves as all being of *amatungwa* descent. In time, they did in fact come to think of themselves as sharing a common origin and culture" (Wright and Hamilton 1989: 72). In a similar manner, the Swazi state was constituted by the coming together of Nguni, Sotho, and Tsonga elements to form a new Ngwane identity (Bonner 1983). These processes were at their initial stages in the early nineteenth century when indigenous states started coming into contact with the expanding colonial and settler forces; they continued to be shaped under the impact of this encounter. (See Wilson and Thompson 1969: 391–446 for the rise of the Sotho state under these conditions.)

Analytically speaking, the obvious point that so far emerges from the comparative examination of indigenous capacities is the marked fragmentation of identity and state structures among indigenous South Africans as compared to indigenous Palestinians. This is not to say that the latter were homogeneous and in possession of a strongly bounded, distinct socio-political organization; however, their structures were clearly more solid and coherent than those of the indigenous people of southern Africa. This contrast had important implications for the ways in which the colonial challenge was handled in the two cases.

Establishment of the Cape Settlement

With the establishment of a European-dominated settlement at the Cape, radically new political and ethnic elements began to make their appearance in southern Africa. The period of Dutch East India Company rule (1652 to 1795) witnessed the almost simultaneous introduction of several new groups: European settlers and company officials, slaves of various backgrounds, and Khoisan who started falling under European political, cultural, and economic domination with the collapse of precolonial political structures.

The Cape of Good Hope colony began its history as a relatively insignificant part of the worldwide possessions of the Company, a capitalist trading enterprise that formed a state within a state in the Netherlands. The colony was strategically significant, located as it was on the road between Europe and the East Indies. Its importance grew during the eighteenth century, together with British naval threats to the Dutch monopoly on trade routes to the Orient. The Company, however, never intended to transform the Cape into a full-fledged settlement colony, since it saw such a development as an unnecessary and costly project, the potential benefits of which were at best dubious. Its interests could have been defended by a small garrison maintaining friendly relations, regulated by treaties, with the indigenous Khoisan. Indeed, in the early years of settlement, Company policy was opposed to enslavement or otherwise undue interference with indigenous independence. This policy was consistent with the Dutch preference for indirect rule in other colonies, in league with local elites (Fredrickson 1981: 17–21, 28–34; Schutte, 1989). Cape realities proved very different from those of Southeast Asia, however, moving colonial-indigenous relations away from the patterns established there.

Cultural Heterogeneity

The Cape population almost immediately acquired a unique character, setting it apart from other colonial territories of the Company. Cape Town itself, together with its agricultural hinterland dominated by wheat and wine farms, was inhabited primarily by two categories of people distinguished by their legal status and origins—the white settlers and the slaves, both equally foreign to the country. While similar groups subject to Company rule were not unknown in other colonies, their proportion of the population in South Africa, relative to Company officials and indigenous people, was exceptionally high due to sparse precolonial settlement patterns. The numbers of the western Khoisan rapidly fell even further as a result of epidemics, military defeats, and social and political dislocations. Out of this encounter between people of different geographical, ethnic, and linguistic backgrounds there emerged a certain measure of cultural synthesis, the major manifestation of which was the formation of a new lingua franca. Malay, Portuguese, and Khoisan vocabulary and grammatical structures gradually joined to transform the Dutch used in South Africa from a European language into Afrikaans, a distinct though closely related language (Valkhoff 1972).

None of the various elements in the colonial population was itself homogeneous in composition. Their heterogeneity contributed even further to the internally diverse nature of the emerging South African culture and society. The widespread view of South Africa as a society historically composed of well-defined groups, living side by side and maintaining rigid racial and ethnic boundaries between themselves, is inadequate. There has always been some measure of cultural intermixture and a crossover between groups, resulting in constant redefinitions of the boundaries separating them. Though the legal system made distinctions between and among white and black categories, these were fluid in nature, especially in Cape Town (Fredrickson 1981: 54–93). Fredrickson's thesis, which emphasizes the less rigid character of early South African race relations as compared to those in the United States, has been subject to criticism. I discuss the debate in its comparative context further on, but at this point it is sufficient to say that incorporation, a process distinct from legal and social equality, was clearly in evidence in South Africa from the earliest times.

The white settlers, mostly from northern Europe, of Dutch and German origin, were servants and soldiers employed by the Company. A few began leaving the Company in 1657 to pursue independent farming, and they were joined in 1688 by about two hundred French Huguenots fleeing Catholic persecution. These people, together with other Europeans, were recruited by the Company to strengthen the Cape settlement. In 1707, fifty years after the first burghers became independent, the Company terminated its short-lived policy of actively encouraging immigration from Europe. As a result, most of the subsequent growth of the settler population during the Dutch period came from natural increase, retirement, or defection of Company employees, and crossovers by individuals of non-European origins (Guelke 1989). The absence of a significant ongoing immigration from Europe for the subsequent century facilitated the crystallization of a distinct settler culture which was extensively influenced by other local elements, such as slaves and Khoisan.

In 1717 the Heren XVII, the governing body of the Company, decided to finally lay to rest the increasingly unlikely prospect of making European immigrants the basis of agricultural production and to reaffirm the continued use of slave labor. Slaves made their appearance in South Africa together with the first Company employees. They originated in several places in Asia and Africa. Data for a fifty-year period (1680–1731) show that about 50 percent of the slaves came from Madagascar, 16 percent from India (Bengal, South India, Ceylon), and a similar proportion from the Dutch East Indies (mostly from the Outer Islands). The rest came primarily from Mozambique and East Africa (Armstrong and Worden 1989: 120–21).

The slaves brought with them a variety of identities, languages, and religions. Their substantial internal diversity became a major obstacle for the evolution of their own distinct culture, unlike the case for other slave societies, especially as they did not reproduce themselves in intergenerational units (Ross 1983). Even those who came in large numbers, such as the Malagasy, could not maintain their separate identities in the face of atomization and dispersal into many small units. Slavery in South Africa was characterized by the absence of the New World plantation-type order in which slaves congregated in large numbers. The prevalent system was that of the "family mode of control," with intense domestic contacts between masters and servants in individual households (Shell 1989). This resulted in a thorough and more rapid linguistic and religious acculturation of slaves into the society they found themselves in, though of course on a radically inegalitarian basis (Ross 1983; Armstrong and Worden 1989). This pattern of slave ownership contributed to the shape of emergent slave identities, though the initial heterogeneity of the people would not have lent itself easily to the formation of a slave culture, rigidly segregated from other elements, anyway.

The nature of the evolving South African culture varied with the differing regional combinations of European, slave, and indigenous elements. In the early period of settlement, from 1652 to the demographic demise of the western Khoisan in the smallpox epidemic of 1713, the assimilation of the latter into the colony was limited. The Company and the church were not interested in actively working toward cultural and religious incorporation, except in so far as labor needs demanded it. Linguistically, there was widespread use of pidgin and even standard Dutch among the Khoisan, arising from Company policy as stated in 1664 that "the natives there shall learn our language rather than we theirs" (quoted in Elphick 1985: 210). Khoisan continued to speak their own languages among themselves, though, well into the eighteenth century. Thus, overall cultural assimilation during that period was more superficial among the Khoisan of the western Cape, compared to the Eurasians of the East Indies under Dutch rule (but not the bulk of the indigenous population there), due to the absence of missionary activity and the relatively lower level of cross-group sexual relations in South Africa (Elphick 1985: 193–214). However, even the limited extent of incorporation at that early stage was more substantial than was the case in Palestine/Israel.

Cape Town and Its Agricultural Hinterland

Cape Town was the only urban center and market outlet for most of the Company period, and therefore the place with the most extensive and regular contacts with Europe. It was the site of administration and courts where High Dutch was spoken and written. Most nonwhites in town were of Asian origins, slaves, political exiles, or free blacks. Consequently, more than any other part of South Africa, Cape Town had a strong Islamic component in its population and generally a more mainstream European orientation. In fact, conversions to Islam continued to occur among slaves throughout the colonial period and were tolerated by local officials and slaveholders (Fredrickson 1981: 82–85; Elphick and Shell 1989: 191–94). The city's people of color (slaves and free blacks) were, on the whole, better educated and skilled than other nonwhite elements in the population in other parts of the colony. The possibilities for individual mobility and freer cultural expression were greater there than in other places, leading to the development of "an urban sub-culture which included the Free Blacks, political exiles from the East, Chinese traders and visiting soldiers and sailors as well as Company and privately-owned slaves" (Armstrong and Worden 1989: 148). Having said that, we should be wary of the "romantic haze which surrounds the early history of the Cape" (Elphick 1983: 507) and not exaggerate the freedom and cultural intermixture in Cape Town, let alone the rest of the colony.

In a controversial statement comparing the eighteenth- and early nineteenth-century Cape to the southern United States, Fredrickson talks about the former's "relative inchoateness or fluidity and . . . the extent to which social class rather than racial caste persisted as the normative basis of social organization" (1981: 88). This thesis has been criticized for underestimating the degree of racial prejudice existing at the time. Giliomee (1983) argues that it could apply to some extent to Cape town, but definitely not to the rural slaveholding districts in which rigid racial norms, strict endogamy, and taboos against social intercourse existed. Social classification, from this perspective, was most meaningfully based on the legal distinctions imposed by the Company that differentiated between employees, freeburghers, slaves, and Khoisan: "It was of the highest importance for subsequent South African history that, in the seventeenth century, each of the legal status groups corresponded almost exactly to a culturally and somatically distinct group . . . this initial correlation of race and legal status was constantly reinforced by the further incorporation of new individuals into Cape society" (Elphick and Giliomee 1989: 529–30).

Elphick and Giliomee portray a picture of race relations virtually unchanged since the seventeenth century. However, much of the evidence contained in the book from which their essay is taken, and which they themselves edited, indicates that the situation in South Africa then was far from a perfect correlation between race, culture, and status. The four groups mentioned above were internally divided, and segments of some of them shared cultural attributes with segments of other groups, breaking down the identity between legal, cultural, and somatic distinctions. The notion that there were clear somatic distinctions between different groups in Dutch South Africa is problematic in itself. What somatic norm, one wonders, served to unite Mozambican and Bengali slaves? Or Chinese and Malagasy? Even Europeans cannot be assumed to have been somatically identical unless one adopts in an uncritical manner latter-day racial categorization.

In any event, of greater interest is the question of culture. Members of all groups increasingly came to share the Dutch-Afrikaans language. Slaves were split on religious grounds, and the Christians among them (and among the Khoisan) had more in common with other Christians than with Muslim or animistic slaves. And it is at least arguable that Company officials and urban burghers showed greater cultural affinity with some of their fellow Capetonians of Asian origins than with many pastoral farmers of European ancestry in the interior, who in turn were close in their material culture to their Khoisan neighbors.

Cultural mixture was more obvious in Cape Town itself and on the colonial frontiers, where conditions were fluid. The most pronounced contrast was between Cape Town and its rural hinterland, whose economy was dominated by slave-based wheat and wine farming. The possibilities there for legal and racial crossover from the status of slave to that of freeburgher were virtually nonexistent. Rates of manumission were low—relative to colonial Ibero-America—especially for the Madagascan and African slaves who formed the bulk of the rural slave force; most emancipated slaves were city-based and of Asian origin. The rural-urban divide was evident with regard to mixed marriages, most of which took place in Cape Town and very few in the rural districts (Elphick and Shell 1989). Gaps in power, social status, and material resources between masters and servants were too wide to be easily bridged in the rural areas. There were few free black farmers, and their ability to survive on the land was limited, leaving city life as the most viable option.

The Frontiers

The situation on the northern and eastern frontiers was more ambiguous. Traditional South African historiography regarded the frontier as the place where racial segregation appeared in its harshest form. Legassick (1980), in contrast, focuses on the more cooperative relations and shifting alliances between white settlers and indigenous people on the frontier. Racism undoubtedly existed there, but it had not yet hardened into a rigid attitude prohibiting social and political intercourse on a relatively egalitarian basis: "White frontiersmen expected all their dependents (save their families) to be non-white: they did not expect all non-whites to be their servants" (1980: 67). In fact, he argues, opportunities for people of color were greater on the frontier than in the western Cape.

Legassick's approach is disputed by Giliomee (1981, 1983) who makes a distinction between the more open relations on the early "pioneering" frontiers and the rigid conditions of group enmity and hostility on the closing frontiers. In a similar vein, Guelke (1989) distinguishes two patterns—the inclusive pluralist community in which settlers mixed with Khoisan, but whose offsprings were denied entry into white society, and the exclusionary orthodox frontier community based on white family units and "racial purity." It seems from the discussion that there are two distinct issues here—the extent of sexual and marital mixture on the one hand, and the extent of cultural and political interpenetration on the other. Both processes were in operation, but it was the latter, on which Legassick focuses, which was more significant historically and of greater consequence for this study.

The discussion so far has portrayed a mixed picture of the extent of incorporation in the sphere of identity in the seventeenth and eighteenth centuries of colonial South Africa. The settlers maintained a distinct sense of identity in terms of their origin (as Europeans), religion (as Christians), race (as whites), and legal status (as free men and women). Linguistically, however, a strong inclusionary dynamic was evident in the creolization of Dutch. In addition, Christianity began to make progress among the slave, Khoisan, and other mixed populations. Communities of free blacks and, on the frontiers, *bastaards* of partial European ancestry came into being. The existence of these intermediate categories and overlapping identity components consequently mitigated, but clearly did not eliminate, the settler-indigenous dichotomies that might have developed otherwise. The lack of consolidated and mutually exclusive precontact identities on the part of both sides of the colonial equation was largely responsible for this outcome. The dominant tendency, then, coming into sharp relief when compared to Palestine/Israel, is the overall pattern of "inclusive expansion" (Giliomee 1981: 76) and the fact that "in whatever capacity, non-whites became integral parts of the total society" (Legassick 1980: 58).

Political Incorporation: The Khoisan

In the sphere of state formation, as in that of identity formation, dynamics of incorporation on an unequal basis were clearly evident. The initial policy of the Company toward the Khoisan was based on the recognition of their independence. The Dutch were only interested in a secure supply of meat, vegetables, and water for their ships, and they saw no need to upset the prevailing political order at the Cape. Costly territorial expansion was not their goal, beyond the establishment of a defensible settlement on the shores of Table Bay, since "empire-building was contrary to the mentality of the Dutch merchants-regents" (Schutte 1989: 292). Nevertheless, their presence unleashed forces that were to result in unforeseen and unintended consequences for indigenous people. European hunger for cattle, grazing land, and labor undermined the bases for indigenous economic and political independence. Dutch-Khoisan relations were quickly transformed from domination by diplomacy and treaties between sovereign powers to the use of physical coercion and the subordination of indigenous chiefs.

As early as 1671, less than twenty years after the establishment of the Cape settlement, the Company's Council of Justice asserted its legal authority over the individual Khoisan residing in the colony. Settlers were also subject to the same system and were liable to be prosecuted for offenses committed against the Khoisan, though they generally faced milder sentences than the latter for similar acts (Elphick 1985: 181–88). At the same time, and more significantly, a gradual process of political subjugation began to affect Khoisan chiefdoms. Taking advantage of indigenous factional conflicts, the Company waged a series of expeditions against leaders who refused to accept its authority. The rewards for the Dutch and their allies were cattle confiscated from, or paid in tribute by, the defeated parties. In the mid-1670s the Company started to directly intervene in internal disputes among Khoisan clans and chiefdoms and established itself as the ultimate source of political authority, in charge of installing chiefs in office (188–92).

The collapse of indigenous people's independence by the beginning of the eighteenth century was not due to an intentional policy on the part of the Dutch: "The Company did not have to be consistently aggressive; to some degree at least, Khoikhoi society fell apart as its age-old weaknesses were exacerbated by interaction with a more cohesive and powerful alien society" (Elphick and Malherbe 1989: 18). Inability to unite in the face of external danger, and the fragile nature of chiefly power, which was dependent on the accumulation of livestock to attract followers, contributed to the failure to effectively resist European encroachment on their land and cattle. The demographic catastrophe of 1713 completed the process of political demise in the southwestern Cape. The loss of indigenous control over material resources, the fragmented nature of their political institutions, and the lack of a strongly bounded exclusionary identity all combined to facilitate the subordination of the Khoisan and their incorporation into the Cape Colony.

The Company

The political authority of the Company was strongest in the southwest—in Cape Town and the neighboring districts—not only in relation to indigenous people but also in relation to settlers. The Company was the only source of political legitimacy for Europeans, its own employees, and settlers. Control over the port, and thus over marketing and import of foreign goods (especially arms and ammunition), gave the Company a large measure of power over its subjects. Its power was further enhanced by the large number of officials at the Cape, exceeding the number of adult male burghers for the first century of settlement (Schutte 1989: 293–97). The dominant role of the Company gave rise to resentment on the part of settlers, and occasional conflicts broke out during the eighteenth century over specific policies and the conduct of officials (Schutte 1989). These clashes, however, did not usually amount to a challenge to Company rule as such; it remained the sole lawmaker and enforcer. There was no real prospect of independent settler organizations to replace the Company. The farmers were too dependent on imported supplies and weapons, and their geographical dispersal and internal divisions prevented them from forming their own coherent structures.

In addition to fulfilling necessary administrative and economic services, such as operating the port and other infrastructural facilities, the Company played an important role in assimilating indigenous people and slaves into the legal order and keeping them in their subservient position. Local officials functioned as the ultimate authority in charge of policing the colony. The Council of Justice and the police were responsible for assuring compliance with the law and punishing disobedient slaves. They also punished, on occasion, excessively brutal masters or supervisors who went too far in "disciplining" their servants and thus threatened to violate the Company's monopoly on legitimate violence. Mild transgressions by slaves were punished by a whipping at the hands of a Company servant. More serious crimes were subject to very heavy and cruel penalties. Policing activities in the rural areas were performed on an ad hoc basis, with commando or vigilante groups used to suppress rebellions or to capture runaway slaves (Ross 1983: 11–37).

Whereas the slaves were mere objects of the law, subject to penal sanctions without any say in the colony's affairs, free people of color had been initially incorporated into the system on a more meaningful legal basis. A Company proclamation of 1752 asserted that they "enjoy all privileges and rights of burghers" (Elphick and Shell 1989: 215). They did enjoy property rights and access to the courts, carried arms and formed militias, but they fell short of full legal equality. Their status seemed to deteriorate toward the end of Company rule and in the first years of British rule (214–24). Their political incorporation, however, had already been completed by that time in the sense that they did not have recourse to alternative indigenous sources of authority, nor did they challenge colonial rule as such. The dissolution of Khoisan institutions and the inability of uprooted slaves to resurrect their preenslavement structures, or construct new ones in the context of fragmentation and dispersal, left little alternative to colonial power.

Political Relations on the Frontiers

On the northern frontiers similar processes of incorporation took place during the eighteenth century. In contrast to the southwest, though, settlers rather than the Company played the most active role in subjecting indigenous people to colonial domination (Penn 1989). The Khoisan's loss of independence was accompanied by their transformation into colonial subjects, partly as a result of the commando system, which functioned as an ad hoc mobilization of armed settlers. Toward the end of the Company period, the commando became the chief instrument of colonial expansion in the northwestern Cape, where it killed or drove away the nomadic San and coerced the still independent Khoikhoi into the labor market. It was also a means of institutional incorporation as the majority of troops were colonial Khoikhoi or *bastaard Hottentoten*—people of mixed Khoisan-European and Khoisan-slave descent who were Dutch-speaking Christians; they were eligible, in the settlers' eyes, for military service though not for full civil rights (Penn 1989; Elphick and Malherbe 1989). In the military field, collaboration across the colonial divide was an important feature of the open colonial frontiers (Legassick 1980). The lack of unified precolonial identities and institutions, and the localized universe within which people operated, facilitated the cooperation between settlers and some indigenous elements against others, a recurrent theme in South African history. The contrast with Palestine/Israel in this respect is obvious.

The territorial expansion of the colony, motivated by the search of pastoral farmers for free land and cheap labor, brought settlers into contact with the indigenous communities of the Xhosa people in the east in the 1770s and the Tswana in the north after 1800. After the Khoisan, these were the first Africans to feel the pressure of the moving frontier of white settlement. The encounter between settlers and Africans, with Khoisan chiefdoms squeezed in between, created a frontier zone in the Zuurveld—the area between the Sunday and Fish rivers in the eastern Cape—in which no central authority prevailed and people of different origins lived side by side in an unstable coexistence (Giliomee 1981; 1989a).

Initially, the settlers made little attempt to incorporate Africans in the colony in any capacity. The Xhosa, for their part, showed no signs of following the road taken by the western Khoisan, whose loose and fragile sociopolitical organization disintegrated under the impact of colonial demands for cattle, land, and labor. The Xhosa proved a serious obstacle blocking further settler expansion. Their structures and mobilizing capacity were strong and flexible enough to enable them to resist initial settler encroachment, exploit internal divisions among their opponents, construct alliances, and keep or regain contested territories. Their own political segmentation, together with internal conflicts among settlers and between them and the Cape government, created a fluid political situation whereby elements on opposing sides of the colonial boundaries collaborated against common enemies. Settlers and colonial authorities tried to enlist Xhosa help against each other or the Khoisan, and offered help to some indigenous leaders against their factional opponents (Peires 1981b: 50–63; Giliomee 1989a).

The settlers were mostly interested in driving the Xhosa to the east, beyond the Fish River, and gaining sole land and grazing rights to the Zuurveld. They had already satisfied most of their labor needs through Khoisan clients, though they occasionally used Xhosa labor on a temporary basis. The Xhosa, for their part, were willing to accommodate the presence of settlers in the area, as they did not regard claims to land as necessarily mutually exclusive. In the past they had assimilated foreigners into their society and established relations of cooperation and clientage with various other peoples, such as the Thembu or the Gonaqua Khoisan; they did not see ethnic or "racial" differences as particularly problematic.

Their identity boundaries were open and inclusive, as compared to those of settlers. Few of them regarded settler culture as superior, or initially showed an interest in abandoning their own religious identity and embracing Christianity or in adopting aspects of European culture other than material artifacts such as cloth, blankets, and guns. Like the Khoisan (first in the west, then in the east) before them, indigenous people turned to new ideologies and ways of life in significant numbers only after the collapse of their independent social and political bases. As long as chiefs could secure for their followers access to land and cattle, and consequently maintain their allegiance, indigenous stability was largely intact. Only marginalized people, individuals who did not find a place within traditional social structures, were attracted to the new religion and to the missionary stations established from the earth nineteenth century onward (Elphick 1981; Peires 1981b: 70–74).

The process of social dislocation which facilitated indigenous conversions to Christianity was more pronounced on the eastern frontier among the Khoisan than among their Xhosa neighbors; consequently, missionary activities among the former bore more fruit (Sales 1975). By the beginning of the nineteenth century the eastern Khoisan had been transformed from external clients and enemies into an internal segment of colonial society, thus following the road taken by their western brothers a century before. In addition to settling on mission stations, the Khoisan occupied an integral but subordinate part of colonial society, as expressed in their joining the ranks of the Cape Regiment—the Hottentot Corps—which was founded in 1793, and in fighting alongside settlers and colonial troops against internal dissidents and external enemies (Elphick and Malherbe 1989: 35–43).

Mission stations and military service were seen by many Khoisan as alternatives to labor service on settler farms, although they did not manage to break out of their subordinate position in that way (Freund 1989a: 339–43). While incorporation implied a loss of political and cultural independence, it was preferable to economic dependence on individual masters. An even better alternative, for some, would have been the overthrow of colonial rule altogether. Sporadic arts of resistance against subjugation climaxed in the third Frontier War of 1799–1802, when the eastern Khoisan collaborated with the Xhosa in a last major attempt to regain political autonomy. Despite impressive military victories for the alliance, the Cape government succeeded in buying off some of the leaders through small grants of land and promises of better treatment on farms, to be governed by contracts. Internal divisions within the alliance and the fact that the government appeared to play a mediating role between the conflicting parties, rather than being a tool to further settler interests, contributed to an uneasy truce between the parties (Giliomee 1989a: 441–43).

The British Takeover

The Dutch East India Company period was brought to an end with the first British occupation of the Cape during 1795–1802, and a new era opened when the

British took over on a more permanent basis after 1806. The British period witnessed massive territorial and demographic changes, affecting the size, composition, and geographical spread of southern African populations. British rule coincided with, but did not always directly lead to, growth in internal diversity, with the introduction of new populations onto the scene. Relations between settlers and colonial authorities, on the one hand, and African chiefdoms and states on the other increasingly occupied a central place in the political process. Colonial expansion resulted in a growing influx of African farmers and laborers into the territory. By 1865, when the first census was taken at the Cape Colony, the group of African farmers and laborers had grown to 100,000, classified as Kafirs, or 20 percent of the total population of 500,000. The rest were of mixed descent—classified as Hottentots and Others, and 43 percent of the total—and Europeans, at 37 percent of the total (Houghton and Dagut 1972:3. 31–32).

Two other important political and demographic processes occurred in the same period. The first was the consolidation of larger, more stratified and centralized African state structures, and consequent wars and disruption (Peires 1981a; Wright and Hamilton 1989). Indigenous state formation took place concurrently with the movement of large numbers of Dutch-Afrikaans settlers and their servants from the eastern Cape into the interior, and the establishment of new political entities—the settler republics of the Orange Free State and the Transvaal (on its various divisions), and the British colony of Natal. Thus, African ethnic and state consolidation got entangled within an overall restructuring of political relations in southern Africa. The extent to which the two processes were causally linked has long been subject to historiographical and political debates, the most recent academic manifestation of which is known as the Mfecane debate. Without going into detail on the substance of the debate (see discussion in Hamilton 1993, chaps. 3 and 4), it is clear that the interpenetration of political interests in the southern African context was much tighter than was the case for the equivalent processes in Palestine/Israel.

The New Colonial State

The change to British rule had long-term implications not only for indigenous-colonial relations but also for the status of people of color in South African society. Before the nineteenth century the colonial state (in the form of the Company) kept only a handful of officials in charge of a population thinly spread over a large area. Its own military power was insignificant, and it relied on the settler-dominated commando system to deal with external enemies. Its coercive power vis-à-vis settlers was limited as it did not have a monopoly on the legitimate means of violence. While it was the sole nominal political authority, its capacity to control relations on farms was restricted; masters and servants were largely left to their own informal devices to manage the situation. The new British rulers, in contrast, possessed the necessary resources and will to establish effective authority in the colony. They put strong emphasis on the creation of reliable administrative and legal frameworks to handle both subjects and outsiders. (See Crais 1992 for an extensive examination of the innovative role of the British colonial state.) Their goal was to establish a stable political order and minimize the costs of the administration to the British colonial purse. Initially they continued to rely on the existing social institutions and intervened on the side of settlers to help them maintain orderly rule throughout the colony, in particular on the frontier. The Cape Dutch ruling class kept its economic and administrative power, though within the framework of British rule (Atmore and Marks 1974; Freund 1989a). In this vein, the Hottentot Proclamation of 1809, together with other regulations in subsequent years, established for the first time the legal rights and liabilities of the Khoisan, granting them recourse to the courts to protest mistreatment and violations of contracts while maintaining restrictions on their freedom of movement, ownership of land, and choice of employment (Macmillan 1968: 155–70).

In the context of these policies, another step aimed at stabilizing the political situation was the sustained military campaign in the fourth Frontier War of 1811–12, which resulted in the eviction of the Xhosa from the contested Zuurveld—for long the chief demand of settlers in the region. The British-dominated state enjoyed a major military advantage over their African opponents, whose forces, like those of their erstwhile settler adversaries, consisted of "mobilized citizenry," as Peires (1981b: 141) puts it. Indigenous people had great difficulties in offering a sustained challenge to the total war waged by British troops, who were full-time soldiers and possessed more sophisticated weapons and much greater firepower. The technological gap between the two sides eventually proved of tremendous benefit to colonial expansion.

As the Cape was gradually incorporated into the British Empire, economic and political realities inherited from the Company period gave way to new attitudes and practices. A reform process had been set in motion by the 1820s, adapting government structures to those prevalent elsewhere in the empire. The corrupt and inefficient government, which was used for the personal enrichment of officeholders and their cronies, was replaced with a better organized and more professional civil service, regional administration, and independent judiciary. The political power of the dominant slave-owning and merchant classes was curtailed, but not eliminated, by depriving them of direct access to the central government (Peires 1989a: 490–99).

The British ideology of economic liberalism, combined with a growing humanitarian sentiment at home fueled by the activities of missionary societies in the colonies, contributed to the elaboration of a new spirit at the Cape. Officials came to regard existing restrictions on the free movement of labor—such as slavery, pass laws, or indenture—as obstacles to the spread of civilization and progress in South Africa. In the minds of liberal missionaries and their like-minded officials, these concepts stood for a Christian way of life, fixed residence, production of cash crops, and the acquisition of a work ethic of hard labor and desire for material improvement (Comaroff 1989). From the British point of view, Khoisan and Africans primarily, but also white pastoral farmers, were lacking in those attributes. The abolition of obsolete social relations was seen, in addition, as necessary for making the country economically viable and competitive in international markets (Atmore and Marks 1974; Newton-King 1980).

Emancipations

Changes in labor policies in the 1820s and 1830s were linked to changes in the legal status of different groups. Ordinance 49 of 1828 liberalized the labor market by lifting the ban on the employment of African "Frontier Tribes" in the colony. It was immediately followed by Ordinance 50, which repealed the previous repressive regulations regarding the "Hottentot and other free persons of colour." The greater significance of these ordinances was that they effected a major move toward the transition from Hottentot to Eurafrican as Macmillan (1968) puts it, and that "after the passage of Ordinance 50, the legal category 'Hottentot', ceased to exist" (Newton-King 1980: 197). At the same time, the new policy of official toleration of Africans in the colony was the beginning of their transformation from citizens of independent chiefdoms to colonial subjects. This was particularly the case with the Mfengu, refugees from the Mfecane Wars in Natal and the interior, whose tribal or chiefly affiliations were disrupted by conflict and dislocation. The loss of their coherent social structure, land, cattle, and political organization made them less immune to missionary influences and more open to military and political collaboration with colonial forces against fellow indigenous people (Moyer 1974).

Following the ordinances of the late 1820s, and along similar politico-ideological lines, slavery was abolished in 1834, with final emancipation four years later. By 1838, then, all people of color who had been subjected for almost two centuries to numerous regulations drastically limiting their freedoms, if not eliminating them altogether, had become theoretically free, equal, and fully incorporated into the colony. In the words of Andries Stockenstrom, lieutenant governor and a prominent representative of liberal attitudes, "we will never again see the day when under British rule different degrees of rights and privileges will exist for different classes of His Majesty's subjects" (in a letter to N. T. van der Walt, 9/20/1837, in Du Toit and Giliomee 1983: 118).

The practical implementation of these lofty principles proved much less idyllic, however. Formal equality before the law did not mean social or economic equality. It entailed, rather, the adoption of criteria for the allocation of power and privilege which were nonracial in their appearance but racial in their consequences. As Marais puts it, "although 'class' [meaning here race] legislation became taboo in 1828, laws passed after that date continue to bear unmistakable testimony to the presence in the Cape Colony of large masses of backward people. In this sense 'class' legislation, in fact if not in form, continued to find its way onto the Colonial statute-book" (1957: 158). The Masters and Servants Ordinance of 1841, the Cape

Constitution of 1853, the Masters and Servants Act of 1856, and the qualified franchise of 1872, as well as other laws and regulations, were all formally colorblind; they did not discriminate on the basis of race or origin. They did make distinctions, though, on the basis of wealth, residence, and occupation, all of which frequently were the functional equivalents of race. Having said that, one should not minimize the importance of this legal transformation which did give some people of color real political and social rights and made them all, in principle, citizens of equal status fully incorporated in the colony.

The abolition of slavery brought about the emergence of a new social category comprising Khoisan, free people of color, and the emancipated slaves. Together they became known as Cape coloreds. They were Afrikaans-speaking and the majority belonged to the Dutch Reformed church, though there was a substantial Muslim minority, especially in Cape Town. The extent to which they developed a group identity superseding previous particular affiliations is debatable and the evidence fragmentary and inconclusive. Whereas Macmillan argues that "there was never anything like a distinct 'Coloured' national consciousness or pride of race" (1968: 287), Lewis (1987: 1–20) and Ross (1989b) portray a more ambiguous picture of Cape Town colored politics and social life in the second half of the nineteenth century. In this respect it is interesting that in more recent times the Population Registration Act of 1950 used subcategories such as Cape coloureds, Cape Malays, and Griqua until its abolition in July 1991. Significantly, language and religion, two important cultural elements common to the majority of colored people, were also shared by the majority of settlers, hence the common reference to coloreds as "brown Afrikaners."

Relations on the Frontiers

A corollary of the internal legal changes in the Cape Colony was the short-lived attempt following the sixth Frontier War of 1834–35 to stabilize conditions on the eastern frontier, through a system of treaties with African chiefdoms. The border areas were regarded as a buffer between the colony and the Xhosa, to be settled by colonial Khoisan, as in the Kat River settlement of 1829. The rationale behind this policy was that indigenous chiefs' control over their subjects, rather than direct colonial control, was more effective in keeping order and was cheaper and less troublesome for the Cape authorities. As Andries Stockenstrom put it in a letter to Lord Glenelg in 1836, "every measure tending to lower the importance of the Chiefs is calculated to weaken the hold we have on the people, as it is by means of these Chiefs we will soonest succeed in securing peace and promoting civilization. The supersession of their authority by that of our magistrates . . . [will create] a discontent which cannot fail to break forth with destructive violence as soon as it gets vent" (quoted in Du Toit and Giliomee 1983: 174).

The border policy encountered difficulties in the face of the persistent drive of settlers for land. The spread of wool farming in the 1840s gave rise to a powerful lobby for the continued dispossession of Africans and Khoisan from land suitable for sheep raising. Settlers were pressuring the government to "tame" the undisciplined "natives" and open up new territories for commercial exploitation. On the other side of the frontier, "trade, mission activity and labour migration had already bound the Xhosa inextricably to the Cape Colony" (Peires 1989: 490). In the late 1840s, the seventh Frontier War laid to rest the possibility of peaceful coexistence between the colony and independent African chiefdoms as separate, though allied, political entities. The breakdown of the treaty system thereafter led to its demise (Kirk 1980; Peires 1981b: 127–34, 150–58 deals with the circumstances of the War of the Axe of 1846–47).

The renewed expansionist drive of the colony brought about the occupation of more territories densely populated with Africans. The district of Victoria, between the Fish and the Keiskamma rivers, was annexed to the colony, and the area between the Keiskamma and the Kei rivers was administered for the Crown by High Commissioner Harry Smith as the province of British Kaffraria. Smith envisaged total incorporation of the territories and their people as he spelled it out in his address to the first public meeting with Xhosa chiefs: "Your land shall be marked out and marks placed that you may all know it. It shall be divided into counties, towns and villages, bearing English names. You shall all learn to speak English at the schools which I shall establish for you. . . . You may no longer be naked and wicked barbarians, which you will ever be unless you labour and become industrious" (quoted in Peires 1981b: 166).

A pattern similar to the one experienced by the Khoisan in the previous two centuries applied here as well: annexation, dispossession, and limited incorporation. However, the political structures and cultural identity of the Xhosa proved more resilient than those of the Khoisan. In a sense, the logic of Andries Stockenstrom, advocating indirect rule through treaties with African chiefs, was still operative, though in a modified form, governing internal rather than external relations. The mass of Africans kept their language and traditional institutions, but their chiefs were not independent as before. Rather than being equal sovereign parties in their treaties with the British, many of the chiefs were reluctantly transformed into intermediary agents subordinated to British and Cape officials. The more direct incorporation of the Khoisan (and the slaves), who were dispersed in small units and were largely left without leadership, was not generally repeated in the case of the Xhosa. Only a minority of Xhosa underwent conversion to Christianity and more comprehensive incorporation into the Colony as "de-tribalized natives." Their loss of land and cattle was not as thorough as was the case with the Khoisan, and the greater cohesion of precolonial Xhosa institutions allowed for longer and more sustained resistance to foreign control.

Settler Differentiation

The British takeover of the colony, and the administrative, economic, and legal changes introduced in its aftermath, affected relations within the settler population as well. A new element was introduced in 1820 with an influx of British immigrants into the frontier areas. Though a minority among settlers, and initially concentrated in the east, they had a strong impact on the colony's economy. Many became traders and land speculators, and their presence had the effect of increasing pressures toward a fully commercialized agriculture. Hailing from a fully capitalist society, the 1820 settlers were better fit to operate in an economic environment based on principles of liberalism, professional civil service, and "free" labor, that is, free from noneconomic constraints. They showed little interest in playing the role assigned to them as indentured servants, farmers, and a human buffer between the colony and independent Africans (Newton-King 1980; Peires 1989: 472–80). Consequently, they became a small but important constituency for economic and administrative changes.

The new and more professional style of government did not sit well with many of the settlers of the eastern districts, who favored a decentralized system of rule in which local farmers and their representatives exerted a strong influence on government policies. Their economy was based on expansionist pastoralism, which was only partially market-oriented and was dependent on the use of coerced labor. The changes introduced by the British from the 1820s onward made it difficult for these settlers to survive in the old way because their access to the administration was significantly reduced: "Now we have a Civil Commissioner to receive our money for Government and for Land Surveyors, a Magistrate to punish us, a clerk of the Peace to prosecute us . . . but no Heemraad [fellow settler-official] to tell us whether things are right or wrong" (a frontier farmer in 1830, in Peires 1989: 499). Dissatisfaction with the new British administration was magnified by an economic squeeze that resulted from growing pressure on land in the colony and blocked opportunities for further eastward expansion. Interference with their authority over laborers, the emancipation of the Khoisan and the slaves, and fears of being marginalized by a (highly unlikely) British-Khoisan-Xhosa alliance contributed to a feeling among many of the Dutch-Afrikaans settlers that the only way out of this situation was to leave the colony altogether. Their migration became known as the Great Trek.

The racial discourse within which their reactions were formed was, of course, a major element in the decision to move, but it was not explicitly expressed in their documents; they portrayed themselves rather as victims of, among other things, the "continual system of plunder . . . endured from the Caffers and other coloured classes" (manifesto of Piet Retief, 2/2/1837, in Du Toit and Giliomee 1983: 214, also 16–22, 213–17). In a less formal testimony to the spirit of the migrants, an 1843 letter written by Anna Steenkamp, Retief's niece, talks about the effects of the emancipation of slaves, of "their being placed on an equal footing with Christians, contrary to the laws of God and the natural distinction of race and religion, so that it was intolerable for any decent Christian to bow down beneath such a yoke" (quoted in Thompson 1985: 149). Steenkamp did not refer directly to color or language in her letter but instead counterposed "slaves" and "Kafirs" to "Christians," rather than blacks to whites. The distinctions the migrants made between their white, Dutch-Afrikaans, and Christian identities are un-clear. At that point in time, and for a long while after that, it seems that Afrikaner identity was not in existence: "Although the Dutch-Afrikaners did possess by 1850 certain common cultural traits in the form of generally endogamous marriage patterns, membership of the Dutch Reformed or Lutheran churches, and a common language (or variants of it), it was difficult to find any self-conscious sense of ethnic unity among them" (Giliomee 1989b: 23).

The Trekkers

The Great Trek of the late 1830s extended settler presence into the interior of southern Africa. White control became thinly spread out over a vast area populated by a large number of indigenous people. Ethnic and political complexity in the region increased enormously as a result. New political entities were created, constructing networks of relations which shifted between war, collaboration, and tense coexistence with existing African chiefdoms and states and their diverse peoples. In the Cape Colony itself, the departure of the migrants did not halt the drive toward the east which resulted in even more African territories and populations brought under British control. Despite the fact that one of the motivations of the migrants was their disapproving attitude toward what they perceived as equality between whites and blacks in the colony, their approach to the indigenous societies they encountered was not invariably hostile. The migrant leader Louis Trichard even contemplated at one point an anti-British alliance with the Xhosa and was willing to live under their rule (Peires 1989: 506–8). The migrants did not believe in granting citizenship or civil and political rights to their black servants, but they entered agreements and cooperated on many occasions with various African forces. They clearly perceived themselves as an integral part of the regional political environment and were pragmatic in building alliances and offering and receiving military help from their neighbors. As another leader said in his address to the Philippolis Griqua, "we are emigrants [and] together with you dwell in the same strange land and we desire to be regarded as neither more nor less than your fellow-emigrants, inhabitants of the country, enjoying the same privileges with you" (A. Potgieter in 1844, in Ross 1976: 56). The locus of political incorporation for them, however, was at the level of external rather than internal relations.

The statement above was not merely lip service. White settlement beyond the Cape Colony was widely dispersed, and the political organization of the settlers was decentralized. They possessed arms and horses but their military power was not enough to compensate for numerical weakness. Consequent problems in imposing their economic and political rule over indigenous societies forced settlers to reach an accommodation with the large and relatively powerful African states. The latter were willing, in turn, to grant land concessions to settlers in exchange for their help in their own factional fighting; as "there was no well-developed sense of racial identity among Africans, sectional advantage was placed before wider interests, and views of the most appropriate strategy differed as much as they do among black South Africans today" (Saunders 1981: 162).

Interactions between Indigenous People and Settlers

The fragmentation of indigenous people (and settlers) was especially common in the region between the Vaal and Limpopo rivers (Transvaal). The settlers were divided into several competing regional centers in the west (Potchefstroom), east (Ohrigstad), and north (Zoutpansberg). They frequently formed politico-military alliances with indigenous people. The Pedi under Sekwati, for example, joined forces with settlers under Potgieter to attack the Kgatla in the northern Transvaal in 1847; then, in 1852, Transvaal Ndebele collaborated with two settler parties to attack the Pedi; and in 1857 the Lydenburg Republic reached a mutual recognition agreement with the Pedi (Delius 1983: 30–40). In Zululand/Natal, settlers and British officials intervened in factional fighting for succession in the Zulu kingdom (Ballard 1989; Colenbrander 1989). Similar political relations of conflict, interspersed with military collaboration, existed between Transvaal settlers and the Swazi, who occasionally joined forces against the Pedi and the Zulu (Bonner 1983: 65–84). Complex maneuvers took place in the territories between the Orange and Vaal rivers. The Basotho, led by Moshweshwe, the Griqua, the British, and the settlers fought over land and political power. The outcome, specified in the Bloemfontein Convention of 1854, was the emergence of two states, the settler Orange Free State and Basutoland, both coexisting under British hegemony, which turned in 1868 into British annexation of Basutoland (Wilson and Thompson 1969: 414–24, 442–46).

In general, throughout the period, indigenous factions attempted to enlist the help of settlers and colonial officials against fellow Africans, and also to use intercolonial rivalries between settlers and the British to protect themselves from settler encroachment on their land. African state formation was enhanced by the ability of some political elements to wisely maneuver between different power centers, isolate their rivals, and consolidate their own rule. Loss of nominal independence was sometimes the price paid for greater security of land and eventual independence. Thus, the existence of Botswana, Lesotho, and Swaziland as legitimate independent states since the 1960s owes its origins to their prior history as British protectorates since the nineteenth century. Settlers, for their part, used these same rivalries to establish their initial political presence and then to increase their power, territorial control, and influence in the region. No undisputed dominance was achieved, however, until the significant increase in colonial and settler power in the wake of the economic transformations of the 1870s and 1880s (Atmore and Marks 1974; Saunders 1981). To be sure, though, alliances between settlers and indigenous people as external parties did not mean that the latter were granted political citizenship rights in any white political entity outside the Cape Colony.

Incorporation and Exclusion of Indigenous People

The co-optation of indigenous people into settler-dominated political structures posed a new dilemma. The Khoisan had had a weak and decentralized leadership, which disintegrated almost completely within decades of the initial colonial encounter. Most slaves arrived, of course, totally disorganized. The newly encountered indigenous Africans, in contrast, had their traditional leadership largely intact, even when defeated and conquered by colonial forces, as was the case with the Xhosa and later on with the Zulu kingdom. Those Africans who were not bound by the authority of chiefs, many of them Christianized refugees in the eastern Cape and Natal, soon began demanding representation in parliamentary and governmental structures. The outcome of ensuing struggles over incorporation was largely determined by the balance of interests of various forces: British administrators, Cape and Natal merchants, indigenous political elites, African peasants, and settlers.

Two principal modes of partial inclusion, and one of exclusion, characterized the response of white-ruled states to the challenge of indigenous groups. The first became known as Cape liberalism. It was a continuation of British policy as reflected in Ordinance 50 of 1828, which established legal equality for the Khoisan, and in the emancipation of the slaves. Its underlying assumption was that European, and more specifically British, supremacy could be maintained by using economic mechanisms of control without recourse to explicit racial legislation (Marais 1957; Newton-King 1980). The extension of qualified franchise to people of color was seen by liberal state officials as a way of dividing people of color into an educated and prosperous elite, committed to Western values and class domination, and the illiterate poor devoid of their natural leadership. The same policy was to be applied to Africans, who could thus be incorporated in a manner similar to the way the Khoisan and slaves were incorporated into a stable social-political order.

As discussed in chapter 3, white traders and missionaries saw the franchise as a way of creating a Christian-oriented, surplus-producing indigenous peasantry, free of the control of chiefs (Trapido 1980). Liberal policies were thus an instance of the collusion of material (trader), ideological (Christian), and state (Cape administration) interests. The issue also resulted in a clash of interests between the British colonial state, which was interested in political stability and working within wider frameworks of imperial strategy, and local settlers and their political representatives, who were more concerned with satisfying their immediate economic greed for land and labor. (Comaroff 1989 conceptualizes such conflicts in terms of the three models of state, settler, and civilizing colonial domination.) Among the indigenous people themselves, these liberal policies benefited all those who could and would incorporate themselves in colonial society—prosperous peasants, mission-educated intellectuals, and Christians. The mass of the indigenous population who continued to rely on homestead subsistence production had less to look forward to from such an incorporation.

The second mode of limited inclusion, applied in Natal and to some extent in the eastern Cape, consisted of indirect rule over the African population through traditional leaders, though it was based on a stated ideological commitment to color-blind principles. Lord Stanley, the British colonial secretary, posed a condition at the time of the annexation of Natal to the empire in 1842 that "there shall not be in the eye of the law any distinction of colour, origin, race, or creed; but that the protection of the law, in letter and in substance, shall be extended impartially to all alike" (quoted in Wilson and Thompson 1969: 372). These words were reflected in the 1856 Charter of Natal, which in theory did not make racial distinctions regarding franchise qualifications (Eybers 1918: 188–94). In practice, however, the vast majority of indigenous people could not meet the requirements for the vote since they were "placed under special control, and made subject to their own laws, customs and usages, and are consequently only partially brought under the operation of the general Laws of the Colony" (195). It was deemed "inexpedient" to allow them to exercise the franchise. Only Africans who had lived in the colony for twelve years, had been exempted from the authority of "native law" for seven years, and were proven loyal to the Crown were granted the vote. Naturally, very few passed these stringent tests (Guest 1989).

The Natal innovative mode of dealing with indigenous people became known as the Shepstone system, after Theophilus Shepstone, the longtime leading Natal authority on "native affairs." The essence of this policy of indirect rule consisted in the superimposition of British administrative and legal institutions on top of precolonial African social structures. Chiefs and village headmen were incorporated into the machinery of control and received a share of the spoils in the form of fines and tributes. To some extent, this system did not merely use traditional institutions but also reshaped or even created them. As a result of the Mfecane disruptions and large-scale movements of refugees into Natal, many Africans congregated in newly designated reserves and locations and did not live under hereditary chiefs: "Consequently, he [Shepstone] had to make 'tribes' and chiefs. In some cases, he attached individuals and fragments of chiefdoms to existing chiefs. In other cases, he rewarded trusted African assistants by putting them in charge of entirely artificial chiefdoms" (Etherington 1989: 178). This policy was based on a collusion of interests between British authorities and local chiefs who shared in the revenues generated through taxation. As in the Cape, the interest of the colonial state in political stability and large tax revenues clashed with the desire of settlers to gain unlimited access to indigenous land and labor and get rid of chiefs as intermediary powers. The colonial state was engaged in a larger strategic project of empire building, which transcended the narrow interests of settlers and allowed more space for indigenous incorporation.

The settler republics of the Transvaal and the Orange Free State did not attempt politically or ideologically to incorporate nonwhites. Driven by hunger for land

and cheap labor, they had no use for the more strategic arrangements implemented in the Cape and Natal, and backed by the interests and resources of the British Empire. In addition, their exclusionary identity and state institutions were premised on the explicit rejection of British practices in the Cape. Replicating the same arrangements which drove them from the Cape in the first place would have made no sense. The republican constitutions were explicitly racial. An early 1844 Potchefstroom constitutional document excluded "half-castes, down to the tenth degree" from citizenship rights (Eybers 1918: 350). In 1855 "all coloured people" were excluded from a voting franchise provision in the South African Republic and were "never [to] be given or granted rights of burghership" (362), and the 1858 constitution of the South African Republic established the principle that "the people desire to permit no equality between coloured people and the white inhabitants, either in Church or State" (364). Similar provisions applied in the Free State, in which citizenship rights were limited to white persons (286). Numerous restrictions on freedom of movement, property rights, and employment were imposed on indigenous peoples, though the capacity of the republics to enforce these was uneven (Thompson 1990: 87–96, 100–109).

Conclusions

By the end of the 1860s, four white-dominated political entities had come into being: two British colonies—the Cape and Natal—and two settler republics—the Orange Free State and the South African Republic. Alongside them, many autonomous and independent states of indigenous peoples continued to exist, including the Zulu, Sotho, and Swazi kingdoms, and various Mpondo, Tswana, Venda, and other chiefdoms. People of mixed origins established the autonomous political communities of Griqualand East and West. Even within the boundaries of white-controlled states there was a large degree of local autonomy, especially in the Transvaal and Natal. The interpenetration of colonial, settler, and indigenous spheres of influence was based on the inability of parties to achieve a decisive victory over their political opponents. This made for some flexibility in relations among the various states whose formative processes got entangled, as well as for a lack of rigid separation between them. The situation was far from harmonious, though, with constant fighting and readjustment of boundaries.

Ethnically and politically, many of these units were far from homogeneous, comprising people of diverse backgrounds with differing relations to the state. The Cape Colony had gone farthest toward the political incorporation of people of color, though in a qualified manner. Other white-dominated states adopted different forms of indirect control, but none established a coherent identity operating in similar exclusionary ways to those of the Jews and Arabs in Palestine/Israel. To take the example of language, Dutch-Afrikaans was the official language in the settler republics but most inhabitants were speakers of Bantu languages. In Natal, English was the official language but it was spoken by a tiny minority of the population. At the Cape, the most bilingual of all four (as far as whites were concerned), both European languages had official status, with English clearly predominant in government, law, and education, causing resentment among Afrikaans speakers, among whom were included the majority of colored people (Wilson and Thompson 1969: 283–86). Indigenous languages were completely displaced as mediums of administration in the colonial and settler states, though they continued to be spoken by Africans; Khoisan languages were not used except in isolated communities, and the original languages of slaves had long since been forgotten. Bantu languages were, of course, widely used in the still independent African chiefdoms and states.

The intermixture of ethnicity, religion, language, and factional affiliation, brought about by long historical processes of encounter, conflict, and interaction between groups with relatively permeable boundaries, presented serious obstacles for the formation of exclusionary national or political entities. Space for politics of inclusion was created by default, if not always by design. Incorporation in the realms of identity and state was not based on egalitarian foundations, but it had an important impact on future trends nonetheless. South African intergroup relations increasingly unfolded on a terrain shaped by struggles for equal rights within the system rather than attempts to leave the system or destroy it altogether. Strong exclusionary and separatist tendencies continued to exist, but their weight as a component of political dynamics shrunk over the years and, in the case of the slaves and the Khoisan, all but disappeared.

Comparison and Conclusions

I have discussed identity formation and state formation processes in the same chapter because of the difficulty of separating them in the historical narrative. For analytical clarity, however, I deal with their effects separately. The distinction is artificial but it allows us to focus systematically on the operation and importance of each of the processes.

IDENTITY FORMATION

In the sphere of identity formation, intergroup relations in Palestine/Israel and South Africa unfolded in distinct ways. The major process affecting Palestine/Israel was the creation of clearly defined external boundaries *between* groups and the (at least partial) dissolution of internal boundaries *within* them. The result was the consolidation of two relatively coherent and mutually exclusive identities. In South Africa, on the other hand, a complex process involving the simultaneous creation and dissolution of boundaries between groups took place. The result was the coexistence of multiple and partially overlapping identities, with no clear correspondence between color, language, religion, and legal status.

World-Historical Context

The rise of Zionism, the Jewish settlement of Palestine/Israel, and the beginning of the Arab-Israeli conflict took place in a period in which nationalist ideologies and movements had already emerged as important forces in European politics. Central and eastern Europe in particular, the regions with the largest concentrations of Jewish populations, became arenas for fierce battles over sovereignty, cultural autonomy, and self-determination waged by national minorities residing within the boundaries of multinational empires. In southeastern Europe, similar dynamics had tremendous impact on the organization of the Ottoman Empire, including its Middle Eastern territories, which became exposed to the operation of nationalism in the form of separatist revolts. These developments eventually led to the breakdown of the empire and the formation of numerous national states in Europe and the Middle East, including republican Turkey.

In late Ottoman Palestine/Israel, then, settlers and indigenous people encountered each other in an environment increasingly dominated by nationalist principles by which the world was understood to be composed of discrete units with their own exclusive territories and identities. Furthermore, even before the rise of the idea and practice of nationalism to such a prominent place in history, Jews, Muslims, and Christians in the Middle East and elsewhere had been conscious of their adherence to different and mutually exclusive world religions. The process of identity formation in Palestine/Israel consequently unfolded in an environment based on exclusivity, religious as well as national in nature.

In southern Africa, in contrast, colonization took place initially in a different world-historical context; nationalism had not yet appeared in Europe, let alone in other parts of the world. The notions that societies should be based on ethnic homogeneity, that all speakers of a language should be part of the same political unit, and that rulers should speak the same language as their subjects were not widespread at the time. Most Europeans lived in multiethnic and multilingual societies well into the nineteenth century. In southern Africa at the same time, the small scale of most political units made internal ethnic unity more likely than in Europe, but there was no correspondence between linguistic and political boundaries, nor was there any movement to match the two.

Racial and religious distinctions did form an important part of the European way of looking at the different populations of the world, but in the seventeenth and eighteenth centuries they had not yet hardened into the rigid biologically based racist ideologies of the nineteenth century. There was room within this framework for sexual and marital contacts between people of different backgrounds as testified to by the existence of such mixed populations as the Eurasians of the East Indies and the mulattos of the Caribbean. The indigenous people of southern Africa did not regard racial distinctions as crucial to the way they perceived the new groups of European settlers and slaves of African and Asian origins. In fact, their own previous history had been one of mixing between people of different somatic and cultural characteristics, such as the Khoisan and the Bantu-speaking populations. Settlers and indigenous people in southern Africa, then, interacted in a historical environment which created some space for a variety of ethno-religious combinations or crossover between groups.

Indigenous Capacities

The transformation of the focus of identity in Palestine/Israel, from one based on religious-denominational foundations (the *millet* system) to one dominated by ethno-national groups, was expressed in the move taken by Arabic-speaking Christians and Muslims toward an inclusive Palestinian-Arab identity based on shared language and territory. This move was made possible by the fact that both Christianity and Islam had a transnational and trans-ethnic character almost from their beginnings, and that even before the rise of nationalism the prevailing religious boundaries rigidly separated Jews from other communities. As far as most Muslims and Christians were concerned, there was no inherent contradiction between the maintenance and dissolution of boundaries in the religious sphere and the creation of a comprehensive new community in the national sphere. In fact, that kind of compartmentalization of identities can be found in numerous local variations all over the Christian and Islamic worlds. This is manifested in two forms: (1) world religions whose adherents are people of various national groups, for example, Irish, Italian, and Polish Catholics or Iranian and Lebanese Shi'ite Muslims; (2) national groups internally divided by religion, for example, Muslim and Coptic Egyptians or Catholic and Lutheran Germans. Historically, the second case has been more problematic in its implications for the prospect of a unified identity.

The ability of indigenous people to construct a coherent national identity, subsuming but not displacing religious-communal affiliations, if only in a rudimentary form, allowed them to maintain their ground and not be submerged when confronted by the Jewish settlement project. There was virtually no movement on the part of Palestinian Arabs to adopt any of the cultural attributes of the settlers, such as language, religion, or ethnic identity. Islam, Christianity, and the Arabic language were all indigenous forces capable of investing struggles with powerful ideological and political meanings with no need to borrow from the Jewish or Zionist arsenal of symbols. In this respect, in Palestine/Israel, indigenous people maintained their cultural independence and consequently were not open to incorporationist dynamics in the realm of identity, unlike their South African counterparts.

In both countries processes of forming new nations or imagined communities were woven out of preexisting materials. In Palestine/Israel, to follow up on that terminology, a large stretch of the imagination was needed to bring into being an identity comprising both Jews and Arabs, as a result of the relatively impermeable boundaries of their historical identities. In South Africa, on the other hand, the construction of a shared identity in the Cape Colony was less taxing on the imagination, though by no means easy. The lack of prior consolidation of coherent indigenous identities of the Khoisan facilitated a process through which "they literally acculturated themselves out of existence" (Marks 1972: 77). This was the historical background for the limited cultural and biological intermixture between settlers, Khoisan, and slaves which took place in the colonial period. It was expressed in a gradual process of fusion that had led, by mid-nineteenth century, to the appearance of a large number of Dutch-Afrikaans-speaking Christians (as well as Muslims) who became known collectively as coloreds. For most of the Dutch East India Company period, and well into the second half of the nineteenth century, the various ingredients that went into the making of the category "coloreds" outnumbered settlers in the Cape Colony. Their presence served to mitigate the dichotomy between settlers and indigenous people that might have developed otherwise.

The case with the Bantu-speaking people of the eastern coast and the interior was different. Their ethnicity was more strongly bounded and their cultural identity more resilient than that of the Khoisan. They showed few signs of losing their distinct cultural heritage or become at that time incorporated into any comprehensive South African identity (with the exception of the mission-educated Christian minorities in the Ciskei and Natal). Similar to the Khoisan, however, they did not develop a sense of belonging to the same race or nation among themselves. Their myths of origin and historical memories continued to refer to specific localized identities (Xhosa, Mpondo, Zulu, Sotho) rather than to an inclusive indigenous category, be it defined as African or black. In this sense, they did not develop a sense of common destiny capable of politically and culturally uniting them in struggle through the dissolution of internal boundaries, as both Arabs (Muslims and Christians) and Jews (Ashkenazim and Sephardim) did in the case of Palestine/Israel. Indigenous capacities, then, facilitated the rise of multiple groups with partially overlapping boundaries in South Africa, as compared to the creation of two clear and mutually exclusive groups in Palestine/Israel.

Settler Strategies

Both indigenous capacities *and* settler strategies pushed in an exclusionary direction in Palestine/Israel. Local Jews did not take part in the process of Palestinian-Arab identity formation but engaged instead in their own formative processes, because historically Judaism evolved as a religion with a specific ethnic content, allowing no separation of religious and national identity. We cannot rule out the possibility that the Arabic-speaking Jews of the Middle East in general, and Palestine in particular, would have joined the mainstream of Arab nationalism had Zionism not emerged as an alternative, exclusively Jewish, national movement in late nineteenth-century Europe. However, given the self-definition of Jews as a people (or nation), not only as a religion, it is unlikely such a development would have taken place. Thus Jewish was counterposed not only against such concepts as Christian or Muslim but also against Polish or Arab. This was not the case, however, for national identities defined in terms of citizenship, such as French or American, rather than in ethno-religious terms; no contradiction is generally perceived between being Jewish and belonging to these national collectivities. The full complexity of the issue cannot be discussed here, but the crucial point is that Jews were different in this respect from such other non-Islamic religious minorities as the Greek Orthodox and the Catholics who were incorporated in Arab nationalism.

In any event, Zionism appeared on the scene and exerted a strong influence on the direction identity formation processes took. Moreover, since the early nineteenth century, Ashkenazim started immigrating in growing numbers into the country, thus making the non-Arab, foreign character of the local Jewish population more pronounced. The rise of the new Jewish community, the revival of Hebrew as a means of daily communication, and the consequent relaxation of intra-ethnic tensions within the Jewish community further served to fortify the boundaries between Jews and Arabs. The Zionist movement targeted the territory for settlement, with the prospect of the reconstitution of independent Jewish national life there; this made the implicit clash over the national identity of the country into an explicit one. Two competing national movements thus emerged, both of which regarded Palestine as their patrimony in mutually exclusive terms. Historical heritage, culture, religion, and language combined to create two communities with little common ground between them.

Seen from this comparative angle, the most remarkable feature of European settlement in the South African context is its nonnational character. Settlers were of various origins, though most were Dutch, and their arrival in the country and subsequent settlement and territorial expansion had little to do with any national project comparable to Zionism. They did not operate in South Africa as representatives of a well-defined group seeking to found a national home for its people, nor were they concerned in particular with the creation of boundaries rigidly separating themselves from indigenous people on the one hand and other Europeans on the other. Their major motivation for settlement was socioeconomic, and they did not put forward as conscious goals the formation of a particular version of identity and the creation of the political circumstances enabling its realization. In that, they were very different from Jewish settlers in Palestine/Israel.

All of this should not be taken to mean that settlers in South Africa had no interest in identity. They did create boundaries and were very conscious of their distinction from indigenous people and slaves. They approached the issue of identity boundaries, however, from a more utilitarian perspective without attempting to follow a clear ideological blueprint. Of course Israeli-Jews did not follow Zionist blueprints to the letter either; their nationalist designs could not have been implemented without major modifications and internal contests in light of local realities. Their mere existence, however, served to impart an overall sense of direction to the Zionist project that was absent in South Africa. As a result, settlers in South Africa were more flexible than their Israeli-Jewish counterparts and more tolerant of transgression of boundaries. More space for incorporation was thus created in South Africa.

STATE FORMATION

The analysis of state formation requires a focus on the creation of political and administrative structures and their effects on the unfolding relations between indigenous people, settlers, and colonial authorities. From the late nineteenth century onward, Palestinian Arabs and Israeli Jews increasingly tended to regard each other as external political elements. This trend intensified with the rise of the Zionist movement, as the intercommunal struggle centered on the question of which of the two mutually exclusive emergent sets of national-political institutions would become dominant in the country. In South Africa, on the other hand, relations between indigenous people and settlers were initially governed by treaties and external relations, but came increasingly to be dominated by struggles over terms of incorporation within a single set of political institutions. These changes in the locus of conflict, from internal to external in Palestine/Israel and from external to internal in South Africa, came about as a result of the operation of the following three factors.

World-Historical Context

The encounter between indigenous people and settlers in Palestine/Israel took place in a historical context that saw the rise of centralized state institutions as the principal form of political organization in Europe and gradually in the Middle East as well. The social and political reforms in the Ottoman Empire, the Tanzimat, were initiated in the nineteenth century in order to enable the state to defend itself against foreign intervention and participate on an equal footing in the European state system. Reforms came against a background of centuries-long involvement of the Ottomans in relations of cooperation and conflict with other European powers. This pattern of relations was disrupted in the nineteenth century with the rise of better organized and more powerful European states whose authority was based on recent advances in industrial production, military technology, and the professionalization of bureaucratic apparatuses.

The formation of political institutions in South Africa unfolded in a different world-historical framework. The European state system of the seventeenth and eighteenth centuries was divided among land-based continental empires, maritime-based commercial empires, and a host of smaller political units such as the German and Italian principalities. Centralized states working within clearly defined boundaries, and based on principles of separation of powers and professional civil service, were hardly known at the time and did not become important until well into the nineteenth century. States extended their control over diverse territories and populations, which frequently enjoyed a large degree of autonomy, especially in frontier regions that passed back and forth between empires. Boundaries were not fixed, and the relations between territorial rule and citizenship rights were subject to frequent shifting. Overall, the system was less organized than it later became with the division of spheres of influence and the Vienna and Berlin conferences in the nineteenth century.

The effects of these different backgrounds on settlement and resistance processes in the two cases varied. For South Africa, the loosely structured system of interstate relations in which context the colonization the country unfolded, allowed experimentation with varied institutional arrangements. There was no single overriding model of colonial expansion and settlement followed by all, and the diversity made possible various modes of incorporation (and lack thereof, including physical extermination) of indigenous people. The historical context did not mandate any particular form of rule but, unlike latter-day modes of colonial domination, neither did it exclude any.

The latter historical period in which the Jewish settlement of Palestine/Israel took place was more rigid in this respect. Relations between European powers and indigenous forces became more systematized and uniform as various powers competed with each other in the scramble for Africa. Greater emphasis on racial exclusivity, segregation from the "natives," and clear distinctions between colonial and indigenous institutions were the norm. Consequently, colonizers in the latter period were less open than their early counterparts to transgression of boundaries. While this attitude did not determine on its own the pattern of settlement in Palestine/Israel, it did exert an indirect influence on the terms within which settlers viewed the nature of their project.

Indigenous Capacities

When indigenous Palestinians began confronting the Zionist settlement project, they had already acquired some experience in the modus operandi of European-style state institutions. Notions such as politics of public pressure, legal action, parliamentary work, and international forums were introduced into the country through indigenous regional channels and were not a foreign imposition. Of course the Ottoman state was not a full-fledged parliamentary democracy. Furthermore, the political reforms it went through were not entirely generated from within; European pressures played a significant role in the design and implementation of a reformist agenda. Nevertheless, the administrative capacities of indigenous people in the realm of state management owned nothing to settlers in this respect.

Prior exposure to the operation of a large-scale state apparatus increased the capacity of indigenous people to use existing political structures and create their own modes of organization in order to meet foreign challenges. Settlers did not enjoy any inherent advantage over indigenous people in that respect. Both groups could compete in the political arena on terms that, if not entirely equal due to better education and training of settlers, were sufficiently similar to enable indigenous people to construct movements, parties, and institutions without adopting settler modes of organization. They thus avoided incorporation in a subordinate position. In addition, Palestinians could rely on the tacit and sometimes open support of state officials, and the potential solidarity of the popular masses in other parts of the region. The Zionist movement thus could not base its project on "non-European foundations," as neither indigenous people nor elements within the state had much to gain from such collaboration. They were engaged in their own process of state formation, which did not leave much room for competition, or much need for help, from the outside. Indigenous and settler political projects were seen, then, as inherently incompatible by both sides.

In southern Africa, on the other hand, the state principle, as distinct from organization based on kinship, was in its early stages. Territorial rule in the form of chiefdoms was based on the effective decentralization of control and tributary relations among chiefs of different ranks and between them and commoners. No permanent and professional military, budgetary, and administrative structures existed independently of the court prior to the nineteenth century. Even in later periods, with the emergence of larger and better organized indigenous states, the scale of organization was small. Political units were frequently fragmented, with numerous factions competing over land, cattle, followers, and revenues.

The fragmented nature of the political organization of indigenous people facilitated the ability of colonial forces to conquer them, take over their resources, and politically incorporate them in a subordinate role. Fighting among Khoisan chiefs allowed the Dutch East India Company to construct alliances with some indigenous leaders and use its interventionist capacity to impose its authority on all of them, loyal and dissident alike. Similar processes took place about 150 years later, with the British and the Xhosa chiefs on the eastern frontier. The latter, though, unlike Khoisan chiefs, managed to maintain limited political power because of their more resilient culture and their continuing access to land and cattle resources, essential in recruiting and retaining followers.

The military assistance provided to the European side by indigenous groups, such as the colonial Khoisan troops and the Mfengu, proved crucial for colonial conquest and subjugation. Access to superior weapons played an important role in the willingness of indigenous people to become involved in military cooperation with colonial authorities and settlers in South Africa. African political factionalism combined with the potential benefits of alliances with European forces to build an indigenous foundation for foreign rule, and thus made colonial expansion easier.

These factors were not operative to any significant extent in the relations between Jews and Arabs in Palestine. Day-to-day contact and cooperation at the local level between Jewish settlements and Arab villages were common, but there was no political, let alone military, collaboration at the national level. Settlers had no privileged access to firearms, and their own military capacity was limited; they thus did not carry with them to any potential Arab partners the promise of military-political benefits. The long-term involvement of the Ottoman Empire in European affairs (through wars, alliances, and training) meant that Jewish settlers enjoyed little technological advantage over indigenous people; their situation was thus different from that of their South African counterparts. As a result, no interpenetration of political interests was evident in Palestine/Israel. In the sphere of state formation, then, the exclusionary nature of Palestinian/Israeli developments can be contrasted with the more inclusive, though limited and inegalitarian, nature of relations in South Africa.

Settler Strategies

Settlers in Palestine/Israel were highly politicized as a community by virtue of the fact that they owed their existence in the country to conscious choices by individuals and movements. Their main goal was the establishment of an independent political community (or state), and they resorted to building their own institutions rather than seriously trying to manipulate existing ones to their advantage. Having no imperial or colonial power directly behind them, and being few in number, settlers were unable to challenge the vast powers (relative to their own) of the Ottoman state. Under these conditions, direct confrontation with the indigenous state would have been disastrous for them; an attempt to incorporate themselves within existing political institutions would have put them in a disadvantaged position vis-à-vis indigenous people. The latter were capable of using their citizenship status, access to the state, and larger numbers to block the progress of the Zionist project to some extent and to prevent state officials from granting it major concessions. The most reasonable course of action open to settlers at the time, then, was to organize autonomously, cultivate contacts with foreign powers, and prepare for the imminent demise of the Ottoman Empire.

Settlers in South Africa, on the other hand, were never left to their own devices. European settlement was sponsored at first by the Dutch East India Company, and then became part of the British Empire. The more extensive military and financial resources possessed by these international enterprises were put, at least to some extent, at the service of settlers in their struggle with indigenous people over territorial and political control. Consequently, they could face the indigenous people of the Cape from a powerful position and establish a strong beachhead in the region. Later in the nineteenth century, British military force proved decisive for further territorial advances of the colony. Given their relatively secure position, settlers could embark on the political incorporation of indigenous people in a subordinate role without having to worry too much about adverse consequences.

5 | Development, Dependency, and Dispossession

In this chapter I continue my analysis of land and labor relations between settlers and indigenous people. During the British rule of Palestine/Israel (1917–48), distinct patterns of exclusionary land policies, labor relations, and economic development were established, reaching a climax with the partition of the territory in 1948. In South Africa during the period in question, we see the conquest of hitherto independent African territories, rural dispossession, industrial development, and segregationist incorporation, beginning with the mineral discoveries of the late nineteenth century and culminating in 1948 with the rise of the white supremacist National Party to power.

The focus in much of the existing literature on the interests, visions, and designs of settler and colonial forces is inadequate for coming to terms with the processes discussed here. We have to go beyond these concerns to explore indigenous social structures and the processes they underwent independently of, but also in response to, colonial challenges. Encounters between settlers and indigenous people in the field of land and labor did not result in a simple and unilateral imposition of colonial schemes on indigenous populations. Internal social and political differentiation and multiple struggles among various indigenous and settler segments, as well as tactical alliances across colonial boundaries, made the picture more complex than that of a conflict between two clearly defined groups, the results of which were determined in advance.

Palestine/Israel

The period of British rule over Palestine/Israel brought about important changes in the relations between indigenous people and settlers. During that time, Palestinian-Arabs and Israeli-Jews consolidated their independent social and economic structures, strengthened their collective identities, constructed political institutions, and engaged in an organized struggle over political and territorial control. The exclusionary patterns of economic relations that began to be evident in the late Ottoman period became dominant and were consolidated during the British period. The Mandate for Palestine, administered by the British government under the authority of the Mandates section of the League of Nations, provided the terrain on which the conflicting parties formulated their interests and fought for their realization.

The British Role

The Balfour Declaration of November 1917 publicly expressed for the first time the willingness of the British government to recognize the Jewish claim to Palestine/Israel as articulated by the Zionist movement. Lord Balfour, the British foreign secretary, stated that his government viewed with favor "the establishment in Palestine of a national home for the Jewish people, and will use their best endeavours to facilitate the achievement of this object" with the provision that "nothing shall be done which may prejudice the civil and religious rights of existing non-Jewish communities in Palestine or the rights and political status enjoyed by Jews in any other country" (League of Nations 1922: 2). The principles of the declaration were incorporated into the preamble of the mandate, stipulating that Britain as the mandatory power "shall be responsible for placing the country under such political, administrative and economic conditions as will secure the establishment of the Jewish national home" and "shall facilitate Jewish immigration under suitable conditions and shall encourage, in co-operation with the Jewish agency [meaning the Zionist Organization] . . . close settlement by Jews on the land, including State lands" (p. 3, articles 2 and 6).

The overall political framework of the mandate meant that relations between Jews and Arabs developed in an environment more favorable to the interests of settlers than was the case in the preceding Ottoman period. The existing restrictions on Jewish immigration, capital imports, and land transfers were substantially relaxed, though they did not disappear altogether and some were reimposed at a later stage. The government, however, provided no more than the elementary economic infrastructure and the legal mechanisms that regulated the economic transactions that actually took place in the country. It did not actively intervene to promote Jewish settlement through purchasing land, encouraging immigration, and subsidizing labor costs as the Zionist movement expected it to do. On the other hand, the government did not block controversial land deals as long as they did not blatantly infringe on the limited rights of cultivators for compensation, as defined by law. In other words, the crucial issues of land ownership and labor policies were primarily handled by individuals and organizations in the communities concerned themselves, though these were affected by the overall economic policies of the government. In this sense, the Palestinian-Israeli conflict developed in a different institutional environment than the South African conflict in which the British colonial state played an active role, alongside settlers, in the subjugation, dispossession, and exploitation of indigenous people.

Palestine/Israel emerged into the British mandate from a long and devastating war that had caused a great deal of destruction. During the war and its immediate aftermath, economic activities were paralyzed to a large extent and no land transactions could have taken place. The activities of the Zionist movement had to be suspended, and some of its leading activists, along with large numbers of settlers who held Russian citizenship, were forced out of the country. In 1918, with the imposition of a British military administration, normal life resumed. It was only in 1920, though, that the new civilian government created the legal framework for the continuing process of Jewish settlement as part of the construction of a Jewish National Home in the country.

The dissolution of the Ottoman Empire, the formation of the newly unified political unit of Palestine/Israel, and the establishment of the mandate brought about changes in government economic policies as well. The British government firmly believed in fiscal restraint and the free operation of market forces; they therefore restricted their intervention in the economy to those aspects deemed essential to their overall strategic interests. Gross (1984) identifies six main, and somewhat contradictory, British policy objectives that had important economic implications for the country. These were derived in the following order of importance from imperial geopolitical considerations, metropolitan economic interests, and specific mandatory obligations. All were served by developing internal and external communication and transportation networks, maintaining a stable and legitimate rule, keeping a balanced budget, helping British exports, promoting modern and capitalist cultural and economic standards, and avoiding the disruption of local customs and social structures. (See Gozansky 1986: 91–96 for emphasis on the colonial character of British policies.)

These priorities made it unlikely that Britain would satisfy the demand of the Zionist movement that the British mandatory power be empowered to "propose measures for the close settlement, intensive cultivation, and public use of land, where necessary by compulsory purchase at a fair prewar price and further, by making available all waste lands unoccupied and inadequately cultivated lands or lands without legal owners and state lands," to be taken over by a proposed Jewish Council representing Jews in Palestine and elsewhere (statement of the Zionist Organization to the Paris Peace Conference of 1919, in Kaplan 1983: 96). The Zionist view was that this council should participate in the development and administration of immigration, land, public works, credit, and all other issues pertaining to economic conditions in the country.

The Land Question

Those steps, if taken, would have further alienated the representatives of the Arab population of Palestine, who were strongly opposed to the whole Jewish National

Home concept from the start. British officials were well aware of the explosive potential of the transfer of Arab land to Jews. As Major General H. D. Watson, chief administrator of the military government, expressed it in August 1919, "the natives of the soil" were very hostile to the Jewish National Home scheme because they "foresee their eventual banishment from the land" (report to the Foreign Office, in Ingrams 1972: 81). Two years later, following outbreaks of public disorder in the country, the Haycraft Commission reported that "the general belief that the aims of the Zionists and Jewish immigration are a danger to the national and material interests of Arabs in Palestine is well nigh universal amongst the Arabs," citing among the reasons for that the perception that public jobs are being monopolized by Jews (Palestine 1921: 45).

Despite these sentiments, the organized Palestinian-Arab national movement did not treat land and labor questions as particularly urgent in the early years of British rule. It did deal with them occasionally, though. A March 1921 deputation from the Arab Executive Committee claimed that "Palestine suffers . . . from her Jewish colonies. Wherever these exist the surrounding peasant population has had to sell out and migrate. Because of their clannishness Jews will, as far as they help it, not employ a native, or buy at his store or benefit him in any way" (Colonial Office 1921: 146). A year later, in correspondence with Winston Churchill, secretary of state for the colonies, the Palestinian delegation complained about Arab railway employees "being turned out of their jobs in order to make room for [immigrant] Jewish employees" (Palestine 1922: 25). The Fifth Palestine Arab Congress in August 1922 discussed land sales to Jews and appointed a committee to examine the issue, though no further steps seem to have been taken by the Congress in subsequent meetings (Porath 1977: 90–91).

These and other references to land and labor issues were vague. Anti-Zionist arguments in the early 1920s were primarily concerned with overall legal, diplomatic, and political issues. The Palestinian-Arab national movement attempted to nip the Zionist project in the bud rather than fight specific manifestations of it. Another reason for the Arabs' relatively meager engagement with land issues during that period was that the exclusionary nature of Jewish settlement had not been very pronounced during the late Ottoman period. Obvious exclusionary tendencies were expressed by the Zionist labor movement, however, and they did increase political tensions in the country, but they also coexisted with, and were thus mitigated by, a large measure of economic interaction between Jewish farmers and Arab laborers and tenants. Settlement strategies were a focus of internal conflict within the Jewish community over the policy of Jewish labor, rather than a major cause for intercommunal conflict. As the country moved deeper into the British period, however, accelerated Jewish immigration and land purchases pushed land and labor issues to the center of the national political conflict, especially in the 1930s.

The potentially problematic nature of the land question was recognized by the Land Transfer Ordinance enacted in October 1920. All land transfers required official authorization, and specific clauses ensured the continuing economic viability of the direct cultivators. The district governor had to "withhold his consent of a transfer, unless he was satisfied that in the case of agricultural land either the person transferring the property, if he is in possession, or the tenant in occupation, if the property is leased, will retain sufficient land in the district or elsewhere for the maintenance of himself and his family" (Palestine 1930b: 115). In addition, restrictions on the size of transactions and on speculative land transfers were attempted. As a result of combined pressure by Zionist organizations and Arab landowners interested in removing obstacles to the operation of free market in land, these latter restrictions were abolished soon after with the amended ordinance of December 1921. A further change in the regulations was the exclusion of agricultural laborers and small owner-peasants, more than 80 percent of all cultivators, from legal protection. Only with regard to tenants had the previously mentioned restrictions been maintained (Granott 1952: 305–6; Stein 1984: 44–52).

For much of the 1920s, land sales involved transfer from big (mostly foreign) absentee landowners to Zionist and other Jewish organizations, a continuation of the pattern established in Ottoman times. The proportion of land acquired from small peasants was negligible—less than 2.5 percent of the total in the years 1920–27 (see figures in Granott 1952: 277). About 97 percent of the purchased lands were not previously cultivated by their owners, so the crucial questions to be considered are: Who were the direct producers and what happened to them as a result of these transactions? At the time these issues were of great importance and in one way or another they continue to be crucial to scholarly and political debates about the nature of the Zionist settlement project and its impact on Palestinian-Arab society.

Tenancy and Dispossession

Most of the large tracts of land purchased from the large absentee landholders had been acquired by them for speculative purposes in the late Ottoman period. Located primarily along the coastal region and in the interior valleys, the tracts were sparsely inhabited and extensively cultivated. Relatively little of that land was found in the densely populated areas of the central hilly districts. It was rarely managed in large productive units because this would have required substantial capital expenditure and constant supervision, efforts not appealing to landowners who were seeking easy profits. As a consequence, the numbers of tenants, agricultural laborers, and grazers on these lands were low though not insignificant.

There are no exact figures on the number of persons displaced by land sales to Jews, and the estimates vary a great deal depending on the definition of dispossession and the reliability of data. The official guidelines used by the Development Department in the Palestine administration, echoing the position taken by the Jewish Agency for Palestine, defined the landless as "such Arabs as can be shown to have been displaced from the lands which they occupied in consequence of the lands passing into Jewish hands, and who have not obtained other holdings on which they can establish themselves, or other equally satisfactory occupation" (Government of Palestine 1931: 31). This restrictive definition excluded tenants who found land elsewhere or who received monetary compensation when evacuated or moved to the cities in search of employment. By 1935, as a result of this definition, 664 tenants were recognized as having a valid case out of the 3,271 who claimed to have been dispossessed.

Based on these numbers, Granott asserts that the charges of widespread dispossession were rooted in distortion and exaggerated figures and were used as a weapon by forces opposed to Jewish immigration and settlement. He attributes the low numbers to the decline of this particular form of cultivation: "In Palestine tenancy is dying out along with the disappearance of large land ownership. As the large estates are converted into small [Jewish] peasants' holdings there is no longer any room for tenants . . . in view of the extensive areas which had been acquired from the large landowners (and it was only on their properties that tenants were to be found), it would seem that already at the end of the first World War tenancy had declined in the country" (1952: 302–3). Tenant rights became a contested political issue, however, precisely because of the assumption, a central component of Zionist discourse, that there was no room for Arab tenants once the land was transferred into Jewish hands. Contrary to the impression Granott seeks to create, there was no necessary economic rationale for the disappearance of tenancy; in fact, it persisted in various forms throughout the period in the Arab-dominated agricultural economy (Firestone 1982). Tenants were removed, regardless of the size and the economic potential of the holding on which they resided, in conformity to a Zionist view that assigned prime importance to land as a territorial and political, rather than merely an economic, asset.

The low official figures for the dispossessed have been challenged by many writers. Porath, for example, uses a more comprehensive definition to include among the displaced those who used to work on the land without clear tenancy agreements as well as those who later found some other kind of land or employment. Consequently, he raises the estimate to a few thousand families (Porath 1977: 87–90); other critical Israeli writers adopt the same or similar findings (Kimmerling 1983: 106–21; Gozansky 1986: 154–61). Much higher figures are offered by Palestinian sources. Kanafani (n.d.: 8) talks about 20,000 displaced families for the entire British period, 8,730 of them evacuated from the Valley of Esdraelon alone. Several other writers adopt his figures as authoritative, although he does not provide sources for them. The difficulties of reaching agreement on the numbers are huge, and it is highly unlikely that conclusive figures will emerge at this point in time. (See the appendix at the end of this chapter for further discussion of this issue.)

The crucial point for understanding the implications of the issue, beyond the conflicting estimates, is the role of land as a material, political, and symbolic asset.

As Kimmerling argues, regardless of numbers, "the existence of *fellaheen* who saw themselves as unjustifiably evicted from their lands created an awareness within the Arab agrarian sector that this was a possible fate for every *fellah*. This made the struggle over land concrete and relevant for every individual in the Arab community" (Kimmerling 1983: 106). That this was the case in the 1930s was attested to by the British high commissioner, who remarked that the fear of takeover of land by the Jewish community was felt in 1935 "in every town and village in Palestine" as "about one fifth of Arab villagers are already landless. Village communities are well aware that they have sold, or their neighbours have sold, large sections of their land to Jews and that they have not permanently benefited by the transaction. Their money has gone, the shortage of land has increased. Their fear that the process will continue till the bulk of the land is gone is genuine" (quoted in Lesch 1979: 70). It is unclear to what extent these feelings were common throughout the period; the big land purchases by the Zionist movement in the early 1920s did not go unchallenged, but neither did they give rise to much organized Arab agitation. They did, however, create latent fears, which began emerging with the growing crisis of peasant agriculture.

One reason the land transfers of the 1920s did not attract much attention was that the parties to the land transactions wanted to settle the fate of the cultivators outside the public view. Regulations for protecting tenants from dispossession proved incapable of achieving their goals. The collusion of interests between Arab sellers and Jewish buyers, both of whom regarded interference with land transactions as a nuisance, made enforcement of legal restrictions very difficult, even without the (suspected) connivance of local government officials. In a 1929 testimony given before the Shaw Commission, the director of lands claimed that, by the time the district officer inspected a deal, "he would go out to the village and in some cases he would find that the whole population had already evacuated the village. They had taken certain sums of money and had gone. . . . In other cases it was found that a large percentage of the population had already gone before the transaction came to us, and we could not find out who the tenants were, they had no written contracts, and we did not know what compensation they were getting" (Palestine 1930b: 115).

This pattern was consistent and devised by the interested parties precisely to prevent the tenant question from becoming an open political issue. The strategy proved successful until the late 1920s, when it led to the 1929 Protection of Cultivators Ordinance, which gave official sanction to the principle of monetary compensation (which was widely practiced anyway) and generally made it easier to vacate tenants from the land. The lack of organized and vocal opposition to land sales should not, however, be interpreted as lack of concern for their effects. Under the surface, Palestinian anxieties about the implications of land transfers were widespread, though not necessarily clearly articulated and accessible to outsiders. (See Khalidi 1988 for the problems in relying on written Jewish, British, and even urban Arab sources to analyze peasant feelings and attitudes.) These anxieties were not limited to the fate of the cultivators but reflected concern about the future of the country as a whole.

The sudden shift of interest in the land question, beginning with the Arab-Jewish clashes of 1929, the Shaw Commission of Inquiry and the Hope Simpson report of 1930, and the work of Lewis French and his successors at the Development Department with regard to landlessness in 1931, was probably not generated by current events. The quantity of land bought in the early 1920s was larger than that bought in the late 1920s and early 1930s, yet the public outcry and political reactions were much more intense during the latter period. The Zionist movement did engage in a large-scale transaction involving the eviction of tenants in 1929—from the Wadi Hawarith lands—but the consequent political developments mentioned above were unlikely to have resulted from this deal alone. Other factors were operating, primarily the crisis in peasant farming and the growing feelings of political insecurity which were triggered, in part, by the Zionist settlement strategy.

Zionist Settlement Strategies

The discussion so far has not extensively dealt with the most crucial aspect of the question. Land transfers in themselves were not necessarily problematic from an Arab point of view. After all, in many cases land changed hands both among Arabs before and during the mandate, and also between Arabs and Jews, without giving rise to antagonistic political reactions. The issue would have acquired a very different meaning had not land sales to Jews been equated with the automatic eviction of tenants (with or without compensation). The Zionist movement and its settlement agencies had no use for the tenants, however; their retention would have interfered with the strategic goal of consolidating a viable Jewish agricultural base, essential for the success of the nation formation project that was the rationale for the entire settlement enterprise. The effects of this attitude were analyzed by John Hope Simpson in his *Report on Immigration, Land Settlement and Development*. In it he argued that the land bought by the Jewish National Fund (JNF) "has been extra-territorialised. It ceases to be land from which the Arab can gain any advantage either now or at any time in the future. Not only can he never hope to lease or to cultivate it, but, by the stringent provisions of the lease of the Jewish National Fund, he is deprived for ever from employment on that land" (Palestine 1930c: 54).

Hope Simpson's attitude is particularly noteworthy in that he did not regard Jewish settlement in itself as necessarily harmful to Arab peasants. He contrasted the JNF colonies with the older Palestine Jewish Colonization Association (PICA) colonies—the *moshavot* established during the Ottoman period—and claimed that "the policy of the PICA was one of great friendship for the Arab. Not only did they develop the Arab lands simultaneously with their own, when founding their colonies, but they employed the Arab to tend their plantations, cultivate their fields, to pluck their grapes and their oranges. As a general rule the PICA colonisation was of unquestionable benefit to the Arabs of the vicinity" (Palestine 1930c: 50). We can be skeptical of the great friendship supposedly existing between commercial farmers and their agricultural laborers and tenants, but it is hardly doubtful that the principles of exclusion of Arabs from Jewish-owned land, and denial of employment in Jewish-owned enterprises, were detrimental to intercommunal relations.

The twin strategies of conquest of land and conquest of labor had been advocated by the Zionist labor movement since the beginning of the twentieth century as the only way of securing a healthy foundation for a new Jewish nation, society, and state in Palestine/Israel. These policies were gradually implemented as the official guidelines of the various bodies affiliated with the Zionist Organization. Thus the constitution of the Jewish Agency for Palestine, adopted in 1929, declared that "land is to be acquired as Jewish property, and . . . the title to the lands acquired is to be taken in the name of the Jewish National Fund, to the end that the same shall be held as the inalienable property of the Jewish people. The Agency shall promote agricultural colonisation based on Jewish labour, and in all works or undertakings carried out or furthered by the Agency, it shall be deemed to be a matter of principle that Jewish labour shall be employed" (Kaplan 1983: 42–43).

Hope Simpson brings many examples of the application of these principles to agricultural settlement. He quotes from a draft lease issued by the JNF to prospective Jewish renters in which "the lessee undertakes to execute all works connected with the cultivation of the holding only with Jewish labour" on pain of fines and, for repeated offenders, loss of the land without any compensation whatsoever. Similarly, the Palestine Foundation Fund required the Jewish settler in its colonies to undertake "that he will during the continuance of any of the said [monetary] advances, reside upon the said agricultural holding and do all his farm work by himself or with the aid of his family, and that, if and whenever he may be obliged to hire help, he will hire Jewish workmen only" (Palestine 1930c: 53). Often a big gap exists between written obligations and actual implementation, but in this particular case there was a very high degree of compliance with the regulations. Many of the settlers were financially dependent on the Zionist movement and ideologically subject to very strong group pressure, especially in such collectively oriented communities as the moshavim and kibbutzim which were created as experiments in new forms of agricultural settlement.

Experimentation of that kind started in the late Ottoman period, with settlements established by the Palestine Land Development Company and run by workers' cooperatives (Bein 1954: 56–93), and was continued on a much larger scale during the mandatory period. The basic principles of this type of rural settlement were mixed farming—growing cereals and vegetables as well as engaging in animal husbandry—a primary orientation toward subsistence production, with marketing of surplus, and most importantly, self-labor. Self-labor was the only alternative to the massive employment of non-Jewish labor, due to the historical impossibility of creating a viable class of agricultural workers out of eastern European Jews (Ruppin 1925: 10–24). As Ruppin later argued in his testimony to the Palestine Royal Commission in 1936, those Jews had no rural habits and no training in agriculture: "They had, on the other hand, distinctive intellectual needs; they could not live according to the Oriental standards then prevalent in Palestine. They had needs which a man born and educated in Europe could not do without" (Palestine Royal Commission 1937a: 102). In other words, national strategic and cultural considerations, rather than socialist ideals, were behind the support given by the Zionist movement to collective agriculture.

The adoption of a Zionist strategy that focused on the creation of a large number of relatively small cooperative settlements brought about an effective closure of the new settlements to all Arabs, in whatever capacity. Close ties between community members and the high involvement of the collective in private life made it virtually impossible for individuals to breach the rules. In addition, settlers in the moshavim and kibbutzim did not have an independent economic base (unlike the farmers of the *moshavot*). They did not own the land and were frequently dependent on external subsidies for economic survival. As a result, they could not violate the segregationist principles established by the Jewish national institutions even if they wanted too, which in any event they very rarely, if ever, did.

These policies applied only to land held by Jewish national institutions. Privately owned land, such as that of the *moshavot*, was the focus of bitter struggles over this issue. One side to the dispute were the farmers, individually and collectively, who argued against the policy of Jewish-only labor as damaging to profitability and therefore undermining the economic viability of private agriculture. They saw private farming as the most important economic branch of the community and therefore as an activity that was the foundation of the Jewish National Home: "We alone among the entire Jewish people redeemed with our own efforts, with our blood and money, a quarter of a million dunums. We are the first ones in the land of our forefathers who live only on the fruit of our land. We are the pioneers of Jewish agricultural exports to the world market" (from *Bustenai*, the newspaper of the Farmers Federation, August 1929, in Shapira 1977: 105). On the other side of the dispute was the Zionist labor movement, led by the General Federation of Jewish Workers in Eretz Israel (the Histadrut), which advocated Jewish labor as the only way of guaranteeing the long-term viability of the Jewish National Home project and, at the same time, serving the more immediate needs of Jewish workers for employment.

The Campaign for Jewish Labor

The basic assumption of the labor movement, as expressed by David Ben-Gurion in his 1925 article "The Jewish and Arab Worker," was that only workers could lead the Jewish national movement because they were the only class among which existed an organic identity of the national and class vocation. The realization of Zionism could only be accomplished through the insistence on the principle of Jewish labor: "To subvert this crucial principle is to undermine the construction of the entire Jewish community and to utterly destroy any hope for Jewish national salvation in this country. The Jewish worker in his difficult struggle for Jewish Labor . . . does not only perform his class mission but also performs a crucial national mission" (Ben-Gurion 1931: 104).

From this perspective, then, it was imperative that the Zionist project not be governed by profit motive alone since that dictated a search for the least costly source of labor, namely, local and foreign Arab workers. Exclusive or even substantial use of Arabs on Jewish farms, and elsewhere in the Jewish-owned economy, would have undermined the ability of the Zionist movement and the Jewish community to absorb Jewish immigrants arriving without sufficient financial resources. Immigrants stood little chance of competing successfully with the more experienced and cheaper Arab agricultural laborers in a free market, without the introduction of extra-economic criteria for work eligibility. Since continued immigration and satisfactory absorption of newcomers were essential to the success of the Zionist project, the Jewish national institutions shared an interest with the labor movement in the closure of the Jewish-owned economy to Arab labor. On the other hand, higher labor costs and consequent declining returns on capital investments seemed likely outcomes of the political preference for Jewish labor. Profitability concerns could have been ignored only at the risk of undermining business confidence and hurting the economic viability of the National Home enterprise. There was room for flexibility on the issue, however, as Zionist funds came in part from hundreds of thousands of small donors who wanted their money to be used for national reconstruction rather than for generation of profits. The ability of the movement to centralize control over these widely dispersed resources was an important consideration in its strategy.

A possible solution to the dilemma consisted in subsidizing the private sector in agriculture in order to induce it to employ Jewish labor, without an increase in the costs of production. The limited funds of the Zionist movement made it unable to afford such a policy on a massive scale, though some steps in that direction were taken. The problem did not seem urgent in the early 1920s, a period of economic growth and larger demand for labor in the economy as a whole. In addition, the emergence of the small-scale cooperative form of settlement gave Jewish workers an alternative to employment in the *moshavot*. The issue of Jewish labor resurfaced, however, in the late 1920s with the crisis of the urban economy, especially in Tel Aviv, and the appearance of a large number of unemployed Jewish workers, many of whom were recent immigrants. Thousands moved from the cities into the *moshavot* in search of work. As the economy of the large *moshavot* was based on exports, they were unaffected by the urban crisis and thus became an arena of struggle over labor policies.

Isolated conflicts between Jewish workers and farmers started in 1926 and continued at different levels of intensity throughout the late 1930s. Workers formed picket lines at the gates of citrus orchards and other places of work to protest the employment of Arabs by farmers. In 1926 in Haderah and Rehovot, clashes broke out over this issue. During the 1927–28 fruit-picking season, Jewish activists prevented Arab laborers from entering orchards in Petah Tikvah, the oldest and largest of the *moshavot*. The protests turned violent in some cases, and the police were frequently invited to remove the demonstrators (Shapira 1977: 38–42). Not until 1929, though, did the conflict over Jewish labor become a major political concern, as the labor movement struggled for political power in the local Jewish community and in the institutions of the Zionist movement worldwide. It also contributed to political tensions between Jews and Arabs and was one reason for the increasingly violent climate in the country.

Arab Employment in the Jewish-Owned Economy

When we evaluate the issue of intercommunal labor relations in the 1920s, we must take into account the actual extent of the employment of Arabs in the Jewish-owned economy. Numbers varied from time to time, especially in the seasonal orchard-based economy, but data from 1931 mention 5,500 workers in the *moshavot*, about 20 percent of the total number of Arab agricultural laborers. These laborers represented no more than 4.5 percent of the 122,000 Arabs employed in agriculture, most of whom were independent small-scale farmers (Abramowitz and Guelfat 1944: 33). In other words, Arab laborers employed by Jews were a minor element in the Arab population. They *were* significant for the *moshavot*'s economy since their numbers exceeded those of Jewish agricultural laborers, 4,000 of whom were employed during the high season. However, as most Arabs were hired on a temporary basis, during the low season they were outnumbered by tenured Jews who, moreover, performed other nonseasonal jobs such as construction and services (Shapira 1977: 50–52).

In other branches of production Arabs were employed by Jews to a lesser degree. Accurate statistics are difficult to come by, but there seem to have been no more than 2,000 Arab workers in Jewish-owned construction, transportation, and manufacturing companies in the late 1920s and early 1930s. These workers were a substantial part of the total number of Arab industrial workers, but mainly because there were so few to begin with. A few hundred Jewish workers were employed for a while in Arab companies and towns, but most were dispensed with once there were enough skilled Arab workers to take their places (Abramowitz and Guelfat 1944: 59–65; Sussman 1974: 36–41). Compared to the laborers in the *moshavot*, Arabs were not a substantial proportion of the employees in the Jewish-owned urban economy. In addition, the Jewish labor policy in the urban economy had less explosive potential than that of labor in agriculture. It did not carry with it the enormous symbolic importance of the land issue, and there were other sources of employment for the relatively few Arab workers who moved into the cities in search of jobs. Most were employed by government departments—primarily Public Works, international enterprises, and Arab employers.

Rural Conditions

The issues of land sales, tenant dispossession, and employment on Jewish farms, important as they may have been to the development of the national conflict, directly affected only a segment of the Palestinian-Arab people in the 1920s. Rural Arabs, a majority of the population throughout the mandatory period, faced other economic problems with which they were preoccupied and which influenced the way they reacted to political events. Access to land, a big debt burden, increasing internal inequalities, the destabilizing effects of market pressures, and the declining viability of subsistence production all contributed to a sense of insecurity that was compounded by the presence of the alien force of the Zionist settlement project. Internal and external factors thus combined to effect social and political changes in the Palestinian-Arab countryside.

Although market forces had been present in Palestinian agriculture since the late nineteenth century, the bulk of small-scale peasant production was still used for subsistence. The Johnson-Crosbie Commission of 1930 estimated that only 20 percent of total village production was marketed. Wheat, barley, and legumes were mostly consumed by the household, whereas durrah, watermelon, and sesame seed crops found their way in varying degrees to the market (Government of Palestine 1930: 23). The rate of market dependency of the Arab peasant farm around 1930 did not exceed 20 percent, as compared to 47 percent for the Jewish cooperative settlements, 60 percent for the Jewish private small-holding settlements, and almost 100 percent for the fruit-growing (largely citrus) farms (Himadeh 1938: 346). These are national averages and in some regions the rates were much lower (see Graham-Brown 1982 for the example of Jabal Nablus, "a periphery within a periphery"). The comparatively low rate of market dependency (45 percent overall, excluding oranges) could be attributed to several factors, prominent among which were the land tenure system (in particular the *musha'* system and the relations of tenancy), poor marketing and transportation facilities, and the low capital investment in production, which inhibited agricultural intensification.

One of the first actions of the new British administration in 1919 was to abolish the payment of taxes in kind and require cash payments instead. The *'ushr* (tithe) tax continued to be the main source of revenues in the early period of British rule as it had been in the Ottoman period. Its monetary value was assessed by special commissions according to local market prices. Peasants apparently continued to pay in kind for a while, though this form of taxation slowly disappeared toward the end of the 1920s (Himadeh 1938: 509–10; Graham-Brown 1982: 95–96). Tenants continued to pay rent through various combinations of sharecroppings agreements, dividing the produce between the four basic factors of production: land, labor, seed, and ploughing stock, though cash rents were increasingly demanded by landlords. (See Firestone 1982 for examples of different arrangements in the relatively less monetarized region of northern Samaria.)

Probably the most important problem facing Arab peasants, including independent owner-cultivators and tenants, was debt. In 1930 the Johnson-Crosbie Commission estimated that the average family's debt was equal to its annual net income and that about 20 percent of the income went to pay interest on loans. Hope Simpson quotes the director of education as asserting that "the economic state of the agricultural population is desperate. Hardly any Arab village exists which is not in debt. . . . Money is so scarce in some places that the people purchase the necessities of life by barter, and they cannot pay the tithe without further borrowing. This means increasing their already overwhelming debt to the moneylender" (Palestine 1930c: 65). The need for money to provide for times of drought and plague, to buy seeds, implements and livestock, and to pay taxes and rents when required to do so in cash forced many peasants to borrow money at very high interest rates under conditions where regular credit facilities hardly existed. Only well-off peasants with individual title to the land could possibly get credit at reasonable rates, the rest having no choice but to rely on landlords, merchants, and moneylenders. Insolvency could have led to loss of the land that served as collateral (Abramowitz and Guelfat 1944: 37–43: Stein 1984: 19–20).

Against this background, a process of social differentiation took place expressed in an increase in internal inequalities and a growing dissolution of the village community. A gap opened between those peasants who managed to take advantage of the new economic opportunities presented by British policies, and the fast-growing market for agricultural produce created as a result of Jewish immigration, and those whose economically precarious position was further undermined by these same factors. Under conditions of massive influx of capital into the country, the growth of the coastal urban economy, and the transformation of land into a commodity, the British concern for the continued existence of viable peasant communities, as expressed by the Johnson-Crosbie Commission and other official reports, could not be realized. This was especially the case as the government refrained from taking any steps that would have involved a large financial commitment and could have upset customary power relations in the villages (Miller 1985: 79–89). Given the power relations in the Palestinian-Arab countryside, the professed British concern with rural welfare and political stability was self-contradictory: "The chronic indebtedness of the *fellaheen* was clearly the main barrier to the development of production and the stabilising of the peasantry on the land. The mandatory state was not prepared to break the power of the class of landowners and money-lenders whose exactions were the main cause of this indebtedness, any more than it would give priority to curtailing land sales to the Jews" (Graham-Brown 1982: 98).

Though the poor were the majority among peasants, a substantial minority of them were better off. The Johnson-Crosbie Commission gave the following breakdown of village population: 29 percent had no official title to land, though they were not necessarily without access to it (this included tenants, laborers, and other nonagricultural workers); 5 percent had very small plots but without fields; 36 percent were poor peasants with land but in insufficient quantity; 14 percent were middle peasants with sufficient land; and 16 percent were wealthy peasants with a surplus of land (Government of Palestine 1930: 21, table 17). This social heterogeneity affected the responses of different strata to economic challenges, and their reactions were far from uniform. The variety of responses can serve to question the modernization perspective, which views the Zionist project as beneficial to the Palestinian peasants because it introduces modern methods of cultivation and organization (Granott 1952; Assaf 1970), as well as the dependency perspective, which sees in the same process the subordination of the precapitalist Arab sector to the capitalist Jewish sector (Asad 1975).

The upper layers—the wealthy and perhaps also the middle peasants—could benefit from the economic changes triggered by British rule and Zionist settlement. Poor peasants did not possess the basic capital requirements necessary for the intensification of production and the marketing of surplus. On the contrary, many of them actually lost their land as a result of inability to pay back their debts. According to the French Report of 1931, in addition to land sales to Jewish individuals and organizations, there were on-going land transfers among Arabs. In one hilly district (where Jewish presence was nonexistent), 30 percent of the land changed hands in the 1920s alone. This process was described as "the absorption, gradual but inevitable, of the Arab peasant proprietor by the Arab *effendi* or capitalist landlord" (Government of Palestine 1931: 19). Rich peasants and urban speculators could also buy shares in *musha'* land, even though they were not members of the community. High Commissioner John Chancellor described a process whereby "the fellaheen vendors were in many cases in debt to money lenders for money borrowed at usurious rates of interest. When pressed by their creditors they sold their share in village land in order that they might discharge their liabilities, they were usually allowed to remain in occupation on the lands as tenants" (quoted in Stein 1984: 15). In contrast to absentee landlords, wealthy peasants were likely to enter into tenancy agreements in which they maintained some control over the production process, especially when opportunities for marketing surplus increased (Firestone 1982).

Tenants themselves were divided according to their possession of other capital assets in addition to their labor, and some of the better-off among them even hired their own laborers or croppers (Graham-Brown 1982: 121–23). In addition to subsistence crops, small cultivators (whether owners or tenants) with sufficient land and capital produced cash crops that did not require large and risky investments or major changes in the techniques of production, such as vegetables (tomatoes, potatoes), fruit (olives, grapes, figs, almonds), dairy products, poultry, and eggs. Other crops such as oranges and bananas were more capital-intensive and required large sums of money. The overall share of land allocated to cash crops was quite low, estimated at 8–10 percent, though the income from it was much higher than that generated by the extensive cultivation of cereals (Abramowitz and Guelfat 1944: 31–32, 49–53). Only farmers with a surplus of land could afford to experiment with resolutely market-oriented capitalist agriculture, frequently selling excess land to Jews in order to get the necessary funds. This road was not open to the majority of peasants, for whom survival on the land was not guaranteed and who frequently resorted to wage labor in order to supplement their meager family income.

This intensification of agriculture, even on a small scale, clashed with the continued existence of the village community—the *musha'*. The process of dissolving communal ties fitted into the British program of rationalizing and modernizing the peasant farm. The absence of private title to the land prevented peasants from using the land as collateral for low-interest loans. It also was considered an obstacle to the introduction of new and more efficient agricultural techniques because the benefits of the improvements would be lost to the innovator as a result of periodic redistribution of village lands. For most peasants, however, the benefits of the privatization of village lands were theoretical, since they did not have the necessary capital to invest in production anyway. Communal land tenure was supposed to guarantee minimum availability of land to everyone in the village and to prevent it from being transferred to outsiders. The latter effect was realized to a limited extent as far as land sales to Jews were concerned, but not with regard to land transfers among Arabs. Nevertheless, the system did act as a safety net to retard, but not eliminate, market pressures on subsistence-level peasants who were unable to respond to economic opportunities because of lack of capital, and for whom the benefits of stronger market orientation were mostly academic (Graham-Brown 1982: 124–25).

Although the low level of agricultural commodification was bemoaned by the British and Zionists alike, their reasons were different. The British considered commercial agriculture the cornerstone of a prosperous and stable rural life, in Palestine as well as elsewhere. They were opposed to the "extravagant use of land" entailed by the communal system, which excluded the fellah from "the advantages of mechanization and irrigation" and destroyed "the incentive to improve the land" (Government of Palestine 1946: 278). Zionist officials were uninterested in modernization for its own sake or out of a general preference for commercial agriculture; rather, their main concern was the release of "excess" land onto the market. Their opposition to communal landholding was motivated by the obstacles this form of tenure placed in the way of acquiring land for the Jewish National Home. Their solution to indigenous agrarian problems consisted of an intensification of production that was to be financed by the sale of land. The two elements were tightly connected, and Zionist land experts were opposed to providing cheap credit to Arabs, to be used for agricultural improvement and irrigation, if it was not accompanied by a transfer of land into Jewish hands, regardless of the long-term consequences for future generations of rural Arabs.

Maurice Hexter, head of the Colonization Department of the Jewish Agency for Palestine, stated the Zionist view clearly in his testimony to the Royal Commission in 1936: "Every generation works out its own problems without providing for reserves for future generations" (Palestine Royal Commission 1937a: 159). Addressing the issue of long-term credit schemes for Arab peasants, he added: "I hope I have not left the impression we were in favour of such long term loans for such development as to enable the Arab to intensify his cultivation *and leave us out in the cold*" (159; italics added). In other words, although Jews were entitled to worry about the availability of land in the long run (in fact, the entire Zionist strategy was precisely about that), Arabs apparently were not. Differences between Jews and Arabs in this respect, resulting from the greater strategic planning among the former, were summarized by an Arab spokesman as follows: "The Arab obtains immediate relief for a while only to find himself in the course of time without money and without land; while the Jews hold the land in anticipation of the time its use may insure the success of the national home policy" (Abcarius 1946: 136). Of course, this was true only for those Arabs who had no other means of subsistence; many Arabs benefited from selling their land at a high price. Most peasants, however, were unable to invest in advanced technology and production and fared poorly as a result of the commodification of land.

In any event, the process of *ifraz*—the permanent division of community lands into private plots—continued throughout the 1920s and beyond. The percentage of land held as *mushaʿ* fell from 56 percent at the beginning of the decade to 44 percent in 1930. Thus, the pressures of internal processes of social differentiation combined with the transfer of land to Jews to bring about a decline in the rural poor's access to land. The result was an increase in tensions in the countryside and the creation of fertile ground for political turmoil. The danger, from a British point of view, was that rural dislocation would undermine political stability in the country: "A continued increase in the class of landless Arabs was a social peril against which steps should be taken without delay. . . . There was the risk of the landless Arab class producing economic results which would serve as a focus of discontent and might even result in serious disorders" (High Commissioner Wauchope in 1932, in Graham-Brown 1982: 100). And indeed, social discontent and disorder were a prominent feature of politics in the 1930s.

Economic and Political Turmoil

A period of violent clashes opened with the Wailing Wall conflict of 1928–29. The turmoil was further fueled in subsequent years by Palestinian anxieties over the perceived threat to their personal and national birthright by Zionist settlement. A number of commissions of inquiry, formed in the wake of the 1929 violent Arab-Jewish clashes, did not focus on social and economic issues but directed attention to the land question in general and to the plight of peasants in particular. The main area of confrontation in 1929 was not related to land sales, nor were the new Jewish agricultural settlements specifically targeted. In fact, the worst incidents took place in the strongholds of the old Jewish community, Hebron and Jerusalem, whose residents did not take part in the Zionist project but nevertheless suffered the major burden of Arab attacks, and with scores of Jews killed, raped, and forced to flee their homes. It was clear, however, that Jewish immigration, settlement, and political and institutional buildup played a major role in the overall increase in political violence. As the Haycraft Commission argued with regard to the 1921 riots, "during the riots all discrimination on the part of the Arabs between different categories of Jews was obliterated [and] . . . they became merged in a single identity" (Palestine 1921: 50).

Some of the major recommendations of officials following the 1929 events dealt with the issues mentioned above. High Commissioner Chancellor claimed early in 1930 that "no cultivable land now in possession of the indigenous population could be sold to Jews without creating a class of landless Arab cultivators." Rather, "legislative measures [should] be taken in order to insure that the indigenous agricultural population shall not be dispossessed of its land" (quoted in Stein 1984: 84). These concerns were shared by the Shaw Commission, which was established to study the causes of the 1929 turmoil and whose report advocated imposing restrictions on land transfers from Arabs to Jews. The official British position was expressed in the Passfield White Paper of 1930, which was based on Chancellor's proposals and the Shaw and Hope Simpson reports. It attempted to balance the exercise of Jewish rights to immigration and land acquisition—guaranteed by the mandate—with the imperatives to help Arab cultivators keep their land and to resettle landless Arabs on state lands. No effective steps were taken to implement these goals, though (Palestine 1930d; Stein 1984: 88–120; John and Hadawi 1970: 217–35).

The links between the crisis of the peasant family farm, land sales to Jews, and social dislocation in the countryside became more pronounced as many small owner-cultivators were increasingly pushed to sell their land and look elsewhere for employment as a result of their inability to manage their growing debt burden. Young males frequently moved to the cities to supplement the family income (as revenue from the land was insufficient) or to become main providers if the family did not own any land. The scale of this change can be seen in the following figures showing the share of land bought by Jewish organizations from small cultivators: from less than 2.5 percent in the period 1920–27, it jumped to 18.3 percent in 1928–32, and to 22.5 percent in 1933–36. In absolute terms, the quantity of land sold by fellahin since the late 1920s was twice of that sold since the beginning of the century (Granott 1952: 277). If we add to these figures land transferred between Arabs, whether for its own sake or as a step toward ultimate transfer to Jewish ownership, the figures would undoubtedly be much higher.

This change was of great political significance. Land deals in much of the 1920s, and before that, usually involved sales by absentee landlords (largely foreign speculators) and were frequently followed by the eviction of relatively marginal tenants and agricultural laborers, with or without compensation. In the late 1920s and the 1930s, this state of affairs began to change by increasingly involving sales by the actual cultivators, the small peasants, who were the numerical as well as the symbolic core of Palestinian-Arab society. Peasants who sold land could not be seriously accused of acting out of pure greed or lack of patriotism, charges frequently directed by nationalist activists against landowners who bought and sold land for investment purposes. This change prompted calls for abolishing the right to sell land, since "a member of any community should not be allowed to dispose of his property in a manner which may prejudice the rights and position of the community as a whole" (Mogannam 1937: 210).

The economic predicament of peasants—each a member of a village community—was indicative of an overall crisis of subsistence felt throughout the country. What seems to have been their central concern was not so much their ability to survive physically or feed themselves—they sought and usually found jobs with (mostly Arab) employers in the rural areas and the cities—but the threat that their way of life, their *moral economy*, would collapse. For peasants, land was the substance of life, the source and guarantee of their long-term security, and not merely an economic asset. Potential higher incomes in wage labor could not compensate for the lack of sense of stable, although poor, existence. As the Palestinian activist Emil Ghori put it, "prosperity and economic improvement are not everything of worth in life. . . . [The Arabs] prefer to be destitute and poor, but independent and free, in their country, than prosperous and rich in a country which will in a few years time be theirs no more" (letter to the *Observer*, 10/4/1936, in Abboushi 1985: 82–83), a point repeatedly made by other activists. Of course neither Ghori himself nor most other speakers for the Arab cause were peasants, and it was easy for them to make such statements as their own destitution and poverty were not at stake. For the majority of peasants, however, the dilemma between prosperity and independence was not concrete, and the eventual loss of land, economic security, and national independence were all part of the same process that culminated with the War of 1947–48.

Compared to the Southeast Asian colonial cases discussed by James Scott (1976), who popularized the moral economy concept, the crisis of the Palestinian peasantry had more far-reaching implications. The national community as a whole was beginning to perceive itself as facing an existential threat. Individuals and organizations expressed a growing premonition that the continuation of peasant land sales, rather than merely losing economic resources vital to Arab peasants, put the viability of Palestinian-Arab national life in danger. As the activist Izzat Darwaza argued, when the Arabs object to the sale of land, "they do not object to it because it deprives the fellah of his only means of livelihood, but they object to it because land is one of the matters that deeply affects the existence of a nation. . . . The uprooting of a people from a life in which they had their roots might cause serious moral injury to them and to the community" (Palestine Royal Commission 1937a: 315). More dramatically, Hajj Amin al-Husayni expressed the same sentiments in apocalyptic terms, addressing fellow Arabs and Muslims in other countries: "If you remain indifferently watching this catastrophe, a catastrophe matching the loss of Andalusia [Spain], you will not be pleasing God, His Prophet and the Historical Traditions of Islam which has created all Muslim brethren" (speech to a national religious conference in Jerusalem, 1/25/1935, in Jbara 1985: 135).

The 1930s saw the intensification of Palestinian-Arab national mobilization aimed at putting an end to land sales to Jews. The political leadership seems to have realized by the beginning of the decade that the key to this problem was more than ever in the hands of the Arabs themselves. In the framework of this more active approach, the Arab press campaigned against land transfers, activists went to villages to explain the threats facing the national community, and tenants were given legal support in resisting eviction. Modeling themselves on such Zionist organizations as the Jewish National Fund, the Palestinians formed committees such as Sunduq al-Umma (the National Trust) and the Arab Committee for the Defense of the Land, which encouraged Arab owners not to sell land to Jews. The Supreme Muslim Council, headed by Amin al-Husayni, played an important role in these campaigns by organizing conferences, issuing religious edicts (*fatwas*), excommunicating people involved in land transactions, preaching, attempting to register land as (untransferable) *waqf* property, buying shares in *musha'* land and thereby blocking its sale, and appealing to the government to prohibit land purchase by Jews (Porath 1977: 122–27; Jbara 1985: 125–36; Kupferschmidt 1987: 240–47).

These efforts were not very successful. The plight of the peasants could not have been alleviated by appeals to patriotism not materially backed up by anything other than the meager resources of the national movement. Peasants squeezed off the land frequently moved elsewhere in search for work. There developed a specific pattern of urbanization which did not usually consist of a complete transition from the countryside to the cities. Most rural migrants continued to maintain some form of contact with their villages of origin through ties of kinship and solidarity. Many moved to the urban areas on a short-term basis, saving money or sending it to their relatives who were left behind. In the words of a trade union activist, Haifa became an "America," a place to which people moved to make money and then returned home (Waschitz 1987: 116). State policies encouraged this process of temporary movement into labor without permanent urbanization. The Public Works Department, a major employer of labor for construction of roads, railways, and harbors, recruited workers through village-based networks. The preservation of rural ties was seen by British officials as a way of avoiding full-scale proletarianization with its consequent social and political destabilizing effects (Taqqu 1980: 266–72).

These migrant peasant-laborers frequently remained attached to their community through working with fellow migrants, sharing living quarters, organizing on the basis of village affiliation, and helping each other in need. The difficulties of finding cheap housing and the resulting growth of shantytowns increased the distance between the migrating peasant-laborers and the settled urban population, thus providing a basis for solidarity among the former (Yazbek 1987; Swedenburg 1988). They found employment in public works, construction, industry (both Jewish- and Arab-owned), quarrying, and unskilled trades and services. It is difficult to arrive at any precise figures because of the undercounting of casual and seasonal labor, but an estimate of 15,000 to 20,000 (without the self-employed) seems plausible for the first half of the 1930s (Taqqu 1980: 264; Abramowitz and Guelfat 1944: 61–63).

This process of temporary urbanization had already started in the early 1920s, when it was pushed forward by labor surplus on the family-labor farm. It became a significant social phenomenon when the agricultural crisis of the early 1930s coincided with economic prosperity and a growing demand for labor in the cities, fueled by the massive wave of German-Jewish immigration. After a reversal during the Revolt of 1936–39, the urban economic boom continued in the first half of 1940s to meet the demands of the British war effort. The urban Arab population, especially in the coastal centers of Haifa and Jaffa, had thus expanded to include a new element of a pronounced rural character (Arnon-Ohana 1981: 149–53).

The radical political and military activities of the movement associated with Sheikh ʿIzz al-Din al-Qassam were an instance of the developments that accompanied the changes in rural and urban social relations. Al-Qassam, a Muslim preacher and activist, was deeply involved as a teacher and organizer of rural migrants in the 1920s and early 1930s. He managed to extend his influence from his initial base in Haifa throughout the northern region of the country with his appointment as a marriage registrar for the Haifa Shariʿa court in 1929. His message, a mixture of religious and nationalist elements, called for a regeneration of Islamic purity as a basis for an anti-British and anti-Zionist revolutionary struggle to save the Arab homeland from foreign control (Schleifer 1979; Lachman 1982).

His disciples were mostly of peasant origins, a few of whom were still living in villages while the majority had already moved to the city and found temporary and sometimes more regular jobs. Most sources on the organization Ikhwan al-Qassam (the Qassam Brothers), emphasize the novelty of the movement's reliance on peasants and urban migrants in the context of a national movement, which had been based until then on elite politics. His appeal was greatest among the unskilled migrant working masses in Haifa who were drawn to the expanding economy in such sectors as construction, railways, port, and oil refineries (Schleifer 1979). In that sense, the Qassam movement is a significant element in what Lesch (1979) defines as the transition from the era of mobilization from above (1917–28) to the era of mobilization from below (1929–39). The experiences of rural dislocation and uprootedness were clearly linked to the growth of radical sentiments, and more specifically to "the fact that as fellahin, they [the activists] were well aware of the threat of spreading Jewish colonisation" (Lachman 1982: 77). Their organization thus offered a mutually reinforcing combination of nationalist and materially-rooted motives (Kanafani n.d; Swedenburg 1988; see also Porath 1977: 132–39; Kayyali 1979: 180–83).

These developments should be set against the background of the transformation in the capacities of the Jewish community at that time. Following the Nazi rise to power in Germany, a huge wave of Jewish immigration into the country resulted in massive growth of the Jewish population (which almost doubled in size) and in considerable strengthening of the economic and political viability of the community. These developments contributed to a new sense of political urgency among Palestinian Arabs. Capital transfers into the country increased enormously. They were used, among other things, for the purchase of land and for investment in construction and industrial production. The threat which the development of the Jewish National Home posed to the prospects of Palestinian independence was strongly felt among the Arab political leadership and masses alike. When Awni Abdulhadi declared to the Royal Commission in 1937 that "we have reached a stage where it is extremely detrimental to the national existence of the Arabs to accept an additional immigrant from any country whatever" (Palestine Royal Commission 1937a: 312), he was most probably reflecting a sentiment widely felt among all segments of the Arab population since the early 1930s.

Jewish and Arab Labor in the 1930s

The sense of impending doom was compounded by the fact that Palestinian Arabs were excluded, to a large extent, from the economic opportunities that opened in that period. The principle of Jewish labor was reasserted and implemented, at least in the urban areas. The influx of a large number of European Jews increased the size of the work force available for sustaining infrastructural and industrial growth in the Jewish-owned economy. The match between (Jewish) capital and labor imports left little room for the employment and economic incorporation of Palestinian-Arab laborers. The economic boom was based on industry and services which required different skills than those essential for agricultural work. The main assets of unskilled Arab workers in the competition for jobs in commercial agriculture—their work experience and low cost compared to those of Jewish workers—did not prove as lucrative to potential Jewish employers in the urban sector; the latter required different kinds of skill and were more dependent on the internal Jewish market than were their agricultural counterparts.

The dimensions of Arab employment in Jewish-owned enterprises varied throughout the 1930s. In the *moshavot*, the struggle for and against Jewish labor policies continued after the 1929 countrywide armed clashes, during which many Arab workers temporarily abandoned their jobs. In 1930–31, a period of economic recession, several *moshavot* experienced violent intra-Jewish protests, including demonstrations and pickets that resulted in physical damage and many arrests of unemployed Jewish workers. The protestors were demanding a reduction in the number of Arabs employed in citrus orchards, if not their complete replacement by Jews (Shapira 1977: 89–96). Data for the rest of the 1930s show a mixed picture. Initially, the proportion of Jewish workers was high. In August 1933, the low season, there were 4,246 Jewish workers as compared with only 2,000 Arabs (4,519 during the February 1934 high season). The number of the latter rose rapidly, however, with the extension of the cultivated area, and reached a peak of 8,000–10,000 by 1935 (Shapira 1977: 154–57). These numbers declined with the Arab general strike of 1936, back to about 4,000 in February 1937. The continuation of the Arab revolt led to a drastic decline in Arab workers to the point of zero in March 1939. With the end of the revolt and the economic prosperity of the early 1940s, the employment of Arab workers was resumed, though they were fewer in number (272–77).

In evaluating these figures we must keep two things in mind. First, even during the peak period, Arab workers employed on Jewish farms were no more than a small part of the total number of Arabs for whom agriculture was a major occupation. In other words, the vast majority of Arab agricultural employees were either self-employed or employed by other Arabs. Second, the weight of citrus production in the Jewish-owned economy significantly declined after the 1920s. The economic boom which followed the immigration wave of the early 1930s primarily affected the cities. Even as the number of Arab workers in the *moshavot* rose toward 1935, their overall impact on the Jewish-owned economy was reduced due to the reduction in the weight of the rural sector. The economic center of gravity of the Jewish community permanently moved from the orchard-based agricultural settlements—its mainstay since the turn of the century—into the fast-growing industrializing cities of Tel Aviv and Haifa.

The role of Arab workers in the Jewish-owned urban sector was generally less important than their role in the agricultural sector. Data from 1936 give the number of Arabs employed by Jews as 12,000, 14.6 percent of the total number of employees in the Jewish sector (there were 70,000 Jewish employees). Arabs formed 35 percent of the employees in agriculture (7,000 people); their proportion in transportation and harbors was 25 percent (1,000), in construction 12.4 percent (1,700), in industry 8.7 percent (1,900), and in commerce 6.7 percent (400). Their proportion among unskilled workers was much higher though (Sussman 1974: 40). The 5,000 Arabs employed by Jews in the urban economy were a small segment of the urban Arab employees, about 18,000 of whom were employed by various government departments (Sussman 1974: 41) and an undetermined number (perhaps as many as 30,000) in Arab-owned industrial enterprises, home manufacturing, and services, including owners and their family members (see several somewhat contradictory estimates in Gozansky 1986: 203–7). All of these coexisted with a large number of unemployed people. The crucial point here is that in the urban economy, just as in the agricultural sector, most Arab workers (up to 90 percent of them) were *not* employed by Jews. Although labor relations between Jews and Arabs did develop, and were important for some branches in the

Jewish-owned economy, they were not generalized throughout the economy and did not become the main form of Palestinian social structure in the 1930s, as they did become in South Africa in the same period.

One obvious reason for the meager presence of Arab labor in the Jewish-owned urban economy was the demand of the Labor Zionist movement that Jewish enterprises not employ Arab workers. It is not easy to evaluate the effects of this policy since, in contrast to the extensive documentation of the struggle for Jewish labor in the *moshavot*, there is little material concerning the way in which the issue was dealt with in the urban sector. (Incidents in which Jewish workers picketed mixed work sites in Haifa and Jerusalem in 1934 are reported in Shapira 1977: 161–62, 229–33.) While these campaigns were not as extensive as those waged in the *moshavot*, and did not involve as many people, they did have a strong impact on public opinion since "every single case of removal of Arab workers—and in many cases the operation took the form of ugly scenes of violence—was reported in the Jewish press and reverberated in the Arab media creating an atmosphere of unprecedented tension" (Flapan 1979: 206). Arab workers organized protests against their exclusion from Jewish-owned work sites in Jaffa in 1935 (Barbour 1969: 161–63), and Arab labor activists voiced their complaints about their constituency being driven out of work by Jewish laborers "for racial and economic reasons" (see the testimony of George Mansour, secretary of the Arab Labor Federation, in Palestine Royal Commission 1937a: 340–43). It seems, however, that the symbolic importance of these campaigns outweighed their actual material effects, which were restricted to a small number of people.

The Jewish Labor Debate

Many writers attribute Jewish labor policies to the socialist nature of the leaders of the Zionist movement. Flapan, for example, claims that "as class-conscious socialists and as Zionists, the Third Aliyah [1919–23] immigrants believed it was their duty to eliminate the exploitation of cheap unorganized Arab labour by Jewish settlers" because "the exploitation of cheap Arab labour was incompatible with their vision of a socialist society. They thought that by forcing Arab workers to seek employment in the Arab sector, they would stimulate the class conflict in Arab society and prevent the Jewish-Arab national conflict from attaining as well a class dimension" (Flapan 1979: 201). This may be a reasonable account of the way activists felt about the issue, and the way they justified their positions to themselves and others. It leaves unexplained, however, how an authentic socialist vision could be reconciled with the blatantly antisocialist practices of segregation and exclusion of workers who do not belong to the right national group.

A different explanation is offered by Shalev (1989), along lines similar to those offered by Shafir (1989), whose work was discussed in chapter 3. Working from the perspective of a split labor market, Shalev argues against granting major importance to ideology. He analyzes Jewish labor policies as serving the class interests of organized and expensive Jewish workers who enjoyed the support of the Zionist movement in preventing competition from unorganized and cheap Arab laborers. The basis for the alliance of Jewish workers and the Zionist movement was their mutual interest in blocking Arabs from entering the labor market and preventing them from squeezing out overpriced Jewish workers. The erection of barriers to Arab employment was a way of simultaneously guaranteeing jobs for Jewish workers and serving the Zionist goals of enhancing Jewish settlement and achieving economic self-sufficiency.

This explanation is problematic. It posits the existence of an expensive stratum of Jewish workers as the starting point of the analysis without asking how these workers came into that position in the first place. Most of them, in fact, were immigrants who had recently moved to Palestine/Israel as a result of their allegiance to Zionism. Jewish emigration from eastern Europe had an economic rationale, of course, but one that directed people to western Europe and the Americas, not specifically to Palestine (the destination of a small minority of the Jewish emigrants). Focusing on the nationalist motivation for immigration to Palestine is essential if we are to understand why unorganized and cheap Jewish workers were considered by the organized Jewish labor movement as potential allies who could and should be incorporated, whereas Arab workers facing similar market conditions were excluded. The starting point of the analysis should be the prior structuring of the labor market on the basis of national affiliation rather than on the basis of the hypothesized class interests of abstract capitalists and "expensive" and "cheap" workers, as if these workers had no national identity. To talk about a collusion of interests between Jewish workers and the Zionist movement, as Shalev does, is to forget that these same workers assumed specific class positions in the country precisely *because* of Zionism. They were not an external element to the national project but part and parcel of it. Thus, no explanation can proceed without considering the nationalist discourse that made sense of the class position of workers and provided the context within which they formed and fought for their interests (but see Bernstein 1992 for a version of split labor market analysis that avoids the reduction of national conflict to class imperatives).

Another explanation, attempting to deal jointly with Zionist ideology and class processes, argues that the imperatives of Jewish nation building took precedence over, and shaped the processes of, Jewish class formation: "The working-class agents [Zionists labor parties and unions] were the predominant powers in nationalistic politics. They opted for an integration of class formation and nation-building formation and explicitly preferred the nation building. The alternative option, which meant giving priority to the process of class formation, as class for itself, was considered inexpedient by the working-class agents, who had much to lose regarding their position in the Yishuv" (Ben-Porat 1986: 212). In the 1930s in particular, "politics and, to a certain extent, ideology were predominant in the social formation of the Yishuv. . . . The allocation of economic resources, and, in part, the reallocation of surplus value, were determined by politics" (213).

This analysis avoids the economism of the split labor market approach in that it explicitly introduces notions of politics and ideology and their articulation with class interests. It conceptualizes politics too restrictively, however, confining it to intra-Jewish institutional and party developments. Ben-Porat discusses modes of production and their ideological, economic, and political instances only as they pertain to the organized Jewish community. He hardly deals with the Jewish-Arab struggle over the future of the country. The exclusion of this central political concern from the analytical framework is unwarranted, though, especially since most of the internal debates, conflicts, and alliances among Jewish political forces specifically revolved around issues that had a lot to do with Jewish-Arab relations.

In contrast to the approaches outlined above, the position adopted here maintains that the labor and land policies pursued by Jewish and Arab forces should be analyzed in the context of a national conflict over territorial expansion and political control. Processes of immigration, industrialization, and urbanization did not lead in themselves to an increase in political tensions and hostilities. If they did have this result, it was because they unfolded within the framework of exclusionary discourses (articulated by Arabs and Jews alike), shaped by a variety of material and institutional factors. The interests of Jewish workers in finding decently paid employment played a role in the outcome, of course, as did the material interests of Arab workers in getting and retaining jobs, of Arab peasants in keeping their land, and of Jewish and Arab capitalists in lowering the costs of labor, gaining access to markets, and making profits from real estate. These material dimensions affected the ability of political leadership to formulate and gain support for their policies. This was done, however, within parameters set by a conflict focused on the fundamental political issue of the national identity of the country. Without analyzing this issue in further detail here (it is discussed in chapters 4 and 6), it should be mentioned that the rise of nationalism to a dominant position within the European and the Middle Eastern political arenas since the late nineteenth century made a crucial contribution to these developments.

The Arab Revolt

The social and economic pressures discussed above reached their political climax with the Great Arab Revolt of 1936–39—the most significant expression of sustained and organized Arab opposition to British rule and the Zionist settlement project during the entire period. While no immediate land and labor issues were involved in the outbreak of the general strike and the consequent armed rebellion, social dislocation in the countryside was an important background factor that affected the responses and differential participation of Arab forces in the ensuing political struggles.

As early as 1933, a rise in political agitation was felt in the cities in protest against the rapid increase in (German) Jewish immigration. Palestinian-Arab political parties were formed, with similar programs calling for a national representative government and independence (Mogannam 1937: 237–42). These demands increasingly acquired an anti-British dimension as the government seemed unable or unwilling to take any effective steps against the continuation of Zionist settlement. On November 25, 1935, the leaders of the main Arab political parties presented the government with a set of demands, including prohibition on transfer of Arab-owned land into Jewish hands, protection of small cultivators, and a halt to Jewish immigration (John and Hadawi 1970: 253–54). These demands were motivated more by a concern about the consequences of land sales for the viability of the national community as a whole than by a specific preoccupation with the fate of the peasantry. The massive influx of Jewish immigrants, with their capital resources and technological capacity, into the country was seen as a dangerous development that had to be confronted before the economic, institutional, and military power of the Jewish community grew so strong as to become unstoppable in its attempt to take possession of the country.

Beginning with clashes in Jaffa in late April 1936, the country was soon engulfed in turmoil that led to the declaration of a general strike and the formation of a Palestinian-Arab national leadership, the Arab Higher Committee (AHC). The leadership of the strike, which meanwhile had spontaneously spread nationwide, was officially taken over by the AHC, which decided to continue with it until the demands of putting an end to Jewish immigration and land purchases were met (Porath 1977: 162–66). As was the case with earlier manifestations of urban-based nationalist activities, the demands were articulated by the leadership as national and general in nature rather than as social and specific (Arab Higher Committee 1937). Even the issue of land sales, the only issue with clear social implications, was phrased in nationalist terms as "the immediate and complete prohibition of the sale of Arab land to the Jews" (13), rather than in terms referring to the plight of the peasantry. And yet the events of 1936–39 *were* distinct from previous political protests, as they eventually turned out to be, in that the rural population played a direct role in the struggle.

The responses of the urban masses to the call to strike were mixed. Nationalist appeals clashed with the workers' fears of losing their jobs. The Jewish labor policy was used by the nationalist leadership as a major rallying cry in its attempts to mobilize workers' support. The Haifa-centered Palestinian Arab Workers Association emphasized that the policy of the Jewish National Home inflicted unemployment and starvation on Arabs who had been expelled from their places of work in the Jewish-owned economy as a result of Jewish labor policies and the competition offered by the growing number of Jewish immigrants (Porath 1977: 167). It was precisely this factor, however, that made the success of the strike more problematic. The availability of Jewish workers ready to take over employment from striking Arabs played an inhibiting role, to some extent deterring the Arabs from rushing into the front lines of struggle. Indeed, whenever Arabs left their places of work in agriculture, transportation, industry, and construction, Jews moved in to fill their place, sometimes on a permanent basis. A general strike involving only a segment (although a majority) of the population could not have achieved its goals "when a highly organized and largely self-contained one third of the population could act as a buffer in the crisis and even derive benefit from it" (Waines 1971: 232).

The revolt began spreading to the countryside a short time after declaration of the strike. Already in May 1936, urban political activists toured villages and conducted meetings to mobilize support for the national struggle. A meeting of the rural national committee in Nablus argued for a refusal to pay taxes, denounced the building of police stations in villages, and called for establishment of rural national committees throughout the country (Kayyali 1979: 192). Around the same time, peasants started organizing for armed action, sabotaging roads and Jewish agricultural production. Their participation was facilitated by the decline of the urban job market to which they usually turned at that time of the year. Initially these activities were conducted in areas close to Jewish population centers, primarily along the coastal region, because the presence of the British government and Jewish settlement was felt more strongly there (Arnon-Ohana 1981: 275–78). Also, proximity to cities encouraged the formation of mixed rural-urban armed bands, but as the conflict's center of gravity moved away from the cities after 1937, the urban leaders' control over the direction of the revolt rapidly declined and it acquired a predominantly rural character.

With the termination of the general strike in October 1936 and the conclusion of the work of the Palestine Royal Commission in 1937, the center of the revolt decisively moved into the rural areas. The urban Arab population could not sustain the political-military campaign because it directly confronted the Jewish economic sector, which was larger, better organized, better financed, and enjoyed, in addition, the active support of the government in its struggle for self-sufficiency. Despite short-term economic dislocation, the strategic alliance between the organized Jewish community and the British government, both of which were threatened by the revolt, proved beneficial for the long-term development of the infrastructure of the Jewish community. Far from bringing it to its knees, the strike allowed the Jewish leadership to move forward with plans for national autonomy based on economic and military self-sufficiency, whose imperative was articulated by Ben-Gurion: "To liberate ourselves from economic dependency is not just a question of physical security, but a fundamental question of our existence and revival. Economic independence means a Jewish port, government institutions in Jewish population centers, Jewish agricultural produce and raw materials" (quoted in Amikam 1976: 370).

The conditions in the countryside were more conducive to the revolt. Physical isolation, subsistence production, and the small size and relative intimacy of village communities provided logistical resources, unavailable in the cities, for sustained resistance. These factors combined with peasants' profound social grievances resulting from the pressures of indebtedness, and with increasing internal inequalities and land sales, to lead the rebels to target government forces, Jewish communities, and the Arab landholding urban elite. All of these were seen as jointly responsible for undermining the ability of peasants to survive independently on their land.

No clearly articulated ideology emerged to unify the different strands in peasant resistance. Although it had a clear social basis, it was not organized as a class movement as such. A number of writers emphasize the multifaceted character of the revolt. It is referred to as "a racial, religious, colonial, familial and peasant struggle intermingled" (Bowden 1975: 147) and as "a congealing of nationalism, religious revivalism and class consciousness, no element of which can be neatly disentangled from the others" (Swedenburg 1988: 196). A stronger focus on the class content of the revolt is offered by Kanafani (n.d), who argues for recognition of the revolutionary role of the peasants who organized to fight for their class and national interests, only to be betrayed by the reactionary feudal and bourgeois leadership. What is particularly interesting in this respect, however, is that the specifically class components in the armed and political activities of the rebels were expressed primarily, if not exclusively, against other Arabs and only indirectly if at all against Jews. The opposition to Jewish settlement was not expressed in any social-class terms, but in the form of a nationalist rejection of foreign elements who conspired to take over the country from its rightful Arab owners. This can be primarily attributed to the fact, mentioned earlier in the chapter, that exploitative labor relations between Jewish farmers and Arab tenants affected only a small minority of the rural Arab population, especially in the hilly core of the country where Jewish settlement was minimal. Arab anti-Zionist discourse was articulated and acted upon in overall nationalist and religious terms, then, with few distinctions between different social forces.

At the height of the revolt, 1937–38, the rebels managed to gain effective control of much of the hilly countryside and, for periods of times, cities such as Nablus and Jenin, as well as Jaffa, briefly. In military terms the revolt reached its highest point in summer 1938, when the general officer commanding the British troops reported that "the situation was such that civil administration and control of the country was, to all practical purposes, non-existent" (Gen. Robert Haining, 8/30/1938, in Lesch 1979: 223). The main constituency of the revolt, as sympathizers, activists, and leaders, were of peasant origins. The vast majority were Muslim, and an important role was played by activists who were adherents of the religious and nationalist teaching of al-Qassam (Lachman 1982: 78–86). The rebels formed their own courts and collected financial contributions from villagers, landlords, and urban businessmen, frequently using force and intimidation in the process. They generally attempted to form an alternative unified command to replace the authority of the state as well as that of the urban leadership. The latter, represented by the AHC, was banned by the British in 1937, and some of its leaders were forced into exile, most prominently Amin al-Husayni. As part of a specific social program, the rebels proclaimed an indefinite moratorium on debts and on the payment of rents to moneylenders and property owners. They ordered urban people to adopt the typically peasant headdress for tactical purposes—to avoid detection by government forces, but also to assert symbolically the domination of the countryside over the cities (Porath 1977: 260–69; Kayyali 1979: 209–16; Arnon-Ohana 1981: 279–88).

Despite temporary victories, the government's intensive military campaign, in collaboration with Zionist organizations, eventually repressed the revolt. A major factor in the ability of these forces to achieve military victory by 1939 was the exhaustion of the peasants. They were subjected to fierce repressive measures by the British forces (Barbour 1969: 179–93; Abboushi 1977: 35–37) and found it increasingly difficult to support the rebels, who became abusive themselves, coercing the population into providing financial and logistical assistance. Those who refused to aid the rebels, or those who were suspected of collaborating with the government, were physically harassed and frequently executed. (See Miller 1985: 128–36 for the problems facing government officials in the rural areas.)

The deterioration of the revolt into a cycle of internal violence and the consequent dilemmas facing the peasants are captured in a petition by a villager submitted to the high commissioner: "We the Fellahin are falling between the devil and the deep blue sea; on one hand the rebels come to our villages, take our money, food, and sometimes kill some of us, on the other hand, the Police come to our villages following these rebels with their dogs. . . . The rebels take money from the rich people only, but the Police take it from the poor as well. The rebels are more merciful than the Police" (petition from the village of Wadi Sarar received on 7/5/1938, in Miller 1985: 127). Regional, religious, familial, and class factionalism grew as the rebels were pushed back by government forces and the revolt turned in on itself. (See Abboushi 1985: 92–102 for the social divisions that contributed to the failure of the revolt, especially the rural-urban and the elite-masses divisions.)

The spontaneous and local character of rebel activity was their greatest source of strength but also their ultimate undoing. Their parochialism did not allow much coordinated action and produced an "unsystematic, unstable insurgency prone to anarchic lapses" (Bowden 1975: 169). The prominence of local considerations and the factional legacy of Palestinian politics nationwide (discussed more fully in chapter 6) resulted in the death of many hundreds of Arabs in a spate of violence that left its marks on national politics for years to come. The weaknesses of the revolt should not make us forget, though, that even with the best organization, it is highly doubtful that the Palestinian movement could have won militarily against the formidable combined strength of British and Zionist forces (Swedenburg 1988).

The World War and Its Aftermath

The decline of the revolt and its final demise in 1939 coincided with the start of the Second World War in Europe. The closing of the Mediterranean to Allied shipping in 1940 forced the Palestinian economy to reduce its reliance on external markets as sources of imported goods and as outlets for exports. The citrus export–based economy contracted as a result, forcing hundreds if not thousands of agricultural laborers and port workers out of their jobs. Soon after, however, the redirection of production toward meeting local needs, and the presence of large British military concentrations participating in the North African campaign, brought about a massive rise of industrial capacity, rapid expansion of the labor force, and an overall growth of the local economy, fueled above all by British wartime consumption (Abramowitz and Guelfat 1944; Owen 1988).

The increase in the recruitment of laborers from the Palestinian countryside and from neighboring countries reversed the trend toward the de-proletarianization of migrant workers that was evident during the revolt and the general economic depression of the late 1930s. Beginning in 1941, government and industrial demand for large numbers of unskilled and semiskilled workers reached unprecedented levels. In 1942 the Labor Department assessed the number as about a hundred thousand, including peasants in temporary and seasonal employment (Taqqu 1980: 266–67). Wage labor, especially of the temporary kind, did not necessarily involve moving to a city. About half of the jobs offered by the War Department and most of the jobs in Public Works were outside the urban areas and frequently involved commuting rather than permanent urbanization. In times of economic depression, a retreat back to agriculture was still possible. The majority of those positions called for unskilled and casual labor, usually for specific local projects. It allowed peasants to supplement their income from agriculture but was not a substitute for it. The low wages would have made it very difficult for most rural workers to survive without maintaining any base in the village; during the war, however, their situation improved since they could combine income from selling agricultural produce in the market and from wage labor (Graham-Brown 1982).

The rise in the size of the Arab labor force, more specifically in the urban and industrial sectors, brought Arab and Jewish workers into more direct contact with each other. Ownership of the enterprises in which large numbers of people of different communities were jointly employed was largely in the hands of the government, the military, and international companies. The extent of Arab employment in the Jewish-owned sector itself continued to be small. Various estimates agree that the bulk of Arabs were employed by other Arabs or by the public sector. Likewise, most workers employed by the Jewish sector were Jews. Arab-owned manufacturing and services grew together with the rest of the wartime economy and absorbed the supply of large numbers of Arab unskilled laborers. (See Gozansky 1986: 206–10 for occupational breakdown of workers and P. Smith 1984: 55–57 for the growth of the Arab bourgeoisie.) Economic growth and proletarianization thus did not lead to the establishment of overall communally based hierarchical economic relations. In contrast to South Africa, no pattern of indigenous "servants" working for settler "masters" emerged. The relations of mastery and servitude that did develop were largely intracommunal, giving rise to economic conflicts among segments of the same national community. Conflicts between Jews and Arabs retained a national-political focus that was not directly concerned with class issues.

The most important feature of the communal patterns of economic relations in Palestine/Israel was the role played by indigenous structures and capacities, clearly seen when compared to South Africa's situation (and many other colonial-type settlement projects). Arabs had independent access to technology and capital outside the control of settlers. Their social differentiation was "advanced" enough to allow the accumulation of resources and the development of capitalist agriculture and industry through their own channels. This was facilitated by the fact that the British colonial state was not settler-dominated. The demand for indigenous workers came mostly from nonsettler (indigenous and international) sources. Furthermore, when peasants were squeezed off the land and went through processes of proletarianization and urbanization, they did not invariably enter into settler service as indigenous people did in South Africa.

It would be instructive at this point to examine some of the economic statistics compiled toward the end of the mandatory period. Arabs controlled over 90 percent of the land and produced most of the grain, vegetable, and fruit crops (Government of Palestine 1946: 323, 327). Their share in commercial agriculture—citrus, bananas, and other plantations—equaled or exceeded that of Jews (566, 725), though they lagged far behind Jews with regard to industrial production (567). Overall, ownership of capital was roughly equal, £132.6 million owned by Arabs and £125.7 million by Jews (569), though on a per capita basis the Arab share was half the Jewish share (and the highly inegalitarian social stratification made poor Arabs much poorer and rich Arabs much richer than their Jewish counterparts). Jews possessed almost six times more industrial capital than did Arabs, but the share of industry in overall capital assets was low, just below 10 percent for Jews and 1.6 percent for Arabs. These data indicate that while Jews were more wealthy, technologically advanced, and capitalist-oriented as a group, Arabs were by no means reduced to a state of economic subordination or dependency.

A far-reaching attempt by economist Atef Kubrusi to quantify the value of Arab property lost as a result of the 1948 war, only a segment of the total value of Arab property at the time, puts it as £743 million, or $92 billion in 1984 U.S. dollars (Hadawi 1988: 115–89). The data may be subject to criticism as grossly inflated. For example, the *Survey of Palestine* (Government of Palestine 1946) lists total Arab industrial capital as £2.1 million for 1945, whereas Kubrusi asserts that the volume of industrial capital *lost* in 1948 amounted to £11.4 million. The overall magnitude and value of Arab assets cannot be disputed, however, and the role of indigenous forces in the development of exclusionary patterns of economic relations needs to be fully acknowledged.

The End of the Mandate

In addition to the social factors mentioned earlier, the intense political conflict between the national communities made the Arab labor force seem undependable, because of the history of boycotts and counterboycotts that plagued Jewish-Arab economic relations during the mandatory period, reaching a climax with the revolt of the late 1930s and continuing through the 1940s (Assaf 1970: 233–37; Flapan 1979: 219–23). Relations of trade involving mostly (Arab) agricultural and (Jewish) industrial products continued to exist, but the wider economic, ideological, and political circumstances pushed the two communities into ever increasing separation from one another.

An exception to the situation of economic separatism was the wartime employment of Jews and Arabs in military installations and other public sector occupations (Gozansky 1986: 216–24). Despite the few strikes and other joint campaigns, however, no permanent binational organizations emerged. There were some prior attempts by Jewish unions to organize Arab workers in the 1920s and the 1930s, though on a basis separate from Jewish workers. The Histadrut trade union federation was perhaps the most important Zionist organization of the period, but it was not acting as a class institution. It consisted of a network of unions, settlement movements, businesses, production and marketing cooperatives, and cultural and youth organizations, all linked as elements in a federated structure. Defined as the General Federation of the Jewish Workers in Eretz Israel, it was just that: a set of organizations operating within the framework of the general national effort but attempting to represent the interests of a specific segment of the national community. Its aim was to lead the Zionist political project in a process termed by Ben-Gurion "from class to nation," and it had never subordinated national goals to class interests. Arab unions were similarly organized on a national basis and were affiliated with various Palestinian political parties. Even the Palestine Communist Party (PCP) could not sustain a unified organization. The strain of the national conflict had caused estrangement between its Jewish and Arab members since the late 1920s, culminating in a formal split in the early 1940s and the formation of a leftist Arab party, the National Liberation League (Budeiri 1979: 153–84, 212–42).

With the conclusion of the period, a large degree of separatism between the national communities had been established in the economic sphere. The UN Committee on Palestine referred to this situation as a "complex phenomenon of two distinct economies—one Jewish and one Arab, closely involved with one another and yet in essential features separate." Economic separateness did not correspond to any clear territorial division, however (United Nations 1947: 19). The committee noted that virtually no Jews were employed in Arab undertakings and few Arabs were employed by Jews. Despite unified administration, trade, transport, and currency policies, "the economic relations between the two groups have something of the character of trade between different nations" (20). Hierarchical labor relations did not develop between Jews and Arabs as in South Africa. Jewish land acquisitions and capital imports were used to develop an autonomous economy based on exclusionary principles; no significant incorporation of Arabs occurred. Arabs similarly concentrated on investing their resources in their own sector. The result was a growing separatism, reflected in the partition resolution adopted by the United Nations on November 29, 1947.

South Africa

It is argued that in South Africa, in the aftermath of the mineral discoveries of the late nineteenth century, the processes of capitalist development in agriculture and industry, and the consequent transformations of class structures, should be seen against a background of preexisting patterns of landholding, labor recruitment, and productive relations. New economic opportunities and challenges were met in a historical context that imposed economic and political constraints on the options of social actors. I combine an emphasis on the social and political changes brought about by the rise of industrial capitalism, with a focus on continuities in racial attitudes and systems of political domination. Both elements are crucial to the discussion of the formation of socioeconomic structures, collective identities, and political institutions.

South African developments differed in several crucial respects from the developments in Palestine/Israel. The capacity of indigenous people in South Africa to retain independent access to land and to develop their own industrial and urban infrastructure was limited in comparison to that of indigenous Arabs. As a result, Africans who were squeezed off their land and looking for jobs had to move into employment in the white-controlled industrializing economy. This fitted with the strategies adopted by white capitalists, who primarily relied on Africans for their labor needs. The relations of white mastery and African servitude were sustained by the various colonial and settler states that played an active role in restricting indigenous people's access to land and in pushing rural people to move from independent agricultural production into the rural and urban labor markets.

The period covered in this section, stretching from the 1870s to the 1940s, was decisive in the formation of modern South Africa. During that time the white-dominated colonies and republics merged politically in 1910 to form the Union of South Africa, forcibly incorporating in the process the remaining African territories, some of which had maintained their independence until the end of the nineteenth century. In the economic realm, the same period saw major transformations in the forces and conditions of production, with the introduction of large-scale industrial operations that were both capital and labor intensive.

The Mineral Revolution

A period of accelerated economic growth followed the discovery and commercial exploitation of diamonds and gold at Kimberley and on the Witwatersrand respectively. These precious minerals, which were sold on the world market, raised state revenues and allowed for enormous increases in the imports of capital, technology, and skilled and unskilled labor from overseas and from all over the southern African region. Secondary industry serving the mines and producing consumer goods rapidly developed. Expanding internal markets resulted in a growth in commercial agriculture that found ready consumers for its output. These changes took place in the context of an established racial system, a major feature of which was the existence of large numbers of black servants (by no means all or even the majority of blacks) who were coerced into providing labor services to meet the demands of white masters (who comprised a large part of, but not the entire, white population). The logic behind the racial system of forced labor was articulated in 1876 by John Ayliff, acting secretary for native affairs in the Cape Colony, who argued that experience has shown "that they will not labour from free choice, and that there is no necessity sufficiently pressing to induce them to labour continuously, [so] it is surely no injustice to expect that in return for the many benefits we confer, they should supply that moderate amount of labour which will prevent positive perpetual idleness" (quoted in Godlo 1933: 101).

Land and labor relations between and within racially identified groups; the control and destination of agricultural production, manufacture, and the transportation and communication networks; and the relations of South Africa to the world system—all were deeply affected by the social and economic upheavals resulting from the rise of the mining industry to a prominent place in the southern African economy. These processes gave rise to new social groups and classes that became locked into a pattern of conflict that has characterized, with numerous adaptations, South African society ever since. How these developments were set in motion, beginning with the discovery of diamonds in 1867, is the main topic of the rest of this chapter.

The Diamond Mining Industry

The Kimberley diamond industry started as a highly decentralized business, with small claims divided between thousands of black and white diggers. Regulations formulated by diggers and other proprietors limited the size of holdings to tiny parcels. The technology used was rudimentary, little capital was invested, and marketing was done on a personal basis—from digger to dealer. The initial boom of the early 1870s ran into difficulties, however, with exhaustion of the easily accessible surface diamond deposits. The consequences were a rise in the cost of labor, fragmentation of claims, and technical and organizational problems that increased as the continuation of profitable mining required a move into deep-level digging. The local state, Griqualand West, which effectively came under British rule, in 1876 abolished size limitations on claims and opened the way to large-scale capitalization and industrialization of the mines; it thus moved into "that wide region where the laws of trade are all powerful; laws of capital and labour and of supply and demand [to which] its future development must be committed" (editorial in the *Diamond News*, 11/23/1876, in Worger 1987: 37).

In the following decade small claims were combined into ever larger units held in ever fewer hands. The establishment of joint stock companies accelerated the process of amalgamation, which eventually led to the domination of the field by two powerful companies, Kimberley Central and De Beers Mining (Worger 1987: 44–63). By 1888 the two joined to form De Beers Consolidated Mines, and a virtual monopoly on diamond production was established three years afterward (Turrel 1987: 211–25). The centralization of production was accompanied by a more organized system of labor regulation and control that primarily affected African workers who migrated to the mines from all over the region; the same system also affected white workers but to a much lesser extent. In this respect, Kimberley became the first town to experience the open and massive conflicts over the social position of African as compared to white labor, which became a prominent feature of the South African political economy for much of the twentieth century.

The role of African laborers in the process of diamond production was crucial from the beginning of mining operations. They outnumbered whites at all times, even though in most cases, unlike whites and especially Afrikaners, they did not bring their families along with them. It was in Kimberley that the major institutions controlling black lives, their movements, residence, occupation—the entire complex known as the Pass Laws—first emerged in their modern form and were tested; later they were extended throughout the economy. Not all Africans in Kimberley were manual laborers, however, though most manual workers were African. Initially, some of them, largely those coming from the Cape Colony, were claim holders. The majority were migrants who stayed for periods of three to six months before returning to their homes. In the early 1870s, 50,000 to 80,000 Africans came and left every year, though not more than 15,000 of them were employed at any given time due to the high rate of turnover (Turrel 1987: 19–25). They worked long hours in units of fifteen laborers on the average; they picked, shoveled, hauled, and sorted earth, earning wages that were higher than those paid to Africans in any other place in southern Africa. Their numbers declined in later years due to mechanization of production and reorganization of the labor force.

The Migrant Labor System

Data for the years 1873–76 show that the main sources of migrant labor in the Kimberley mines came from the eastern Transvaal and southern Mozambique, followed by migrants from Basutoland. The largest numbers came, then, from far away and not, as might be expected, from neighboring territories (with the exception of Basutoland). Consequently they tended to stay longer at work on the average (Worger 1987: 71–75). The numerical dominance of these three sources continued through 1885, though with some variation between the four major mines (Turrel 1987: 92–94).

The common wisdom in South African studies used to be that the migrant labor system was a strategy devised by mining capitalists to lower the price of labor. With this system, the wages of migrants could be kept low because they were meant to support only the migrants themselves, not their families, who were left behind at home in the native reserves and satisfied their own needs through subsistence agricultural production. The articulation of modes of production resulted, then, in the precapitalist sector subsidizing the capitalist sector. These exploitative relations were imposed by coercion, conquest, and political domination as well as by such related economic mechanisms as the imposition of hut taxes, payable in cash. (See the classical theoretical statement by Wolpe 1972 and a restatement of the thesis within a comparative perspective in Burawoy 1976.)

More recent historical scholarship indicates, however, that in the early years at least, much of the migration was voluntary and did not originate in societies under the control of the mine authorities. In fact in 1880, only 4 percent of the mine work force were the Griqua, Kora, and Tlhaping residents of the colony itself. Direct coercion, then, could not possibly have played an important role in the migration of Africans to the mines. To understand the reasons for the massive influx of workers, many of whom faced long and risky journeys to get there, we venture beyond the needs of the mining economy for cheap labor (since demand by itself does not explain its own fulfilment) and consider precolonial gender and age divisions and the political strategies pursued by indigenous states.

Africans in the eastern Transvaal, for example, regarded labor migration, long before the opening of diamond mines in Kimberley, as a kind of initiation ceremony, a stage through which youth were supposed to go in order to acquire guns and ammunition (Delius 1983: 62–66). The relatively high wages paid in the mines were advantageous because they enabled migrants to achieve the goal of purchasing arms in a shorter period of time. Guns were used for hunting and consequent trade in game and were essential for defense and expansion of territory. In addition, young male migrants used their income to purchase cattle, thereby expediting their marriages, which were dependent on payment of *lobola* or bride-price. Thus they helped reproduce the relations of authority that gave elder male homestead heads control over access to cattle, women, and land. The indigenous leadership, paramount and chiefs, sought to structure labor in a way that would give them a claim over a portion of migrant incomes. They even attempted to reach agreements to that effect with mine authorities (72–79).

Similar factors operated among the people of southern Mozambique in the late nineteenth century. Harries (1982) focuses on kinship as an alternative explanation to the articulation of modes of production thesis in accounting for the origins of labor migrancy. Younger men were dependent on their elders for access to cattle and through it to women and to their own economic and political autonomy. Migrant labor provided these young men with an opportunity to acquire independent economic resources and thus to escape the control of elders and chiefs. The latter responded with raising the bride-price and imposing taxes on returning migrants. Both sides to this age-power conflict attempted, then, to use migrancy to consolidate their own positions; they did this at the expense of women, whose share in the burden of agricultural production increased to compensate for the absence of young men. As Bozzoli (1983a) suggests, the ability of chiefs (and men in general) to subordinate women's labor in this way was the foundation of the initial emergence of migrancy in southern Africa. (See Walker 1990 for a survey of the role of gender in the development of the migrant labor system.)

The struggles over internal production, rate of exploitation, and surplus appropriation were complicated by the fact that the migrants themselves benefited from the system. When they were away their families were protected by elders, and elders helped them increase their own negotiating position and decrease the external rate of exploitation by mine owners. Overall, relations of authority became less stable as younger men challenged the power of elders, prompting the latter—the "uncles"—in 1895 to seek Portuguese help "in order to get back the power that they had formerly exercised and put aside their nephews" (a contemporary observer, in Harries 1982: 154; see also Kimble 1982, who focuses on internal factors and in particular on the need of the Sotho state to accumulate arms in order to withstand colonial encroachments).

This account of the factors internal to African societies in the emergence and spread of migrant labor does not imply that the mining industry had nothing to do with development of the system. Neither does it imply that the system remained unchanged from its earliest days to the present. With the passage of time, and as mine authorities together with the colonial and settler states became better organized, the benefits to indigenous social forces declined relative to the benefits derived by capitalists from the system. It is important to realize, however, that the system emerged in a historical process that involved multiple struggles between and within indigenous and colonial forces. It was not simply an outcome of the ability of capitalists to impose their grand design in order to secure for themselves the best possible arrangement, minimizing their costs and maximizing their profits.

Discipline and Control

As diamond mining went through a process of amalgamation, labor recruitment and control became more organized and created important precedents for disciplinary and surveillance institutions in South African society. In the beginning, white small-claim holders could not control the movements and therefore the costs of black laborers, leading the *Diamond News* to complain in 1872 that African workers were "the most expensive in the world" as well as "the most unmanageable" (Worger 1987: 112). While this seems a gross exaggeration, two factors made it particularly difficult for employers to impose their will on workers. First, workers maintained their access to the means of production in the countryside, and therefore had an alternative to selling their labor power in the mine. In addition, there was no strong state, or a centralized employers' organization, that could have intervened on the side of mine authorities. The Kimberley region was in a transitional stage, moving toward but not yet fully incorporated into the Cape Colony, and it took some time before secure political control was established.

Repressive regulation was constantly attempted by the authorities. In that sense, South African labor relations were crucially different from those prevailing in Palestine/Israel during the mandatory period; in the latter case the state did not actively intervene to help settlers establish and sustain control over indigenous people. In 1872 a Pass Law was decreed, obligating "servants" (a color-blind term referring, in effect, to Africans) to register for work, carry passes, and show them on demand. This act curtailed neither the free movement of workers nor their insubordination because its enforcement was ineffective. In the late 1870s a stronger commitment by the state to maintain order led to the establishment of compulsory residential locations for Africans and to intensive pass raids, arrests, trials, and convictions. These steps, however, did not result in lowering wages or preventing employees from leaving en masse when conditions did not suit them (Worger 1987: 111–31).

This state of affairs changed around 1880 with the annexation of Griqualand West to the Cape Colony and the centralization of the mining industry. The mechanization of production and the transition to deep underground mining made the transition to a smaller but more reliable labor force seem more profitable. The alliance between capital and the state enabled both for the first time after more than fifteen years of mining, to enforce tight regimentation of the labor force by new means of surveillance, most importantly the recently invented (1885) segregated, closed compound. As a result, for African workers "there was little discernible difference between the workplace, the compound, the location, and the jail in Kimberley; all were part and parcel of the same system of labor control" (Worger 1987: 146).

These disciplinary devices were not used to control white workers, who, in contrast, were given much higher wages and co-opted into the machinery of supervision in collaboration with management (Turrel 1987: 149–55). A system of industrial racial segregation thus came into being. Its essence was the coexistence of different strata of white and black workers in the same work places. Whites jealously guarded their respectability and privileges by distancing themselves from and using color bars against Africans, who formed the bulk of the labor force. This segregated system was anchored in a discourse that regarded indigenous people, irrespective of their individual circumstances, as inherently subversive of authority. The "rule of law" was invoked to neutralize the danger of subversion (Worger 1987).

The mining industry set in motion a process of socioeconomic transformation that affected many rural communities throughout the region. Those who lived closest to the mines experienced mixed benefits. Southern Tswana, for example, saw a rapid depletion of such natural resources as game and wood as a result of the growing needs of the Kimberley population for meat and fuel. In the 1870s short-term material gains, an outcome of production for the urban markets, were thus translated into long-term loss of vital community resources. This was followed by increased pressure on the land as a result of settler expansion (Shillington 1985: 62–70, 99–106). While many African farmers initially benefited from the growing demand for grain, vegetables, and stock, they later faced difficulties; these increasing opportunities opened up just as the means necessary for realizing them—indigenous people's access to land—was taken away, first by "legal" white settlement, then by political annexation and in many cases by military defeat (Kallaway 1981).

The very geographical proximity to colonial markets, which at first promoted a certain material prosperity among indigenous people, also facilitated the economic and political subordination of those same people, who faced the impact of colonial expansion immediately and directly. The strategic and economic importance of diamond mining to the British Empire and the Cape Colony led the colonial state to intervene to ensure the profitability and stability of the enterprise. (According to the figures in Turrel 1987: 10, the total exports and imports of the colony more than tripled between 1869 and 1888.) Indigenous people residing in the vicinity of the mines were squeezed off their land if they stood in the way of settlers and mining capitalists. In other, more geographically peripheral areas of southern Africa not exposed to colonial power so directly, such as the Transkei, pressures on indigenous people's land were not so strong in that period. They could thus take advantage of the opportunities opened by the growth of internal markets, without immediately suffering the consequences in terms of land dispossession (Bundy 1979).

The Gold Mining Industry

In retrospect, the effects of diamond mining were but a prelude to the more significant economic, social, and political transformations that accompanied the development of the gold mining industry on the Witwatersrand. These processes, in many respects a larger-scale version of developments at Kimberley, were set in motion with the 1886 discovery of gold at a site in the South African Republic (Transvaal) that was to become the city of Johannesburg. The Kimberley system of labor control had already reached its more organized and repressive phase by the time gold mining made its appearance. This historical coincidence influenced the patterns of class relations developed on the Rand, though these were not a mere imitation of the earlier experiment. (See Bozzoli 1981: 30–33 for the role of Kimberley as a model.)

The most important characteristic of the Rand gold deposits was that they were rich in quantity, stretching along forty miles of almost unbroken reef, but at the same time they were poor in quality. To facilitate their profitable exploitation in the South African circumstances, it was deemed necessary to invest in sophisticated machinery and employ large numbers of workers who would extract the gold ore, which was thinly and deeply spread. Individual prospecting could not have gone beyond scratching the surface. Constraints of a geological, technological (reliance on costly imported machinery), and financial (the determination of the price of gold by external factors) nature thus pushed capitalist entrepreneurs to lower expenses in areas over which they could exercise some degree of control, such as the price of labor power and other productive commodities (Richardson and Van-Helten 1982). The latter, primarily fuel and explosives, were difficult to control and so, argues Johnstone, the central imperative for guaranteeing the "profitability of the mining companies of critical importance to the very existence of the gold mining industry was the ultra-minimisation of labour costs" (Johnstone 1976: 20).

As a result of these conditions, struggles over the recruitment, control, and cost of labor power became crucial aspects of the expanding economy. It is no exaggeration to say, as many have done, that modern South Africa, and indeed even its very existence as a unified political entity, would have taken a very different shape without the prior development of the gold mining industry. Having said that, we must take account of the fact that the growth of the mining industry took place in a specific historical and institutional context that placed limits on the ability of the industry to act on the imperatives of cost minimization and affected the role it has played in shaping the South African economy, race relations, and social and political conflicts.

The gold mining industry became the largest employer in southern Africa within a few years of its emergence. It grew continuously, overtaking Kimberley by far. By 1897, 80,000 people were employed there on a daily basis, 70,000 of them Africans. The number rose to 122,000 by 1907 (105,000 Africans) and more than 200,000 by 1912, more than ten times the number of workers at Kimberley (Richardson and Van-Helten 1982: 82–83). For a period of time at the beginning of the twentieth century, indentured Chinese laborers numbering in the tens of thousands were employed. Labor was seen as the crucial scarce factor of production that could have enabled an "enormous industrial development . . . if only workmen can be found"; the Chinese, or "Asiatics" in general, were seen, in the absence of a sufficient number of white and black workers, as "a temporary expedient, but for the time being essential" (Lord Milner in a letter, 4/1/1903, in Houghton and Dagut 1972: 2.81–82). Only a few remained after 1907, however, when political pressures led to a prohibition on their importation and to their complete repatriation by 1910 (Richardson and Van-Helten 1982: 88–90; Van Onselen 1982: 1.25–26). In terms of volume and value of production, the Rand overtook Kimberley as early as 1893 (Houghton and Dagut 1972: 1.272–75). Its share in the world gold output grew from 0.16 percent in 1886 to 27 percent by 1898, to 40 percent by 1913, attracting vast amounts of capital imports to finance the increase in productive capacity. The sum invested by 1914 was £125 million, almost three times the total of all Canadian and Australian mining operations combined (Kubicek 1990: 68–74).

Recruitment and Control of Labor

Whereas during the early period in Kimberley the workers largely migrated voluntarily and stayed there for short periods of time, on the Rand more elaborate, though initially fragmented and inefficient, networks for the procurement of labor developed almost from the beginning. The mining companies found it impossible to rely on unplanned migration because their scale of operation was large, and they required a stable and dependable pool of workers. There was no guarantee that their needs would be met without an active campaign of promotion and organization of the process of recruitment. Also, mining companies attempted to control labor and centralize recruitment to reduce competition and thus lower the cost of the operation. Their goal, in collaboration with the Native Affairs Department, was to find a replacement for the initial system of touting—recruitment through bidding by different mine agents—a system they regarded as unsatisfactory, "evil," and "obnoxious" because it facilitated "desertion" by workers who took advantage of the competition between different employers (see the 1903 report by the Transvaal commissioner for native affairs, in Houghton and Dagut 1972: 2.77–78). The reorganization of recruitment was a long process, and only by 1920 had the mining houses managed with the help of the state to coordinate their activities and to operate more effectively (Jeeves 1985: 3–21). The state intervened on the side of capitalist and settler forces to facilitate control over and exploitation of indigenous people. The contrast in this respect with the role of the British state in Palestine/Israel is obvious.

Many indigenous Africans in need of cash preferred to concentrate on agricultural production for the growing urban markets and on finding employment in the fast-growing industrial and service sectors in Johannesburg and other cities. They chose to avoid the mines, if possible, which had acquired a reputation for harsh, repressive, and unrewarding conditions. Consequently, the industry attempted to secure access to labor from all over the southern African region to supplement the frequently unavailable local Africans. Data for the years 1903–20 show that the single largest group of workers were from southern Mozambique. Their percentage declined from a high of 67.3 percent at the beginning of the period to an average of around 40 percent by the end, but remaining at a steady level of 75,000 to 80,000 people on the average. About 5–10 percent came from other territories, the British protectorates and "the tropicals" of Malawi, Zimbabwe, and northern Mozambique. The rest of the workers came from South Africa itself, with the percentages rising from 25–30 percent to about 45–50 percent toward 1920. The total number of workers in 1920 was around 100,000 persons, most of whom came from the Cape Province (Jeeves 1985: 265–69).

It seems that in the early period the majority of local South African migrants came voluntarily, without having been brought there by the Witwatersrand Native Labour Association (WNLA) networks. An exception were the migrants from Pondoland, who preferred to sign contracts to receive advance payment in cattle. In 1908, 80 percent of them were recruited in this way. Other migrants from different regions in the eastern Cape were also recruited in this manner: 13 percent from East Griqualand, 25 percent from Thembuland, and 43 percent from Gcalekland and Fingoland (Beinart 1982: 56).

The recruitment of migrant workers was just one aspect of a series of practices aimed at stabilizing the supply of workers, lowering their cost to the industry, and disciplining them through tight regimentation of their living and working conditions. Thus the alliance between the Chamber of Mines and the state acted to restrict the mobility of workers, enforce their compliance, and prevent acts of resistance. Penal sanctions for an employee's breach of contract were mandated by Masters and Servants laws. Pass regulations such as Law 22 and 23 of 1895 subjected workers to registration and curfews and regulated their movements in order to prevent desertion (Hindson 1987: 22–25). The compound system made the surveillance of illicit and subversive activities, and the isolation of miners from urban Africans easier though far from complete. Together, "the combination of the these various systems of coercive labour control—the contract system, the pass system and the compound system served to secure and maintain the extreme exploitability of African mine workers" (Johnstone 1976: 39).

Class, Race, and Migrant Labor: Theoretical Considerations

Johnstone's work is an influential landmark in the development of the radical school in South African historiography. His insistence on the crucial role of capitalist imperatives in determining the nature and function of racial institutions—in particular the mining industry's exploitation color bars—has shaped the theoretical debates in the field. With different emphases, two other studies share this place—Wolpe (1972) and Legassick (1974). Their argument is that the process of capitalist accumulation, which is structured by exploitative class relations, is the essential element in understanding racial policies and practices. This approach, itself a reaction to the scholarly focus on beliefs and attitudes which had previously dominated the field, suffers from several problems dealt with in the next section.

There is little doubt that the benefits derived by the mining industry from the creation of an internally disorganized and coercible pool of workers governed by contractual obligations were important for the emergence and shape of the racial order. However, capitalist interests did not operate in a purely economic environment; they were affected by other forces, primarily those of state and race. State and class interests were not necessarily antagonistic, but no set of interests can be reduced to the other. State institutions have their own concerns, and although their ability to pursue their agendas is constrained by dependence on revenues generated by material production, they can constrain, in turn, the conditions and possibilities of realization of profits. Such constraints were imposed by the mandatory racial division of labor, known as the color bar, which dated back to the mid-1880s and was codified and sanctioned by the Mines and Works Act of 1911 (see the Gold Law and the Mines and Works Act, in Houghton and Dagut 1972: 2.11–16, 116–18).

The Mines and Works Act limited the options of mine management in organizing the labor process in that it allocated job certificates and supervisory positions on the basis of race rather than competency and efficiency. Initially, white immigrants were indeed the only ones with the necessary mining skills; many Africans were quick to acquire such skills, however, but were prevented from exercising them due to the color bar. Many whites, on the other hand, reached their positions without possessing the necessary skills, leading the Mining Department of the Transvaal to complain about the "plentiful supply of all classes of whites for the mines, with the exception of first class miners, who are scarce." The department further attributed the large number of industrial accidents to these miners' lack of training and their drinking habits (Annual Report of the Government Mining Engineer for 1907, in Houghton and Dagut 1972: 2.106). The racial order that resulted in the reservation of skilled jobs for members of one group (only some of whom were skilled) and the exclusion of members of other groups (not all of whom were unskilled) from these same jobs can hardly be seen as acting in the interests of the mining industry.

In order to arrive at a more satisfactory understanding of the racial order and the particular shape of the migrant labor system, we must take into account concerns other than those of capitalist interests. Labor relations cannot be separated from considerations of power and control over urban space. An influx of a large number of Africans into the cities, most particularly Johannesburg, threatened the social and political stability of white-dominated society and state. An organized and tightly regulated system of labor control, including a segregation of migrants whose permanent residence would be elsewhere, was seen by white officials as a way of lowering the perceived risks, fueled by racist fantasies, of having the unruly and materially deprived masses roam the streets. Such an influx into urban areas did not actually take place until the 1920s, when it became a major concern for state officials (Ashforth 1990: 82–90). Long before that, however, some people warned of the dangers of indigenous urbanization and called for a policy that would "prevent our simply turning him [the African] loose in the country and allowing him to find his own level, for whatever veneer of civilization he may have acquired will rapidly under these circumstances disappear, and unless he is controlled, he will rapidly relapse into barbarism, in which condition he will be a source of endless trouble and difficulty to his white neighbours" (J. H. Pim in 1904, in Dubow 1989: 24).

From this perspective, then, the insistence of the state on the temporary nature of the African urban presence, as provided by the system of migrancy, served political and racial, rather than merely economic, imperatives of containing the "dangerous classes"—the unemployed and the criminals—separating them from the white laboring classes, and maintaining law and order. Labor policies were formulated in terms of a racial logic that defined the "natives" as potential subversives, objects for state regulation, rather than elements as potentially assimilable and co-optable as their fellow urbanizing white workers. Keeping dangerous elements under control was an important concern for local and state authorities alike, especially in the aftermath of the Anglo-Boer War (See Van Onselen 1982 for different aspects of the issues of vice and morality in early Johannesburg.)

The problems posed by the social effects of proletarianization, urbanization, and unemployment were not unique to South Africa. What *was* unique is the particular racial logic that operated in these circumstances. The prospect of a permanent migration of African workers into the cities challenged not social stability as such but the racial character of the state, particularly in the Transvaal. In the South African Republic, the rise of the mining industry and the consequent urban population boom undermined the foundations of the preexisting political relations between African peasants and tenants and their white landlords. Seen against this background, the system of labor migrancy established the essentially foreign nature of African workers and thus deflected, to some extent at least, their political incompatibility with the racially based state. There was an inherent contradiction between the economic incorporation of Africans, essential to white prosperity, and their political exclusion. The principle of migrancy was developed under these circumstances in order to legitimize the maintenance of racial political structures. This exclusionary political rationale, which went together with an incorporationist economic rationale, continued to operate after the takeover of the territory by British forces and the Union of 1910 which consolidated white power. The more recent strategies of Grand apartheid and the homelands, which were implemented after 1948, essentially manifest a similar logic. In this sense, analytically, one cannot detach migrancy and labor relations from the relations of political power and racial identity in which they were deeply implicated.

Relations in the Countryside

Discussion of the labor policies adopted in the wake of the spectacular growth of the mining industry should not lead us to forget that the vast majority of indigenous South Africans continued to reside in the rural areas and were engaged in agriculture and stock raising. Though most of them remained physically remote from the centers of economic transformation, their lives were deeply affected by the expansion of industrial production, the growth of cities and urban markets, and the increasing demands by commercial farmers and urban capitalists for a steady supply of workers to meet their labor needs. The relations of land and labor in the countryside, and the social and political conflicts between indigenous people, settlers, and the state should be analyzed in the context of these profound changes. In recent years, a large body of scholarship has debated the timing, process, and interpretation of the rise of agrarian capitalism in South Africa. What is not in dispute is that the overall trend, seen in retrospect, was toward squeezing Africans off the land and into working as tenants and laborers on white-owned farms and industries. Africans were thus increasingly incorporated into the expanding South African economy on terms largely favorable to white employers. This process was not linear, however; its results were not inevitable, and its protagonists (indigenous peasants) had shown considerable resiliency in confronting attempts to dispossess them, as is shown in the following sections.

The rise of mining at Kimberley and on the Witwatersrand created a huge increase in demand for food products (grain, vegetables, and meat), stock, and services. Tens of thousands of European and African migrants flocked to the newly established cities in search of jobs and prosperity, and their subsistence needs had to be satisfied by local agricultural production. Though commercial farming had existed before then, supplying the older cities of Cape Town, Port Elizabeth, and Durban and directed to the world market, its scale increased many times with the process of industrialization. Not surprisingly, African farmers wasted little time in responding to the new opportunities. In the 1870s and 1880s, for example, the independent people of Basutoland expanded their cultivation of cereals, wool, and other produce to be exported to the mines and the neighboring white communities, successfully competing with the Free State white farmers in the process. African farmers continued to enjoy access to markets with the 1886 gold rush on the Rand; into the twentieth century they worked their own land or that of white-owned farms (Keegan 1986a: 9–19).

The people of Basutoland initially enjoyed the geopolitical advantage of being close enough to both major industrializing centers to benefit from the rise in demand for agricultural produce, but not so close as to fall under direct colonial domination as southern Tswana did (for the latter see Shillington 1985). Their political autonomy, in the form of a British protectorate, and their military power relative to their white neighbors allowed them to maintain access to land and to resist demands that they enter service on white-owned farms. In that, they were strategically aligned with white traders who marketed their produce, and with white absentee landowners and companies with whom they entered sharecropping agreements. They also cultivated land owned by white farmers to whom they paid rent in kind, cash, or the labor services of young family members (a practice that became known as squatting). Whether working on their own land or not, in most cases they effectively controlled the means of production and the production process. The African family-labor farm proved, when given a chance, a suitable competitor in the field of commercial agricultural production, latter-day notions of its traditional and stagnant nature notwithstanding. As Keegan puts it, "by the end of the nineteenth century it had by no means been established that white capitalism rather than black peasant production was eventually to dominate the countryside" (Keegan 1986a: 18).

In several other regions of the country, such as the eastern Cape, African peasants responded to market demands in similar ways, though not under the same political circumstances. Their ability to farm and produce surplus created new opportunities and at the same time new pressures by white interests. The growing prospects of commercial agriculture, supplying the mining economy as well as other growing urban and regional markets, made the question of indigenous access to land a hotly debated issue among white farmers who regarded African cultivators as competitors and, at the same time, as potential laborers. Industrial capitalists expressed similar dissatisfaction with the continued ability of Africans to fend for themselves and thus avoid having to work for wages. As the Cape Labour Commission of 1893–94 concluded: "The mere necessities of life are few, and are obtainable with little effort. These people do not therefore feel impelled to work. . . . A cause of the insufficiency [of labor] may also be found in the fact that some natives are in some sense land or rather lease-holders . . . on shares as it is called. . . . The natives are also in another sense landholders, where they cultivate their own fields in the parts of the country called Native Locations or Reserves" (quoted in Bundy 1979: 114).

All of the different arrangements described in the previous paragraph—independent farming, tenancy, and sharecropping—had in common a continued indigenous link to the means of production. In response to this situation, white farmers and state officials in different South African territories devised a series of laws and regulations aimed at detaching cultivators from their land (see the survey of legislation affecting Africans, in South African Native Affairs Commission 1905: A1–A72). Once again, the role of the South African settler and colonial states differed from that of the British colonial state in Palestine/Israel; the latter did not assist settlers in dispossessing indigenous people of their land, though it did not do much to prevent it either.

From the 1870s onward, several legislative acts proclaimed various measures with the purpose of forcing Africans to provide labor services for white employers. In the Orange Free State, for example, as early as 1872 the republican Volksraad imposed a hut tax on African tenants whose numbers were in excess of five families for a farm. In 1881 that limit was made mandatory by Ordinance 7. In 1889 a mounted police force was formed to enforce Pass and antisquatting laws. In 1892 stricter Pass Laws were enacted, and in 1895 Act 4 reinforced the limit on the number of tenant families on farms in order to distribute African labor among settlers. Africans themselves, as well as the large-landowning whites and companies who benefited from tenancy agreements, opposed this legislation. The ability of the state to enforce it was limited, however, and tenancy in multiple forms continued to be practiced (Keegan 1986a: 225–35).

Similar attempts were made in the Cape Colony. Location Acts were passed in Parliament in 1869, 1876, and 1884 to limit the numbers of African "idle squatters" on white farms. The extent of tenancy was very large. All over the eastern Cape, tenants rented land from white owners. In the district of Fort Beaufort, for example, it was reported in 1875 that "vast numbers of Kafirs have been allowed by landed proprietors in this district to hire ground from them" (quoted in Bundy 1979: 79). Passage of these laws disrupted tenancy but on an irregular basis, not enough to actually overturn the situation. White merchants, missionaries, and liberal state officials were opposed to the enforcement of such regulations, whereas white farmers and their elected representatives were the ones pushing for them (78–83; Trapido 1980).

The influence of the Cape liberal tradition waned with an accelerated drive for industrialization, spurred by the mineral discoveries. In 1892 Act 33 limited the number of tenants on white farms. In some cases tenants were forced to become laborers, but generally the act was not implemented. A more notable effort to achieve the same effect was the Glen Grey Act of 1894. The act aimed at driving Africans in the Transkeian Territories off their land, to which they maintained access, and into the colonial labor markets. The act called for the introduction of private rather than communal tenure (guaranteed to deprive inefficient farmers of the cushion of access to tribal land); it provided for a labor tax on those farmers who did not work for wages, in order to "give some gentle stimulus to these people to make them go on working" (C. Rhodes in Parliament in 1894, in Beinart 1982: 43). The law was passed but its effects, at least in Pondoland, were not significant due to the resistance of cultivators and other administrative difficulties (43–44). In general, these various regulations were not very effective. As the Departmental Commission on Occupation by Natives complained in 1908, "the ease and liberty of the situation [of tenancy] appeals to the ordinary Native peasant . . . and he will usually prefer it to daily toil at the mines or ports or in towns or on farms." The commission suggested that "if the system were placed under greater restriction a large number of these Natives would be compelled to go out to labour" (Bundy 1979: 136).

In Natal, similarly, a campaign directed against independent African homestead production, including squatting-tenancy, got under way with the growth of colonial markets. After 1897 the government was controlled by white farmers who used their influence to increase pressure on Africans to enter the labor market in the colony. Pass laws, hut taxes, and prohibition on sales of mission and crown land to Africans, combined with military defeats, draughts, and plagues to undermine the position of peasant producers, leading to an increase in migrant labor. By 1904, out of an African population of 608,527, about 30,000 were farm workers, 71,299 were migrant laborers within the colony, and 32,878 were migrants outside Natal (Lambert 1989: 386–87). According to Slater (1980), by the early years of the twentieth century the economic tide in Natal turned decisively in favor of white commercial farmers and against the advocates of tenancy, though homestead production continued for a long time afterward. This was especially the case in Zululand, where peasant farming never really took hold, and the foremost way of procuring cash was migrant labor and permanent migration out of the colony into Johannesburg (Guy 1982).

In the Transvaal, peasant production was still dominant in the first decade of the twentieth century. By 1904, out of more than 900,000 Africans, 438,000 were rent tenants on private land owned by whites, 180,000 leased Crown lands, and 130,000 farmed their own land. Only a small minority, 50,000, were full-time employees (Bundy 1979: 209). As the 1903 Transvaal Labour Commission put it, "African natives are in possession or occupation of large areas of land suitable for both agricultural and pastoral purposes. . . . The occupation of the country by Europeans is too recent to have brought about any change in the conditions governing the native occupation of the soil, and consequently throughout the whole of the territory under review, the natives are living practically under the same economic conditions as they were before Europeans came into the county" (Houghton and Dagut 1972: 2.87). This state of affairs prompted the commission to recommend changes in the existing land tenure system in order to channel labor into the market, "mainly for the reason that while the present facilities for obtaining land exist, the native is in a position to meet his wants and his small need for money by the sale of the produce of his land" (2.89). At the national level, in 1905 the South African Native Affairs Commission (SANAC) recommended a series of measures "to stimulate industry among the Natives," consisting of restrictions on tenancy, tax increases, enforcement of antivagrancy laws, and encouragement of education among the natives "with a view to increase their efficiency and wants" (South African Native Affairs Commission, 1905: 82–83).

In general, it seems, the more resilient cases of tenancy throughout the country benefited white absentee landlords and speculative land companies, in addition to Africans themselves. The Vereeniging estates in the southern Transvaal, for example, was a commercial enterprise based on production by self-exploiting tenant families. It worked well for a while, serving the interests of large-landowning whites and African tenants who operated in the framework of "a labour-shortage, land-surplus political economy" (Trapido 1986: 339). White nominal landowners provided access to land and grazing rights to tenants who provided labor as well as capital in the form of stock, seed, and implements. The produce was divided between the two parties. Small- and medium-sized white farmers, on the other hand, had much to gain from undermining indigenous peasant production. As Keegan argues for the Free State, "the smaller the property and the smaller the African community, the more disruptive the labour demands of the white farmer were likely to be, and the greater the degree of conflict and resistance implicit in the relationship. The social engineers, those who sought an 'equitable distribution' of black families [among white farmers], were those without the landed resources necessary to offer attractive terms to peasant communities" (Keegan 1986a: 236).

The Natives Land Act

The Anglo-Boer War of 1899–1902 and the Act of Union which established a politically unified South Africa by 1910 strengthened the coercive capacity and unity of purpose of the state, and its farming and industrial constituencies, in tightening control over indigenous land and labor. As early as 1905, the South African Native Affairs Commission condemned the "evil of absentee landlordism" and the "pernicious" type of land occupation known as "squatting," and called for their abolition since they restrict the supply of labor and fill up "with Natives much land which would otherwise be better utilised and developed" (South African Native Affairs Commission 1905: 31). To facilitate that, the commission recommended that land for locations and reserves "be defined, delimited and reserved for the Natives by legislative enactment" and that "thereafter no more land should be reserved for Native occupation"; at the same time, the commission called for "the creation, subject to adequate control, of Native locations for residential purposes near labour centres or elsewhere, on proof that they are needed" (39).

The Natives Land Act of 1913, an important landmark in the process of solidifying hierarchical relations between white masters and African servants, was in line with these recommendations. The act did not by itself transform land and labor relations, but it contributed to the overall trends of growth of white rural capitalism and the dispossession of African cultivators. It restricted Africans, who at the time made up about 67 percent of the population, to scheduled native reserves comprising 7.5 percent of the country's territory (later extended to 13 percent by the end of the period discussed here), prohibiting them from buying land outside those areas except from fellow Africans. It outlawed sharecropping in the Orange Free State, and it expressed the intention to do the same in the rest of the country, putting pressure on Africans to enter into relationships of dependency with white farmers as wage workers or labor tenants, though it did not mandate these arrangements immediately (see text of the act, in Plaatje 1982: 61–69).

The effects of the act, and similar pieces of legislation, on the nature of rural social relations have been the focus of much scholarly debate. There can be no doubt that at the time of its implementation the act left its mark on many individual tenants who had to submit to the loss of their economic autonomy or leave. Its effects were reflected in a famous song of the period, "iLand Act," written by the African musician Reuben Caluza. In the song, the "children of Africa . . . Zulu, Xhosa, Sotho" were bemoaning "A terrible law that allows sojourners/To deny us our land," crying "for the children of our fathers/Who roam around the world without a home/Even in the land of their forefathers" (quoted in Coplan 1985: 73).

The act also deeply affected contemporary political observers and African organizations in particular. In July 1913 a notable spokesperson for the latter, Sol Plaatje, traveled by bicycle through the Orange Free State; later he powerfully conveyed in his book *Native Life in South Africa* the dislocating effects of the act on the sharecroppers and tenants who were forced to move out. These people, in their desire to find a place where the act was not in force, were "moving to every point of the compass" (Plattje 1982: 87). They were "driven from home, their homes broken up, with no hopes of redress, on the mandate of a Government to which they had loyally paid taxation without representation—driven from their homes, because they do not want to become servants" (17). In a letter to the Lovedale College publication *Christian Express*, in December 1913, Plaatje described the unforgettable scenes of "families living on the road . . . their attenuated flocks emaciated by the lack of fodder on the trek, many of them dying while the wandering owners ran risks of prosecution for travelling with unhealthy stock" (quoted in Willan 1984: 165; see Plaatje 1982: 199–272; Karis and Carter 1972: 1.82–88, 125–133; and Walshe 1970: 44–50 for the campaign waged by the South African Native National Congress against the act).

While the hardships inflicted on Africans cannot be doubted, much debate has focused on the capitalist character of the relations of production established in the aftermath of the act. Morris (1980, 1987) argues that by the second decade of the twentieth century, concurrent with passage of the Land Act, capitalist production had come to dominate South African agriculture. For all intents and purposes, tenants had lost control over the means of production and became wage workers in all but name. Yet Keegan (1986a), Beinart, Delius, and Trapido (1986), and Bradford (1987), put a much stronger emphasis on the resilience of peasant homestead production and the continued, if tenuous, African access to land. (See Bradford 1990 for an overview of the debate.) The most important point that seems to come out of the debate is that the economic subordination of indigenous peasant producers was a discontinuous process with no predetermined results. It proceeded through protracted struggles between different class, race, and state forces and was not an outcome of the inevitable logic of capitalist accumulation.

From the perspective adopted in this work, the act can be seen as one important component of the trend of economic incorporation of indigenous people and settlers, albeit on terms increasingly unfavorable to the former. When Cell (1982: 79) describes it as "the foundation, the single most important piece, of the legislative program of segregation that white South Africans were steadily and very consciously constructing," we must keep in mind that the process involved a specific coercive form of incorporation, the terms of which were contested, rather than the assertion of an exclusionary principle. White farmers did *not* seek to exclude Africans altogether, that is, to treat them as an external element. On the contrary, they wanted to control them tightly as an internally subordinate part of their economy and society. As the 1916 Natives Land (Beaumont) Commission argued on the basis of a wide range of testimonies, white farmers were primarily interested in the supply of labor which had been drifting from the farms to the urban areas, and they objected to any arrangement in which "Natives could easily obtain land and so free themselves from the obligations which attach to residence on private farms" (Union of South Africa 1916: 3).

Geographical racial segregation was deemed impracticable by the Beaumont Commission since it was "too late in the day to define large compact Native areas or to draw bold lines of demarcation; for reserves, mission lands, Native farms and other lands solely occupied by Natives are, with the exception of the Transkeian Territories, scattered in all directions and hopelessly intermixed with the lands owned and occupied by Europeans, whose vested interests have to be considered" (Union of South Africa 1916: 4). As a result, the commission concluded, "in whatever way the segregation of European-owned and native-owned lands may be attempted, it is impossible to avoid the inclusion of much European-owned and occupied lands within proposed Native areas" (11). Of course this proposed step encountered stiff resistance from white farmers and their parliamentary representatives and consequently was never taken.

In fact, there was never any serious intention by supporters of "segregation," then or at any other time since, to remove all Africans from white-classified areas. If that was the intention, two additional steps that no white political party was willing to consider would have had to have been taken: (1) the allocation of sufficient land of good quality to be used by those Africans who were removed from "white" areas, as a viable basis for economic self-sufficiency; and (2) the restructuring of the white-owned economy in a way that would make it independent of African labor. As long as these steps were not even meaningfully contemplated, let alone implemented, white calls for segregation remained empty rhetoric (see in this respect the discussion by Brookes 1934: 53–77, still remarkably applicable to current calls for white or Afrikaner "self-determination").

Rural White Dispossession

To analyze more fully the indigenous peasants' relationship to the land, it is instructive to compare them with rural whites. The history of the *bywoners*, white "squatters" without title to the land, is of crucial importance for understanding the racial character of rural dispossession and incorporation in twentieth century South Africa. The land and labor issues which confronted the *bywoners* were similar in some respects to those with which Africans had to deal, but their overall fate proved very different. The existence of a poor rural white population of significant size dates to the nineteenth century, when they became a concern for state authorities. In the Cape Colony in particular, since the 1850s, the numbers of white landless tenants, or holders of nonviable tiny plots, increased rapidly. Growth in the prospects of commercial agriculture, especially sheep and ostrich farming, created an economic boom that benefited the better-placed white farmers but impoverished others who could not keep up with rising prices and rents (Bundy 1986).

In the northern Boer republics, the growth of the *bywoner* class can be primarily attributed to the period of mineral discoveries. The rise in land values prompted large landholders to survey and fence their possessions and insist on a respect for private property. Mineral prospecting and a growing demand for the commercial production of food made the extensive use of land, which previously had been central to the rural white economy, an inefficient and wasteful use of resources. This meant that large landowners could capitalize on new economic opportunities, while rural whites without secure title to the land were facing increasing difficulties in maintaining their way of life, making them more vulnerable than Africans to economic pressures: "They were in some sense the victims of their own society's entrenchment of private property in that they had no access to communal tenure land when ejected from farms. As tenants they were often less attractive to landlords than African families whose households were both more exploitable and more productive. As laborers their cost was far higher. . . . They were thus shaken out of the rural areas more rapidly" (Beinart and Delius 1986: 42).

African tenants' reliance on kinship networks for assistance and the self-exploitation of all family members as agricultural producers made them more competitive as rent tenants. White *bywoners*, in contrast, did not use family labor on the same scale, particularly women's labor, making it more difficult for them to survive on the land (Keegan 1986a: 29–33). This was especially the case since intensive farming had not been their primary economic activity to start with. Their reluctance to engage in what they considered degrading activities, contemptuously known as "Kaffir work," was reinforced by their sense of identity as masters in a racial system, incorporated at the level of identity and state politics with other whites on an equal basis in the independent Boer republics.

Related developments resulted in landless whites' decreasing ability to resort to alternative means of making a livelihood to which they had turned in the past. Depletion of game resources undermined hunting activities; the advent of the railways made transport-riding obsolete to a large extent; the formation of professional merchant companies made small-scale trading less profitable. In addition, their general lack of education and the process of deskilling explain why "the collapse of the hunting/trading/trekking economy left [them with] little alternative to a slow, bumpy slide into a new, white, industrial lumpenproletariat" (Keegan 1986a: 23). The strong emphasis on self-reliance in rural white culture made the loss of economic independence and the need to enter into the service of others intolerable alternatives. In comparison, city life must have looked more promising even if very far from satisfactory (see the 1908 report of the Transvaal Indigency Commission, in Houghton and Dagut 1972: 2.98–105).

We must keep in mind that urbanization did not necessarily mean proletarianization. For the white Afrikaans-speakers moving into the cities as much as for rural and urban Africans, wage work was something to be avoided if possible. As long as the newly urbanized could make a living by self-employment, in the Witwatersrand region in particular, they attempted to do that, regarding wage labor as the last resort. Initially, indeed, many of them managed to find work in Johannesburg as transport riders, cab drivers, and brick makers (Van Onselen 1982: 2.111–21). The growth of capitalist industry and services did not allow them to continue this kind of activity for a long time though, and many were forced into the growing ranks of urban employees and unemployed. Their road into the working classes consisted, then, of a two-stage process—first rural and then urban dispossession. Their capacity to organize, resist absolute immiserization, and fight for their rights, however, gained them concessions from employers and municipal and state authorities in the form of limited welfare, charity, relief works, and access to jobs and higher wages (2.125–58).

Black and White Labor

These developments bring us to the most crucial question concerning the evolution of political conflict in South African history: why did official policies define the *inability* of white farmers, tenants and industrial workers to compete freely in the market place and to supply their own needs as urgent problems calling for state intervention on their behalf, at the same time that they defined the *ability* of African peasants and urban residents to provide for their own subsistence as a threat to be contained and eliminated? This radical divergence in state policies was underwritten by a specific racial logic. The operation of this logic becomes even more obvious when we realize that in both cases the state was *counteracting* trends established by the economic processes of capital accumulation, free of direct political intervention. In other words, left to care for themselves, white and black social forces would have ended up in very different positions from those in which they actually found themselves due to state intervention. What was it, then, that made the state regard these eventualities as serious dangers? In answering these questions we need to address class interests as shaped by identity and state formation processes.

Two class-based explanations have been offered to account for these developments—the theses of cheap labor and of a split labor market. The first focuses on the imperatives of capitalist accumulation which dictated that unskilled black, rather than white, workers be employed on a massive scale as the chief source of labor in the mines. The reason was the differences in black and white proletarianization processes. Africans faced coercive and repressive campaigns by the mining industry to drive them into wage labor, while whites moved to the cities as an unintended consequence of other processes and "had not been subjected to any of the particular exploitative institutions associated with the migrant labour system, and they had no base in any 'reserve' economy" (Davies 1979: 58). They thus became "relatively expensive" as unskilled laborers and therefore unattractive to the mine owners, as compared to Africans who were "ultra cheap." Under these circumstances, whites were restricted to supervisory and mental positions in the production process, fulfilling the role of the necessary allies of the capitalist power bloc "in the absence of any potential supportive classes among the black population" (79). Davies considers identity and state forces, but regards them as the mere effects of struggles between capitalist factions and their responses to threats to their material interests.

This historical materialist analysis is based on a circular logic in its claim that the "power bloc" incorporated unskilled white workers in a supportive role since they were available, whereas black supportive classes did not exist. In fact, the supposed presence of these white allies of capitalism, and the absence of African counterparts, was *a result* of the racial policies devised by this same power bloc, rather than the independent material foundation for its policies. Supportive or subversive classes, as opposed to mere aggregations of individuals with similar relations to the means of production, do not have any existence prior to their construction as such in the course of political struggles over social meanings. The focus on the need of the mining industry to fill pregiven empty places in the division of labor with appropriate social agents prevents us from realizing that the very conceptualization of the productive process as requiring a division between unskilled, artisan, and supervisory positions (Davies 1979: 52–53) was not an objective material necessity. It was shaped in its specific South African form by perceptions of the availability and exploitability of labor, which was seen in terms of the existing definitions of some groups as potential servants and others as potential master and allies. Supervision and coordination may well play an essential role in any production process, but without acquiring a necessary racial character. Even if the mass of workers had to be African simply because of the prevailing demographic realities, no inherent economic logic prevented the urban "de-tribalized natives" from occupying higher supervisory positions, controlling in the process of production African migrants whose base remained in the rural native reserves. Blacks and whites were heterogeneous groups, and state and capital did not have to regard them as undifferentiated social forces.

An alternative class theory emphasizes the interests of white workers rather than the imperatives of capital as the determining factor in state policies. Bonacich, starting from the premise of the cheapness of African labor, argues that racial segregation emerged under conditions of a labor market split by job competition between high-priced white labor and cheap African labor. White workers attempted to prevent capital from using Africans, and therefore "the impetus for restriction on full African participation in the capitalist sector . . . [was not] an effort by capital to keep African labor cheap, but an effort by white labor to keep capital from displacing them with African cheap labor. Capital wanted to do away with the color bar; white labor fought to maintain it" (Bonacich 1981: 255).

The split labor market thesis suffers from many of the same problems as the cheap labor thesis. Both approaches are premised on the implicit assumption that African workers had to be treated by capital, the state, white workers, and presumably themselves as a homogeneous group. Africans, however, came from widely varying backgrounds, not only geographically and ethnically but economically as well. They maintained divergent relations to the means of production and to the native reserves, and were not all "cheap" in the same way. Whites were similarly divided on social and economic grounds. As the report of the Low Grade Mines Commission of 1920 puts it, a situation developed in which on the one side there was "a considerable body of more or less skilled and partly educated natives who clamour for opportunity to improve their pay and their station in life, and on the other a large number of whites who, through no fault of their own, have had no training in any particular trade. They claim protection against the competition of natives who are still in an inferior stage of civilisation, and *are strongly supported in their attitude by their more fortunate skilled fellow-workmen*" (report on the Low Grade Mines Commission, in Houghton and Dagut 1972: 3.33; italics added).

Economic processes created a labor market that was differentiated on the basis of skill and efficiency, not merely race. Identity formation processes intervened to prevent these same economic forces from consolidating the divisions among members of the white community; they achieved this goal by defining all whites as potential fellows. It is precisely this racial mobilization of skilled whites (who were not in danger of being replaced), in support of the cause of unskilled whites (who were in such danger), that is left unaccounted for by the split labor market thesis. In fact, capitalist interests might have been served equally well if not better had the mass of African and white workers been disaggregated on the basis of education, skill, occupation, and ties to the countryside rather than rigidly differentiated into distinct racial groups, to be uniformly exploited, co-opted, or excluded.

Many liberal writers and even official commissions of inquiry suggested just such a differentiation, arguing that in order to detach African workers from class radicalism there is a need to create cross-racial common interests and open "doors of opportunity enabling the ambitious member of the [African] proletariat to escape into the governing class, at the very least by ostentatious professions of a single national unity transcending class distinctions"; otherwise, the alternative would be that "class becomes associated with something definite and tangible such as colour" and "the stage is inevitably set for the 'class war'" (Brookes 1934: 42). No inherent class logic prevented the formation of a multiracial labor aristocracy, as classes need not have been either white or black in their entirety. Neither capital nor white workers, however, seriously attempted to mobilize potential class allies among Africans, at least not before the First World War. (The report of the 1908 Transvaal Mining Industry Commission, for example, presents the opposed policies of the Chamber of Mines and of white organized labor, neither of which saw any role for Africans other than that of cheap labor; in Houghton and Dagut 1972: 2.114–16). To explain the origins of this attitude, we have to go beyond the taken-for-granted assumptions of both approaches (see in this respect Omi and Winant 1986: 30–37 for a similar critique of the application of class analysis to racial divisions in the United States.)

In contrast to the class approaches presented above, I regard processes of identity and state formation as essential for understanding labor market dynamics.

The labor market had already been shaped by the presumed existence of racial groups that were differentiated on the basis of their origins into exploitable and co-optable groups. White material discontent was seen as a serious threat by the mine owners. As one member of their ranks argued in 1902, "if they [the white unemployed] become a starving and disorderly rabble it will cost us money, exertions, repute and stability ten times what it may cost to tide them through the period until they can be absorbed into the working community" (J. F. FitzPatrick, in Van Onselen 1982: 2.132). White troublemakers, unlike their African counterparts, enjoyed prior political incorporation, military training, access to arms, and a sense of inalienable right, guaranteed by the state, to earn a "decent" livelihood. In addition, a racial identity common to white workers and capitalists made them more likely partners even if no love was lost between them. Their attitudes had less to do with racist prejudice but rather with the prior formation of colonial and racial identities acting to exclude certain class options regardless of their potential profitability. When whites of all classes defined their interests, they did it in the framework of a racial discourse that defined the "natives" (making no internal distinctions among them) as backward people who were useful in servicing white needs but should not be independent and posed a threat to "white civilization." Even leading mining magnates opposed to the color bar expressed deep apprehensions about being dependent on African labor and regarded the removal of all racial restrictions as "an absurdity because, for the proper working of the mining industry a large number of skilled White men of all kinds are essential." This was due to the "actual inferiority" of Africans in doing "any work requiring initiative, fortitude and intelligence" (Lionel Philips in a 1922 letter, in Marks and Rathbone 1982: 36).

The greater sensitivity to the concerns of white workers can be attributed to the state's need to acquire political legitimacy from its white constituency. This need limited the ways in which capitalists could act on the imperative of accumulation. The state was similarly constrained in its ability and willingness to repress white workers, although this did not prevent fierce assaults on white workers when they seemed to be threatening political and economic stability in the country as a whole, as in the Rand Revolt of 1922. The need for white legitimacy was not the only constraint on the operation of the state. It has to be seen within a larger context in which the excluded presence of Africans was the foundation of the entire social order. Africans, though physically present, were excluded by the state as subjects with a legitimate voice in shaping their own future. At the same time, they made their presence clear, as Burawoy (1981) argues, in resisting the system and thus giving rise to disciplinary institutions, commissions of inquiry, parliamentary debates, and an elaborate surveillance apparatus dedicated to monitoring and controlling the activities of workers and the urban population. Overall political control was at stake, not only the specific interests of capitalists.

Industrialization and Segregationist Incorporation

The period from the end of the First World War to the late 1940s saw the intensification of the trends discussed in the previous sections. The South African political economy continued to be characterized by such racially specific processes as the exertion of pressure on indigenous people's land by the state in collaboration with white farmers, the undermining of independent farming by peasants, and the movement of rural Africans into the cities and urban employment. These processes gave rise to acute social and political conflicts: the growing incorporation of Africans into white-dominated economic structures was coupled with energetic attempts to impose legal and coercive measures of racial segregation that would rigidly separate blacks from whites in terms of economic rights and status. The capacity of Africans to resist incorporation on highly unequal terms was gradually eroded, though not eliminated, in the countryside. At the same time, the potential for resistance in the cities grew together with the creation of settled African urban communities. The process of permanent urbanization of Africans was, in effect, posing a challenge to the fundamental premise of the twentieth-century South African racial order: the existence of the native reserves as the true home of Africans, and hence the temporary nature of the urban African presence.

The development of industrial infrastructure, the manufacture of consumer goods, and growth in the public and domestic service economy increased the demand for labor much beyond the needs of the mining industry. The strict control associated with the hostels, mining compounds, and the migrant labor system was an unsatisfactory tool for the creation of a sizable and suitably qualified labor force to meet the needs of multiple, small-scale enterprises and private employers. These employers, unlike mine owners, did not have the financial and organizational resources necessary to create and sustain a system of recruitment, allocation, supervision, and discipline of labor without the help of the state. However, the state had less of a direct interest in intervening in processes of production that were not as strategically important as mining. It was concerned, rather, with the creation of a comprehensive legal framework to determine and control the freedom of movement of Africans, their residence rights, and the terms on which they migrated into and resided in the urban areas.

An effective system of control was difficult, if not impossible, to establish given that the state apparatus did not possess a high degree of efficiency and organization. This state of affairs stimulated intense policy debates and investigations into various aspects of labor, wage, land, and social conditions. A long series of policies, laws, and regulations was devised by Parliament, official commissions of inquiry, and government agencies in order to ensure that the incorporation of African labor be carried out on terms most favorable not only to their white employers, and to the South African racial economy as a whole, but to "white civilization" as well (though, of course, what that term meant was hotly disputed among whites themselves). Africans, in response, formulated their own strategies of survival and resistance. The ensuing clashes over terms of incorporation took the shape of localized (thematically and geographically) struggles waged in a variety of social and political settings.

The urban African population experienced continued growth throughout the period. It became not only larger but more settled, expanding from 587,000 in 1921, to 1,141,642 in 1936, to 1,719,338 in 1946, or 42 percent of the total urban population as compared to whites, who were only 40 percent of the urban population at the time (Union of South Africa 1948: 6). If counted together with colored people and Indians, whites were outnumbered in the cities by blacks as early as 1921 (6). More significant, perhaps, were changes in the composition of the population. Data for Johannesburg show that the sex ratio of Africans declined from 772 (in 1921) to 276 (in 1936) to 178 (in 1946) males for every 100 females, reflecting an increase in the number of women migrants and entire families settling in the cities. Other indicators pointing to the same trend were the increase in the proportion of children, and the decline in the percentage of the potential labor force (those aged 15–54), from 93 to 84, to 78 in the same period (Proctor 1987: 255–58). The Johannesburg municipality estimated that about 40 percent of Africans were living with family in 1935, with the proportion increasing to 66 percent in 1951 in the western areas of the city, and even to 89 percent in more established townships (Cobley 1990: 18). This trend went together with a decline in the proportion of male migrant workers employed by the mining industry in the total urban African population and a rise in the number of workers in other occupations. The official goal of keeping the urban areas white, allowing only for the temporary presence of African workers, became ever more remote.

The state attempted to control urbanization at the national, regional, and municipal levels by using Pass Laws to maintain an orderly flow of Africans into the cities without creating, at the same time, a large group of unemployed people. Two major official reports addressing African urbanization were submitted in 1922, one by the Inter-Departmental Government Committee on the Native Pass Laws (the Godley Committee) and the other by the Local Government Commission appointed by the Transvaal Province (the Stallard Commission). Both reports, despite their differences, had great impact on legislation in subsequent years. Of the two, the Godley Report adopted a far more liberal attitude, which tacitly acknowledged the futility of attempts to halt or reverse the process of African urbanization. It suggested ways of coming to terms with the process, without abandoning the principles of segregation in housing and occupation. The Stallard Report, dominated by more rigid local white concerns, was more resolute in its rejection of any role for urban Africans other than that of temporary service. The debate between these two approaches foreshadowed future arguments which have shaped white responses to racial issues ever since (see discussion of the reports in Hindson 1987: 32–39).

The Godley Report made basic distinctions among categories of indigenous people, differentiating between the permanent and the temporary sections but at the same time regarding both as in need of surveillance. It called for the abolition of passes and for the provision of a "suitable accommodation . . . attractive and properly controlled native townships or locations for the more permanent section of the native population, supplemented by efficiently conducted hostels and rest houses for natives temporarily sojourning in these areas" (Union of South Africa 1922: 11). In this way, it was assumed, all Africans would "be continuously under proper supervision and control and the temptations and dangers to which unsophisticated natives are now subjected would be minimised" (11–12). In addition, the report advocated exemptions from tight control of movements and the employment for women, chiefs, skilled artisans, educated Africans, and generally "all natives of good character who have arrived at such a scale of civilisation and education as no longer to require special measures of protection and control, beyond those extended to other sections of the community" (15).

In contrast to the Godley Report, the Stallard Report articulated an overall logic of segregationist incorporation (an inherently unstable concept but not a contradiction in terms) to maximize economic benefits for white employers and externalize the social and political costs onto the native reserves. It refused to accept any permanent presence of Africans in the cities as legitimate. Africans should be available when their services were required and would disappear from the scene once they were no longer needed: "The native should only be allowed to enter urban areas, which are essentially the white man's creation, when he is willing to enter and to minister to the needs of the white man, and should depart therefrom when he ceases so to minister" (Province of Transvaal 1922: 13). The commission saw the presence of "the masterless native in urban areas" (47) as particularly dangerous and called for the creation of "native villages" that would "be reserved exclusively for the residence therein of natives so long as they are in the employment of European masters or have definite work to do for the good of their own community" (49). No exemptions on grounds of education, skill, status, or basis in the reserves were to be recognized.

In practice, the Godley and Stallard approaches were largely reconciled in the 1923 Natives Urban Areas Act. The act encouraged the establishment of municipal locations for permanently urbanized Africans, but imposed strict control on the influx of job seekers from the rural areas and penalized the chronically unemployed, who could be sent back to the reserves or condemned to forced labor (Hindson 1987: 39–41). Since the late 1920s, the attempt to accommodate these partially contradictory approaches has increasingly given way to a stronger assertion of Stallardist principles. Amendments to the act in 1927 and 1937 tightened supervision over the "redundant native population." The rigid and more exclusionary version of segregation associated with Herzog and his government was strengthened at the expense of the more liberal incorporationist version of Smuts. Both versions, we should keep in mind, were informed by a white supremacist logic and were aimed at the defense of white domination (Dubow 1989: 123–27).

Both shared the implicit assumption that black labor should continue to form the foundation for white prosperity. Their disagreements were over the manner in which Africans could be incorporated into the white-dominated economy without posing a fundamental threat to the existing socio-political order. Liberals were willing to allow a measure of interracial legal and political incorporation with a view to promoting social stability, but they did not usually tackle white supremacy directly. Nevertheless, despite its limitations, the liberal approach resulted in the creation of political openings which allowed black and white forces to mount attacks on the system.

The need for African participation in the urban economy was not seriously disputed among whites. White workers who resented competition from cheap labor usually saw their own role as that of supervising Africans rather than replacing them altogether. In that sense, the economic incorporation of Africans was indeed permanent as it was widely acknowledged to be indispensable for whites. As the report of the Mills Commission said in 1926: "Nothing is more striking than the interpenetration by the native of every accessible phase of the life of the white community. One asks, 'What is the foundation of agriculture, of mining, of industry generally?' To this question there is but one answer: the native" (Union of South Africa 1926: 209). This was a result of successive South African governments' policy of undermining any independent basis for indigenous people's economic development. Africans were left with little alternative to employment in white service. Under these circumstances, calls for segregation were deemed impractical by the commission since "the contact of native and European has lasted too long, and their economic cooperation is too intimate and well-established, for the native to be excluded from European areas and European industries. The provision of adequate native reserves has been delayed too long for it to be possible now to provide reserves within which it would be possible for the present native population of the Union to live without dependence on outside employment" (152). This was the case throughout the country, even in the Transkei and Zululand, which contained the most substantial and solid blocks of indigenous-held land available.

The majority of Africans continued to live in rural areas through the end of the 1940s. For example, in 1946 about 77 percent of them lived in rural areas, but only 52 percent of these (or 40 percent of the total African population) lived in the native reserves, with the rest living on white-owned land and in the cities (Union of South Africa 1948: 7–8). The viability of independent African agricultural production was continuously undermined in the 1920s and 1930s. The deterioration of economic conditions in the reserves, coupled with the growing pressure on the land by white farmers supported by the government, served to push reserve dwellers out of their areas into work on white farms and in the urban areas. Despite their declining share in the African population, the absolute numbers living in the reserves actually increased during the period. This led to overgrazing, drying up of springs, deforestation, soil erosion, and "robbing the soil of its reproductive properties, *in short the creation of desert conditions*" (Union of South

Africa 1932: 11; italics in the original). The result was a decline in agricultural productivity and a decreasing ability to provide basic needs, leading the commission to conclude that "the carrying capacity of the soil for both human beings and animals is definitely on the downgrade" (10).

Comparative data for the district of Victoria East in the Ciskei in 1875 and 1925, representative of conditions in other regions, show that whereas the population more than doubled in those fifty years, reaching a point of "supersaturation," the market value of local agricultural production declined by half (or even more, if inflation is taken into account). Furthermore, food accounted for 64 percent of the total external purchases in 1925, a sharp rise from 20 percent, the figure for 1875 (J. Henderson, "The Economic Condition of the Native People," [1927], in Houghton and Dagut 1972: 375–77). This situation led to a growing need to resort to wage labor in order to supplement subsistence production.

The trend in other regions was generally similar, though with local variations. In 1930 it was estimated that, on the average, every male African of working age in the reserves worked one-third of his time for white employers, and that this amount of time was on the increase (Robertson 1934). This figure varied across regions. Some areas such as Pondoland went through the process of dispossession at a slower rate. A measure of self-sufficiency was maintained through the 1930s. The soil was in better condition, there was more room for agricultural expansion, and the homestead economy was less dependent on wage labor (Beinart 1982). In the Transkei in general, peasant alienation from the means of production was clearly taking place and eroding the ability of producers to survive independently, without recourse to migrant labor, but "proletarianisation seeped rather than swept through the communities. People clung tenaciously to their rural identities and productive resources, and questions of land and livestock continued to dominate their political responses" (Beinart and Bundy 1987: 3). In a similar manner, the pressures on the reserves in the eastern Transvaal gave rise to a mass movement focused on access to land, reflecting Africans' resistance to becoming wage workers devoid of ties to land and cattle. (See Bradford 1987 for the profoundly rural and preservationist nature of political struggles in the 1920s.)

Outside the reserves, in the western Transvaal, sharecropping arrangements between white landlords and black tenants continued into the 1940s, despite the fact that the arrangements had been banned for decades. There was a collusion of interests between the more wealthy white landlords with a surplus of land and the African tenants who maintained their autonomy, "for the native provides his own seed, his own cattle, his own labour for the ploughing, the weeding and the reaping, and after bagging his grain he calls in the landlord to receive his share, which is fifty percent of the entire crop" (Plaatje 1982: 87). This cooperation was resented by smaller white farmers, who felt they were deprived of access to African labor by wealthier landlords able to offer better conditions to tenants (Van Onselen 1990).

Many examples show the persistence of homestead production in the reserves, and the continuation of sharecropping arrangements outside of them, giving tenants a large degree of autonomy well into and even beyond the 1920s and 1930s. As a result of the difficulties in implementing the Natives Land Act of 1913, an observer concluded in 1934, many Africans "have legally remained the sole occupiers of European-owned land in the Transvaal and Natal, while there is general agreement that much illegal squatting continues both in those provinces and in the Free State" (Robertson 1934: 144; in this connection see the stories of the sharecroppers Nkgono Mma-Pooe in Matsetela 1982 and Kas Maine in Nkadimeng and Relly 1983). This evidence should not lead us to believe, however, that the processes of (white) accumulation in the countryside and cities and (African) rural dispossession were not real. The significance of the evidence is that it indicates that the incorporation of Africans into the white-dominated economy in a subordinate position was a prolonged process; its results were not guaranteed in advance but rather were the outcome of struggles over the terms of incorporation between different white and African interest groups. These struggles took place within the framework of official segregationist incorporation, which saw the "natives" as having a distinct and subordinate place and, at the same time, being an indispensable ingredient of the South African economy. Parliamentary debates and government policies were premised on the notion that some kind of balance had to be maintained between the social and political exclusion of indigenous people and their continued economic presence.

To preserve this duality, parliamentary legislation was passed to force independent African producers off their land and into labor on white farms under conditions that would prevent them from moving around freely. The 1925 Native Taxation and Development Act, the extension of Masters and Servants and Pass Laws in the following year, and the 1932 Native Service and Contract Act were all meant to force Africans into farm labor. This process culminated with the Natives Land and Trust Act of 1936, which extended the scheduled areas proclaimed in the Natives Land act of 1913, and established a state-controlled Native trust to consolidate the areas and impose administrative and financial control over their inhabitants. The act aimed to formalize the division of the country into white and native reserve areas. It also reinforced the drive toward greater subordination of tenants by penalizing Africans who engaged in tenancy without providing six months of compulsory labor service to white farmers (Greenberg 1980: 79–85; Lacey 1981: 164–80).

The Road to Incorporation

By the early 1940s, with the introduction of large-scale mechanization in white-owned agriculture, the struggle of African tenants to maintain their autonomy was basically lost. Their bargaining power, previously based on the supply of ploughing stock and implements, was considerably reduced with the advent of tractors subsidized by the government (Keegan 1990: 54–55). There were pockets of subsistence production in the reserves and outside of them, but the prospects for survival on the land were diminishing. The only way independent agriculture could possibly be sustained under these conditions was by massive state investment in the modernization of production and the education of the rural population; this was highly unlikely given that a government "representing the interests of white South Africa must regard the reserves primarily as sources of labour for the mines and European farms" (Roux 1949: 190). No South African government dependent on white voters was likely to channel resources to the reserves, even though such a policy would have contributed to the goal of curbing the uncontrolled movement of African urbanization. It is significant in this respect that even the Native Economic Commission of 1932, which centered its report on the need to develop the reserves, refused to specify where the necessary funds for such a project would come from, for fear of alienating their white constituencies.

An increasingly popular response to the deterioration of rural conditions was the movement of Africans into urban areas. Migrants took advantage of the industrial growth of the 1930s and 1940s, especially on the Rand, where over 40 percent of South Africa's industrial activity was concentrated. Between 1932–33 and 1939–40 the industrial work force grew from 131,906 to 282,779, and then to 422,013 in 1945–46. More than half the latter figure were Africans (Freund 1989b: 92), which constituted a shift in the composition of the industrial labor force from earlier years, when white workers played a prominent role, especially in state employment. White workers benefited from the civilized labor policy, which promoted the creation of jobs for and the employment of whites. It was defined by Prime Minister Barry Herzog in October 31, 1924, as mandating that "wherever practicable, civilized labour shall be substituted in all employment by the Government for that which may be classified as uncivilized. Civilized labour is to be considered as the labour rendered by persons, whose standard of living conforms to the standard generally recognized as tolerable from the usual European standpoint. Uncivilized labor is to be regarded as the labour rendered by persons whose aim is restricted to the bare requirements of the necessities of life as understood among barbarous and undeveloped peoples" (quoted in Houghton and Dagut 1972: 360).

Industrialists began to introduce more African workers to make up for the limited size of the white work force and with a long-term view to benefiting from the growing potential African consumer market. This policy went hand in hand with a drive by capitalists to loosen influx control restrictions, legitimize the permanent presence of urban Africans, and stabilize a healthy, settled, and organized labor force, though on a segregated residential basis (Hindson 1987: 52–59; Freund 1989b: 102–5). The industrial boom of the war years attracted a large number of Africans who, in the absence of any social welfare system and affordable housing, were forced to survive under very difficult conditions. The Smit Commission of Inquiry, formed to study the social and economic conditions of urban Africans, was impressed above all "by the poverty of the Native community . . .

the ill-effects of which permeate the native's entire social life" (Department of Native Affairs 1942: 1). The commission went on to advocate a progressive policy based on the need of the state to come to terms with the permanence of urban Africans, given that "the belief that the situation can be met by developing the native Reserves is illusory" (4).

Calls for the amelioration of living conditions in the cities, and in particular the provision of accommodation, went unheeded. Many migrants created illegal squatter settlements, necessitated by the shortage of official and affordable housing, which grew to "unmanageable proportions" (Union of South Africa 1948: 5). Attempts to evict these squatters were generally unsuccessful. As one of the squatter leaders put it: "The government was like a man who has a cornfield which is invaded by birds. He chases the birds from one part of the field and they alight in another part of the field. . . . We squatters are the birds. The government sends its policemen to chase us away and we move off and occupy another spot" (quoted in Stadler 1979: 19).

The rapid wave of African urbanization in the 1940s, coupled with the growing militancy of African communities, squatter movements, and trade unions, confronted the state with new challenges. Two contradictory responses were offered. On the one hand, white liberals accepted the inevitability of the permanent urbanization of Africans. Whoever wanted to reverse it, as Jan Smuts is reputed to have said in the early 1940s, might as well try to sweep the ocean back with a broom. This version of liberal (though limited) incorporation was elaborated further by the 1948 Fagan Report, which argued that movement from country to town had as a background economic necessity; therefore, "it can be guided and regulated, but it is impossible to prevent it or turn it in the opposite direction." One has "to accept the fact that there is a permanent urban Native population" (Union of South Africa 1948: 49; see discussion in Ashforth 1990: 114–39). The commission advocated a differentiated, controlled, and supervised incorporation of Africans into the urban areas in terms of housing, employment, and legal rights. In doing that, it explicitly rejected the Stallardist approach to segregation as utterly impracticable due to a division of labor in which "the economic structure of South Africa is based on the one hand on European initiative, organisation and technical skill, on the other hand no less on the availability of a few million Native labourers" (Union of South Africa 1948: 17).

Hardline segregationists were represented by the National Party, whose policies found expression in the 1947 Sauer Report. In contrast to the liberals, they called for strict enforcement of influx control and for vigorous attempts to reverse the process of African urbanization. This strategy was, of course, to be implemented under the name "apartheid" after the 1948 election. Even the Sauer Report, however, did not clearly pose an immediate challenge to the fundamental economic role of African labor in the white-dominated South African economy (Posel 1991: 58–60). The demise of independent African agriculture, the consequent migration out of the rural areas, and the incorporationist dynamics of urbanization and industrialization seem to have gone too far to be turned back. Although white nationalists rejected the notion that the situation was irreversible, they were unwilling to pay the full price of inverting these processes by investing massive resources in the reserves, and by restructuring the South African economy so that it would cease to depend on African labor. In fact, one of their major policy goals was to insure a steady and organized supply of labor to different white employer interests. In that sense, they never offered any serious alternatives to economic incorporation.

Africans, for their part, could not sustain a viable economic basis that would enable them to survive independently, outside the framework of the white-owned economy. Their organizational, financial, and technological resources were generally too meager, relative to those of whites, to allow them to compete effectively in a capitalist-driven market economy. Their direct access to land was limited to about 10 percent of the territory, and their per capita share of the national income was only 8 percent of whites' share in 1936; even if combined with the income of colored people and Indians it was no more than 10 percent (Department of Economics 1949: 345). Those Africans who managed initially to thrive were incapacitated by the political and legal liabilities endured under settler rule. Lack of indigenous people's access to the settler-controlled South African state became a major obstacle to their economic success, which is clearly visible when compared to the case of indigenous Palestinians and the British colonial state. As a result, the march toward complete economic (though not political and social) incorporation seemed unstoppable. Not even the white nationalist government that took over in 1948 could seriously contemplate reversing the trend in this respect.

Comparison and Conclusions

In both Palestine/Israel and South Africa the period from the 1870s through the 1940s brought about important economic transformations. A large increase in capital and labor imports and accelerated processes of industrialization and urbanization were crucial ingredients of these changes. Differences in the ways in which economic developments shaped, and were in turn shaped by, relations between various groups in the two countries were also evident. In both cases settlers accumulated large areas of land originally owned by indigenous people, but whereas in South Africa this was largely the outcome of military conquest, in Palestine/Israel, land transfers were the result of economic transactions until 1948. In the field of labor relations, Jews and Arabs generally did not enter into hierarchical master-servant relations. Most of the labor services rendered to Jewish and Arabs employers were provided by employees who belonged to their respective communities. In South Africa, in contrast, Africans became suppliers of labor for the white-dominated economy, primarily in agriculture and mining, and no significant indigenous rural or urban bourgeoisie ever emerged.

In the following discussion I account for these divergent developments by concentrating on two factors: indigenous capacities and settler strategies. The world-historical context, discussed in previous chapters, is not considered for the period covered here; given that similar time frames were involved, its role was roughly the same for both countries.

Indigenous Capacities

The capacity of indigenous people to engage in sustained economic development and maintain their independence in the process of production has been underrated in the historical literature on both countries, and especially in the case of Palestine/Israel. Analyses written from the modernization perspective emphasize the conservative nature of traditional agriculture, deemed incapable of using new technologies and adopting attitudes conducive to improvements and achievement. Starting from radically different premises, the dependency and world-system perspectives reach similar conclusions with regard to indigenous capacities. Indigenous people are seen as having been crushed by settler colonial forces with little ability to stand their ground and take advantage of newly opened commercial and financial opportunities. Neither approach gives adequate consideration to indigenous initiative and to the ways in which they managed to transcend their relegation to the role of either obstacles to progress or passive victims of capitalist development.

Having said that, we should not overstate the case by ignoring the extent to which indigenous economic structures *were* frequently modified or destroyed in processes of conquest and settlement. Furthermore, we should keep in mind that the ability of indigenous people to maintain their economic independence and avoid falling under settler domination varied enormously across time and space. There was no uniformity in their responses to, and successes in meeting, colonial challenges. Indigenous Arabs in Palestine/Israel were capable of maintaining a large degree of independence in pursuing their own interests and policies in the economic field. They were more successful in achieving that than indigenous Africans were. Many Arab entrepreneurs, though not a majority of the indigenous population by any means, took advantage of the huge increase in the influx of capital, and the growing commodification of the economy that resulted largely from the impact of the British and Zionist presence. In South Africa, on the other hand, the advantages to indigenous people were fewer to begin with and more difficult to sustain.

In this section I examine the differences between the capacities of the two indigenous groups by focusing on three related issues: (1) indigenous people's access to land and capital resources; (2) internal social differentiation; and (3) the role played by the colonial state.

ACCESS TO LAND AND CAPITAL

In the beginning of the British mandatory period, Palestinian-Arabs were in nominal and effective control of most of the cultivated and cultivable land in the country. By the end of the period they were still in possession of about 90 percent of the available land (and more than 75 percent of the cultivated land), despite massive transfers into Jewish hands. In other words, the access of indigenous people to, and control over, the means of production *as a group* was not seriously affected by the Zionist presence, though many tenants and grazers lost access to land *as individuals*. Indigenous South Africans, in comparison, had a more tenuous link to the land. In some regions, by the beginning of the period they had already lost nominal ownership of the land, though not necessarily effective access to it, due to internal and external wars of conquest. In other regions they maintained ownership of the land but were faced with settler encroachments, frequently backed by the military power of colonial states. The prevalent African pattern of extensive use of land, dispersed homestead units, and stock keeping, as compared to the dominant Palestinian-Arab pattern of settlement in densely populated villages and intensive agriculture, made indigenous hold on the land in South Africa less stable and easier to dislodge.

Access to capital was another important factor. Indigenous Arabs were able to mobilize capital resources and gain access to productive technology through sale of urban or agricultural land, commerce, and credit facilities. They were not dependent on settlers for access to capital, nor were settlers the first to introduce capitalist trading activity, productive relations, and banking into the country. Indigenous Palestinians could engage, then, in their own intensified production and marketing processes without falling under settler domination. None of these avenues to capitalization were clearly open to indigenous Africans, who came from nonmonetarized societies in which land was held communally and assets were accumulated above all in the form of cattle. These resources could and were used initially to compete successfully with small white farmers, and to take part in sharecropping arrangements with white landowners on relatively nonexploitative terms. Africans, however, proved ultimately unable to withstand the pressures on their land and labor exercised by white capitalist landlords supported by massive state subsidies and physical coercion. As a result, Africans were increasingly forced to resort to the sale (or rent) of their labor in order to supplement their incomes and be allowed to retain even limited access to the land.

INTERNAL DIFFERENTIATION

Indigenous Palestinians were more stratified than indigenous Africans, that is, they had more internal differentiation. Of course African societies were not truly egalitarian, but they were characterized by a relatively less skewed distribution of resources. Processes internal to Palestinian-Arab society generated a surplus of labor (provided by the landless and owners of tiny plots) which was usually employed by other, more wealthy, rural and urban Palestinians. In other words, there were enough indigenous landlords, industrialists, and entrepreneurs in Palestine/Israel to provide most of the dispossessed from their own community with jobs. Indigenous people looking for work had no need in most cases to enter labor relations with settlers, though some of them did do that. Settlers were not the only, or even the most important, sources of employment; indigenous employers and government enterprises coexisted with a settler-owned economic sector.

In South Africa, in contrast, indigenous people's wage labor almost always meant providing labor services for settlers and other foreign employers. No substantial economic demand for labor ever emerged from indigenous people themselves. Most enterprises owned by them were small in scale and of the self-exploiting family labor kind. As a result of these differences, when indigenous people were similarly squeezed off the land, in South Africa they almost inevitably entered into settler service, but not in Palestine/Israel.

ROLE OF THE STATE

The third aspect of indigenous capacities is the role of the colonial state. The dispossession of indigenous people and their movement into the labor market were facilitated in South Africa by the intervention of the colonial state in passing legislation to that effect and using its repressive apparatus to enforce compliance. Even when the state was not directly controlled by settlers, it was generally sympathetic to their concerns. British officials perceived African land usage as wasteful of precious resources, unproductive, and uncivilized. Even if not entirely committed to settler causes, the state actively collaborated with them in the subjugation of indigenous people in order to serve settler demands for land and labor. In Palestine/Israel, on the other hand, the state was neutral. Both sides to the conflict accused the British of being partial to the interests of the other side, but in no case did the state intervene clearly and massively on the side of settlers, nor did it ever actively coerce indigenous people off their land and into providing labor for settler farms, as it did in South Africa. The British mandatory state set up a legal framework that gave all residents the same civil rights, though with a bias toward settler political interests in the form of the Balfour Declaration. For the most part, the state left the management of land and labor relations to the national communities themselves. In that sense, indigenous people in Palestine/Israel were capable of using the state, or at least preventing it from intervening on the side of settlers; they were not politically disadvantaged by colonial rule in the same way that their South African counterparts were. Indigenous South Africans did not enjoy any direct access to the state, in contrast to white settlers, and in addition they were forced to confront the active mobilization of the coercive and legislative capacities of the state in the service of settler domination.

Settler Strategies

The strategies adopted by settlers were influenced by indigenous capacities and state policies as well as by their own interests and designs.

IDEOLOGICAL IMPERATIVES

Settlers in Palestine/Israel were motivated by a vision that pushed them to seek to build their lives in a new country to which they felt historical affinity. Their nationalism was ethnically specific in the sense that it was a conscious creation, focused on finding a solution to the problem of the dispersed Jewish people. It was not a territorial nationalist movement which could have been, at least in principle, open to members of other national and ethnic groups living in the same territory. In addition, the process of settlement made the creation of jobs to accommodate newcomers a necessity. Both imperatives, the ideological and the practical, acted to promote exclusionary economic strategies.

Settlers in South Africa, in contrast, were not driven by sentiments of a nationalist-religious kind, but rather by material concerns. Most of them were attracted to the region by the promise of economic opportunities, especially with the industrial boom which opened with the mineral discoveries of the late nineteenth century. Their main concern was to improve their economic position; their interest in the territory of South Africa was not due to specific religious or nationalist considerations. Unlike the Zionist-inspired Jewish settlers, white settlers in South Africa did not engage in a conscious nation-building project, the success of which might have required exclusionary economic policies. They sought solutions for their own local and territorially limited problems, unlike the problems of an extraterritorial people in search of a homeland. As a result, they were more pragmatic in their orientation.

MATERIAL IMPERATIVES

The other aspect of exclusionary settler policies, that of securing employment for newcomers moving into the cities (whether from abroad or from rural areas), played an important role in South Africa. It took place, however, in a different economic context than that of Palestine/Israel. White workers felt that they were facing unfair competition from cheaper and unorganized African workers and that their very access to many positions was consequently blocked. They organized campaigns to implement segregationist policies and put color bars in place to insure that certain jobs were reserved for whites. In the Rand Revolt of 1922, hundreds of striking and protesting miners were killed, wounded, and arrested in clashes with the state and their employers over the threat to the white workers' positions. Settler workers, however, never demanded an end to the employment of indigenous people. They asked, rather, for guarantees that they themselves be employed, preferably in higher-skilled positions. In the context of a capital- and labor-intensive economy, dominated by primary industries using vast numbers of unskilled laborers, settlers could not substitute for the entire indigenous labor force.

In Palestine/Israel, on the other hand, the Jewish-owned economy was dependent on capital imports, which were usually accompanied by matching imports of (settler-immigrant) labor. With the exception of the export-oriented citrus plantations, most of the economic development that took place was directed toward production for the local markets. Supplies of Jewish capital and labor did not usually lag far behind one another. No development similar to the emergence of the mining industry and its reliance on indigenous labor in South Africa took place in Palestine.

The dominant pattern in South Africa became one of segregationist incorporation in the form of massive dependence on the indigenous labor force, coupled with job reservations and "civilized labor" policies for settler workers; in Palestine/Israel the dominant pattern became one of an exclusionary labor market, expressed in policies of Jewish labor that in principle did not permit employment of indigenous workers, even in a subordinate position. The indigenous people who *were* employed in the settler economy were few in number, both in proportion to the total number of the economically active Palestinian population as well as in proportion to the total number of employees in the Jewish-owned economy.

THE ROLE OF THE STATE

As mentioned earlier, colonial and settler states in South Africa intervened in the sphere of land and labor relations on the side of settlers. This was clearly the case with the white supremacist Boer republics but also to a lesser extent with the British colonies of the Cape and Natal, especially after they were granted representative government. The British shared with settlers an interest in the profitable exploitation of the mineral riches of the country. They regarded these as important to their dominant position in the world system. They also developed broader strategic concerns related to the survival of the empire, and consequently they saw political stability as a necessary ingredient of economic prosperity and secure imperial control. Though the British were not committed to supporting white supremacy on settlers' terms, they shared with settlers a worldview that perceived indigenous people as an unruly mob, incapable of providing a solid foundation for imperial rule. Generally speaking, then, they promoted a state of affairs in which indigenous people were under the trusteeship of colonial domination for the sake of creating and sustaining a stable business environment. This was true even more, of course, for the Union of South Africa, which came into being in 1910 and directly represented settlers.

In Palestine/Israel the colonial state was also British, but it was inserted in a different position within the imperial system. The British had no direct economic stake in the country as in South Africa. They assumed mandatory powers because of their strategic interests in securing the Suez Canal, the road to India, and access to Middle Eastern oil resources. There were no material assets in Palestine/Israel equivalent to the Rand gold mines, and consequently no need for the subordination of indigenous labor. There was no compelling state interest in promoting the incorporation of Palestinians into Jewish-dominated economic institutions. In fact, the state developed an interest in developing a prosperous indigenous economic sector, which was seen as conducive to greater political stability.

Overall, then, indigenous capacities, settler strategies, and state interests intersected in South Africa to produce a large degree of economic incorporation. The result was the formation of a class structure in which indigenous Africans played a subordinate role in a system dominated by white settlers. In Palestine/Israel, on the other hand, these forces gave rise to a situation in which exclusionary economic institutions developed without being dependent on labor relations between settlers and indigenous people. More space was thus created for exclusionary socio-economic developments (on a mutual basis) in Palestine/Israel and incorporationist developments (on a racially hierarchical basis) in South Africa. These divergent trends in the history of the two countries were reinforced by developments in the spheres of identity formation and state formation, topics dealt with in the next chapter.

Appendix: The Politics of Sources

Few issues have been more contentious in the history and historiography of the Israeli-Palestinian conflict than the question of numbers. Basic demographic data have been in dispute since the beginning of the systematic analysis of the conflict, and we are probably as far from a satisfactory settlement of such issues today as we have ever been. The most hotly debated question (in addition to the number of people Israeli forces pushed out of the territory in the War of 1947–48, an issue that falls beyond the scope of this work) is the number of tenants and other peasants displaced by the process of Zionist settlement in the pre-1948 period. The problematic nature of the sources used to establish these issues becomes apparent once we realize that not only Jews and Arabs produced highly politicized accounts and figures but the ostensibly neutral British contributed their own share to the confusion, though in a less conspicuous manner.

As early as 1929, when the Shaw Commission of Inquiry began its deliberations, sharp differences over the number of tenants who used to live in the Valley of Esdraelon (the single largest piece of land bought by Jews during the entire mandate period) came to the surface. The commission did not produce its own figures and was satisfied to report the competing claims. Curiously enough, the much-quoted figure of 8,730 *people* (not *families* as some later writers such as Kanafani asserted) appears in the official report (Palestine 1930b: 118) but not in the testimony of Saleem Farah from Nazareth to whom it was attributed. His own estimate was about 1,670 families or 7,500–10,000 people, and he nowhere mentioned the 8,730 figure (Palestine Commission 1930a: 445–56). His data were primarily based on acquaintance with the pre–World War I conditions in the area. His figures were thus not entirely firsthand but derived from fifteen-year-old memories. This does not mean that his data were unreliable, of course, but it does call for caution.

The data provided by Zionist representatives were problematic as well. In 1929 Arthur Ruppin quoted a figure of 700–800 *tenants* for the Valley of Esdraelon (mysteriously reduced to 664 *for the entire country* in his testimony to the Palestine Royal Commission in 1936), conveniently forgetting that these individuals were heads of *families*; the result is an undercount by a factor of five or so. The evidence for these and similar figures was usually to be found in internal Zionist documentation and was thus of questionable external validity. To complete the picture, the British figures for this case were somewhat over 5,000 people (Palestine 1930c: 51; or more precisely, 5,138 according to Memorandum 17, in Government of Palestine 1937: 56–57). The displaced people thus comprised about a third of the population of the entire district of Nazareth.

It is unlikely, then, that 25,000 tenants could have been dispossessed from the Valley of Esdraelon alone (as claimed in Arab Office 1947) if the entire rural Arab population of the district of which it formed a part was about 15,000 people at the time of the 1922 census (Government of Palestine 1937: 5). In addition, the same figure of twenty-two villages destroyed as a result of the transfer of land in the Valley of Esdraelon is repeated several times over the entire period (in the 1930 Shaw Commission report and in the testimonies of Jamal al-Husayni to both the 1937 Royal Commission and the 1946 Anglo-American Commission of Inquiry). This indicates that few if any other villages were destroyed (though individuals were displaced), thus casting doubt on the claim that tens of thousands of peasants (119,000 people according to one version) were displaced all over the country throughout the period. It is hard to believe that such a massive number of individuals could have been uprooted and dozens of villages demolished without leaving a trace in contemporary or more recent records.

Zionist accounts putting the figure in the range of a few hundred are equally untenable. The most reliable estimate continues to be that provided by Porath, who sets it at a few thousand families (Porath 1977: 87–90). The exact number of displaced peasants cannot be established with precision and perhaps is not of great importance in itself. Nevertheless, the discussion here demonstrates the problems involved in such an endeavor both during the period itself as well as in its historical reconstruction. Even though hearings on the issue were first held only a few years after the land in question had been transferred into Jewish hands, none of the parties involved—Arabs, Jews, and the British—managed to produce a single witness who had actually lived on the land before it was sold.

British data themselves are not beyond suspicion, as two other documents from the same period demonstrate. In a study widely referred to but seldom read, known as the Johnson-Crosbie Report (Government of Palestine 1930), two government officials conducted a survey of rural conditions using a questionnaire administered to a large sample of families in Arab villages. It was the only study conducted on such a massive scale during the period and is therefore of great value, but there are several problems with the report that are rarely mentioned. The report is based on self-reporting by the objects of study, which would not necessarily be a major problem if the researchers were careful to observe that the terms used by respondents and researchers had a clear and agreed-upon meaning. But it is unclear exactly what is meant by such categories in the report as "owner-occupiers" and "labourers," especially since the crucial and contested category "tenants," possibly falling in either of the above, does not appear in the report for the purposes of land ownership classification.

Sharecroppers, who lived and worked on land nominally held by absentee landlords, usually controlled all factors of production, except for legal ownership of the land. They frequently regarded themselves as practical owners. They possibly could have defined themselves as "owner-occupiers" in one of the two subcategories provided in the report (those living exclusively on their land or those who also work as laborers), but whether they actually did so cannot be established from the report. A similar confusion is created with regard to laborers. Some of them were tenants and others were agricultural workers. The two categories, the distinctions among which are crucial to our understanding of landlessness, are conflated in the report.

The problem is far from purely terminological. In calculating the breakdown of holdings, Johnson and Crosbie assert that 6,940 families out of a total of 23,573—29.4 percent of the sample—were laborers (Government of Palestine 1930: 21). This figure has gained currency in much of the literature on the issue, beginning with the Hope Simpson Report (Palestine 1930c) and the subsequent Passfield White Paper of October 1930 (Palestine 1930d). In these latter documents, Johnson-Crosbie's "labourers" appear as "landless," a definitional transformation that was valid for some, no doubt, but not for all.

Several logical possibilities for interpreting these concepts emerge at this point. If all the "labourers" were landless, then that category would have excluded tenants who had access to land. In other words, tenants would have been included among the "owner-occupiers." This interpretation is inconsistent with the text of the report, which does make a distinction between tenants and owner-occupiers (Government of Palestine 1930: 22). On the other hand, if the category "labourers" did include tenants, they would not all have been "landless," and the equation between the two concepts made in the Hope Simpson Report and in the Passfield White Paper of 1930 would be false. There is a third possibility, which is that all tenants were indeed regarded as landless. In such a case, however, the entire controversy over the dispossession of tenants would become meaningless: tenants could not have been dispossessed of what they did not possess in the first place.

Without belaboring the issue further, the crucial point is that we must be cautious in using any set of figures, whether coming from clearly partisan or from "official" sources. The British had their own agendas, though their reports were clearly not as partisan as those produced by the direct parties to the conflict.

The difficulties involved in definitions and determinations of numbers are compounded by the tendency of various writers to attribute causality to descriptive statements. The Johnson-Crosbie Report presents data on the distribution of land; it is not an analysis of the historical causes of landlessness. At no point does it assign responsibility for the existing patterns of landholding to Zionist settlers, British officials, or any other force for that matter. Hope Simpson goes beyond descriptions to criticize Zionist policies for increasing landlessness, but he nowhere claims that all 29.4 percent of the families who were landless, or any identifiable portion of them, reached that condition because of Zionist settlement. In fact, precisely when and how people became landless was a question explicitly left open in his report; no subsequent account of the issue managed to give a satisfactory answer to it.

To make a convincing case for the historical effects of any factor, be it political or economic, we have to show how the situation "before" changed as a result of factor X, to produce the situation "after." In the absence of reliable data on the patterns of land distribution in earlier pre-Zionist periods, we cannot reach any conclusions with regard to the increase (or otherwise) in the frequency of landlessness in the 1920s. In the absence of historical data on the circumstances in which 29.4 percent of Palestinian-Arab families lost their land (if indeed they had possessed any before), no solid conclusions about the effects of Zionist settlement on rural landlessness can ever be reached. This is not to say, of course, that one has no basis to maintain that Zionist settlement exacerbated the problem of Palestinian-Arab landlessness, but rather to assert that landlessness cannot be attributed *tout court* to Zionism on the basis of the available data.

Having said that, I hasten to assert that the conclusions above should not be taken to mean that the effects of Zionist settlement on the pre-1948 Palestinian-Arab society were not destructive. What I argue, rather, is that we can attempt to trace the operation of internal and external factors in the making of Palestinian history without hoping to find any hard numerical data that would conclusively prove the validity of one thesis over another. In that sense, the "primary" sources eagerly sought by historians are no less implicated in power and conflict relations than "secondary" sources. Both types of sources should be subject to constant interpretation and reinterpretation. This is the only way to reach sound historical conclusions, the validity of which, however, would continue to be subject to political and academic challenges.

6 | Nationalism, State, and the Struggle for Power

This chapter continues the discussion of the processes of identity and state formation along lines similar to those pursued in chapter 4. It covers the period of the British mandate in Palestine/Israel, beginning in the aftermath of the First World War and ending with the partition of the territory, the establishment of the State of Israel in 1948, and the creation of the Palestinian refugee population. In the case of South Africa it covers the period that started with the conquest of the remaining independent African territories, proceeded with the union of white colonies and republics in 1910, and culminated with the elaboration of a national policy of segregation and the rise of the white supremacist National Party to power in 1948. I focus on the extent to which political movements came to articulate visions of society in terms of mutually exclusive group identities, as in Palestine/Israel, or in terms of inclusive and partially overlapping group identities as in South Africa. All of these options were open *in principle*, though the prior operation of identity formation processes in the earlier period had excluded some of them *in practice*. Throughout the chapter, the role and the activities of indigenous people and their political movements receive particular attention.

Palestine/Israel

During the period of the British mandate, the Arab and Jewish movements in Palestine/Israel established themselves as representatives of their respective constituencies and created an institutional infrastructure for separate political developments. Distinct national identities were shaped in opposition to each other, leading to a conflict between irreconcilable claims to the territory. The resulting clashes left little room for attempts to construct inclusive identities and institutions.

The organized Palestine-Arab national movement first emerged in the aftermath of World War I, largely in response to the Balfour Declaration of November 1917. In that document, the British government committed itself to supporting the Zionist project of a Jewish National Home in Palestine/Israel. The Zionist movement thus for the first time managed to gain international recognition of its claim to the territory. The struggle for control over the country, which had already started in the late Ottoman period, intensified as a result. The British mandate period, which concluded with the U.N. partition resolution of November 29, 1947, was characterized by frequent violent clashes between the national communities. The outcome of the period was the War of 1947–48 and the partition of Palestine/Israel into the predominantly Jewish State of Israel and the exclusively Arab regions of the West Bank and Gaze Strip (respectively controlled by Jordan and Egypt until 1967), with no equivalent State of Palestine in existence. A large Palestinian-Arab refugee population came into being in the course of the war, giving the Israeli-Palestinian conflict its most important distinguishing feature, which has characterized it ever since.

The two groups entered the British period in possession of partly formed corporate national identities, the external boundaries of which were better defined than the internal boundaries; the latter were still shifting and open to modifications. In the subsequent three decades, a more elaborate expression was given to the sense of nationhood in the form of organized mass movements, institutions, and symbols. The basic motif running throughout the period was the twin processes of the dissolution of internal boundaries within each group (though sometimes creating new ones in the process) and the further consolidation of external boundaries between them. This chapter deals with these developments and with the extent to which the two national movements managed to achieve their goals.

The Political Framework

The overall historical context for the struggle over political and territorial control in Palestine/Israel was established by external events, external in the sense of being beyond the control of the parties involved in the conflict as well as in the sense of owing little to the internal dynamics that developed in the previous period and governed the relationship between the parties. These new circumstances were created by the defeat of the Ottoman Empire in the First World War, the takeover of the territory by British forces in the military campaigns of 1917–18, and the grant in 1922 of a League of Nations mandate to Great Britain to administer the country and prepare it for independence.

Even before formalizing its control, Britain had already taken a major step toward creating a framework for the political development of the country in the form of the Balfour Declaration of November 2, 1917. The declaration was addressed to Lord James Rothschild, a leader of the British Jewish community, requesting him to communicate its message to the World Zionist Organization. It expressed sympathy with "Jewish Zionist aspirations" and proclaimed British support for "the establishment in Palestine of a national home for the Jewish people," without prejudicing the "civil and religious rights of existing non-Jewish communities in Palestine, or the rights and political status enjoyed by Jews in any other country" (preamble to the mandate, League of Nations 1922: 2).

This statement, arguably the most important political document of the period, was based on two assumptions crucial to our understanding of the specificity of the conflict. First, it recognized the right of the Jewish people to the territory. It did not derive this right from the existence of a Jewish community in the country; in fact, it did not even mention that such a community had already come into existence. The basis for the declaration was the abstract and general rights of the extraterritorial Jewish people wherever they were, rather than the concrete rights of the specific and territorially based Jewish community of Palestine/Israel. Second, the statement did not acknowledge the existence of an Arab, or a Palestinian-Arab, *national* community in the country. Rather, it referred to a plurality of non-Jewish communities, defined by religion (or rather by lack of adherence to a particular religion), residing in the territory but, unlike the Jewish people, with no identifiable legal and historical relation to it.

In both of these aspects the declaration ignored the prior operation of identity formation processes that had taken place in the period preceding the First World War. In practice, as soon as the world war came to an end it became evident that circumstances in the country itself were rather different from what they appeared to be from the outside, primarily in London. Arab (and more specifically Palestinian-Arab) national identity had already begun to emerge and thus made the passive role that the declaration envisioned for the "non-Jewish communities" untenable. Furthermore, the formation of a cohesive and numerically substantial local Jewish community, capable of sustaining a viable claim to the territory on behalf of the Zionist movement, proved a problematic and complex process. The Jewish National Home had to be created in the country itself, assembled locally out of largely imported materials; it could not have been transplanted fully formed from elsewhere.

The legal framework established by the Balfour Declaration, and later ratified by the League of Nations Mandate for Palestine in 1922, could not by itself determine the future of the country then. It was, however, crucially important in that it created the political terrain on which the Jewish-Zionist and Palestinian-Arab national movement constructed the identity of their constituencies, conducted their conflicts, and formed their own institutions with a view to gaining eventual control over the country as a whole. The creation of a British administration, even if only for the express and limited purpose of preparing the country for independence, allowed a degree of mediation between the conflicting parties, neither one of which enjoyed obvious political dominance. In this sense, Palestine/Israel was different from South Africa, in which white-dominated colonial and settler states clearly operated to promote settler causes without attempting to maintain even a modicum of neutrality.

The Emergence of Palestine

Palestine (or the Land of Israel) was a relatively unproblematic territorial concept for the Zionist movement and the British government, though its boundaries were never precisely defined. It had been a central element in Jewish and Christian religious discourses for millennia, and the Balfour Declaration took its definition for granted. This was not so obviously the case for Palestinian Arabs, Muslim in their majority, who were confronted with contradictory pressures as a result of the subjection of the country to special treatment by the international community. On the one hand, the demarcation of Palestine from other Arab territories, in a conceptual rather than mere geographical or administrative sense, was a process that began in the late nineteenth century and was accentuated under the impact of Zionist settlement. The unique status of the country within the general mandate system—a consequence of the Balfour Declaration—forced attention to its distinct identity. The rise of Arab nationalism in the aftermath of the world war, on the other hand, reaching a climax with the independent Arab government headed by Emir Faysal in Damascus in 1918–20, created an alternative focus for national identification. The early years of the British period, then, saw a struggle between these two tendencies. Local Palestinian-Arab patriotic nationalism (*wataniyya*) competed with, but was also embedded within, general pan-Arab nationalism (*qawmiyya*). The two foci of identity were not mutually exclusive organizing principles of identity. They reflected varying emphases and priorities rather than irreconcilable differences.

The establishment of an Arab national government in Syria was seen by many as a prelude to national independence in the entire region. Consequently, numerous Syrian, Palestinian, and Iraqi activists flocked to Damascus to bolster the new regime against European threats to its sovereignty. Of particular concern were the French, who were strictly opposed to Arab independence. They considered Syria (in addition to Lebanon, over which they had already established control) as part of their zone of influence, in accordance with their wartime 1916 Sykes-Picot agreements with the British. The division of the Arab lands of the Middle East between Britain and France in the aftermath of the world war was detrimental to the prospects of a unified Arab government. It created inevitable splits between the concerns and interests of the various constituencies of the Faysal government. External factors operated against a background of internal tensions and clashes between different regional factions; Arab unity was thus made difficult to achieve in practice, though it was retained in principle as the foremost goal at the level of identity politics (Muslih 1988: 115–29; see also Muslih 1991 for a more focused discussion of internal Arab factors).

The first General Syrian Congress, convening in Damascus in July 1919, became an arena for political debates and clashes between different nationalist factions. The result was a victory for the advocates of an inclusive Arab nationalism within which Palestine was seen as part of the Syrian and Arab homeland. The resolution adopted by the congress, which claimed to be speaking for Christians, Muslims, and Jews, expressed its opposition to the Zionist demand that "the southern part of out country, i.e., Palestine, be made a National Home for the Jews, and that Jews be allowed to immigrate to any part of our country, as they have not the least claim thereto." It went on to distinguish Zionism from Judaism by asserting that "our brethren the Jews, who originally inhabited the country, shall have the same rights and be subject to the same obligations as ourselves" (quoted in Mogannam 1937: 119).

The pan-Arab tendency was significant among political activists in Palestine itself at the time, though political organization there started with a strong focus on local concerns. Muslim-Christian Associations were established in various cities in 1918 to protest the implications of the Balfour Declaration. They called on the British authorities to take indigenous rights into consideration and refrain from determining the future of the country without soliciting the opinion of the Arab population (Muslih 1988: 107–9). They regarded the country as Arab in terms of the identity of its inhabitants, land ownership, and the language most commonly spoken by the people (Kayyali 1979: 57–58). A large number of organizations and individuals signed a petition on November 8, 1918, identifying themselves as "Arabs, Muslims and Christians" and claiming Palestine as "the Holy Land of our Fathers and the graveyard of our ancestors," a country "which had been inhabited by the Arabs for long ages who loved it and died in defending it." At the same time that they rejected the idea of a Jewish National Home in the country, the petitioners asserted their desire "to live with our brothers the Jews of Palestine in peace and happiness and with equal rights" (quoted in Lesch 1979: 86).

The point of most interest emerging from these documents is the coexistence of religious, ethnic, and territorial principles as bases of identification. The first two principles singled out Jews as religiously and ethnically distinct. The only basis, in fact, for constructing a national entity uniting Muslims and Christians and excluding Jews was the common Arab ethnic identity of the former two groups. This identity was not shared with Jews, not even with those who were Arabic speakers. The exclusionary ethnic character of historical Judaism (perceived by its own adherents, as well as by others, as a people religion, unlike Christianity and Islam, which remained open to people of various backgrounds) made Jews distinct in more than merely a religious sense. The third basis of identity, that of a Palestine-bounded territorial nationalism, was open in principle to the Jews residing in the territory. The indigenous nature of the Jewish community of Palestine, however, was in a steady process of decline as immigration (inspired by Zionism and religion) became an even more important source of population growth toward the late nineteenth century. In effect, this development led to excluding the option of a broad territorially based national identity. Jews were seen as distinct at multiple levels of identity, with few cross-cutting affiliations between them and Arabs in terms of religion, language, and history.

The differences and tensions among the (not mutually exclusive) national, territorial, and religious components of Palestinian-Arab identity have never been resolved. They have become its permanent feature, with some of its elements being submerged only to resurface at another point in time. Identity formation is a process that may involve shifting foci rather than the necessary emergence of one overriding principle at the expense of all others. While the boundaries between the Jewish and Arab identities maintained their rigid character throughout the period, the internal boundaries within these groups on religious and ethnic grounds were more flexible and open to contestation and change. In more recent times, the same trend manifested itself in the move of Palestinian political consciousness from a strong focus on pan-Arab nationalism in the 1950s to a territorial emphasis in the late 1960s, with the aftermath of the June 1967 War and the rise of the Palestine Liberation Organization. The local dimension was powerfully reasserted in the Intifadah of the late 1980s, but lost some ground to a resurgent Islamic focus in the early 1990s, with a brief interlude of greater concern with pan-Arabism during the Gulf crisis of 1990–91.

It is significant in this respect that even as the Muslim-Christian Associations were expressing opposition to Zionism and the Balfour Declaration as repugnant and prejudicial to the interests of the Arab inhabitants and their historical links to the specific territory of Palestine, their early 1919 Jerusalem congress adopted resolutions in which they demanded that "Palestine be considered as an integral part of Syria, from which we were never severed, and with which we are united in race, religion, language and economics." On the basis of that assertion, they went on to insist that "our territory, Palestine, be attached to the Independent Arab Government of Syria within an Arab Union" (quoted in Mogannam 1937: 116).

The idea of Palestine as southern Syria was never universally accepted. It encountered resistance by some forces among the urban elite in Jerusalem as well as other cities because it reflected a power struggle within the movement between older activists whose local power was well established and younger and more militant activists who stood to gain from unity with a Syrian regime controlled by their like-minded peers (Porath 1974: 70–85). The appeal of Arab nationalism was much wider than that of providing activists with positions of influence, however. Its power was primarily derived from patriotic sentiments and pride in the first Arab independent government as well as from strategic thinking motivated by fears of Zionism. Palestinians frequently looked for their defense to larger frameworks, the Ottoman Empire and Arab nationalism, each of which was seen in its time as a defensive shield capable of warding off the British-Zionist incursion (Muslih 1991).

As Kamil al-Dajani, a Palestinian activist from Jaffa, argued, "Syria would serve as a wider protective circle from which we [the Palestinians] could derive the strength to fight against the Zionist onslaught" (quoted in Muslih 1988: 186). This logic made sense at the time, but affiliation with Syria, and with Arab nationalism in general, could and did have opposite effects as well. The willingness of the

Hashemite family (headed by the two brothers Faysal and 'Abdullah) to reach agreements with the Zionist leadership, and to compromise on what they regarded as narrow Palestinian interests for the sake of their own larger vision of Arab unity, was a preview of the potential dangers Arab nationalism held for Palestinian national concerns. Pan-Arab national identity was open to multiple interpretations at the leadership as well as at the grassroots level.

In any event, the fortunes of pan-Syrian and pan-Arab unity as a practical organizing principle, not merely an abstract ideal, were not long-lasting. The collapse of the Faysal government with the capture of Damascus by French troops in 1920 forced Palestinians to redirect their attention to the local scene. The defeat of Arab nationalist forces in Syria was but one aspect of the overall stabilization of the postwar situation in the Middle East. The various international committees and conferences that convened under the auspices of the League of Nations to deal with conflicting claims to the region generally deferred to British and French interests. The legal, political, and scholarly debates over the validity of the contradictory wartime commitments made by the British to their European allies, to Arab nationalists, and to Zionists continued unabated. (See Antonius 1965 for a survey from an Arab nationalist perspective.) In practice, though, the status of Palestine was settled by the late 1920 San Remo conference, which made Britain the mandatory power for Palestine. This resolution was ratified by the League of Nations in 1922.

The Mandate for Palestine granted international legitimacy to the creation of Palestine/Israel as a distinct political entity within boundaries which persisted until 1948. Pan-Arab nationalism continued to hold great appeal for Palestinians, who have referred to themselves as the Palestinian-Arab *people*, a part of the larger Arab *nation*, ever since. Only rarely, however, has Arab nationalism reached a position as the principal component of Palestinian identity; its changing fortunes never allowed it to displace the ethnic-territorial component altogether. While indigenous identity fluctuated between general and territorially specific ethnic nationalism in Palestine/Israel, it always retained its clear separation from settler identity. In South Africa, however, the less rigid boundaries of indigenous identities allowed more interpenetration between settlers' and indigenous people's identity formation processes.

The Mandate, the Jewish People, and the Jewish Community

The mandate incorporated the Balfour Declaration and recognized "the historical connection of the Jewish people with Palestine . . . [as] the grounds for reconstituting their national home [there]" (preamble, League of Nations 1922: 2). It recognized the World Zionist Organization as a public agency entitled to represent the interests of the Jewish population, facilitate Jewish immigration into the country, and assist the British administration in its National Home efforts (articles 4 and 6, p. 3). At the same time, the mandate called for the development of self-governing institutions for the country as a whole and for safeguarding the civil and religious rights of all inhabitants of the country irrespective of race and religion (article 2).

It established common citizenship and guaranteed equal rights to all, proclaiming that "no discrimination of any kind shall be made between the inhabitants of Palestine on the ground of race, religion or language" (article 15, p. 5). In this spirit it made English, Arabic, and Hebrew official languages (article 22, p. 8). It recognized religious communities and their rights to cultural autonomy, but did not grant recognition to Arabs (other than as non-Jews, Muslims, or Christians) and did not grant them political status *as a group* (not merely as individuals), similar to that given to the Jewish people. In this sense the mandate reinforced the basic asymmetry created by the Balfour Declaration between a unified national-religious Jewish group with a claim to the country, and fragmented group(s) of non-Jews who have civil rights of residence in, but not an internationally recognized claim to, the territory.

The development of Jewish political institutions was facilitated by the conditions created by the mandate. In addition to the World Zionist Organization and its agencies, officially in charge of representing the interests of the Jewish people, there were two other institutional networks affiliated with the Zionist movement though without directly falling under its control. The first was the labor movement with its parties, unions, cooperatives, and cultural associations organized in the framework of the Histadrut. The second set of institutions consisted of local civic and communal structures, such as the municipalities of Jewish settlements, the autonomous parliamentary and executive bodies of the community, and a host of other associations and parties whose constituency was the specific local Jewish population, as distinct from the Jewish people worldwide. (For tensions between the local and world Zionist organizations, see Horowitz and Lissak 1978: 42–49.)

In 1926, the local civic network was granted recognition by the government as a corporate body which was more than a religious community along the lines of the Ottoman *millet* system. It extended to cover the entire set of national institutions under the name of Knesset Israel (the Jewish community); membership in it, save for some exceptions, was compulsory. Its most important components were the parliament, Asefat ha-Nivharim (Delegates' Assembly), which elected the Ha-Vaad ha-Leumi (the National Executive) (Rubinstein 1976: 151–95). The Parliament defined itself in its first meeting of October 1920 as "the supreme institution for handling the public and national affairs of the Jewish people in Palestine [Eretz Israel] and its only representative internally and externally" (quoted in Atiash 1963: 33). It elected the National Executive to manage its affairs and declared that "the Jewish community in Palestine accepts the authority of the World Zionist Organization in everything to do with the establishment of the National Home" (34).

The formation of political institutions representative of the Jewish population as a whole was not a smooth process. Two other foci of Jewish identity, religion and ethnicity, affected the way the national-communal institutions were composed. Orthodox Jews, especially strong in Jerusalem, refused to accept the authority of secular institutions which advanced a concept of Judaism as a national, rather than religious, identity (Friedman 1978). Many of them boycotted the elections to the Delegates' Assembly and even withdrew from the community altogether. Although they won the right not to fall under the authority of the organized community, over the objections of the latter, their defiance did not amount to a serious challenge to the national institutions. Their numbers were few, and their weight in the Jewish population was constantly diminishing with the increase in secular immigration into the country. The other challenge was that posed by some of the oriental Jewish communities; they did not reject national organization as such, but wanted to modify it so as to increase their representation as groups and not only as individuals. Debates over forms of representation were not conclusively settled until the end of the period, but the legitimacy (among Jews) and viability of the strong political center created in the framework of the mandate were well established by then (Horowitz and Lissak 1978: 37–41).

As early as 1922, when the British government published its official policy statement known as the Churchill White Paper, the Jewish community appeared to have enjoyed a large degree of autonomous organization with "its own political organs; an elected assembly for the direction of its domestic concerns; elected councils in the towns; and an organization for the control of its schools. It has elected Chief Rabbinate and Rabbinical Council for the direction of its religious affairs. Its business is conducted in Hebrew as a vernacular language, and a Hebrew press serves its needs. It has its distinctive intellectual life and displays considerable economic activity. This community, then, with its town and country population, its political, religious and social organisations, its own language, its own customs, its own life, has in fact 'national' characteristics" (Palestine 1922: 19; see also an evaluation of Jewish cultural developments in Palestine 1925: 38).

This description was not written as a disinterested observation but was part of an argument by the British for the continued implementation of policies treating Palestine as a special case in which political principles applicable elsewhere—the right to self-determination, representative government, and majority rule—were rendered invalid. British policies created the legal framework for some of these autonomous developments, the results of which were then used to justify these very same policies. The issue here, in any event, is not the extent to which the Jewish community had acquired an autonomous national character by that time, but the political implications of its development. All sides were similarly convinced that the new Zionist-dominated Jewish community and its institutions were distinct from the rest of society and that they represented a force for change. They disagreed on the desirability of such change, the prospects that were opened as a result of it, and the rights and liabilities these imposed on different segments of the population.

The Zionist Organization, speaking for a minority seeking to establish a secure and legitimate position in the country, adopted language that emphasized the supposed benefits to Arabs from the growing Jewish presence. It declared that "the two brother nations, Jews and Arabs, working together in peace and harmony, are destined to bring about the cultural and economic revival of the awakening peoples of the Near and Middle East" (Palestine 1922: 154). It further praised Jewish settlement as having changed "waste areas into flourishing gardens," and "sandy plains" in which "only the herds of the wandering Bedouins grazed" into "fertile fields and colonies" which provided work and food for many thousands of neighboring non-Jews (154). As local Zionist officials made clear, however, such cooperation was possible only within the framework of Jewish demographic and political predominance. They saw no room for an Arab national home in the same territory as that of the Jewish national home. Their argument was that only after a large number of Jews had entered the country, and built up their civilization and culture, could the population be deemed fit by their experience and political judgment to rule themselves by a representative government (see the statement of David Eder, acting chairman of the Zionist Commission in Palestine, in Palestine 1921: 57).

The British largely adopted this logic. The rationale for their policies was articulated by Lord Balfour, who argued in an internal Foreign Office memorandum that there was no symmetry between Jewish and Arab rights, as "Zionism, be it right or wrong, good or bad, is rooted in age-long traditions, in present needs, in future hopes, of far profounder import than the desires and prejudices of the 700,000 Arabs who now inhabit that ancient land" (memorandum addressed to Lord Curzon, 11/8/1919, in Ingrams 1972: 74). Herbert Samuel, the first British high commissioner for Palestine, made similar points. In a report submitted in 1921 he counterposed "the legitimate aspirations of the Jewish race throughout the world in relation to Palestine" with "a full protection of the rights of the existing population." Fourteen million Jews have a right to ask that "this home [Palestine] should possess national characteristics in language and customs, in intellectual interests, in religious and political institutions," though the degree to which these aspirations could be fulfilled "is conditioned by the rights of the present inhabitants" (quoted in Esco 1947: 275–76).

This definition of the situation, echoing Zionist arguments, was the crucial element in dispute—the source of the problem as far as Palestinians were concerned. The Zionist movement, the British government, and the League of Nations all operated in the framework of the Western discourse of the "Jewish question" as an international issue that should be of prime importance as far as the question of Palestine was concerned. Palestinian Arabs, in contrast, regarded the rights and privileges of the local inhabitants of the specific territory of Palestine/Israel as the focus of consideration. From their perspective there were no fourteen million Jews (overshadowing the 700,000 Arabs in the territory) with national rights to the country, but at most the 100,000 Jews who actually resided there at the time.

The point Arab representatives contested most fundamentally in that state of affairs was the introduction of a totally foreign element, in their view, into the picture. They regarded Zionism as an illegitimate external element with which no reconciliation was possible "because the immigrants dumped upon the country from different parts of the world are ignorant of the language, customs, and character of the Arabs, and enter Palestine by the might of England against the will of the people. . . . Nature does not allow the creation of a spirit of cooperation between two peoples so different, and it is not to be expected that the Arabs would bow to such a great injustice" (Palestine 1922: 28).

The indigenous pre-Zionist Jewish community was not seen as foreign, but its weight in the total population constantly diminished as Jewish immigration continued to increase and became the major source of population growth. The demographic and cultural marginalization of Arabic-speaking and native-born Jews reduced any intercommunal affiliations and made the overlapping of ethnic origin, language, religion, and cultural identity among members of each of the Jewish and Arab groups more pronounced. Consequently, the boundaries between the communities became even more rigid than they had already been. This can be appreciated when seen against the South African situation in which fragmented indigenous identities and the development of an intercommunal cultural syncretism were less conducive to (though without precluding) clear distinctions between indigenous and foreign elements in the population.

The circumstances in which Palestinian Arabs found themselves were anomalous as compared to the legal status of Arabs in other countries; their demographic majority was not translated into commensurate political power, even if only a potential one. (See Boustany 1936 for a critique of the disadvantaged position of Palestinians within the general mandate system.) This was due to the special position of the Jewish community under the mandate. Democracy as a form of majority rule was rejected by the Zionist movement and by the British. As the Jewish nationalist leader Ze'ev Jabotinsky put it in 1918, Zionists "do not want to have a normal constitution here, since the Palestine situation is not normal. The majority of its 'electors' [meaning Jews all over the world] have not yet returned to the country. If there is a normal constitution here, responsible to the [Arab] 'majority,' then the majority of us would never enter . . . the country" (quoted in Caplan 1978: 151).

A more explicit rejection of the concept of majority rule and self-determination under the prevailing demographic conditions is found in Jabotinsky's 1923 article, "The Morality of the Iron Wall." He argued there that since "the civilized world" had recognized that Jews all over the world were in principle citizens of Palestine and had the right to return to it, the local population should not be allowed to block their return in the name of democracy. Democracy should be premised on the existence of two national groups: the Arab one residing in the territory itself, and the Jewish one forcibly removed from the territory in ancient times and now seeking to return. The latter among the two groups is larger, thus making Zionist principles compatible with democracy as majority rule (Jabotinsky 1969). Similar arguments for collective group rights were advanced by labor leaders who regarded parliamentary rule as incompatible with the right of the Jewish community to maintain its independence of language, education, settlement, family, and other national institutions (Gorny 1985: 178–84). The suspension of democracy in practice, not in principle, was defended by Ben-Gurion, who argued in 1924 that "any political program accepted now must logically correspond to the current balance of forces. Such a program would of necessity work against us. We have to evaluate the various forces not only according to their current weight but with a view to the future" (Ben-Gurion 1931: 73). This line of thought was implicitly accepted by the British authorities, who devised constitutional arrangements premised on the existence of a distinct Jewish community whose political autonomy should not be submerged by the Arab majority.

The Boundaries of Identity

Given those conditions, Palestinian Arabs were faced with a need to devise a strategy to deal with their new political status. The Third Palestine Arab Congress which convened in Haifa in December 1920 was the first congress to deal exclusively with Palestinian affairs rather than Arab ones, and thus to confront the specific character of the national struggle in the context of mandatory Palestine. Its resolutions reflected the change of focus, advocating Palestinian-Arab nationalism to the exclusion, but not negation, of general Syrian and Arab nationalism. The congress called on Britain to establish a "national [*wataniyya*] government in Palestine responsible to a representative council, to be elected by the Arabic speaking people who were living in Palestine at the outbreak of the Great War" (quoted in Mogannam 1937: 127). It emphasized the national unity of Muslims and Christians *as Arabs*. It modeled its demands on the example of Iraq and Trans-Jordan, thereby refusing to bestow special status on Palestine as a result of the Jewish National Home policy. It rejected the validity of the Balfour Declaration and its implications—the official role of the Zionist Organization, the right to Jewish immigration, and the decision to grant Hebrew an official language status.

The rejection of Hebrew was linked to an argument over the name of the country. The English (Palestine) and Arabic (Filastin) names were not controversial, but the Hebrew name gave rise to a heated debate. Jewish representatives argued for Eretz Israel, as the country has always been referred to in Jewish tradition; Arab representatives argued for Palestina. The resulting compromise was Palestina (EI), using the Hebrew initials in parentheses. This did not satisfy everybody, and in 1925 Jamal al-Husayni, a prominent Arab activist, submitted a petition in which he argued that he and other Arabs found offensive that they "cannot exercise the legal right of sending letters by post without purchasing and using a document [i.e., stamp] in which their country is described as the Land of Israel" (Memo 33, in Government of Palestine 1937: 159). Not surprisingly, the petition was dismissed by the court.

While the rejection of Zionism by the Palestinian-Arab national movement was very clear, the assertive principle in which name it was rejected was more ambiguous. It is instructive to look at a communication by the Arab leadership in which the coexistence of territorial and ethnic principles, with some religious overtones, is evident in the formation of Palestinian-Arab national identity. In March 1921 the Arab Executive Committee, the congress's leadership body, submitted a deputation to a British conference on Middle Eastern policy held in Jerusalem and Cairo. In it, the Executive asserted the right to speak as "a true representative of Palestine" since it enjoyed support of "all the live aspects of the nation . . . from Dan to Beersheba" (Colonial Office 1921: 142). The nation was geographically bound, not restricted by any ethnic criteria and not extended to include members of the Arab ethnic group from beyond the boundaries of the country. The deputation went on to deny any political validity to religious differences, bringing as evidence the prior acceptance of Jews as equal in Ottoman times and the existing national solidarity between Muslims and Christians.

At the same time, the Executive asserted that "there can be no question that Palestine belongs legally to the Arabs. They inherited it from their ancestors and have been occupying it for more than twenty centuries. The Jews saw, knew and accepted this fact" (Colonial Office 1921: 145). Almost imperceptibly, the nation that had previously been defined in territorial terms acquired an ethnic character. From being the possession of "the people of Palestine" it came to be the property of a segment of that people (though admittedly by far the majority segment). As the document continues, arguments phrased in terms of universal principles of national heritage and historical rights give way to accusations against Jews in particular, appealing to the real or imagined, and presumably shared, anti-Jewish sentiments of the British. Jews are rejected as the "most active advocates of destruction," harboring "pernicious motives . . . towards civilisation" (146), sentiments expressed in their promotion of Bolshevism and attested to by the Protocols of the Elders of Zion.

The demands made by the Executive at the end of the document again reflect a territorial nonethnic nationalism, calling for the formation of "a national government . . . which shall be responsible to a Parliament elected by the Palestinian people who existed in Palestine before the war" (150). This document, indicative of the political tone of the entire period, serves to demonstrate ambiguities in Palestinian definitions of identity. (Similar themes run through other official statements of Palestinian-Arab positions; see in particular Palestine Arab Delegation 1922 and Palestine 1922.) It is crucial that the different definitions rarely if ever explicitly included the majority of Jews of immigrant origins. The changes in identity boundaries took place within specific constraints and were not random.

The contestation over the meanings and boundaries of Palestinian identity was particularly pertinent to issues of self government and political representation. Within the general insistence on a representative government as the only legitimate form of majority rule, the national movement rejected a proposed legislative council which was to be an advisory body subordinate to the government and operating within the framework of the mandate. Only half of the council members were to be elected (on a confessional basis), and the rest were to be government officials. The movement felt that such an arrangement would be premised on the principles of the Balfour Declaration, which they continued to reject. The British clarification that the declaration did not "contemplate that Palestine as a whole should be converted into a Jewish National Home" but only that such a home "should be found *in Palestine*" (Palestine 1922: 18) did nothing to mollify Arab opinion. Consequently, the movement campaigned for a boycott of the elections scheduled for 1923. The boycott was widely obeyed, and only 20 percent of the Arab electors were selected, rendering the council idea inoperative. An advisory council, proposed as an alternative by the British, did not fare much better when most Arab nominees withdrew from it shortly after its establishment (Lesch 1979: 179–86).

In the same year further attempts were made by the government to involve Arabs in governing the country by establishing an Arab Agency which would have "a position exactly analogous" to that of the Jewish Agency with regard to the interests of their respective constituencies (Palestine 1923: 5). Unlike the Zionist Organization, the proposed Arab Agency would not have had any international status and explicit colonizing and settlement purposes. Its creation would have established political parity under conditions in which Arabs were more than 85 percent of the population. The proposal was rejected with the argument that "the Arabs, having never recognized the status of the Jewish Agency, have no desire for the establishment of an Arab Agency on the same basis" (10). Furthermore, they as "owners of the country cannot see their way to accept a proposal which tends to place them on the same footing with the alien Jews. In addition, the name of Arab Agency would make them feel they are strangers in their own country" (response by M. K. al-Husayni, president of the Arab Executive Committee, to the British high commissioner in November 1923, in Lesch 1979: 187).

Advisory bodies of the sort proposed by the British were perceived by the movement as substitutes for independence, rather than as truly national structures that would help prepare the ground for it. In view of this consistent opposition, the British concluded in November 1923 that they "have no alternative but to continue to administer the country in conformity with their undertakings, even though they have to forgo the assistance that they had hoped to obtain from the Arab community" (Palestine 1923: 12). As a result, mandatory Palestine was ruled by a state bureaucracy not limited by any representative institutions conveying the opinions and demands of the population as a whole (Wasserstein 1978; see His Britannic Majesty's Government 1947 for an account of various failed attempts to form consultative and representative bodies).

The refusal of the Palestinian-Arab national movement to grant any legitimacy to the Balfour Declaration, or to accept any arrangement based on principles other than those of majority rule, forced the British in practice to enable both Jews and Arabs "to develop their own separate representative institutions." This served "to increase the enstrangement between the Arab and Jewish communities in Palestine, which became more and more separate political, social and economic entities, bound together by no ties other than the political will of the British government" (Wasserstein 1978: 130). Neither of the contending parties had direct institutionalized access to the state *as a group*, though many members of either group worked in the administration *as individuals*. Both groups focused, rather, on advancing their separate state formation processes, preparing for the struggle for political control once British rule was terminated. This was particularly true for the Jewish community, whose minority status moved it to construct alternative communal institutions with a view to future political independence. Arabs were more dependent on the government for administrative, educational, and political resources in the absence of official corporate elected bodies (Miller 1985: 49–62). The contrast in this respect with the South African situation is clear. South African settlers did not build their own separate institutions, independent and outside of colonial state structures, since state authority was premised on the subordination of "the natives" within its boundaries and the entrenchment of settler domination.

Palestinian-Arab Political Institutions

Nationalist politics found an organizational expression with the Palestine Arab Congress, which convened several times during the 1920s. Its permanent national leadership body—the Arab Executive Committee—was headed by Musa Kazim al-Husayni, a senior public official who had had a distinguished career in the Ottoman administration. The Executive included members from all parts of the country, Muslims and Christians, apparently chosen to enhance the representative character of the movement (see Lesch 1979: 91 for a list). The leadership met on a more regular basis between congresses to discuss courses of action, issue statements, and meet government officials. In all these activities they were effectively acting as the representative body of the political aspirations of the Arab population, though without being granted formal recognition by the British authorities to that effect. Although they were never elected directly by their constituency, the positions they advocated largely corresponded to those of the Arab population at large.

At the local level the movement was based on the Muslim-Christian Associations which gradually but unevenly established branches throughout the country. Centralization at the national level was not tight, though the more provincial associations were generally dominated by the larger Jerusalem, Jaffa, and Nablus branches. The national headquarters operated from Jerusalem and provided the basic framework for the movement, attempting to inform, instruct, and coordinate between local organizations. Despite internal conflicts between and within branches, and weaknesses in their ability to mobilize and act in unison as a mass organization, during the 1920s the movement took steps toward the creation of national-level political structures (Porath 1974: 125–28; 274–93).

In some places local organizations acquired a sectarian character at variance with the national norm. In Haifa, for example, there were separate Muslim and Christian associations which coordinated their activities but continued to maintain separate structures. In other places, tensions and the legacy of latent competition and conflict between Muslims and Christians, dating back to Ottoman times, made the construction of a united Arab front more difficult as religious-confessional solidarities were still powerful. Conscious attempts by the leadership to avert a splitting of the movement along these lines were generally successful insofar as no significant public clashes ever took place on an intra-Arab communal basis.

Nationalist discourse was dominant in the public sphere. It was expressed in the composition of national institutions and official delegations, and in the content of policy declarations that rarely deviated from nationalist orthodoxy, though without necessarily reflecting opinion at the grassroots level. In an important symbolic gesture, the Muslim-Christian Association of Nablus changed its name in 1931 to the Arab National Association, expressing dissatisfaction with the explicitly sectarian, nonnational nature of the previous name (Porath 1974: 277). This and other developments, such as the foundation of the nationalist Istiqlal Party in the following year, coincided with the rise of the Supreme Muslim Council to political prominence in the late 1920s at the expense of the secular Arab Executive Committee. Palestinian identity formation, then, was not a unidirectional process, moving necessarily from sectional to more comprehensive identities. Multiple foci of identity, partly overlapping and partly competing, frequently coexisted in a state of tension.

The extent to which nationalism was widespread among the masses, and the particular interpretations of its meanings, were disputed among observers. As early as 1921 the Haycraft Commission of Inquiry claimed that the anti-Zionist position was "well nigh universal amongst the Arabs, and is not confined to any particular class" (Palestine 1921: 45). The commission went on to assert that "practically the whole of the non-Jewish population was united in hostility to the Jews" (50), without bothering to make distinctions among categories of Jews and their relations to the Zionist movement. On the other hand, High Commissioner Herbert Samuel reported in 1925 that the resolute anti-Zionist position of the Arab leadership was losing ground among the population because they failed to adjust to the new political circumstances (Palestine 1925: 43–47). And yet in 1929 a new outbreak of hostilities was seen by the Shaw Commission to have united Arabs (especially the Muslims among them) on the basis of "racial animosity [toward Jews] . . . consequent upon the disappointment of their political and national aspirations and fear for their economic future" (Palestine 1930b: 150).

Palestinian-Arab attitudes can be conceptualized, as indicated earlier in the chapter, as a combination of ethnic, territorial, and religious-confessional nationalism, the common denominator among which was the rejection of the process of Zionist settlement. Given this lack of clear focus of indigenous identity, and given that all Zionists were Jews—though not all Jews were Zionist—it is not surprising that the boundaries between anti-Zionist and (ethnic and religious) anti-Jewish agitation and activities were difficult to maintain among the masses, although the leadership usually kept to the more strictly defined and acceptable anti-Zionist politics. In practice, the distinctions among the various components of national consciousness were hardly meaningful; the people against whom Palestinian-Arab mobilization was directed were clearly identifiable as Jews, regardless of whether their Jewishness was understood in a political, national, ethnic, or religious sense.

Indigenous consciousness were bolstered by extensive nationalist-oriented cultural activity. Of particular significance in this respect were literature, primarily aimed at urban audiences but reaching beyond them, cultural clubs and discussion societies, and formal education emphasizing the Arabic language and Arab history through the use of textbooks from other countries, newspapers, and popular writing (Abu-Ghazaleh 1972; see also the observations by the Palestine Royal Commission 1937b: 337–40). In all these spheres a particular sense of history, cultivated for its own sake as well as to reinforce contested claims to the country, was in evidence. The search for historical roots and proofs of antiquity resulted in a preoccupation with the specific histories of towns and regions and in the development of "a kind of land survey where the authors seek to repeople the terrain with the thick presence of ancestors" (Khalidi 1981: 68). The threat of the country's takeover by the Zionist movement and fear for the future led people to seek reassurance in the Arab past as a way of reasserting the present against threats to its continued existence.

Intercommunal Political Interpenetration

The move to consolidate national consciousness did not dissolve the different strands of secular (Arab) and religious-confessional (Islamic) nationalism. These were difficult to separate because most Arabs were Muslims and they saw no contradiction between the two identities. The legacy of prenationalist tensions gave Zionist activists an opportunity to intervene and attempt to direct indigenous identity formation processes against those elements who seemed more dangerous opponents. As a member of the Palestine Zionist Executive defined the goal of intervention in Arab politics, "there are many ways of doing political work among the Arabs, and all of them point to one goal: to strengthen the forces and organisation of the moderates and weaken the extremists" (quoted in Caplan 1978: 127).

There were two basic positions among the Jewish leadership with regard to intervention in Arab politics. The majority were convinced that Jewish and Arab political goals were incompatible and attempts to bridge the gap were futile. In a debate on the Arab Question at the meeting of the Provisional Council of the

Jewish community in 1919, Ben-Gurion, speaking from that perspective, argued that "there is no solution to this question. No solution! There is a gulf, and nothing can fill this gulf. . . . We, as a nation, want this country to be ours; the Arabs, as a nation, want this country to be theirs" (quoted in Caplan 1978: 42). By definition, this approach excluded any notion of a comprehensive territorially based identity; it was not an option even worth explicit rejection. Furthermore, compromises on strategic and not just tactical national principles, even while maintaining clear and separate identities, were also excluded.

The second approach, associated with the "Arab work" orchestrated by veteran activist Haim Kalvaryski, saw a potential opening in the ambiguities of Palestinian-Arab national identity. Those interested in this approach did not usually think in terms of constructing a comprehensive identity embracing Jews and Arabs alike, or dissolving in any way the external identity boundaries between them. They believed, rather, that it was possible to prevent the formation of a monolithic Arab camp united by adherence to the tenets of Palestinian-Arab secular nationalism. To achieve that goal they were willing to consider some compromises on Zionist goals. In a way, they attempted to return to the prepolitical times of the Ottoman Empire, a period indeed characterized by relatively good working relations at the level of daily life between the Jewish agricultural colonies and their Arab neighbors. The underlying assumption of this approach was that modern secular nationalism had not yet taken hold on the Arab masses whose life continued to be shaped primarily by parochial identities at the family, tribal, village, and religious-confessional levels. Nationalism was seen as an instrument in the hands of the urban-based landed Arab elite to further their social and economic interests.

Using personal connections and special funds given by the Zionist Organization and the Jewish Colonization Association, Kalvaryski managed to create in November 1921 a Muslim National Association, designed "to weaken the baneful influence of the Muslim-Christian Association" (quoted in Caplan 1978: 100). The power of Islamic solidarity seemed to some Zionist officials an effective weapon against nationalism. The Muslim-Christian Associations were portrayed as dominated by Christians and therefore as serving interests foreign to the Muslim majority of the Arab population (Porath 1974: 216–18; see also Johnson 1982: 22–24 for the conservative political implications of notable-dominated Islam). Many in the Jewish community believed at the time that Christian intellectuals and professionals were apprehensive of the competition offered by skilled Jews; fears of a Jewish-Muslim alliance relegating Christians to an isolated minority position thus led the latter, in this view, to initiate the nationalist movement in order to avert such developments. (See the memoirs of Judge Gad Frumkin, in Assaf 1970: 84–85.) In retrospect, given our knowledge of the importance Islam would acquire in the national movement of the 1930s, this idea seems far-fetched but it was common at the time. It serves to show that religion, like nationalism, can be interpreted and used in different and even directly opposite ways.

The strategy of fostering political divisions among Arabs did not enjoy much success. Regardless of the historical legacies of envy and competition, and tensions among Arabs of different religious and communal persuasions, the ethnic exclusivity of the Zionist movement was not conducive to any strategic political and ideological alliances with significant sections of the Arab population. The few instances of tactical collaboration between Zionist institutions and Arab forces opposed to the nationalist leadership had almost invariably been backed up financially by Zionist funds and would not have been at all feasible without monetary rewards to the concerned Arab activists. Furthermore, these contacts had to be hidden and were denied when exposed for fear of compromising the position of collaborators among Arabs.

The ability of the Zionist movement to manipulate to some extent the internal affairs of the Palestinian-Arab national movement stemmed from the contrast in the organizational character of the two movements. Zionists managed to build a dense network of mass voluntary civil and political organizations that derived their legitimacy from representing the Jewish community on its various tendencies. Palestinian Arabs lagged behind in developing mass-based, grassroots structures. The dominant style of operations during the 1920s was what Lesch (1979) terms mobilization from above. The Arab community exhibited a degree of politicization and organization that was lower as compared to that of the Jewish community. This was the case not because Arabs showed little interest in politics, but because their social and political structures were less conducive than national Jewish structures were to sustained organizational mobilization.

The obvious difference between the two communities was the indigenous character of the Arab population. Palestinian Arabs did not arrive in the country as a result of having taken a conscious decision to relocate, as the majority of Jews did. Arab existence in Palestine was natural, to themselves and to others, in the sense that Arabs had resided in the country for many centuries, without needing to do anything in order to assert their presence under normal circumstances. The circumstances created with the transition to British rule were not "normal," however. They led to rapid changes on an unprecedented scale. Institutional spaces opened up where Ottoman state structures used to be. New civil, political, and religious institutions were created by the British government and the Jewish community, encouraging Palestinians to take initiative in order to claim their place, formulate their interests, and engage in their own institution building. Their capacity to do that successfully was not negligible, though less pronounced than that of settlers, and it seems considerable when compared to indigenous people's capacities in South Africa.

The Supreme Muslim Council

Even as Palestinian Arabs were creating nonsectarian national institutions, they continued to organize on a religious basis as well. This was especially true for Muslims, who had to create new structures to replace the defunct Ottoman institutions. Their most important communal organization, founded around the same time as the Arab Executive Committee, was the Supreme Muslim Council. The Islamic establishment of Palestine had been subordinated before 1917 to the Ottoman religious hierarchy headed by the Sheikh al-Islam in Istanbul. The most important institutions, the court system and *waqf* property, were controlled by the centralized religious bureaucracy in the capital. No administrative unit of Palestine existed prior to the dissolution of the empire; consequently, there was no national religious leadership with authority over the entire country. Furthermore, the direct incorporation of Muslims into the Ottoman state, with no mediating structures such as the *millets* of the religious minorities, left Muslims with no communal institutions at the national level (Porath 1974: 194–96). This created an institutional vacuum, which the British sought to fill in order to enlist the consent of Arabs through the creation of a counterweight to the role of the Zionist Organization in the life of the country, a role written into the text of the mandate itself.

The Supreme Muslim Council provided religious services and officially represented the particular interests of the Muslim community. In practice, its impact was much greater than that. As Muslims comprised the vast majority of the Arab population, about 90 percent of the total, their communal leadership possessed a great deal of potential political power. In addition, the council controlled such public institutions as mosques, courts, schools and welfare, landed property and finances, making it an employer of religious and lay officials, clerks and preachers, some of whom were actually on government payroll but under the council's influence (Kupferschmidt 1987: 59–63). In the absence of any Arab self-governing structures, the council became the most important institution run by the Palestinians themselves. Its authority and budget were ultimately derived from the government, but in managing its internal affairs a large degree of independence was evident, with hardly any outside interference by the British authorities and, of course, none by the Jewish community.

The tasks of the council were self-defined "to manage the affairs of the Muslim *waqfs*, the Shari'a justice and the works of piety and charity," but Amin al-Husayni, its president, added in a 1925 statement the need "to represent the Muslims of this country honourably and properly inside and outside the country" (quoted in Kupferschmidt 1987: 57). Under al-Husayni's leadership, the council indeed acquired such a representative role, moving beyond its administrative duties to become an important player in the political arena. In doing that it used the mosque, a traditional focus of social life, as a forum for political protest and for forging an Arab national identity with a pronounced Islamic core.

The political involvement of the religious establishment owed much to the persuasions and activities of al-Husayni. His career as the mufti of Jerusalem and the *rais al-'ulama*, president of the council, reflected the interplay among the multiple foci of Palestinian identity. Even before assuming any official position he had already gained prominence as a young political activist. Throughout his life he resolutely opposed Zionism from a Palestinian nationalist perspective, though the wider framework within which his patriotism was embedded fluctuated. Born in the 1890s to a distinguished religious-political family, he was educated in the spirit of Islamic reformism in the school of Rashid Rida in Egypt. At the beginning of the First World War he volunteered to join the Ottoman military and was trained as an officer, loyal to the Ottoman state that was defending Islam against Christianity (Mattar 1988: 10–11). His diaries from that time are filled with notes about his love for his country, and poems such as the one that proclaims: "This [Palestine] is my country and the country of my ancestors. I will sacrifice myself for the sake of its sons" (11). Islamic reformism, Ottoman loyalism, and Palestinian patriotism apparently reinforced each other at this early stage, as was the case with other activists and organizations. (See chapter 4 for a more detailed discussion of these trends.)

Disillusioned with Ottoman policies, al-Husayni left the army with the Arab Revolt of 1916 and joined the movement that sought to unite Palestine, Syria, and Iraq under the banner of Arab nationalism. After the war, in 1918, he founded together with other young Jerusalem activists the Arab Club (al-Nadi al-'Arabi), which was distinct from similar organizations in its strong focus on pan-Syrian unity (Jbara 1985: 28–29). The club was apparently an offshoot of a Syrian-based group, with contacts in Nablus, although the Jerusalem activists maintained their organizational independence (Muslih 1988: 167–68). It is also possible that al-Husayni was involved in preparations for armed struggle as a means of opposing Zionism (169–72). Of most significance in his (and many of his collagues') activities is that the same fundamental concerns over the future of Palestine that motivated their early involvement in politics remained prominent in their minds, although now articulated in terms of an Arab nationalist, rather than an Ottoman, discourse.

Al-Husayni's participation and leading role in nationalist-inspired demonstrations, one of which in 1920 was a prelude to armed clashes between Jews and Arabs, earned him a ten-year prison sentence for incitement to violence. He was forced to flee the country, only to return a few months later after having been pardoned by the British authorities. That incident bolstered his radical nationalist credentials, which, together with his family heritage, made him a promising candidate for senior positions. In the eyes of the British he was potentially useful, provided he consented to being co-opted, as symbolic proof that they were not acting in the Zionist interest and were willing to respect Arab rights. The terms of his co-optation, however, were contentious, and he proved himself to be far from a docile tool of the British authorities, their own calculations notwithstanding.

With the nomination of al-Husayni to the post of the mufti of Jerusalem in 1921, and the creation of the Supreme Muslim Council in 1922, he assumed the leadership of the religious establishment in the country as a whole. Although he was not involved for much of the 1920s in explicit political activities, in the sense of directly and publicly addressing the issues of Zionism and British rule, he was busy advocating the Palestinian cause in the world, primarily appealing to Muslim rulers and public opinion in the Middle East and India (Jbara 1985: 61–71). As early as 1922 the council sent a delegation to Mecca seeking support for their cause in the name of "the Islamic Palestine Nation that has been guarding al-Aqsa Mosque and the Holy Rock ever since 1300 years," warning the Muslim world that "the Holy Places are in great danger on account of the horrible Zionist aggressions" (quoted in Lesch 1979: 138; for other appeals of this nature see also 137–41; Kupferschmidt 1987: 187–220).

In addition to these national and religious activities al-Husayni sought to consolidate his personal and political power base relative to other forces in Palestinian society. This was the beginning of a protracted conflict pitting supporters of the council against opposition to its growing power. To a large extent it was an intra-elite fight between the Husayni family and their allies who headed the council and the Arab Executive on the one hand, and rivals who resented their political dominance on the other (Mattar 1988: 27–32). It was also a clash over institutional power between regional and factional interests, and over prestige and influence with the government. This clash became entangled with conflicts reflecting social antagonism and divisions and somewhat different (but mostly unarticulated, with no clear organizational expression) conceptions of patriotism, nationalism and religion.

Internal Conflict: The Opposition

Palestinian internal politics throughout the 1920s and 1930s were dominated by a factional conflict dividing them into two major camps, the *majlisiyyun* (council supporters), and the *mu'aridun* (oppositionists). The conflict operated on several levels, although here I focus only on the dimensions relevant for understanding identity formation processes (thus dismissing the explanatory power of the notions of personal jealousy and conspiracy theories used by Jbara 1985). The creation of a distinct Palestinian political-administrative unit by 1920 did not eliminate overnight the power of loyalties based on religion, region, and clan affiliation. The divisions between the supporters and opponents of the council, as the terms of the conflict came to be known, were not a direct continuation of the factional alignments of Ottoman times. New sources of friction were created with the change to British rule and were responsible for the form and content of the conflict. Frequently, at the local level, the more recent political clashes reflected, to some extent, the preexisting patterns of vertical segmentation that gave rise to clan rivalries and struggles over resources, cutting across communal and urban-rural divisions (Tamari 1982: 185–92).

One particular source of conflict was the centralization of the country. In the late Ottoman period the country was divided into three separate *sanjaks* (districts)—Jerusalem, Nablus, and Acre. The *sanjak* of Jerusalem enjoyed special status and was generally more important than the other two, though the latter were not controlled by it, nor did their social and political elites occupy a subordinate position. With the unification of the territory and naming Jerusalem the capital of the entire country, the leading families of the city acquired an elevated status relative to other urban elites. This development was opposed by some provincial elements who resented being subjected to "the whims of the Jerusalem effendies," as the Nablus historian Ihsan al-Nimr put it (quoted in Tamari 1982: 190). Many traditionally important families in regions other than Jerusalem—in terms of their wealth, prestige, and political power—joined the opposition (Arnon-Ohana 1981: 62–63). In some respects they saw affiliation with the opposition as a way of countering the dominance of Jerusalem and asserting their own claims to equal political influence. This was the case although the opposition itself was led by the Jerusalem family of Nashashibi, though in a decentralized manner. The opposition, however, never challenged explicitly or even implicitly the unification of the country, nor called for its breakup and a return to the earlier autonomous arrangements. The legacy of indigenous political divisions was not very strong, especially when compared to the equivalent South African political alignments, and the scope for divisive strategies on these grounds was consequently limited.

Another basis for political factionalism was the reluctance of traditional elites who had been staunch Ottoman loyalists to transfer their support to Arab nationalism. The Ottomans were no longer present, but the preference for a loosely centralized Islamic identity continued to manifest itself in the form of reluctance to support the brand of nationalism sponsored by the Arab Executive and the Supreme Muslim Council. Joining the opposition was thus a way of expressing reservations about the political changes that resulted from the world war and the dissolution of the Ottoman Empire. Traditional Palestinian elites were similar in this respect to the notables of Damascus, who attempted to obstruct radical pan-Arab nationalism in favor of a locally focused moderate version (Muslih 1988). In this case as well, open and outspoken rejection of nationalism was uncommon, though it was expressed by some, such as As'ad al-Shukayri from Acre, a senior religious official during Ottoman times who continued to be loyal to their ideals even after it became clear the empire would not return (Porath 1974: 208–13).

Following the clashes of 1921, most of the 1920s passed without open, large-scale political confrontation between Jews and Arabs. Internal divisions in Palestinian ranks did not disappear, but a temporary reconciliation between the opposing camps was achieved by the Seventh Palestine Arab Congress of 1928. All that was dramatically changed with the eruption of the struggle over prayer rights at the Jerusalem Wailing Wall in 1928 and the violent countrywide clashes of 1929. These events signaled not only the end of the relatively peaceful period preceding it, but also a shift toward greater emphasis on the Islamic component in Palestinian-Arab identity. This shift converged with the emergence of the Supreme Muslim Council as the most important Palestinian-Arab political organization, with aspirations to the leadership of the national movement as a whole.

The Wailing Wall Conflict

Islam was central to the collective identity of the Arabs of Palestine, only 10 percent of whom were Christian. Though the Arab Executive made an effort to represent both groups, sometimes even giving greater weight to Christians than their numbers would justify, at the popular level Islam and Arab nationalism were frequently conflated. This was especially the case in those parts of the country, such as Hebron and Nablus and many rural areas, where very few non-Muslim Arabs lived. Such conflation was not peculiar to Palestine, of course; it could be found throughout the Arab world. As far as the majority were concerned, the differences between the two identity components were not crucial because both forces confronted the same enemy—the Jewish-Zionist movement which was both religiously and ethnically alien to Arab national identity. In contrast, in South African identity politics, religion was a force bridging the gaps between settlers and indigenous people at some levels, while ethnicity acted to divide both groups internally rather than unify them against each other.

The Wailing Wall (al-Buraq in Arabic) and the adjacent Temple Mount (al-Haram al-Sharif) were simultaneously Islamic and Arab symbols, just as much as their significance for Jews was not only religious but national. The campaign to defend the area, and in particular the al-Aqsa mosque, from what was seen as the danger of falling under Jewish control, became a major cause for the political mobilization led by the Supreme Muslim Council in the late 1920s, both inside the country and outside it among foreign Arabs and Muslims (Porath 1974: 258–65; Jbara 1985: 77–96; Mattar 1988: 33–49). The campaign culminated with a Jewish nationalist demonstration to assert rights to the Wall and a Muslim counterdemonstration in early August 1929, leading to a series of violent attacks by Muslims on Jewish communities, especially Hebron and Safed, in which dozens of Jews were killed and hundreds of Arabs arrested by government forces.

These events became a major landmark in the development of the Israeli-Palestinian conflict. Amin al-Husayni emerged as the most important figure in the Palestinian national movement as a result of his leading role in the agitation and organization of the Wall campaign. (See Johnson 1982: 24–29 for an analysis which emphasizes the attempt by the Husayni faction to use religious symbolism to further its internal and external prestige and power.) By focusing on the sacred al-Aqsa mosque, al-Husayni was able to demonstrate vividly the dangers Zionism held for the Arabs of Palestine, especially but not only the Muslims among them. He was able to speak to the masses using accessible, concrete, and familiar symbols rather than abstract nationalist slogans such as the right to majority rule or self-determination, which did not have much mobilizing power at the emotional level.

The tone for the 1929 events was set by the Committee for the Defense of the Burak-el-Sharif. In November 1928 this organization submitted a statement to the General Moslem Conference presided over by al-Husayni in which it claimed that

"Whereas we, the population of the Holy Land, have been entrusted by God with the custody of this House and His Temple, we deem it our duty to submit to all our brethren in the East and West a statement of the danger which threatens this Mosque owing to the ambitions of the Jews to expropriate it from the hands of Moslems, God forbid" (Palestine 1930b: 32). The conference created the Society for the Protection of Moslem Holy Places to organize a campaign against Jewish designs to extend visiting and praying rights at the Wall. Over the next year, branches were established throughout the country. At the same time, nationalist Jews linked to the Zionist Revisionist Organization formed the Pro-Wailing Wall Committee to fight attempts "to rob a live nation of the last of its relics" and protest "the gross insult of our holy possessions and national and religious feelings" (50). Both sides combined nationalist and religious themes, but the Arab side enjoyed active support at the leadership level, whereas the Jewish side did not. (In fact the Jewish campaign was partly aimed at the internal leadership, which was seen as too moderate.)

The Islamic element was very pronounced at the popular level, but it played a more ambiguous role in the official (and therefore more oriented toward external acceptability) Arab version of the events of 1929, as conveyed in al-Husayni's evidence to the Shaw Commission of Inquiry. His testimony demonstrates an interesting combination of identity components, particularly important as it came from a major spokesperson for Palestinian-Arab nationalism. He began by claiming that in Palestine the Jews intended to take over the places holy to Christianity and Islam, and used as evidence an anti-Semitic French book titled *The Jewish Conspiracy against the Nations*. Muslims believed that the primary goal of the Zionists was "the Temple of Solomon which is and has been in possession of the Moslems for the last 13 centuries" (Palestine 1930a: 1.499; the temple had been at the same site as the al-Aqsa mosque). This general anti-Jewish assertion was qualified, however, by the explanation for his sense of alarm at the increase in Jewish visits to the Wall: "In previous years the visitors used to be orthodox old Jews; now excited [uniformed] young men came to visit it" (1.502). It was not Jewish religious identity—traditionally familiar and tolerated—that posed a threat to Islam, then, but a nationalist version of it, hitherto unknown in the country.

Moving from religious to nationalist concerns, al-Husayni went on to complain about British policy that aimed "at placing this country, which is an Arab country, under such . . . conditions as will make of it a home for another nation which will come from various parts of the world in order to compete with the actual inhabitants of the country and actually take their place" (Palestine 1930a: 1.514). The situation was fraught with conflict as it was impossible "for two nations to live in one country when one of them, which forms the majority, believes that the other, which is in the minority, aims at getting possession of his country and making him the minority and increasing their own numbers" (1.514). At the conclusion of his statement, al-Husayni reaffirmed the standard position, calling for a national representative government in which all inhabitants would have a say in proportion to their group's size. His testimony expresses the conflation of Islamic religious considerations, general Arab nationalism, and territorially specific patriotism—a feature of Palestinian-Arab identity politics throughout the period.

The 1930s and the Arab Revolt

The 1930s were a period of intensified political struggle that reached a climax with the Arab Revolt of 1936–39. Palestinian identity formation went through two important developments during that decade. The first was the emergence of a secular nationalist current which had its origins in anti-British and pan-Arab nationalism. Its direct influence was to a large extent restricted to the urban areas, though its concerns resonated with the nationalist themes of the 1918–20 period in its call for the independence of Palestine within the general unity of the Arab countries (Arnon-Ohana 1981: 166–76). The second trend was the radical Islamic tendency associated with the al-Qassam movement. Although widespread, its influence was unfocused, especially among peasants participating in the revolt. Despite their importance, neither tendency managed to articulate a coherent alternative to the hegemonic ethnic-territorial nationalism, based on the notion of an Arab Muslim-Christian patriotic unity.

Palestinian-Arab national identity coexisted with, but also was challenged by, the use of Islamic symbols in political discourse, which was increasing as mobilization from below replaced mobilization from above. Thus, in a 1935 *fatwa* (religious edict) calling on peasants not to sell land to Jews, Palestine was referred to as the "holy country . . . to which the nocturnal journey [*isra'*] and from which the ascension to heaven [*mi'raj*] of your prophet Muhammad" took place, a country that therefore "should forever remain tinged with the colour of Islam" (quoted in Kupferschmidt 1987: 241). Another *fatwa* adopted around the same time by 248 religious leaders described Arab sellers of land as "preventing the mention of Allah and His name in mosques and striving for their destruction," castigating them as "detrimental to Allah, His Messenger and the faith" (245).

In August 1936, in a less obviously religious vein, the first communiqué by Fawzi al-Qawuqji, commander of the Arab forces during the revolt, included verses from the Qur'an and called on people to take up arms "in defense of the first *qiblah* [Jerusalem in early Islam] and the second of the Noble Holy Sanctuaries" (quoted in Johnson 1982: 55). This call was issued in the name of the "leadership of the Arab revolt in southern Syria (Palestine)," thus showing a familiar combination of religious, pan-Arab, and territorial components of Palestinian-Arab identity, with a bias toward Arab nationalism. The frequent references to jihad (holy war) during the revolt were another indication of the appeal of Islamic terminology at the popular level, though without acquiring a dominant position at the official level. The effectiveness of religious appeals seems to have varied according to the audience. They were useful when directed at the broad masses, and at foreign Muslims whose solidarity was solicited, but were counterproductive when directed at British officials and international public opinion.

The more widespread use of Islamic motifs in political propaganda and mobilization was accompanied by an increase in the political and organizational role of the Supreme Muslim Council. The council, however, did not seek institutionally to replace the national movement, nor did it challenge the nonsectarian mode of political activity. Islamic religious organization was a basis for accumulating and exercising political power, not a substitute for it. The 1930s witnessed growing coordination between the religious and secular wings of the national movement, facilitated by the control of both by members of the Husayni faction. This alliance was cemented by the general strike of 1936, which gave rise to a new organizational expression of the sense of national identity—the Arab Higher Committee. The committee replaced the Arab Executive, defunct since 1934. Its formation was the first time Arab political tendencies managed to unite on the basis of common national demands, confronting both the British and the Jewish community. This political-organizational unity was short-lived, though, and it collapsed a short time after it came into being, with the worst outbreak of internal violence in Palestinian history. It was significant, nonetheless, in that it expressed the comprehensive mobilization of the indigenous population in a campaign articulating their shared grievances and demands. At the same time, the unity shown toward the outside disguised profound internal disagreements over strategy, which became more pronounced as the revolt failed to achieve its goals and turned increasingly into a factional struggle over turf and resources (Abboushi 1977: 39–46).

The solid sense of national identity did not find a commensurate organizational expression, and the Arab Higher Committee lost whatever little control it had over events on the ground. This was due in large part to the fact that even as "the historical experience of being Arab and living in Palestine was creating a new communal identity," it did not replace "older, unchallenged feelings of belonging. These inner struggles produced the intensity of intracommunal warfare and its dissipation in exhausted apathy" (Miller 1985: 125). The coexistence of adherence to the same national goals with loyalty to particular individuals and parties turned the revolt into a series of disparate and localized activities without giving rise to a united and centrally coordinated movement. The extent to which indigenous Palestinians reached a unified collective identity, translated into a set of concrete political demands, is striking when seen from a comparative perspective, though. Indigenous South African activists faced much stronger obstacles in their struggle to consolidate their national consciousness as the legacies of distinct tribal, regional, religious, ethnic, and racial identities proved difficult to overcome.

Palestinian-Arab political factionalism reflected differing power bases as well as dissimilar strategies proposed to achieve the national goals. It did *not* reflect different conceptualizations of identity boundaries or significant variations in the formulation of the goals themselves. The official goals were expressed by the memorandum submitted to the Palestine Royal Commission (Arab Higher Committee 1937). The committee asserted in that document that it acted "on behalf of the Arabs of Palestine" who were deprived of "their natural and political rights," faced with the Jewish National Home which was liable to lead "to the destruction of the Arabs as a national and cultural entity in the country" (5). Arabs were affirmed as "the legitimate owners of the country" (11), and the call for majority rule was asserted in the demand for "an independent national government, constitutionally elected, in which shall be represented all sections of the population" (13). Significantly, specific Islamic language and demands were absent from the document, which adopted an unambiguous secular-nationalist conceptualization of the political situation.

An identical tone was also evident in the testimony of Amin al-Husayni to the commission (Palestine Royal Commission 1937a: 292–99). Al-Husayni asserted that the Jews in the country "will live, as they always have lived in Arab Countries, with complete freedom and liberty as natives in the country" (298). In response to further queries by the commission, though, he confirmed that Palestine could not absorb and digest the 400,000 Jews already there. When the commission chairman suggested that this meant that "some of them would have to be removed by a process kindly or painful as the case may be," al-Husayni asserted in an elusive manner: "We must leave all this to the future" (298). The professed willingness to incorporate all residents equally, consistent with a non-ethnic territorial identity, was thus undermined by the insistence on the essential Arab nature of the country, unmodified by the political realities of Ottoman and British rule and by the changing demographic circumstances due to Jewish immigration and settlement. (The testimony of veteran Arab nationalist and council employee Izzat Darwaza is particularly forceful in this respect [314–5].)

The assertion of the fundamental Arab character of the country was bound to clash with the concerns of the Jewish community, which was dominated since the beginning of the period by the Zionist movement. Most Zionist parties and movements were committed to Jewish communal autonomy leading to national independence, both of which were understood in clearly ethnic and nonterritorial terms. The Palestine Royal Commission did not mince words when it claimed that "the ideal of the National Home is a purely Jewish ideal. The Arabs hardly come into the picture except when they force an entry with violence and bloodshed" (Palestine Royal Commission 1937b: 119). As a result, any notion of intercommunal cultural assimilation seemed unreal, leading the commission to argue that it was time that Palestinian citizenship was recognized as "nothing but a legal formula devoid of moral meaning" (120).

The institutional buildup of the community was geared toward maximum disengagement from both the Arab community and the British authorities. The Palestine Royal Commission used a hyperbole, perhaps, when it claimed that "it would be difficult to find in history a precedent for the establishment of so distinct an *imperium in imperio*" (Palestine Royal Commission 1937b: 49), but without doubt the overall direction of development was toward ever-increasing separation at the levels of identity and state formation. The Zionist view was that a representative government and majority rule, although justified in principle, should not be applied in Palestine/Israel as they would inevitably reflect the current (and hence temporary) demographic realities. The basis for Jewish rights in and to the country in this view was historical, "as old as the Jewish people" (Ben-Gurion, chairman of the Executive of the Jewish Agency, in Palestine Royal Commission 1937a: 288), and it applied to the entire Jewish people "whether we are here [in Palestine] already or whether we are not here yet" (289).

These political claims were bolstered by the success of the Zionist leadership in constructing strong and viable economic, political, and military structures that could successfully confront the revolt and strengthen their own positions in alliance with the British authorities. The gulf created between Jews and Arabs as a result of the revolt was deeper than ever. Long before the period ended it became clear that no unitary solution was possible. As the Palestine Royal Commission, the first to advocate partition, concluded: "An irrepressible conflict has arisen between two national communities within the narrow bounds of one small country. . . . There is no common ground between them. . . . In these circumstances to maintain that Palestinian citizenship has any moral meaning is a mischievous pretence. Neither Arab nor Jew has any sense of service to a single state" (Palestine Royal Commission 1937b: 370–71). As a result, the commission noted, three parallel sets of political institutions (Arab, Jewish, and British) coexisted in a state of tension, with the official administration enjoying the least support among them. Even the limited cooperation at the local and municipal levels was constantly eroding and almost totally collapsed by the time the revolt came to an end.

The Road to Partition

The military repression of the Arab revolt was accompanied by the arrest and exile of a large number of political leaders, most prominent among whom was Amin al-Husayni, who was banned from the country until the end of the period. A period of disarray in Palestinian politics consequently ensued, particularly notable in light of the consolidation of the position of the organized Jewish community. The Second World War and the Holocaust made the Zionist movement's claim to Palestine as a safe haven for the Jewish people much stronger internationally, though it had little effect on the principled refusal of Palestinian Arabs to withdraw their own claims to political independence in the country. Prewar British plans to introduce self-government within ten years with a view to an independent state of Palestine were scrapped. The Zionist leadership rejected the plan for a state "in which Arabs and Jews share in government in such a way as to ensure that the essential interests of each community are safeguarded" (Palestine 1939: 6) as a ploy to keep Jews in a permanent minority in the country. In any event, the changing international scene made the plan obsolete.

With the conclusion of the Second World War, the international community directed its attention to the question of Palestine, seeing it as inextricably linked to the European Jewish refugee problem. This linkage was strongly rejected by Palestinians, who felt they were made to bear a burden not of their own making. As leading activist Jamal al-Husayni put it, "every Jew who enters Palestine is a further step towards our dispossession" (Anglo-American Committee of Inquiry 1946: C8). Arab spokesmen advocated that immigration, like all other issues, be subject to majority control, and they consistently denied any special Jewish right to enter the country. They based their own case "on the natural right of a people to remain in undisturbed possession of their country and on the natural desire to safeguard their national existence" (C2). Al-Husayni coupled the demands for the creation of a sovereign Arab state and the cessation of Jewish immigration with a guarantee that Jews will have the same privileges and rights as Arabs and their status will be similar to that of American or British Jews.

The recognition of the rights of Jews as individuals was not accompanied by an acknowledgment of their rights as a collective. The official Palestinian-Arab position was thus a mirror image of the Zionist position, which advocated a Jewish rather than a secular state (see statements by Haim Weizmann and Ben-Gurion, in Anglo-American Committee of Inquiry 1946: A2–45 and B1–42 respectively). Both parties subordinated their understanding of democracy to ethnic-demographic imperatives. Arab activists interpreted democracy as majority rule consistent with a state with an Arab ethnic character. As a majority whose relative numerical strength was in decline, Arabs were opposed to any delays in the application of democratic principles. In contrast, as a fast-growing minority, Jewish activists demanded that these same principles be suspended until Jews became a majority of the population, or else, in a more conciliatory vein, that communal parity and power-sharing be established regardless of numerical proportions (as Dr. Judah Magnes of Ihud suggested [E1–40]). Neither side seriously considered an arrangement in which political power, land, labor, and immigration issues be decided upon in a non-ethnic manner, independent of the supposed essential Arab or Jewish nature of the country.

Judged by the principles of democracy as commonly understood, Palestinians had a stronger case because they based their claims on the prevailing demographic realities rather than on future prospects, as their Zionist counterparts did. Their case for an *Arab* rather than a *civil* state representative of all its citizens was less sound. Professed guarantees of equal rights for Jews (as in the testimonies of Ahmad Shukayri and Albert Hourani, in Anglo-American Committee of Inquiry 1946: I96–132) were undermined by official Arab demands that land and immigration policies be based on ethnic grounds. On the other hand, although the Zionist case for the suspension of democracy was untenable, the argument that the Jewish community acquired a distinct corporate national character that had to be accommodated in any future dispensation was convincing. Political disputes are not settled on the basis of the merits of the conflicting arguments, however. Palestinians were less successful in getting international support for their cause, their capacity to mobilize resources was lower, and consequently their ability to achieve their goals was eroded throughout the 1940s.

The factionalism that plagued Palestinian-Arab politics during the revolt continued unabated in the last decade of the mandate. The renewed attempts to construct a Palestinian united front in the second half of the 1940s were overshadowed by sectional and personal conflicts as the Husayni faction reasserted its dominance (Khalaf 1991: 91–103, 116–32). Amin al-Husayni once again emerged as the foremost leader of the movement, although he operated from exile. A new Arab Higher Committee was formed with the goal of mobilizing people for sustained struggle. Financial, military, and youth organizations were established all over the country, and the locally based National Committees were supposed to coordinate their efforts. Continuing factional rivalries interfered, however, with the establishment of clear lines of communication and command (146–51). The attempts by al-Husayni to centralize the national effort under his personal control, with no coherent structures to formulate strategy and mediate between the different levels of organization, proved fatal for Palestinian capacity to mount an effective national military and political campaign during the crucial clashes of 1947–48 (for the effects of military factionalism, see 205–10).

Palestinian organizational weakness contrasted with the better-articulated institutional infrastructure of the Jewish community. Having emerged through large-scale immigration and settlement, processes that by their very nature require a degree of conscious mobilization of resources, the Jewish community was better prepared for withstanding the strains of protracted conflict and waging a sustained national effort. The differences in leaderships also played a role in the ability of both sides to achieve their goals. The majority of Palestinian leaders held high social status usually based on land and urban property and on religious and family prestige. Their education was geared toward the humanities, specializing in law and religion as well as medicine (al-Hout 1979). Jewish leaders relied far less on family ties, and their education placed stronger emphasis on the social sciences and engineering—subjects more oriented toward practical matters and conducive to planning social and economic developments (Nashif 1979). Both sides showed great concern with national goals, but with a difference. Whereas among Jews "the gravitating power of national goals outweighed that of partisan personalities," among Arabs the great majority was organized "around leading individuals of social, religious, political and economic prominence" (116). Greater focus on ultimate goals and more professional political operations were distinct advantages that the organized Jewish community possessed over their Arab opponents.

The limitations of Arab organizational capacities relative to those evinced by the Zionist movement played a major role in the eventual defeat of Palestinians in the military conflicts of the late 1940s. Critical Palestinian scholarship has placed a great deal of emphasis on the harmful consequences of factionalism and the failure to overcome parochial, clannish, regional, and tribal legacies (see, in particular, Nashif 1979; Tamari 1982; Khalaf 1991). And yet, when examined from a comparative perspective, it seems that Palestinians actually demonstrated a great capacity to articulate a solid sense of national identity and engage in sustained organizational effort to mobilize and resist adverse political transformations. Within less than two decades of the first crucial encounter with the settlement project (the Balfour Declaration of 1917), they embarked on a campaign uniting them in their majority in a general strike waged on the basis of a common nationalist agenda. This showed a remarkable degree of unity and mobilizing capacity compared to anticolonial struggles in general (one has only to think on the length of time it took indigenous people to mount resistance on a national scale in, say, India or Indonesia), and in South Africa in particular.

Conclusions

From the 1920s through the 1940s, the Jewish community increased its numbers seven times and built a network of social, political, and cultural institutions which consolidated its character as an autonomous national community. Palestinian Arabs also increased their numbers (though not as fast) and retained their numerical majority throughout. Their proportion of the population had fallen, however, from about 90 percent to 66 percent by the end of the period. Palestinians lagged behind Jews in forming their own national institutions and were more vulnerable to British and Zionist intervention in their political life. Nevertheless, they constructed a strong sense of themselves as a people, unified but not homogeneous internally, in possession of strong boundaries toward the outside. Despite sharp political divisions within the national communities, they each maintained their distinct character, leaving little room for shared identities and structures to develop. Exclusion came to be the norm resolutely adhered to by all sides.

It was no surprise, then, that the option of political partition of the country, first advocated by the Palestine Royal Commission in 1937, acquired increasing support. By the late 1940s it became clear that no unitary solution was possible. When the United Nations adopted its November 29, 1947, resolution dividing the territory between two states (the Jewish State of Israel and the not-yet-established Arab State of Palestine), it based its action on the premise that "the claims to Palestine of the Arabs and Jews, both possessing validity, are irreconcilable." Partition, although bound to face great difficulties, was seen as "the most realistic and practicable settlement . . . meeting in part the claims and national aspirations of both parties" (United Nations 1947: 72). The ensuing war and the continued conflict that has afflicted Israeli Jews and Palestinian Arabs to this day demonstrate that a very heavy price was paid for this arrangement. It is ironic then that, almost half a century and tens of thousands of lost lives later, the two sides have come full circle to realize that, despite its limitations, no better solution can be found. Hopefully, the chances of success will be better this time.

South Africa

The processes of identity and state formation in South Africa, from the late nineteenth century through the establishment of the Union of South Africa in 1910 to the rise of the National Party to power and the beginning of the apartheid era in 1948, were varied. During that period, a politically unified state, though one resting on heterogeneous institutional foundations, emerged out of the numerous indigenous, colonial, and settler political systems that had uneasily existed alongside each other. By the end of the formative period discussed in chapter 4, relations of warfare and territorial expansion, frequently interlaced with instances of cooperation and cultural syncretism, had been established between the different polities of the southern African region. In addition to such independent African kingdoms as the Sotho, Swazi, and Zulu states, and several less centralized African chiefdoms, there existed two British colonies of Natal and the Cape of Good Hope and two settler republics of the Orange Free State and the South African Republic (Transvaal). The region was occupied by adherents of a variety of religions, ethnic identities, languages, and cultures, whose boundaries overlapped only partially with political boundaries, themselves subject to frequent shifting.

The Overall Context

During the late nineteenth century, accelerated processes of military conquest and political unification were set in motion which resulted in the defeat and incorporation of hitherto independent African states and chiefdoms and in the Anglo-Boer War of 1899–1902, leading to the formation of a new state—the Union of South Africa. The legacies of political autonomy lived on in the form of provincial divisions and the creation of the native reserves. By the end of the first decade of the twentieth century, however, the modern state of South Africa came into being as a political-administrative unit with an increasing degree of centralization of the legislative, executive, and judicial systems.

Unification did not mean homogenization, however. People of diverse racial and ethnic backgrounds were incorporated in the new state in a differentiated manner. The various citizenship categories created as a result of union opened new terrains for struggle over the extent and terms of political incorporation, giving rise to conflicts between as well as within various black and white groups, themselves internally divided. Debates between white liberal and segregationist political tendencies coincided with clashes and divisions among the proponents of different strategies of incorporation, co-optation, and resistance adopted by diverse black movements. The emerging picture was not that of a black-white dichotomy but rather a complex arrangement involving strategic and tactical alliances between different forces, frequently cutting across racial boundaries (though rarely on an egalitarian basis). The exclusionary political setup that characterized Palestine/

Israel, pitting two mutually exclusive and relatively coherent camps against each other with little common ground between them, did not come to dominate South African state politics.

In close relation, and parallel to developments in the sphere of state formation, were identity formation processes. These led to a certain degree of cultural interpenetration between people of different backgrounds. New groups labeled "de-tribalized natives" came into being in the cities, and these maintained loose connections with the ethnically specific African traditions. The newly urbanized population became a growing constituency for new cultural and political movements articulating conceptions of a comprehensive African, and by extension South African, identity. These emerging identities coexisted with locally based indigenous identities. The strength of the latter was particularly notable in such regions as Zululand and the Transkeian Territories, whose inhabitants retained a vibrant precolonial consciousness. The consolidation of a nationwide identity was clearly evident, but it did not displace specific ethnic and regional identities that persisted throughout the period. These localized identities provided in more recent times, frequently with state help, a foundation for the "creation of tribalism" (see the collection of studies in Vail 1989) and for the emergence of politicized ethnicity in the guise of a return to tradition (see Marks 1986: 110–25 for the case of KwaZulu and the ambiguities of present-day Zulu ethnic nationalism).

Another tendency that began manifesting itself around the same time was the rise, especially in the eastern Cape and Natal, of indigenous intellectual elites consisting largely of mission-educated teachers, journalists, lawyers, and clergy. These elites played a crucial role in articulating the desire of Christianized Africans to complete their integration into British-dominated ideological and political structures. Though a minority among Africans, these people made important contributions to the shape of an African and a South African national identity by establishing the first newspapers and political organizations fighting for equal political and citizenship rights for all. Similar movements emerged among other marginalized groups—colored people concentrated in the Cape, and Indians in Natal and the Transvaal. All of these were forces fighting for political and cultural incorporation, and they found common ground with certain white liberal tendencies, but not with others, as liberalism itself was open to different and contradictory interpretations.

Similar processes of economic change and urbanization brought together the geographically disparate Afrikaans-speaking whites in a unified political framework, thus facilitating the growth of a nationalist movement among them. A major goal of the movement as it became organized in the 1930s and 1940s was the prevention, if not the reversal, of the process of formation of a comprehensive South African identity. Identity formation processes in South Africa thus involved movements in opposed directions and shifting boundaries between and within groups. The dismantling of specific and regional boundaries continued even as new ones were being created. The implementation of a segregationist political program by the white-dominated state in the first half of the twentieth century disrupted but did not arrest altogether the formation of a South African identity out of the diverse raw materials brought together by migration, military conquest, and cultural mixture.

Demographic Changes

The mineral discoveries of the late nineteenth century and the resulting economic transformation of the country gave rise to permanently urbanized and ethnically mixed African communities, perhaps the most significant demographic development of the entire period discussed in this chapter. There were, of course, urban concentrations of Africans even before that, but they were of a different nature, more regionally specific and primarily comprising migrants from the surrounding rural areas. What was new about Kimberley and especially the Witwatersrand was, from their beginnings, their pronounced multiethnic and multiracial character. These urban centers served as foci for people from the entire southern African region, not only from those regions that had already fallen under the direct domination of colonial and settler forces. In addition to Africans, the urban areas attracted large numbers of British immigrants as well as white rural migrants.

In studying processes of indigenous identity formation we make a clear distinction between those Africans employed by mining companies and other urban elements. The former were mostly short-term migrants who came from as far afield as central Africa; they usually returned to their places of origin after earning enough money to satisfy the needs that motivated them to look for work. The more permanent African population, on the other hand, consisted of people employed in a variety of jobs and services who were looking for a settled existence in the towns and newly created locations. They frequently maintained close relations with their families in the countryside but saw their own future in the cities. By the 1930s they had become the largest component of the urban population of South Africa.

The rise of an urban African population was only one aspect of the overall demographic transformation that affected South Africa during this period. In 1891 the Cape Colony had a population of 1,525,739 people, about three times the total of the 1865 census, thus showing a remarkable rate of growth. The "European or White" category numbered 376,812 persons (25 percent of the total), about twice the figure for 1865. There were 847,542 "Aboriginal Natives" (55 percent) compared to only about 100,000 in the earlier census, and 301,385 "all other Coloured Persons" (20 percent), increasing from the 214,253 of 1865 (obtained by collapsing the "Hottentot" and "Other" categories in Houghton and Dagut 1972: 1.31–32; for the 1891 figures see 1.291). Of the different categories, only the colored population owed most of its increase to natural growth. The increase of whites was largely due to European immigration, while Africans increased in numbers primarily because of continuing conquest and annexation of their territories in the eastern and northern part of the colony.

In the British colony of Natal, excluding Zululand, Africans vastly outnumbered all other groups, with 483,690 persons in 1891, about 85 percent of the total of 571,620. Whites numbered only 46,788, 8 percent of the total, and Indians 41,142, 7 percent of the total (Houghton and Dagut 1972: 1.294). Data for the Orange Free State show a relatively large white presence there in 1890, 77,716 out of 207,503 people, about 37 percent of the total. Africans numbered 129,782, 62.5 percent of the total (1.299). In the Transvaal, Africans numbered 655,985 in 1892 compared to whites, who numbered 288,750 in 1898, though it is unclear who was included in these categories and how accurate these statistics were (1.288–90). These figures were still in a state of flux because some African territories later to be incorporated in the Union of South Africa were still independent at the time.

Overall, then, the picture is one of a clear African majority, though differentiated by region. White presence in the Cape and the Transvaal was substantial both in absolute numbers and as a proportion of the population. Those classified as neither African nor white resided in large numbers primarily in the Cape (colored people), and to a lesser extent in Natal (Indians). By the turn of the century, the relative proportions of people of different origins began to stabilize. The demographic differences between the census of 1904 and that of 1911 in this respect are not large. By the time of union, Africans had become 67 percent of the South African population, whites 21 percent, and colored people and Indians 11 percent (Houghton and Dagut 1972: 2.146). The largest concentration of Africans was still in the Cape, with the Transvaal a close second, followed by Natal (2.146–47). By the end of the period discussed here, the Transvaal province had become the largest region as far as population, economic, and political importance were concerned.

Several points are of particular importance in this set of data. The first is that in the short period of thirty to forty years, large numbers of people of disparate regional, ethnic, and religious identities were brought together within the same political and territorial boundaries. The last third of the nineteenth century saw the migration of massive numbers of Europeans, mostly of British origin, into the country, attracted by the new economic prospects associated mainly with the rise of the mining industry. In addition, a smaller number of Indian immigrants arrived, many of whom were equally eager to benefit from commercial opportunities. The biggest source of population increase, however, was indigenous Africans, whose numbers grew by at least five times during that period as a result of being forcibly incorporated into the recently created unified political structures. The result was a sharp rise in internal heterogeneity, and at the same time an elaboration of ways of coming to terms with the new conditions of ethnic and racial diversity. What before had been a series of regional or local issues now acquired a national dimension. The focus of debates became known in official discourse as the Native Question, that is, the question of how to classify, divide, administer, and rule over indigenous people, incorporating them without actually assimilating them fully into the body politic (Ashforth 1990).

The Politics of Incorporation

Independent African states had engaged in relations of trade, warfare, and political maneuvering with white-controlled colonies for many decades, but most of them had not directly fallen under colonial domination until the latter half of the nineteenth century. Indigenous people living in the Highveld republics of the Free State and the Transvaal entered tributary relations with settler authorities but generally managed to retain a large degree of autonomy to run their own affairs, even as they resided within nominal white-defined state boundaries. Settler political institutions did not possess sufficient administrative, legal, and coercive capacities to dominate indigenous people in an effective manner until the beginning of the twentieth century. Only with the emergence of a nationwide political apparatus, following the establishment of union in 1910, could the process of the legal transformation of indigenous people into subjects of the South African state be completed.

The incorporation of indigenous people into the new political structures marked an important shift in the locus of their organization. In earlier times, indigenous struggles focused on military and political resistance to colonial conquest. These extended from the frontier wars of the late eighteenth and early nineteenth centuries in the eastern Cape (for a discussion of which see chapter 4) through the confrontations between British forces and the Zulu kingdom in the late 1870s, to the annexation of the Venda chiefdoms and Pondoland in the 1890s. Even after that, in 1906 the Bambatha rebellion in Natal was conducted in a similar spirit of resistance to colonial expansion. Armed uprisings in certain rural regions erupted in a sporadic manner as late as the 1960s.

Since the turn of the twentieth century, however, struggles for political equality within the framework of white-dominated state institutions, rather than the reversal of conquest, became an ever more prominent feature of the political organization of indigenous people. This tendency had already become evident in the eastern Cape in the late nineteenth century, and its significance increased with the unification of the country. This development was particularly notable given that the dominant trend in twentieth-century white politics was exactly the opposite—the persistent attempt to purge state institutions of any direct indigenous representation. The changes in indigenous political organizations can be contrasted with Palestinian trends. Indigenous people in Palestine/Israel neither sought to persist in isolated enclaves to avoid settler domination, nor did they seek incorporation within settler-dominated structures. Rather, they fought for direct control over state power.

Black Politics in the Cape

The place in which the political and ideological incorporation of all groups was more far-reaching was the Cape Colony (Cape Province after 1910). This was an overall tendency but with pronounced local emphases. Colored-white interaction was most salient in the western Cape, and in particular Cape Town, whereas African-white interaction dominated political life in the eastern Cape. The capital of Cape Town, the oldest and most integrated of all South African cities, combined both racial and nonracial features in its social and spatial organization. A large measure of formal and informal segregation coexisted with a degree of social mixing between whites and colored people, especially among lower classes in neighborhoods where "poor whites and filthy blacks live side by side" (*Cape Argus* newspaper in January 1893, in Bickford-Smith 1989: 54). This state of affairs was replicated in other parts of the colony, such as Grahamstown and Port Elizabeth (52). The Cape Labour Commission of 1893 collected a large body of evidence about cross-racial work, marriage, and sexual relations among the rural and urban poor, testifying to the fluidity of racial categories among certain social groups (Bundy 1986: 116–19).

The economic foundation of the relative permeability of identity boundaries at the Cape, compared to other places in South Africa at the time, is attributed by Bickford-Smith (1989) to the fact that the major occupations in Cape Town were small-scale artisan production, trade, and services. These types of activities did not create a need for a coercive labor-control system similar to that in Kimberley and Johannesburg, whose mines and industry employed vast numbers of unskilled African laborers. There was more to the rigidity of boundaries than the needs of white masters, however. Since the days of slavery, Cape Town had exhibited a long tradition of cultural syncretism that brought together on an *inegalitarian* footing people of different backgrounds; this occurred on the basis of a shared language, Dutch-Afrikaans, as well as a shared religious adherence to the Dutch Reformed church, though Islam was also a strong force in the city. This trend was pitted against the rise in whites' racial prejudice, motivated in part by white artisans' fear of the competition offered by skilled black (mostly colored) labor. Whites' exclusionary sentiments were expressed in craft unions' attempts to block nonwhite employment (Goldin 1987: 12–19). Pressures for segregation and incorporation thus came from multiple directions and were not resolved without struggle.

The operation of contradictory tendencies—segregation in some spheres, such as nondenominational education, and a degree of integration in others such as housing—had been a feature of Cape society for much of the nineteenth century. In other parts of the western Cape, outside the city of Cape Town itself, the balance of forces was more favorable to the segregationist mode. An important element of the incorporationist trend, which remained all over the colony throughout the period, though in a modified and more restrictive form, was the qualified nonracial franchise. The qualifications for voters were raised in the 1880s and 1890s to prevent large numbers of people from the newly conquered Transkeian Territories from joining the electorate (the property and income requirements were tripled and a literacy test was added in Parliamentary Act 9 of 1892; Eybers 1918: 73–74).

Although not directly targeted, many poor colored people (and even some poor whites) who could not meet the new and higher qualifications were disenfranchised as a result. The capacity of colored people and Africans to participate in municipal and parliamentary electoral processes was retained in principle, however, and white political parties competed in several constituencies over black votes. With few exceptions, such as the candidacy of the Cape Muslim politician Ahmed Effendi in the 1893 parliamentary elections, no significant independent political organization emerged among the colored population before the beginning of the twentieth century (for Effendi's campaign see Van der Ross 1986: 12–14). The continuing option of social incorporation, although shrinking, created a situation in which "the Coloured elites aspired towards integration into white society, with all the privileges that this implied, not to a separate Coloured identity with its negative social implications" (Lewis 1987: 13).

The desire for equality was heightened by the expectation, based on British promises, that victory in the Anglo-Boer War would bring an expansion in the political rights of coloured people and Africans. The government reneged, however, on the commitment of such leading officials as Lord Milner to "equal laws, equal liberty" for all races in South Africa if British victory were won (Lewis 1987: 15–16). The British authorities approached the question of race with the imperative of reaching a reconciliation between English- and Afrikaans-speaking whites foremost in their mind. To achieve that goal they acquiesced in the insistence of Afrikaner republicans on the exclusion of all blacks, primarily Africans and Indians but also colored people, from direct participation in state institutions (though the Cape qualified franchise was retained, for the time being). Constrained by their own racial prejudice, the British saw white unity as the key to political stability and regarded as inconsequential the burden blacks had to bear as a result (for Milner's approach see Van der Ross 1986: 24–27).

With the realization that without their own initiative nothing would change their situation in the aftermath of the war, colored and African activists were encouraged to create nationwide political movements for the first time. The most important among these was the African People's Organization (APO), which was founded in Cape Town in 1902 and sought to represent, despite its name, colored people in the Cape and all over the country. The demands of the APO were largely reformist in nature, with a focus on parliamentary politics and demands for incorporation on an equal basis. This was expressed in the goals of the organization, prominent among which were the calls "To promote unity between the coloured races . . . To defend the Coloured People's social, political and civil rights . . . [and to support] the general advancement of the coloured people in

South Africa" (quoted in Lewis 1987: 20). As this document indicates, there was an inherent and unresolved tension between organizing on a specifically colored basis, on the one hand, and fighting racial domination through the unity of all blacks, on the other. While the APO was a colored political movement in terms of its leadership and constituency, at various points in its history it sought alliances with African and Indian organizations to enhance their common cause against white supremacy (59–60, 77–79). The extent to which this reflected grassroots attitudes is unclear. (See Goldin 1987: 19–33 for emphasis on the consolidation of a distinct colored identity by 1904.)

African Politics of the Cape

The emphasis in colored politics on working within the system, on terms set by the elitist though color-blind Cape liberal tradition, was shared by the African political organizations that came into being in the late nineteenth century. These organizations were especially active in regions subjected earlier and more thoroughly to British political and cultural domination—the eastern Cape and Natal. Protest politics in the eastern Cape became a model for other parts of the country due to the privileged political status of Africans there; in other regions, expressions of grievances were generally less organized as a result of the lack of direct access to the political system.

Beginning with cultural-educational concerns, public activities acquired a clearer focus on the political arena at the turn of the century, which was expressed in the efforts of ministers, teachers, and journalists to voice the grievances of their African constituencies over issues such as the Pass Laws, franchise qualifications, and state discriminatory practices. Two Xhosa-language newspapers, *Imvo Zabantsundu* (Native opinion), founded in 1884, and *Izwi Labantu* (Voice of the people), founded in 1898, served to express African complaints and to organize meetings and delegations to protest the restrictions imposed on Africans (for examples of the tone of the former paper, see Karis and Carter 1972: 1.12–17). These newspapers were edited respectively by J. T. Jabavu and W. Rubusana, both of whom gained prominent political status in later years. These protest activities were conducted to a large extent within the framework of white party politics, rather than as part of an independent African project. A crucial change in this respect took place in 1902 when a group associated with *Izwi Labantu* founded a new organization, the South African Native Congress, which became the nucleus of the most prominent twentieth-century African political organizations (Odendaal 1984: 5–16).

In a statement to the British Colonial Office in 1903, the Native Congress expressed its loyalty to the empire and appealed against the danger of disenfranchisement faced by indigenous people as a result of demands by settler leaders in Natal, the Free State, and the Transvaal. The congress was concerned to extend the limited color-blind franchise already enjoyed in the Cape to other regions and to allow all those "fully qualified by education, property and domicile, to vote as free citizens" (statement by the Executive of the South African Native Congress, in Karis and Carter 1972: 1.22). It expressed fear that the rights of indigenous people would be sacrificed to the imperative of "uniting Briton and Boer so as to present what is called a 'solid front' to an alleged 'black menace' " (27), and it appealed to Britain to keep its imperial obligations and protect "His Majesty's black and coloured subjects" (29).

The statement reveals an interesting ambiguity in the manner the congress envisioned its constituency. It was speaking for the rights of all "natives" and the protection of their liberties, but at the same time it rejected the notion of indigenous unity against white rule as unrealistic and contrary to "traditional tribal disunity" (28). Furthermore, it made specific references to "intelligent Natives" who were willing to provide assistance to the Crown in maintaining law and order among the ignorant "mass of the people" (28). The organization of indigenous people, then, was not meant as a vehicle for national liberation but rather as a means of integrating them gradually into the colonial state as imperial subjects, as they become better educated and more "intelligent."

Under conditions of unchallenged colonial domination, the desire of indigenous elites to present themselves as representative of a large number of people, and thus enhance their position vis-à-vis outside authorities, clashed with their need to distinguish themselves as educated and civilized, and thus different from their raw and primitive fellows. If all indigenous people were granted the same political rights, the more "civilized" among them would lose their relative privileges. Of course, we should not take indigenous professions of submission to authority and acknowledgment of inferiority (as a group) at face value. The congress and other political forces operating in the context of colonial rule employed the weapons of the weak to bolster their case in the eyes of the powers that be. They may have calculated that a gradual approach, although falling short of full political equality, was more likely to yield concessions than an all-out assault on the foundations of the system. Even if this indeed was the case, however, the use of an incorporationist language to articulate indigenous demands affected the overall terms within which political debate has taken place at the time, and ever since. This, of course, was very different from equivalent Palestinian attitudes in which no submission (real or feigned) to settler authority was evident before 1948.

Religious Separatism: The Ethiopian Movement

Ambiguity with regard to the extent and meaning of incorporation was also expressed in the religious sphere, though in a different manner, in that religion played a contradictory role. The rise of indigenous Ethiopian churches toward the end of the nineteenth century, coinciding with the conclusion of the period of direct colonial conquest, reflected a growing interest in African administrative and doctrinal religious independence from white control, or perhaps all external control, including that of the black American African Methodist Episcopal (AME) church (see testimony by Rev. Brander of the Ethiopian Catholic Church in Zion to the South African Native Affairs Commission, in Karis and Carter 1972: 1.39–42). The move signified a reaction against incorporation into colonial structures, and it was motivated by a desire to "go and teach our own people by ourselves" (41; Odendaal 1984: 23–29). On the other hand, Ethiopianism was articulated in the language of Christianity, historically a European-centered religion which made its way into southern Africa as part of the colonial enterprise. It thus constituted an implicit assertion of a large measure of incorporation at the level of identity.

The dual nature of religious symbolism and practice, potentially playing a role in both the colonization of consciousness and the emancipation from colonial subjugation, has become characteristic of indigenous South African religious movements throughout the twentieth century. (See Comaroff and Comaroff 1991 for the religious dimensions of the colonial encounter among the southern Tswana.) The drive toward separatist religious organization powerfully asserted the Africans' need for independence from colonial rule, though it was different from the adherence to indigenous religions, still widespread in the countryside. Generally speaking, the Ethiopian and Zionist Christian churches were open to indigenous Africans, regardless of their ethnic and tribal origins; in that sense they consciously sought to transcend precolonial divisions and to act decisively on the terrain created by colonial expansion and conquest.

The Ethiopian movement had considerable political potential. It posed an alternative model to white supremacy and made the authorities nervous. The idea that church organization could be controlled by local leaders was seen as an anomaly, given the close identification between Christianity, colonial conquest, and the subjugation of indigenous people in southern Africa as well as elsewhere. Consequently, the South African Native Affairs Commission castigated the idea as premature and irresponsible and was anxious to discourage "those bodies which owe their existence to the discontent, or . . . to the very misconduct of men who . . . have severed connection with their parent [European] church, and own no competent central authority" (South African Native Affairs Commission 1905: 63). Only churches that retained some form of allegiance to white authority were deemed acceptable by the commission.

South African Native Affairs Commission

The condemnation of religious separatism by the commission was part of an overall evaluation by the state of indigenous people's organization. The first decade of the twentieth century was a period in which political identities and institutions were reshaped in light of the new realities created by the conclusion of the Anglo-Boer War and the establishment of British rule over the entire country. All forces began organizing on the new political-administrative terrain. The new South African polity increased its involvement in the Native Question, the issue that came to dominate state and identity politics throughout the century. Its main goal was to devise a comprehensive policy that would govern relations between the settler state and the indigenous population. The investigative effort, conducted with a view to concrete policy formulation, was informed by "the advisability of harmonising so far as practicable the direction of Native affairs in the various states of South Africa" (South African Native Affairs Commission 1905: 11).

The South African Native Affairs Commission (SANAC), which operated in the immediate aftermath of the war in the years 1903–5, was the first in a long line of official bodies to investigate various aspects of indigenous people's lives at the national level, and to seek to create a uniform policy and administrative machinery to manage them. Indigenous people, the object of state attention, were officially referred to in all-encompassing terms as "natives," a term denoting "an aboriginal inhabitant of Africa, South of the Equator," including "half-castes and their descendants by Natives" (South African Native Affairs Commission 1905: 13). Most colored people were also regarded as natives according to this definition, though in practice they were subject to different treatment. The crucial defining feature of indigenous people in official eyes turned out to be not their ancestry, color, residence, or social class but rather their presumed historical links to the precolonial past in terms of claims to land, ethnolinguistic identification, and loyalty to traditional political institutions; whether these actually characterized the people in question or were long discarded by them (or even their ancestors) was of little consequence. From this perspective all indigenous Africans did indeed have something in common, shared by neither white nor colored people.

At the local level indigenous people were frequently referred to in specific terms differentiating between ethnic, linguistic, and tribal groups (Ashforth 1990: 30–34). For the most part, however, for purposes of administration and control the state tended to treat them as a uniform category. While the state occasionally made allowance for the differences between educated elites and the more traditional masses, in practice this did not mean much as the former were few in number. Since the unification of South Africa in the beginning of the century, the dominant elements in the state attempted (and usually succeeded) to reduce all indigenous people to the same status by removing the political privileges and exemptions enjoyed by some of them but not others.

Given their diverse backgrounds, Africans themselves were not homogenous and obviously did not initially possess a unified sense of identity. The completion of colonial conquest and the creation of the Union of South Africa facilitated the formation of a nationwide indigenous identity. The relations between the components of this identity were unstable, however, with ethnic, racial, and multiracial foci competing with each other. People variously identified themselves as adherents of a local chief (and thus as tribe members), as part of a specific ethnolinguistic group (such as the Basotho), as Africans (or natives and indigenous people), as blacks (meaning all the "coloured races" or non-Europeans), as South African citizens in general, as Christians, or as all of the above with the weight given each element varying by time, space, and the geographical and political contexts. The adoption of the "native" and "African" bases of identification by political organizations (such as the Natal and the South African Native Congresses) was significant, but at least initially these comprehensive identities did not necessarily reflect sentiments at the grassroots level.

Tribalism and Control

A central ingredient of the system of control imposed on Africans was tribalism—a concept based on principles similar to those first devised by Shepstone in nineteenth-century Natal. The overall goal of native administration was to govern effectively and, at same time, to "civilize" indigenous people in conformity with European standards. Old and new modes of control were combined in a process that retained traditional institutions, or created analogous structures where these had not existed before, and at the same time embedded them in new institutional and political frameworks. The resulting arrangements reflected the desire of the state to gain the consent of indigenous people by employing actual or imagined precolonial authority relations, taking advantage of the supposed resemblance of tribal customs all over the country.

Despite the fact that the tribal system was being displaced by or brought under statutory and administrative European control, the SANAC argued, it was still useful for eliciting the consent of the indigenous population. After all, it left behind a legacy of orderly rule and control, because it was "a form of government perfectly understood by the Natives, carried with it mutual responsibility and suretyship, and required implicit obedience to authority. It possessed a ready means of communication and control extending from the Paramount Chief to the individual Native in his Kraal. It embodied an unbroken chain of responsibility" (South African Native Affairs Commission 1905: 41–42). The commission did not call for a wholesale adoption of indigenous laws and customs; it recognized that this would be impossible in circumstances in which tribal rule had already lost some of its characteristics under the impact of colonial conquest. The retention of indigenous law was seen as a temporary measure, with assimilation into ordinary colonial law as the ultimate goal (44–46). This approach was consistent with the view of Christianity as "one great element for the civilisation of the Natives," to be encouraged through "regular moral and religious instruction . . . in all Native schools" (56).

This assimilationist approach, aimed at the entrenchment of white domination, was combined with the SANAC's recommendation for limited political incorporation of indigenous people in order to allow them to express their views and ventilate their grievances. This was to be done, however, "without conferring on them political power in any aggressive sense, or weakening in any way the unchallenged supremacy and authority of the ruling race which is responsible for the country and bear the burden of its government" (South African Native Affairs

Commission 1905: 96). Indigenous participation was to be based on a separate voters' roll and the election of a small number of delegates regardless of the size of the constituency. That way, it was hoped, indigenous issues would be removed from the white-dominated political arena. Even this clearly restricted attempt to provide institutional channels for expressions of discontent went too far for the liking of hard-line segregationists, and SANAC's recommendation was not followed up on.

Union of South Africa

When the Union of South Africa came into effect in 1910, it retained the existing franchise requirements in each of the four provinces. In the Transvaal, Orange Free State, and Natal the vote was denied to nonwhite people, while in the Cape colored people and indigenous Africans were allowed to vote, subject to high property and literacy qualifications, but even they were denied the right to be elected to Parliament. Only a "British subject of European descent" could become a member of Parliament, whether the Senate or the House of Assembly (Eybers 1918: 525; 531), contradicting the principle formally adhered to by the British of equal rights for all "civilized" persons in southern Africa. This promise led the *Izwi Labantu* to proclaim prematurely in February 1909 that "'Equal rights for all South of the Zambesi' is the motto that will yet float at the masthead of this new ship of state . . . and no other will be permanently substituted while there is one black or coloured man of any consequence or self-respect in the country, or any white man who respects the traditions of free Government" (quoted in Odendaal 1984: 153; for the origins of the slogan "equal rights for every civilised man south of the Zambesi" coined by Cecil Rhodes, see Van der Ross 1986: 22–23).

Other responses by black elites expounded a similar line. The APO issued on Union Day in 1910 a proclamation condemning the new constitution; at the same time it advocated a strategy based on proving that colored people were worthy of equal rights: "by a grim determination on the part of every individual, to prove by his life and conduct that . . . [he does] discharge his duties faithfully and fearlessly, we will convince our Union Parliament that a sad mistake has been committed in the insertion of a colour line into the Constitution Act" (quoted in Lewis 1987: 63). The incorporationist tone of this statement is obvious. There is no trace of separatism here but instead an insistence on the right to be incorporated on equal terms within white political structures.

The common predicament in which various black groups found themselves in facing the prospects of union encouraged them to take joint action to address the situation. A joint delegation of "representatives of the coloured and native British subjects" in South Africa, in coordination with Natal Indians, appealed in 1909 to the British Parliament to grant "equal political rights to qualified men irrespective of race, colour, or creed." They expressed fear that "the prejudice already existing in the Transvaal, Orange river Colony, and Natal, will be accentuated and increased" and extended to the Cape as well (petition to the House of Commons, in Karis and Carter 1972: 1.55–56). The intervention of a prominent white politician and former Cape prime minister, W. P. Schreiner, on their behalf did not prevent the delegation from failing to reverse the "Act of Separation" (the Act of Union), and the act went into effect in 1910 (Odendaal 1984: 197–227). The color-blind franchise remained restricted to the Cape, with only one addition: four native senators were to be appointed, one for each province. These were not true representatives of the population as they were nominated by the governor-general and not elected. Although falling far short of what they demanded, the arrangement did provide Africans with an indirect channel for voicing their concerns and grievances.

Faced with their inability to make much progress by relying on the good services of sympathetic white liberals, a meeting of African political organizations was called to create a counterweight to the white political union. In January 1912 the South African Native National Congress (to be renamed the African National Congress or ANC in 1925) convened in Bloemfontein with delegates from all four provinces and the British protectorates, representing chiefs as well as activists. In a call for convening the congress, Pixley ka Isaka Seme, its future president, argued that the lack of unity among indigenous people was the greatest obstacle to progress. To be able to speak for the concerns of indigenous people there was need for cooperation. This meant putting an end to "the demon of racialism, the aberrations of the Xosa-Fingo feud, the animosity that exists between the Zulus and the Tongaas, between the Basutos and every other Native" ("Native Union," in *Imvo Zabantsundu*, October 1911, in Karis and Carter 1972: 1.72). As all Africans were "one people," the congress was meant to be "a National Society or Union for all the Natives of South Africa" (73).

The draft constitution of the congress set as their goals "the promotion of unity and mutual cooperation between the Government and the Abantu Races of South Africa," and "the maintenance of a central channel between the Government and the aboriginal races in South Africa." It additionally defined its constituency as "native people," "black," and "native inhabitants" (Odendaal 1984: 274–75; see also the 1919 constitution of the congress, in Karis and Carter 1972: 1.76–82). Despite this multiplicity of terms, they all denoted indigenous Africans and did not include colored and Indian people. The organization of the congress was premised on the existing racial divisions which set Africans apart from other black people. Its focus was on unity among Africans, and it regarded fragmentation by clan and tribe as a serious danger. Sectional affiliations were not denied, of course, but were meant to be subsumed in a higher pan-African unity through creation of an upper house or a Council of Chiefs; chiefs from all over southern Africa deemed representative of the people in their areas of control were to sit there in an advisory capacity, alongside the presidency and other committees that controlled the day-to-day activities of the congress (Walshe 1970: 205–6).

Tribalism as a Contested Terrain

The continued importance of traditional leadership created a terrain on which the state, political organizations, and rank and file community members in the native reserves vied with each other over access to and support of chiefs. The state sought ways of incorporating chiefs into the machinery of control in order to strengthen its domination over indigenous people by employing traditionally legitimate means of rule. This was accomplished in the Native Administration Act of 1927, which was meant to harmonize and streamline the entire administrative machinery at all levels. The act was modeled on the practice, first established in Natal in the late nineteenth century, of investing the governor with the position of a supreme chief who "exercises in and over all Natives . . . all political power and authority," including the power to appoint chiefs, amalgamate or divide tribes, and otherwise invent and temper with traditional forms of rule (Natal Native Administration Law, 1887, in Eybers 1918: 254). The Natal model was extended to the entire country (except for the Cape Province) in the South Africa Act of 1909, making the governor-general the supreme chief of all indigenous people in Natal, Transvaal, and the Free State (553).

The act established an administrative hierarchy descending from the supreme chief though the chief native commissioners of the Transkei, Ciskei, Natal, Witwatersrand, and Transvaal (including the northern Cape), down to regional, district, and local commissioners, location superintendents, chiefs, and headmen (Rogers 1933: 12–13). All of these, except for the latter two categories, were to be held by whites. The entire machinery was governed through legislation by proclamation, a system that acted to remove "to a great degree questions of Native administration from the arena of [white-parliamentary] party politics" (22). The governor-general, and through him the lower levels in the hierarchy, were given the power to control all political activity in areas of indigenous people and to take all steps they "consider necessary for the protection, control, improvement, and welfare of the Natives, and in furtherance of peace, order and good government" (25; for the specific powers of the different levels, see 259–65; for a survey of the entire apparatus, handling relations between the state and indigenous people, see May 1949: 310–75).

Indigenous chiefs and headmen were incorporated into the native administration apparatus, though a distinction was made among those who were "appointed [by the government] to exercise tribal government and control and to perform administrative functions," and those who were established chiefs in their own right and were consequently accorded "the rank and customary privileges of a Native chief in or over any tribe or portion of a tribe, but do not exercise any administrative or official authority on behalf of the Supreme Chief or the Government over any person or any land" (Rogers 1933: 266). Appointed chiefs were to exercise "general administrative control over their respective tribes and over any other Natives residing within their areas of jurisdiction" (268). Their role was to transmit government policies and orders down to their subjects and report back to the authorities on problems of political agitation, disorder, and anything else that might pose a threat to political stability.

In this mode of rule, indigenous people living in the reserves were subject to a specialized administrative apparatus and were excluded from having any direct say in the legislation affecting them or in the operation of state departments. This was part of an overall segregationist program applied by successive South African governments during the period. There was more to segregation and tribalism than white (indirect) control, however. These policies also satisfied indigenous forces who wanted to preserve customary law and traditional forms of chiefly rule with minimal outside interference. Tribalism was thus politically ambiguous: it gave a measure of control to indigenous leaders who were not entirely in the service of the government, but it also placed limits on their ability to pose direct challenges to white domination, as they were subsidized to a large extent by the state. (See in this respect Marks 1986: 15–41 for the relations between the state, the Zulu monarchy, and chiefs.)

Traditional rule held a resistance potential inasmuch as it was based on an indigenous claim to the land and consequent opposition to dispossession. The persistent political significance of the land question led to a long series of peasant revolts that, due to their fragmented, small-scale, and disorganized nature, generally were short-lived and ended in failure. Although the concern with land was general throughout the South African countryside, its manifestations were always localized, as claims to the land were invariably linked to specific territories rather than to indigenous rights in the abstract. As a result, rural causes were infrequently taken up by urban-based political organizations, and their potential was largely untapped, at least until the late 1950s (Bundy 1987). Even in their failures, these dispersed revolts were a tribute to the resilience of indigenous sociopolitical institutions in face of the colonial onslaught.

Traditional rule was most legitimate in areas that had been conquered in more recent times and that maintained large and dense concentrations of indigenous communities, with only a few pockets of white settlement, in particular the Transkei and Zululand. In these territories, chiefly rule was less disrupted by settler encroachments on land and could therefore provide more solid foundation for an accommodation on relatively equal footing between the state, represented by the Department of Native Affairs, and chiefs. The ability of chiefs to maneuver between their dependence on the state and their power over their constituencies varied in time and space, but generally allowed them to play a dual role: as agents of external domination as well as representatives of the population. Even as chiefs assumed positions within the administrative apparatus of the state, they continued to conduct court cases, collect tribute from followers, and serve as guardians of the communal tenure of land. They were not completely subservient to the state in that they maintained many attributes of autonomous rule which provided a symbolic basis for separatist politics. (See Mda 1929 for the operation of the Bunga—the Transkeian system of chiefly rule; Marks 1986 for the different strands in Zulu ethnicity; and Beinart and Bundy 1987: 106–37 for the case of the Mpondomise chieftaincy.)

Resistance and Identity in the Countryside

Localized resistance politics in the countryside persisted alongside the operation of such national political movements as the APO and the ANC. People in rural areas, especially those who maintained less regular contacts with the cultural and political centers of the country, frequently adhered to tribal, ethnic, and regional identities, leaderships, and organizations with a pronounced precolonial bent. These were perceived as means of confronting the threat to indigenous people's moral economy, centered as it was on access to communal land as the foundation of social life. The increasing loss of land and the growing compulsion to enter colonial and setter-dominated labor markets were a danger not only to material welfare of people but to their entire sociocultural fabric. Access to land in the reserves was dependent on a pledge of loyalty to specific chiefs controlling well-defined territories. The relations between obedience to traditional rule and control over land were vividly captured in the words of a Transvaal chief who complained in the 1920s about the mixed attitudes of labor tenants on white farms toward tradition: in good times African tenants would say, "'I have nothing to do with the native laws, I am living here on the farm of my master, and he is the only one I obey,'" but in bad times when access to farm land was denied, "they will say 'I am a Makwena' or whatever it is, and they say, 'We want our rights'" (quoted in Bradford 1987: 47).

Although much resistance by indigenous people was phrased in terms of clinging to precolonial identities and forms of rule (see Marks 1986 and Hamilton 1993 for the example of Zulu identity), resistance actually emerged in response to the conditions of colonial conquest and socioeconomic incorporation. Traditional symbols were frequently joined with new identities and modes of organization to provide legitimation for defiance politics. Christianity in its Ethiopian manifestations provided one such basis for independent action (for its rapid spread over the period, see Brookes 1934: 193–201 and Mokitini 1949). The Israelite movement of the eastern Cape, although not explicitly political, expressed strong rejectionist sentiments in opposition to white domination and state authority, using a mixture of Xhosa and Christian prophetic symbolism (and influenced by Garveyite pan-Africanism as well, as suggested in Hill and Pirio 1987: 213–14). Its members' refusal to pay taxes and comply with injunctions to move from their camping grounds, relying on a divine order to challenge authority, culminated with the Bulhoek Massacre of 1921 in which about two hundred unarmed believers were killed by government troops (Edgar 1988).

Traditional and Christian religious images combined with modern trade unionism and pan-Africanism in the shape of the Industrial and Commercial Union (ICU) in the 1920s, a union which accepted white members but prohibited them from holding any office (see ICU revised constitution in Karis and Carter 1972: 1.325–26; Bradford 1987: 123–27). This was especially the case in regions in which the legacies of the precolonial past were particularly vivid. The battle cry of "Ama Melika Ayeza" (the Americans are coming) became a popular idea in the Transkei, the territory with the densest concentration of indigenous people in South Africa. It conveyed a vision of a mighty technologically sophisticated black race from overseas who were to come from the sky in their aircraft fleet, destroy white domination, and liberate Africans from their oppression. This was one of a series of apocalyptic revelations articulated by the movement associated with the Garveyite leader Wellington Buthelezi and local diviners, all promising some climatic action annihilating all but the devout, identified in some versions by their ICU membership cards (213–45; Hill and Pirio 1987: 238–42).

The clear rejection of white presence and the symbolic return to the idyllic and supposedly unviolated precolonial past were deployed in more realistic campaigns as well, focusing attention on sociopolitical power and on issues of wages, prices, labor conditions, taxation, and land ownership. (See Bundy's discussion of the Transkei anti-dipping movement in Beinart and Bundy 1987: 191–221 and Beinart 1987a on women's struggles in the eastern cape.) Visions of the past and the future were articulated with present concerns to mobilize people to action, appealing to their spiritual as well as material needs. The centrality of land in indigenous consciousness and the power of the historical memory of independent rule predisposed rural political struggles to be phrased in rejectionist terms. This implied opposition to the entire notion of incorporation, rather than its acceptance as inevitable and a consequent struggle for equal rights within the new political frameworks. The diminishing viability of subsistence production in the reserves, however, gradually undermined the prospects of locally based separatist resistance and directed renewed attention toward the national level, where incorporationist tendencies became ever more powerful after the 1920s.

Rural-Urban Identities and Contradictions

There was an inherent tension between the centralized dynamics of national politics and the fragmentary dynamics of localized struggles. The embeddedness of rural resistance in local and regional practices proved to be its strongest asset, but it also almost invariably led to its demise. To succeed in effecting a meaningful change of social relations in a centralized political system, South African rural movements needed to transcend their confinement to their original boundaries and intervene at the national level; to do that effectively proved extremely difficult when the mobilizing power of such movements was premised on localized identities. This contradiction turned out to be a major stumbling block for indigenous political activity, aggravated by the consciously transethnic and transtribal stance of the major urban-based movements. The desire to build comprehensive African organizations led to the choice of English rather than any of the vernacular languages as the main medium of indigenous people's political life, thus creating a gap between urban and rural constituencies which was not easy to bridge.

A rare combination of rural and urban appeals was evident in the operation of the Universal Negro Improvement Association (UNIA), the pan-African movement led by Marcus Garvey (Hill and Pirio 1987; Cobley 1990: 183–88). As with the ICU and some of the independent Ethiopian churches, support for the Garvey movement was based on its ability to project power and to promise deliverance through association with forces larger than the relatively powerless black South African population. The call "Africa for the Africans" had an enormous unifying potential because it resonated with the universal concerns of all sections of the indigenous population. Despite widespread support at the popular level, the movement was not long lasting. Its millenarian tendencies and dependence on the glorified but problematic figure of Garvey led it to neglect its organizational capacity, thus preventing it from building solid and sustainable structures. The expectations it generated for spectacular change could not have been fulfilled, and the resulting frustration was inevitable. More importantly, the relations between pan-African racial identity and sectional identities were never clearly thought out. The adherence to a global identity did not make other more limited bases for identity disappear. Without elaborating how identities at different levels could be articulated together, pan-Africanism remained an empty shell with much emotional appeal but little concrete political impact.

Struggles waged in the rural areas continued to affect a large number of people, but they generally remained hidden from public and scholarly views (Beinart and Bundy 1987), which paid more attention to the development of urban-based movements. The latter advanced notions of a comprehensive transethnic African identity which, although growing in importance over the years, was facing competition from localized identities. Even long-term urban African migrants (though not the permanently urbanized population) frequently maintained a base in the countryside in which they invested their savings and to which they eventually returned, or at least planned to return, as permanent home. The organization of work in the gold mines and residential patterns in mining compounds and townships on an ethnic basis played a role in inhibiting the development of broad national identities. (See Ranger 1982: 141–42 for an overview of tribalism in the Johannesburg mines and Beinart 1987b for the rural-urban links in the identity in a migrant worker.)

The tensions between centralized and local identities affected national political organizations as well. The African National Congress was plagued by ethnic divisions, a problem decried by many of its leaders. Sol Plaatje, for instance, complained in 1931 that the "failure of our race to unite is due to the failure of its leaders to unite. The demon of tribalism is the great stumbling block to our unity" (quoted in Walshe 1970: 213, who also gives examples of leaders who promoted their own ethnic group even as they were serving as congress officials). Ethnicity was not necessarily obstructive of nationalism, however, since it provided necessary building blocks for constructing a comprehensive African identity and promoting pride in African history within the context of a regeneration of tradition on new foundations (Cobley 1990: 82–88). Pixley Seme, president of the ANC, thus appealed for African national unity by his joint invocation of the images of Shaka Zulu, King Sobhuza of Swaziland, and the Xhosa prophet Ntsikane, all ethnically specific symbols (see his 1932 pamphlet, in Karis and Carter 1972: 1.313–15). Only when ethnicity was constructed as a direct alternative to nationalism (as has been the case with the homelands policy of the apartheid regime after the 1960s) was a clash between the two inevitable.

Segregation and Incorporation at the National Level

As the social bases for exclusionary resistance politics in the countryside gradually eroded in the 1920s, urbanization and industrialization resulted in a rapid increase of the urban African population, which proved to be a constituency for incorporationist (though not assimilationist) identity and state politics. To counter this trend, the state devised an elaborate segregationist legal and administrative apparatus with the goals of containing indigenous people within state structures (and thereby effecting their incorporation) but on a separate basis. White liberals, a noticeable but small minority operating in the framework of state parliamentary politics, advocated an opposite course of gradual political incorporation. They thus found common ground with prominent elements among the urban-based African political organizations. Both groups conceptualized indigenous identity as distinct from that of other groups, yet part of a comprehensive South African collective. In their eyes, membership in the national collective entitled Africans to meaningful political participation, the precise terms of which were subject to debate and modification.

From the perspective of the government, "natives" were different from all other South Africans in that their history and culture made them unable to participate in "civilized" political life. In this respect, no distinctions between ethnic, religious, and regional segments among indigenous people were made, and the machinery of control was applied to all of them. This was the case with the Natives Land Act of 1913, the Natives Urban Areas Act of 1923, the Native Administration Act of 1927, and all other legislation in the 1920s and 1930s that had implications for the political status of Africans. The Native Administration Act, for example, defined "native" as "any person who is a member of any aboriginal race or tribe of Africa"; the specific race or tribe was inconsequential (quoted in Brookes 1934: Appendix III, 231).

The ultimate goal of white segregationists in the political sphere was to extend the racially exclusive franchise throughout the union by abolishing the special status of Africans in the Cape Province. In 1926 the Hertzog government put forward several bills seeking to abolish the nonwhite vote in the Cape. In its stead, Africans would elect white representatives, on a separate basis, to the House of Assembly. In addition, Africans would participate in the election of a Union Native Council (partly elected, partly nominated) to regulate their own affairs. Subsequent years saw intense debates and modifications of these bills until they were adopted in 1936 in a version that allowed Africans to elect indirectly (through chiefs, local councils, and urban native advisory boards) four white senators to the upper house of Parliament, and twelve African members to the new body of the Natives Representative Council (see the Representation of Natives Bill, in May 1949: 351–58). In addition, Cape African voters were allowed to elect three whites for the House of Assembly on a separate voters' roll. The bill was formulated as part of the general policy of segregation at the national level, in an attempt to reverse the growth of the urban, de-tribalized, indigenous population and their political claims (Lacey 1981: 52–83).

The campaign against the abolition of the Cape African franchise brought together a large number of Africans of all political tendencies in the All African Convention (AAC) of December 1935. (A thorough but skewed history of the AAC and its transformations in the 1940s is found in Tabata 1950.) The convention condemned the Native Bills proposed by the government and argued against segregation in political representation and land allocation. It argued that these policies resulted in the consolidation of divisions and the creation of "two nations in South Africa, whose interests and aspirations must inevitably clash in the end and thus cause unnecessary bitterness and political strife" (resolutions of the AAC, in Karis and Carter 1973: 2.31). The convention rejected the denial of common citizenship to Africans and asserted their right to participate in governing their own country, without being subject to the tutelage of their fellow white citizens.

The AAC called for full political rights for all citizens and specifically rejected the notion that African interests were to be realized in the native reserves. The policies of segregation and tribalism were "diametrically opposed to the facts of the South African situation," since "where the interests of the racial groups are inextricably interwoven, the attempt to deal with them separately is bound to defeat its own objects." The only way forward was the adoption of a policy of political identity that will ensure "the ultimate creation of a South African nation in which, while the various racial groups may develop on their own lines, socially and culturally, they will be bound together by the pursuit of common political objectives" (quoted in Karis and Carter 1973: 2.32). The more deferential and Christian tone that characterized early African appeals to the benevolence of the government and the British Crown did not disappear from the resolutions of the convention, but it was considerably weakened. Political incorporation on equal terms, though not assimilation, became the major demand of the movement, thus finding common ground with certain white liberal conceptualizations of the situation (see in particular Hoernlé 1934, with the distinction he makes between political equality and social mixture).

The determination of Africans and their allies to oppose segregation did not amount to a strong enough challenge to the state. An unprecedented white front, with minor dissensions, united to pass the bills in Parliament. The white supremacist National Party supported the removal of Africans from the common voters' roll, though its leader claimed that the continuing ability of Cape Africans to elect members of Parliament on a separate and limited basis contradicted the principle the bill meant to uphold: "The natives in the country will make use of the representation that they have to obtain more and better representation in our European legislative body. Out of that will come an agitation . . . for an extension of a representation of natives, and a conflict between Europeans and non-Europeans in the country, such as has not existed up to the present" (speech by D. F. Malan, in Union of South Africa 1936: 706–7).

Even a would-be liberal like General Smuts, then the minister of justice, supported the bill as an extension of the successful system of native representation in the Bunga—the Transkeian General Council (Union of South Africa 1936: 893–94). Only a few liberals, such as J. H. Hofmeyr, minister of the interior, opposed the bill (but not segregation in principle) because its central feature was "to give to the natives an inferior, a qualified citizenship . . . which bears the added stigma that whatever may be the advance of the native in civilisation and education, to all intents and purposes he is limited for all time to three members in a House of 153" (1085). In a revealing passage, Hofmeyr ascribed the bill to the fear of all whites of "being drowned in a black ocean" and being subject to "race mixture and miscegenation" (1089).

The power of white racial fear was indeed behind the bill. To counter it, Africans needed to mobilize their own sense of racial identity as indigenous people or as all non-Europeans. A major failing of the AAC, despite its broad representative character, was that it did not lead to mass campaigns involving the majority of Africans who did not have much to gain from retaining a system of suffrage from which they were excluded anyway. To facilitate concerted action, in December 1937 the AAC adopted a constitution with a view to the formation of a unified organization, asserting that "the African races of South Africa as a national entity and unit should henceforth speak with one voice, meet and act in all matters of national concern . . . a Central Organisation shall be formed with which all African religious, educational, industrial, economic, political, commercial and social organisations shall be affiliated" (quoted in Karis and Carter 1973: 2.64).

The commitment of the AAC to a policy of political unity and mobilization was not sufficient to transform it into a mass organization. The political energies of most African activists were directed instead toward the new terrain created by the formation of the Natives Representative Council (NRC). ANC leaders in particular decided to contest the elections to the NRC, and they therefore ceased working with the convention (Tabata 1950: 30–43). The first elections based on the new system of representation took place in 1937. Although an advisory body and not a legislative one, the NRC was taken seriously by Africans as, perhaps, a future house of Parliament. These were the only elections at the national level in which Africans could participate, though only adult male taxpayers could vote (with a bias against urban residents). The electorate voted for several seats on the NRC and for the four white senators representing Africans in the Cape, Natal, Transkei, and Transvaal together with the Free State (Roth 1986).

Elections to the council were indirect. Voting units consisted of chiefs voting on behalf of members of their tribes, headmen of locations on behalf of members of the location, and local councils, native advisory boards, and boards of management—all voting as units on behalf of the people under their jurisdiction. Where these bodies did not exist, electoral committees were formed to vote as a unit. The voting strength of each unit was equal to the number of taxpayers it represented. In the Transkei, members of the General Council comprised the electorate (May 1949: 341, 351–58). The striking aspect of the operation of the Natives Representative Council, given these procedures, was that it involved directly and indirectly an unprecedented number of indigenous people in political campaigns, although the power of the council was very limited. By 1946 it had effectively ceased to function as a result of the frustration of its members with their inability to affect state policy in any way. As Z. K. Matthews, relying on African public opinion, explained the suspension of the NRC of which he was a member, "this experiment in political segregation has been given a fair trial by the African people during the last decade. . . . The time has come for them to recognise that the experiment had failed and to embark upon a boycott of the scheme" (quoted in Karis and Carter 1973: 2.233; for the entire affair see 224–61).

The Rise of African Nationalism

The suspension of the Natives Representative Council marked an important transition in African political organization. Together with the changes that took place in the 1940s in such other movements as the African National Congress and the All African Convention, it paved the way for the growth of an overall mass-based African political identity; it weakened, though by no means eliminated, the bases for local and regional politics based on particularist identities and loyalties to traditional leadership. The various African political organizations differed in their ideologies, social bases, and strategies. They shared, however, an appeal to all Africans, regardless of ethnic or tribal affiliations. In other words, by promoting nationally based politics they reshaped African (as well as South African) identity at the national level. A new incorporationist strategy was thus gaining ground among Africans. It expressed a quest for incorporation of all South Africans on an equal basis, and was sustained by the powerful assertion of African identity.

What was particularly distinctive about African nationalist policies of the 1940s was not the call for equal rights as such, but the new assertiveness that underwrote it. The new era of international relations and the anti-Nazi campaign, signified by the Atlantic Charter signed by the Allied forces in the world war, exposed the anomaly of the South African state, which practiced racial discrimination at home while fighting for democracy abroad. In *Africans' Claims in South Africa*, a document adopted in 1943 by the ANC at its annual convention (in Karis and Carter 1973: 2.209–23), the congress proclaimed that "the African people in the Union of South Africa, urgently demand the granting of full citizenship rights such as are enjoyed by all Europeans in South Africa." It further demanded "the extension to all adults, regardless of race, of the right to vote and be elected to parliament, provincial councils and other representative institutions" (217), and the abolition of the entire legal apparatus of racial discrimination and control. The substance, comprehensiveness, and tone of these demands were unprecedented.

The following year saw a step toward the adoption of Africanist principles as the foundation for indigenous organization in South Africa. The ANC Youth League issued its manifesto in which the goals of struggle were explicitly defined for the first time as national liberation and African self-determination (Karis and Carter 1973: 2.300–308). In elaborating further on the meaning of African national identity, Anton Lembede, a prominent member of the Youth League, invoked the historical memory of "the glorious achievements of our great heroes of the past, e.g. Shaka, Moshoeshoe, Hintsa, Sikhukhumi, Khama, Sobuza, and Moslikazi" (article in *Inyaniso*, 1945, in Karis and Carter 1973: 2.315). It is significant that all the aforementioned leaders worked and identified themselves with specific groups rather than with the general African collective. Furthermore, some of them showed far greater readiness to wage campaigns against other Africans than against European colonial forces. At the same time that they were appropriated by Africanists as heroes, they were also claimed by specific ethnic movements in and outside of South Africa. Their relations with the African heritage were thus much more complex than was acknowledged by African nationalists.

Echoing themes first raised by Marcus Garvey, though rejecting his extremism, the Youth League defined Africa as the "Blackman's Continent" (basic policy of the Congress Youth League, manifesto in Karis and Carter 1973: 2.327). It saw a place in the country for other groups but denied them any leadership role in the struggle for national liberation. As South Africa was "a country of four chief nationalities . . . three of which (the Africans, Coloureds and Indians) suffer national oppression" (329), cooperation between all those excluded by white domination was called for, though they were to organize on a separate basis. Nationalism superseded tribal identities, though drawing at the same time on the historical legacies of struggles waged in the name of prenational concerns. With the emergence of nationalism, tribalism became "the mortal foe of African Nationalism," thus necessitating a "relentless war on Centri-fugal tribalism" (330; see, in a similar vein, Tabata 1950: 101–10.)

The Africanist transformation of the ANC, driven by the Youth League, was completed by the adoption of a new program in 1949 in which "National freedom" was declared the foremost goal of the congress (ANC Programme of Action, in Karis and Carter 1973: 2.337). The vehement rejection of white domination and the radicalization of the ANC did not stand in contradiction to the continued emphasis on political incorporation. On the contrary, they asserted the right to full participation on the basis of equality in all state structures. On the eve of the 1948 elections, Dr. Alfred Xuma, president of the ANC, called on Indians, coloreds, and Africans to "organise their respective communities," not to fight whites but to fight "the policy of discrimination and differentiation" in order to attain "common citizenship for all races" (quoted in Karis and Carter 1973: 2.278). The 1949 program of action which signified the triumph of Africanism called for "direct representation in all the governing bodies of the country" and for "the abolition of all differential institutions or bodies specially created for Africans" (337). In this sense, indigenous African politics demonstrated concerns different from those of indigenous Palestinians; the latter struggled for the formation of an Arab national government over the entire country, rather than for representation in the existing state institutions.

A similar consolidation of political identities at the national level took place among other groups. In the case of colored people, a movement toward wide, nationally based affiliations, though with a regional focus as most of them were concentrated in the Cape province, asserted itself. Organizations such as the APO fought for the specific interests of colored people but from a nonsectarian perspective, working occasionally in coalitions with the ANC and other indigenous movements. More radical activists in the National Liberation League and especially the Non-European Unity Movement rejected colored identity and the proposed Coloured Advisory Council, and worked to form a noncollaborationist national united front of all those excluded from political power by white supremacy (Tabata 1950: 76–88; Lewis 1987: 179–244). The position of colored people between the two major groups of whites and Africans meant, however, that their organizations were marginalized in the overall South African political arena.

Urban Life and African Identities

Indigenous people's political organizations fighting for incorporation into state institutions on an equal basis had the rapidly growing African urban population as their social base. In slums and townships a new culture developed, reflecting the aspirations and needs of the African urban masses. These "de-tribalized natives," as they were frequently referred to by anthropologists, were becoming free of the hold of traditional authority structures. Naturally enough, they had great affinity with movements that addressed their concerns as permanently urbanized people seeking a say in determining their life chances in their new place of residence. The move to the cities did not mean a complete separation from the rural areas and the identities and modes of organization that characterized them. It did, however, represent an important shift whose implications were becoming more pronounced with the continued migration.

The new urban culture was syncretic in its combination of diverse ethnic, racial, and religious influences. In places where people were of more homogeneous origins, such as Durban with its predominantly Zulu composition, specific ethnic legacies had a great impact on the emerging culture. Youth associations were based to an extent on the social solidarity of the past, rephrased in the new urban context. Discrete cultural elements "were moulded into a remarkably syncretic ideology of popular protest, overlaid with Zulu nationalism, and continually modified by pre-capitalist ideologies and the less-structured ideas of Durban's labouring poor" (La Hausse 1989: 31). This did not represent a transfer of identities and political loyalties from the countryside to the cities, but the development of a new form of political identity, bearing affinities with the past but separate from it.

In more mixed urban areas, the Witwatersrand in particular, the continuity between rural and urban cultures manifested a more salient African content, transcending but not eliminating the specific ethnic inputs. This was expressed in art, music, dance, literature, and a variety of other associations (Coplan 1982). Strong identification with black American history and culture was evident, helping to shape an African style that freely borrowed from many sources but had its own distinct character. In a remarkable testimony to American influences, the Great National Thanksgiving Celebration of 1934, which was dedicated to the centenary of the abolition of slavery in the Cape, concentrated almost entirely on American slavery (Couzens 1982: 323). The influence of black Americans on religious performance had been particularly notable since the late nineteenth century, when it had an impact on colored people in the Cape (Coplan 1985: 37–40), and it continued in multiple forms in the African townships of Johannesburg and elsewhere (113–39).

Cultural developments were anchored in an urban environment of inner city slumyards and townships. This was the context for the development of the *marabi* cultural style, a term referring to "the whole way of life of a people, the way they earned a living, the class position they adopted, the music they played and the way they danced" (Koch 1983: 159). This lifestyle was centered to a large extent around shebeens and beer halls and was expressed in nontraditional family forms, informal social networks, gangs, burial societies, and mutual aid associations. (See the case of Sopohiatown, in Proctor 1979, and Coplan 1985: 143–80; Koch 1983 focuses on inner city culture.) The emerging culture did not reflect a coherent ideology but celebrated the dignity and experience of ordinary Africans, and their desire for improvement and alternative society (Edwards 1989).

Although urban African culture did not acquire an unambiguous political character, it significantly contributed to the formation of a nationally based African identity and political orientation. The increased centrality of the cities in the rapidly urbanizing South African society allowed the urban African population to dominate the scene of national politics, despite their numerical minority status. They did not abandon their ethnic roots and frequently maintained family and other links with the rural areas. The living circumstances shared by people of various ethnic backgrounds, and their common exposure to the unifying force of the state, predisposed them to act in unison to assert their rights. With no basis (and consequent claims to land and power) in the countryside, they had to operate on the urban terrain, knowing full well that this was where their destinies would be determined.

Afrikaner Nationalism and the Road to Apartheid

The period of spreading African political organization and protest also witnessed the consolidation of white Afrikaner cultural and political identity. It led to the organization of a nationalist movement among the masses of urban and rural Afrikaans-speaking whites that eventually managed to capture state power and harness it to serve the special concerns of a segment of the white population as well as to entrench white domination in general. As individuals, Afrikaner politicians had been in control of the government since the union of 1910; all of South Africa's prime ministers and the majority of cabinet members were of Afrikaner origins, although they did not usually operate as the direct representatives of a specific ethnic constituency. People like Botha, Smuts, and even Hertzog were primarily concerned with securing stable conditions for white rule. It was in direct opposition to their legacy that the National Party, which emerged in the 1930s and 1940s as the party of Afrikaner nationalism, mobilized a divided people and their dispersed resources to take control over the state.

The basis for Afrikaner mobilization was the sense of loss of political independence. The Highveld settler republics of the latter half of the nineteenth century were defeated and conquered by British forces in the Anglo-Boer War of 1899–1902. White political unification, and growing collusion of material and political interests between the English and Afrikaner dominant classes, did not necessarily reflect a sense of common identity among the white masses. One of the crucial developments of the period was the emergence of the Afrikaans language movement. What started as a cultural movement in the late nineteenth century was transformed during the first half of the twentieth century into a comprehensive framework encouraging intense political involvement. The development of Afrikaans as a medium of popular, literary, educational, and political communication culminated in its substitution for Dutch as the official language of South Africa, together with English. It was part of the nationalist project of spreading Afrikaner consciousness in order to mobilize people on the basis of a politically motivated version of history (Moodie 1975; Thompson 1985).

Led by such educated lower-middle-class elements as teachers, church ministers, writers, and journalists, the movement catered to the aspirations of the poor and recently proletarianized working-class Afrikaners. It gave them a sense of belonging in the harsh and alienating urban world. It also served to distinguish them from their black neighbors, decreasing the "danger" of uniting with blacks on the basis of common material deprivation. Communally based social, economic, and cultural institutions provided a platform for aspiring nationalist politicians (most prominently the future prime ministers D. F. Malan in the Cape and H. F. Verwoerd in the Transvaal). They also facilitated the growth of an Afrikaner middle class, challenging English economic dominance and providing a material basis for the nationalist movement (O'Meara 1983; Hofmeyr 1987).

The rise of Afrikaner nationalism intensified existing ethnic divisions among whites. At the same time, it promoted a growing (racially exclusive) South African identity since it developed as a national movement, bringing Afrikaners from all over the country into a common framework. Regional differences did not disappear, obviously, but they existed in the context of a new and more comprehensive identity. Ethnic divisions among whites intersected, though did not overlap, with different positions on the political incorporation of indigenous people. Alongside the consolidation of white racial identity, trends of social integration in the cities gave rise to approaches that advocated a less restrictive social order. A liberal tendency among whites called for the recognition of the permanence of the urban African population, as expressed in the Fagan Report (for a discussion of it, see chapter 5). Liberal support for the incorporation of Africans who severed their ties with the reserves and saw their future in the cities was an alternative to the hardening of segregationist attitudes and practices advocated by the National Party. (For expressions of this liberal approach, see Brookes 1934; Hoernlé 1934; Lewson 1988.) White fears of the Black Peril proved more powerful, however, and the way for the implementation of apartheid was opened after the 1948 white elections.

In conclusion, the period leading up to 1948 can be seen as a struggle over the terms of political incorporation between conflicting interests. The state, especially under Hertzog's administration, adopted segregation as a goal and moved toward the disenfranchisement of colored people and Africans as people with the right to representation as individuals. Instead, the state created intermediary structures to allow representation of people as members of collectives. Tribal authorities, the Natives Representative Council, and the Coloured Advisory Council were attempts to give black elites a (limited) share of control, on a segregated basis, in return for a share in the responsibility for maintaining law and order. These arrangements did not amount to true political separation, on Israeli/Palestinian lines, as "no segregationist is prepared to surrender ultimate control, whatever limited measures of political self-government he might be willing to concede to the Bantu" (Hoernlé 1934: 264).

African political organizations fought for direct incorporation on equal terms, and for the abolition of all the specialized institutions and legislation which set them apart and prevented them from exercising their rights to citizenship. Nothing short of political incorporation could have satisfied their needs. They found common ground with white liberals who advocated the political, but not necessarily social, incorporation of indigenous people in a gradual manner. None of the different parties to the issue seriously regarded total segregation, involving the complete separation of white and black spheres of control, as a practical option. Even the hardline segregationists of the National Party did not envisage a situation in which state institutions would yield their control over "native affairs." The interpenetration at the economic, social, geographical, and cultural levels reached such a degree as to rule out this option.

Comparison and Conclusions

As was argued in previous chapters, indigenous capacities and settler strategies led to stronger incorporationist tendencies in identity formation and state formation processes in South Africa as compared to Palestine/Israel. These tendencies were not clear-cut, resolute forces overwhelming all manifestations of other possible courses of development, but they did push political struggles in the two countries in very different directions.

Indigenous Capacities

Overall, indigenous people in Palestine/Israel exhibited less internal diversity and a stronger sense of a unified identity than did indigenous people in South Africa. Palestinian-Arabs entered the period of the British mandate with a relatively coherent sense of themselves as a distinct group, united by their own language, ethnic heritage, and territory. They shared the first two with other Arabs in neighboring countries, but were internally divided by a fourth factor, religion, between Muslims and Christians. Nevertheless, their national identity was further consolidated during the period, based on two crucial components they had in common among themselves and shared with no others: the specific territory of Palestine (despite the fact that its boundaries were sometimes vaguely defined), and their exclusion from the Jewish-Zionist project. Within a short period of time, a unique sense of identity had developed among Palestinian Arabs, though they were not without their points of contact with other groups (such as Syrians, Arabs in general, and Muslims in the region and elsewhere).

Indigenous people in South Africa, in contrast, had not possessed at the beginning of the period a unified sense of themselves as a group. There were, rather, many indigenous South African groups, divided by language, religion, region, and political affiliation. There was little to unite them in the precolonial period, and they were conquered in a piecemeal fashion by colonial forces, in a process that stretched throughout the nineteenth century. When they entered the political arena of the territorially unified South Africa, they did so at different rates and within different regional constellations of forces. As a result, the process of constructing a grassroots-based, solid national identity that could supersede regional and ethnic identities, and form a foundation for a cross-ethnic and a cross-racial national movement was more problematic. Africans were internally split on many grounds, and they were also distinct in their consciousness, history, and legal status from the other black groups of colored people and Indians.

In addition to the initial heterogeneity of South Africans relative to Palestinians, certain elements of the cultural attributes of settlers and colonial powers managed to penetrate, and to some degree colonize black consciousness. Christianity in particular became both a medium for the articulation of grievances and a language of mobilization for political struggle. While some strong separatist sentiments were expressed through the independent Ethiopian churches, it was significant that they operated on a terrain constructed by colonialism. Indigenous system of beliefs could not have provided a unifying resistance ideology, precisely because precolonial identity as well as political realities were fragmented. To address the new situation of common political incorporation in the white-dominated state, it was necessary to create innovative modes of organization. In a sense, traditionally based exclusionary national politics were a contradiction in terms. Whereas indigenous Palestinians could refer back to their recent history in which they *as a group* were the indisputable majority with unchallenged claim to their territory, indigenous South Africans had to invent such a past, or else operate without such powerful unifying symbols. It was only with the rise of the Africanist tendency of the 1940s that these symbols could be created as part of the general rise of struggles for independence in the continent. Earlier attempts to resort to tradition were largely localized in nature, reflecting withdrawal to specific geographical and sociopolitical niches rather than attempts to transform society as a whole.

A dimension related to the difference between consolidating political identities in Palestine/Israel and South Africa is the character and operation of leaderships. Indigenous political leaders in Palestine/Israel frequently were experienced people who could function in the new arena by falling back on a rich tradition of political activity. They did not derive their experience from, nor were they trained by, settlers. Their political culture was truly indigenous, not in the sense that they had not been exposed to external influences but in the sense that they owed nothing directly or indirectly to settlers in this respect. In South Africa, indigenous elites were usually mission-educated; they organized their local activities in the vernacular, but on a nationwide basis ran their affairs in English. Furthermore, they initially enjoyed the support and guidance of white liberals, missionaries, and politicians, some of whom were possessed with a genuine desire to impart the benefits (or so they perceived it) of white civilization.

These factors acted to promote, even if sometimes indirectly, incorporationist dynamics, as their operation was based on cultural affinities between colonizer and colonized. Obviously, indigenous activists could articulate strongly nationalist and exclusionary messages in English, using Christian symbols, but in doing that they were testifying to the deep impact of some elements of the colonial and settler cultures. Even when these elements were transformed and deployed as weapons against colonialism, they had an inevitable effect on the terms within which struggles were waged. No such adoption of Zionist or Jewish symbols into Palestinian-Arab political culture was necessary or even possible. Islam, Christianity, and the Arabic language were all indigenous forces capable of investing political struggles with powerful ideological and organizational meanings without any need to borrow from the Jewish or Zionist modes of operation. In this respect, then, indigenous people in Palestine were able to maintain their cultural and political autonomy to a greater extent than indigenous people in South Africa and were consequently less open to incorporationist arrangements.

Settler Strategies

Jewish settlers in Palestine/Israel engaged in a conscious and strategically planned project of settlement and institutional buildup. They possessed a strong nationalist motivation for immigrating into the country, a motivation that shaped their strategies and policies with regard to indigenous people once they got there. Ideologically, they had specifically singled out Palestine all along as their desired geographical basis, regardless of their actual numbers in the territory. Their movement was founded on the assumption that a Jewish people with clear identity boundaries existed, and that their historical legacy conferred on them a valid and exclusive claim to Palestine/Israel as a homeland. They targeted the country, the land itself, as their goal and had no interest in the people who were living there at the time as objects of colonization, that is, as providers of labor or other services.

The drive to construct a Jewish homeland was premised on the idea that the constituency was already in existence, that they possessed a sense of themselves as a nation and directed themselves into the territory. The drive contributed to the consolidation of a specific national community in the territory itself. The Zionist leadership saw the emergence of that community as its goal and its own validation. The processes of Israeli-Jewish identity and state formation were thus devised in a way that maintained strong and impermeable external boundaries and weakened the existing internal boundaries (based on Jewish ethnic origin and religious practice), which were deemed divisive. This strategy, although not strictly implemented as initially planned, gave a powerful sense of overall direction to the unfolding of the settlement process.

In South Africa, in contrast, colonization was much less of a planned process. Settlers moved or stayed in places depending primarily on economic opportunities. They did not have a conception of the country as a whole until after they had finished establishing their rule over it, in the same way that indigenous people had not possessed a unified sense of identity before the Union of South Africa actually came into being. Furthermore, for much of the nineteenth century, settlers were internally divided among different political-territorial units and on the basis of ethnicity, religion, and loyalty to the British Empire. They were united, though, on the basis of white racial identity, a concept that came to occupy an important place toward the end of the nineteenth century and the first half of the twentieth. While white settlers were using racialism to distinguish themselves from others and to organize the allocation of power, strong nonracial tendencies were also exhibited in the domains of ideology and polity. Religion provided a counterdiscourse to that of race. Missionaries articulated notions of civilization which were potentially inclusive of all, provided they conformed to a cultural code of behavior. British-inspired Cape liberalism was similarly open, in a qualified manner, to members of all races provided they met standards of literacy and economic occupation. While liberals were by no means free of ethnocentric biases and cultural prejudices, their politics provided more room for the incorporation of indigenous people, as compared with racial politics whose reliance on biology made them very rigid. Seen in overall terms, most of the political debates and struggles among white South Africans throughout the twentieth century can be reduced to the conflict between these tendencies. Despite the strength of the rigidly segregationist tendency since union in 1910, liberal incorporationist trends continued to exert their influence.

Settler strategies, as well as indigenous capacities, were influenced by the role of the state. In Palestine/Israel the state was controlled by an external power, the British Empire, which saw its role as maintaining order, but not necessarily on settlers' terms. Its commitment to provide a secure framework for the development of the settlement project had to be constantly balanced by the need to defend indigenous interests, if only to prevent large-scale political instability. Settlers constructed their own institutions in which to pursue their own policies; the state itself operated under different parameters, including its regional interests and international obligations. It did not perceive its role as that of managing indigenous people on behalf of settlers. After its attempts to construct unified representative institutions failed, the state left the relations between the national communities to the communities themselves. As far as the incorporation of people within state institutions was concerned, in practice the state allowed the principle of *separate but equal* to take effect.

In South Africa, the state was controlled to a large extent by settlers. Even when it was part of the British Empire, the state was run by officials who shared with settlers their goal of managing indigenous people in a way that would secure white domination; it was not neutral in this respect. Whether through direct incorporation (as in the Cape), through indirect rule (through traditional chiefs in the reserves), or through segregated institutions, it took upon itself the responsibility for creating political and administrative structures to govern indigenous people. The South African state, unlike the British mandatory state in Palestine/Israel, made a distinction between citizens and subjects. Both groups were incorporated in the political system but on differentiated and discriminatory bases. The state was thus not external to society but deeply implicated in indigenous-settler relations. As a result, it instituted the principle of *incorporated but unequal* in its relations with the indigenous population.

7 | Historical and Theoretical Implications

When we examine the operation of the three processes of class, identity, and state formation in overall terms, it is clear that South Africa exhibited stronger incorporationist dynamics than did Palestine/Israel. As a result, the class structures, collective identities, and political institutions that emerged allowed members of diverse South African groups to cohabit to varying degrees, but in a state of deep internal conflict over the terms of their relationships. In Palestine/Israel, on the other hand, the unfolding of the three processes exhibited stronger exclusionary dynamics, giving rise to autonomous, though not always entirely independent, communal institutions. Political conflict became conceptualized as external in nature, pitting two mutually exclusive groups against each other.

Palestine/Israel: The Dynamics of Exclusion

From the 1850s to 1948, Palestine/Israel was transformed from a predominantly rural society, most of whose inhabitants engaged in agricultural production for subsistence and, to a lesser extent, for local markets, into a far more urbanized and industrialized society exhibiting a relatively high degree of complex economic activity. This change was initiated by indigenous forces—merchants, landlords, and peasants—who took advantage of the economic opportunities created by their greater integration into the world market since the mid-nineteenth century. Economic development was further accelerated from the late nineteenth century onward under the impact of Zionist settlement, which attracted into the country large amounts of capital and sophisticated technology and production methods as well as many skilled immigrants.

Economic growth proved a mixed blessing for the indigenous population. It affected different strata unevenly, increasing internal disparities. A minority managed to prosper as a result of the commodification of land, the growing commercialization of production, and the creation of large urban markets for agricultural goods. The majority, however, became less secure in their position as the impact of these same processes upset social stability and made their hold on the land more difficult to maintain. Despite the operation of these disruptive forces, throughout the period Palestinian Arabs *as a community* retained control over most of the productive land in the country and did not fall under the economic domination of the settler community. Although many of them lost their land *as individuals*, and some moved into employment with settlers, only a small percentage of the overall indigenous population were engaged in the service of settlers; the rest were largely self-employed (primarily on the land) or were employed by other Palestinian Arabs as well as by state and international companies.

The capacity of indigenous Palestinians to hold their ground, retain independent access to land, labor, capital, and technology, and participate in economic development on relatively solid foundations (though perhaps less solid than those of settlers) was a major reason for the exclusionary direction taken by class relations. It coincided with the dominant settler strategy of building a self-sufficient and viable economic sector that would not be dependent on indigenous labor and would result in minimal contact between the two national communities. These exclusionary trends were facilitated by the British authorities, who largely left intercommunal economic relations to the communities themselves to handle. Communal disengagement was never complete, but the overall tendency was clearly toward ever greater separation between Jews and Arabs, so much so that in 1947 the United Nations Special Committee on Palestine likened the relations between the communities to trade between different nations.

The same period saw the consolidation of mutually exclusive national identities, Palestinian-Arab and Israeli-Jewish, and corresponding sets of independent political institutions. Arabs and Jews had always been distinct from each other in terms of history, religion, and ethnic identity. They entered the period with few overlapping affiliations, and during the course of their encounter even the little they had had in common did not survive. The indigenous Jewish community, which shared to some extent cultural characteristics with indigenous Arabs (such as language and residential patterns), diminished numerically and was marginalized politically. The affiliation of members of both communities to external forces of identity—the Arab nation and Islamic world and the worldwide Jewish people respectively—reinforced their separation from each other.

The sense of totally distinct national identities made the prospect of forming common state institutions very remote. Both groups claimed the country as their own and expressed willingness to share it equally only if the others remained in the minority (Jews in Arab eyes) or became a minority (Arabs in Jewish eyes). As a result, both sides focused on forming their own mutually exclusive and parallel political institutions, with a view to taking over the country once the British forces left. As the British failed in their attempts to construct common state institutions, due to opposition from one side or the other, they facilitated the development of separate representative institutions for each community.

When the final clash of 1947–48 broke out, two separate groups with their own systems of class relations, national identities, and political institutions confronted one another. The coherence of Jewish-controlled structures and their degree of organization were higher than their Arab-controlled equivalents, and as a result they emerged victorious from the conflict. Comparatively speaking, however, indigenous Palestinian capacities to mobilize their resources and organize for political struggle were far greater than those of their South African counterparts, though their defeat was not any less bitter for that.

South Africa: The Dynamics of Incorporation

In South Africa the most significant process that took place from the 1650s to the 1940s was the creation of a society that encompassed within its boundaries people of diverse origins and economic occupations: indigenous hunter-gatherers and pastoralist farmers, slaves and settlers engaged in agricultural and industrial activities. From the beginnings of European settlement in the region to the mid-twentieth century, a dense web of social relations of land dispossession and labor exploitation continuously expanded to cover the entire population. Indigenous people, slaves, and indentured laborers were incorporated within settler-dominated economic structures in a subordinate position, primarily as suppliers of labor to the fields, plantations, and mines. In comparison to their Palestinian counterparts, indigenous South Africans did not manage to hold their ground against the settlers' political-economic encroachment, although dispossession was a long-drawn-out process. The dispersed indigenous settlement patterns, extensive agriculture, and lack of independent access (free of settler control) to capital and to productive and military technology made colonial expansion easier.

The pattern of forcible enlistment of indigenous labor in the service of settlers was coupled with territorial expansion, backed by military power, to bring about the formation of a highly inegalitarian and internally differentiated society, spreading from the western Cape to the northern Transvaal. Regional variations notwithstanding, by the early twentieth century South African social struggles had become focused on internal relationships between different elements in the economic system. Pockets of economic autonomy persisted in the native reserves, and to some extent in "white" territories as well, but their size and spread were constantly shrinking. Consequently, only a small proportion of the indigenous population was able to survive without recourse to employment with settlers. Thus by the end of the period, indigenous incorporation in rural as well as urban areas had become all but complete, prompting the 1948 Fagan Commission to define it as irreversible. Even the persistent attempts after 1948 in the form of apartheid policies failed to effect its reversal.

The trend of incorporation evident in the formation of class structures was also manifested in the spheres of identity and state formation, though in distinct ways. While a comprehensive South African national identity did not come into being, steps toward it were taken on different terrains. In this respect, South African conditions differed from those of Palestine/Israel in two crucial features: (1) members of different groups formed cross-cutting affiliations in the realms of language, religion, culture, and political identity; and (2) the consolidation of solid settler and indigenous identities encountered great difficulties in South Africa, as both settlers and indigenous people were internally divided.

Out of the cultural diversity that characterized the situation in the early days of settlement, a single creolized language—Afrikaans—emerged to become the common mother tongue of the majority of white and colored people. In addition, Afrikaans became the dominant lingua franca in the rural areas of the country. The spread of English was less extensive, but it did become the language of urban black political movements. Indigenous African languages continued to be the chief means of communication for the majority of the population, but none of them emerged to unify indigenous people in a way similar to the role of Arabic in Palestine/Israel. Settlers were similarly divided between Afrikaans and English. The overall result was that language developments in South Africa played a unifying role by preventing the crystallization of a clear linguistic divide, parallel to the racial and indigenous-settler divides.

Religion played a similar role. Christianity in particular became a cross-racial medium that unified people of various backgrounds at the level of consciousness, although at the institutional level racial segregation was prevalent. Even when strong anticolonial separatist sentiments were articulated through the medium of Christianity, as was the case with some of the indigenous Ethiopian churches, the religious discourse cutting across racial boundaries provided a common medium in which people of different backgrounds could communicate.

State formation was the one dimension which showed the least extent of incorporation. The political history of twentieth-century South Africa has been one of ever increasing exclusion of indigenous people from participation in state structures (until the 1980s when the trend began to be reversed). The state, however, took upon itself the responsibility for the governance of and control over indigenous people. This was done in an indirect manner through the tribal system in the reserves, whose operation was regulated by the central state, as well as more directly through the legislative and administrative machinery of the Native Affairs Department, location administration boards, and the Natives Representative Council.

When examined from the perspective of indigenous political institutions, incorporation seems a strong tendency. By the 1940s the predominant theme in African politics had become the demand for equality of political status. While this did not replace regionally based calls for political autonomy and the elimination of white rule altogether, the locus of political activity had decisively shifted toward posing a challenge to the state at the central level, with a view to full incorporation. The character of South Africa as a unified but internally heterogeneous country, in which struggles were waged over the terms of incorporation, was thus powerfully asserted in the sphere of state formation as well as in the spheres of class and identity.

History and Theory

The general point with regard to the study of history that has emerged from the preceding investigations is the need for a historical perspective. This means looking at history as an open-ended process that neither leads in any necessary direction nor has predetermined goals and outcomes. One of the most common methodological fallacies in historical studies is teleology, the assumption, not always made explicit, that what happened had to happen in a particular way because of the inexorable logic of some suprahistorical force, be it defined as the unfolding of the world-spirit, the laws of motion of capitalist development, or the dynamics of system differentiation.

In rejecting this logic, I have attempted to demonstrate that the conflicts in Palestine/Israel and South Africa did not follow a course determined from the outset by their essential nature as settler-colonial societies, capitalist economies, racial orders, ethnic states, or any other similar label that might be attributed to them. The incorporationist and exclusionary dynamics detected in the formation of these societies were not the inevitable products of the clash between settlers and indigenous people or between precapitalist and capitalist modes of production. Rather, these outcomes are best seen as results of multiple and sometimes random factors whose specific combinations cannot be directly derived from the general characteristics which these societies share among themselves and, perhaps, with others as well.

It was the accumulation of numerous events, the building blocks of history so to speak, which led these conflicts in specific directions. At any important historical juncture there were optional courses of development that might have been followed, with the effect of changing historical courses altogether. That certain roads and not others were taken was the result of struggles among diverse class, identity, and state forces, the outcomes of which were never certain. The perception of past developments leading naturally, as it were, to the present is misleading then. To emphasize this point, I have focused throughout this work on the central concept of *formation*. In the sense used here, it indicates a process of becoming; a process of creating new realities out of diverse materials that could have been used for different ends as well; a process of constructing social institutions and shaping their practices in ways that were not always inevitable.

Of course once a certain historical trend asserted itself and reached a degree of institutionalization, it reduced the likelihood of some courses of actions and raised the probability of others. In other words, it imposed limits on the randomness of history by creating specific terrains of negotiation and struggle within given boundaries. These terrains themselves, however, opened new possibilities for the operation of social processes, including the option of reversal of past trends. In the following sections, these abstract meditations are elaborated upon more concretely, beginning with the concept of class.

Class

The most important observation with regard to the operation of class in the context of this work is that class interests are formed in a historical process of conscious reflection. They are not objectively given by conditions which exist independent of the perceptions of various groups and individuals. Abstract class interests, waiting to be discovered and acted upon by human agents, are ahistorical constructs. Class interests have to be *created* and mediated by consciousness and action. Contested historical issues such as the possession of land, the use of cheap labor, or the exploitation of raw materials on the periphery of the world system are perceived in certain ways by people within terms set by specific class discourses. These discourses provide the framework within which interests are defined and legitimate ways of realizing them become available. There are no necessary and clearly identifiable relations between reality, existing on its own "out there," and its multiple representations.

A few examples will help clarify the point. Land at the sparsely populated Cape of Good Hope, in early colonial times, cannot be said to have been unclaimed and therefore free for European colonization or, in contrast, settled by indigenous people in a way that precluded European occupation. Indigenous and settler groups operated within different discourses of land occupancy which defined the ways they responded to material challenges. To be sure, the land itself and questions of access to it were real enough. The material interests that were shaped in relation to land, however, could not have been formulated independent of considerations of who qualified as a fully human being with rights to property, what form of land use was deemed civilized, which type of culture has a superior historical claim to natural resources, and so forth.

In a similar manner, the existence of mineral resources in the interior of South African was not in itself inherently valuable or, to the contrary, a meaningless feature of the natural environment. The value of metals and the feasibility of their extraction were determined by economic discourses which often defined similar material circumstances in widely different ways. Indigenous people were not in themselves sources of cheap labor, petty commodity producers, or potential consumers of European products. They were defined as belonging to one category or another, or any mixture in between, by various class and state actors who attempted to use these definitions to implement policies which were economically beneficial to their own self-defined interests.

Material needs, of course, affected such definitions, but so did collective identities and political programs. Take as an example European views of the economic role of Africans. When missionaries looked at the indigenous people of South Africa and saw millions of potential producers of marketable agricultural goods and consumers of the products of British industry, they were defining those people in a way that made sense within the terms of their liberal capitalist worldview. They saw the ideal of settled, prosperous, and "civilized" indigenous communities as religiously proper, but also as a rational and economically viable strategy of handling relations with indigenous peoples. When Dutch and British settlers looked at the same people and their habitat, and saw vast potential resources that could be used productively in the form of farm labor (if they were human) or be cleared of people to give way to sheep ranching (if it was land), they too were operating in terms of a worldview, albeit a different one.

The point here is not that ideology (religion, for example) matters in the analysis of economic developments, though that is obviously the case. To stay at this point would mean adopting the notion that class and ideology belong to two separate realms, the former objectively determined by economic conditions while the latter subjectively defined. The more basic theoretical point is that classes themselves, and their interests, are constituted within frameworks set by specific economic and ideological discourses. With this approach, concepts such as false consciousness lose meaning because they hinge on the separation between the objective and subjective dimensions of class.

I have illustrated this point several times in the course of the work. The use of indigenous people and slaves as sources of cheap labor in South Africa was possible because certain categories of people were defined in colonial discourse as exploitable and as fit to be enslaved. The economic strategies pursued by settler forces were not the only possible ones, nor were they necessarily the most profitable strategies available. They were adopted by settlers, however, because other options which were theoretically open were deemed unthinkable in terms of the dominant racial discourse. Viable economic options that were *not* acted upon, such as the adoption of the Dutch intensive family-labor farm as a model of settlement in South Africa, the maintenance of continued access of African farmers to land, and the formation of an indigenous labor aristocracy, could all have made the material livelihood of certain white class actors (to say nothing about blacks) at least as secure as the different roads that *were* taken. Nevertheless, to have adopted these strategies would have meant to go against the grain of accepted racial worldviews. Consequently, settlers did not follow those strategies. This is not to argue that the class practices of settlers were economically irrational, only that they acquired their specific rationality in the framework of certain taken-for granted assumptions about the proper class positions of different ethnic and racial categories.

To reiterate this point, class interests can be defined in various ways. We cannot postulate them on the basis of abstract models of modes of production. This is the case not only because reality is always more complex than its models (this is hardly disputed and is not a particularly novel observation), but because the subjective meanings attributed to classes and their perceptions are integral parts of class relations. This becomes evident when we consider the problems faced by the split labor market thesis. To argue in terms of cheap and expensive labor forces that have their own distinct interests is to forget the prior task of explaining how these forces acquired their ethnic and racial character to begin with. A consideration of the identity dimensions of classes is essential for reaching a satisfactory answer to the question of why some groups of unorganized workers were regarded by organized labor as potential allies (such as Jewish immigrant workers in Palestine/Israel or white Afrikaner migrants to the cities in South Africa) and others as dangerous competitors (such as indigenous Arab or African workers) to be eliminated from the scene or restricted in their access to lucrative positions.

Similar problems plague the cheap labor thesis. It fails to reflect seriously on the question of why the plight of destitute workers was seen by the state as a major problem requiring intervention in the form of charity and welfare programs (as was the case with whites in South Africa), while the poverty and destitution of other workers (Africans) were seen either as a positive factor that forced them into the labor market, or, in case they seemed incapable of productive labor, as a social problem to be "endorsed out" of the way and dumped in the native reserves. These issues cannot be adequately addressed by referring to objective class interests without analyzing the discourses of identity that defined some workers as fit to be exploited (or organized, as the case may be) and others as fit to be excluded on racial and national grounds. In short, class analysis has to transcend its material determinism in order to provide an adequate analysis of class issues themselves, let alone an analysis of other issues.

Identity

Identity, like class, is a concept that emerges in a historical process. The existence of nations, or racial and ethnic groups, needs to be problematized. Not only have nations not always existed in a fixed form, but their appearance on the historical arena at a given time is not an irreversible event. They can grow, stagnate, and decline, and the internal balance among the different components of their identity may shift over time, as demonstrated in the discussion of the interplay among the Islamic, Arab, and local-territorial foci in the Palestinian-Arab sense of nationhood. Furthermore, the meaning of terms given to or selected by certain groups is not fixed; the content of identical terms may appear unchanged on the face of it, even when it actually varies in time and space. To give an example, in Ottoman times, even as late as the second half of the nineteenth century, only desert nomads used to be referred to as Arabs. By the 1920s, the term had expanded to encompass all speakers of the Arabic language and had become universally accepted as the standard way of referring to that group of people as well as the preferred term of self-reference. Another example would be Jews who have existed as a group for millennia, but have been variously regarded at different times and spaces as a non-Christian religious minority (in Europe), a white ethnic group (in North America), or a national community (in Israel). The same group of people may define their identities differently, depending on the historical, geographical, and ideological contexts within which they find themselves.

The important point here is that we should treat national and racial groups as unstable in nature, not as immutable entities. In posing questions about the origins of conflicts between groups, we must simultaneously raise the issue of how these groups came into existence, or modified their character, in the course of the conflicts themselves. We should not assume that they necessarily existed in the same form prior to the beginning of the conflicts. This is obviously the case with immigrant groups whose arrival in a different territory can be traced with precision, but it also applies to indigenous groups. Indigenous South Africans did not exist in precolonial times as a group with its own clearly bounded identity and culture. There were, rather, *many* indigenous African groups and cultures. Commonly used concepts such as blacks, coloreds, Africans, Bantu speakers, Tswana, and Zulu are all relatively recent creations which emerged and became consolidated in a long historical process. The same is true for the concept of Palestinian Arabs. The focus on the formation of identities should thus direct our attention to the constantly (but not randomly) changing nature of groups and the conflicts in which they are implicated.

I have approached identity (and more specifically nation and race) in terms of the notion of boundaries—external dividing lines which separate groups from each other. Within groups, these lines may shift among different foci of identity. There are no necessary connections between the external and internal boundaries. These notions allow us to introduce change and contingency into concepts that have frequently been treated ahistorically. Instead of positing the existence of blacks and whites in South Africa (and Palestinian Arabs and Israeli Jews in Palestine/Israel) as cohesive parties to conflicts, we have to account for the process through which they acquired the group identities they possess at any given time.

In dealing with formative processes of national and racial identities I have extended the meaning of identity to include material and institutional practices. Identity is thus not synonymous with ideology. In the sense used here, the concept of national or racial identity is different from common perceptions of ideology which focus on the conscious beliefs of individuals. There is a need to emphasize the diachronic nature of identity as a process rather than as a system of beliefs and attitudes which are relatively fixed in time. In addition to consciousness, or the subjective dimension of identity, other important aspects are language, religion, and education, all of which shape identity, but not necessarily in a conscious way. Linguistic assimilation such as that existing between white Afrikaners and colored people, or English-speaking whites and Indians in South Africa, does not necessarily translate into conscious political attitudes and organization but nonetheless exerts a powerful influence on tendencies of incorporation and exclusion. The same can be said for the adoption of Christianity by indigenous Africans, and for the lack of common identity attributes between Jews and Arabs in Palestine/Israel. In conclusion, we have to move beyond purely subjective conceptions to explore other crucial aspects of identity.

State

State formation is frequently treated as a unidirectional process of extension of territorial and political control from the center to peripheral regions. In this work, I have expanded the term to cover not only the operation of the centralized legal and administrative systems, but also the political organization of elements external to the state, though working in relation to it. The concept of political-institutional power has thus been decentered to some extent; it has come to include organizations, activities, designs, and programs articulated by state-oriented actors, even if they operate outside the boundaries of the state proper. The attitudes taken by indigenous organizations in favor of equal rights for all persons in South Africa (civilized or otherwise) can thus be regarded as a moment in the state formation process. It is not only when the state opens its institutions to people and groups that had not previously had access to it that a process of incorporation can be said to have occurred. When elements barred from direct access to the state knock on its doors to be let in, using inclusive discourses in the process, they strengthen the incorporationist character of the political system in general, not just the state apparatus in a limited sense. The approach adopted here, then, creates a broader conceptual terrain for the study of political organization and struggle.

The historical discussions of state formation in South Africa and Palestine/Israel can provide insights into theoretical debates over the relations between class, identity, and state. In critical junctures in South African history, racial identity and state organization intervened to tilt the balance in favor of one political-economic strategy among several alternative policies, all of which could have served capitalist interests well. A case in point is the economic reliance on African migrant labor and the implementation of apartheid. Alternative liberal policies based on the creation of a settled indigenous labor force in towns and the partial political incorporation of "de-tribalized" urban Africans were defeated because of the strength of white racial (and Afrikaner ethnic) mobilization and the capacity of the settler state to block policies deemed threatening to its version of white domination. No

Historical and Theoretical Implications | 273

proper understanding of economic strategies can thus be gained without the incorporation of state and identity factors as well as other forces.

World-Historical Context

In addition to the concepts of class, identity, and state, the historical study points to the importance of the world-historical context for the analysis of colonial settlement and indigenous resistance. The colonization of southern Africa took place as part of the expansion of commercial and industrial capitalism in the seventeenth to the nineteenth centuries. It did not reflect any prior interest on the part of settlers and empires in the country and its peoples in anything other than their economic utility. The Jewish settlement of Palestine/Israel, in contrast, targeted the country itself as a solution to the economic and political problems of European Jews. The Zionist movement was interested in the land and the economic and human resources of the country only inasmuch as these were essential to the process of forming an independent state based on Jewish national identity. The entire settlement project took place as part of the late nineteenth-century awakening of central and eastern European nationalisms from which Jews were implicitly or explicitly excluded. It was facilitated by the self-exclusion of historical Judaism from its non-Jewish environments. This difference in the basic drives and historical contexts of the respective conflicts is of crucial importance in accounting for the differences between their trajectories.

The world-historical context shaped the three formative historical processes. Land and labor relations between settlers and indigenous peoples were affected by the opportunities offered and constraints imposed by the development of the world economic system. Colonization took place in southern Africa before production for the world (or even regional) markets became an important economic trend. Class differentiation was not very pronounced among indigenous people, and surplus labor was not available, as it was in Europe during the same period. Consequently an important element of the conflict revolved around the attempts of the settlers to coerce indigenous people into working in their service. In Palestine/Israel, market relations, integration within the world system, and land dispossession had all been more thoroughly advanced processes. The conflict revolved around the exclusion of the indigenous people from the settler economy rather than their forced inclusion in it.

In a similar manner, processes of identity formation were affected by the differential consolidation of national identities and movements in the various contexts of Europe, the Middle East, and southern Africa. The European settlement of southern Africa began to unfold at the early stages of modern nationalism in Europe, and at a time when it was completely unknown in southern Africa. The Zionist settlement project in Palestine/Israel took place at a later stage, when nationalism had already left its full mark on Europe and to a lesser extent the

Middle East as well. The construction of settler-dominated state structures was similarly affected by the prior existence, as in Palestine/Israel, or lack thereof, as in southern Africa, of centralized state systems in the region and internationally. In all respects, the encounters between indigenous people and settlers cannot be properly analyzed without paying attention to the world-historical context within which they unfolded.

Indigenous Capacities

The last point in this chapter concerns the choice of the precise object of inquiry. Though the assertion made here seems obvious enough, it needs to be stated explicitly: conflicts, or any other type of social interaction, involve by definition more than one side. All too often, however, scholars have implicitly, if not always explicitly, assumed that in order to understand the nature, direction, and outcomes of conflict situations it is enough to observe the dominant side—its interests, capacities, concerns, and strategies. This tendency is apparent in many studies of colonial processes that relegate indigenous people to the passive role of being physically present (or absent) in a given territory, without acknowledging their role in acting, reacting, and otherwise shaping the nature of the societies in question.

The same tendency is exhibited in most of the comparative studies of South Africa and Palestine/Israel, which as a rule do not take seriously the indigenous populations' capacities, initiatives, and visions as factors in the evolution of conflicts. To counter this bias, I have attempted to demonstrate throughout the work the crucial importance of looking at indigenous people not as passive victims or mindless obstacles to change, but rather as actors in their own right. This has profound implications for the question of the dynamics of exclusion and incorporation. No valid answer or explanation can be given without taking into consideration indigenous inputs. We have to go beyond concepts of resistance (which frequently imply mere responses to actions taken by others) in order to evaluate the pro-active role of indigenous people's strategies of material subsistence, identity reconstitution, and institutional buildup, as constitutive of all the formative processes discussed in this work.

On a general note, my point is not to elevate one concept to a position of supremacy or to keep adding concepts to the analysis to obtain theoretical pluralism. The crucial point, rather, is that the analytical concepts on which we focus never exist in isolation and can only be understood in their specific historical articulations with all other concepts that modify their dynamics *from their inception*. Thus, material production cannot take place even at the most basic level in the absence of rudimentary notions of collective identity (who is "us," who is "not-us," even in the smallest groups), political organization (who has the authority to decide what to do and how to do it), as well as gender (the sexual division of labor; organization of the family). These concepts have no distinctly identifiable dynamics existing outside networks of articulation that have to be studied historically. The creation, elaboration, and modification of analytical frameworks in close conjunction with specific historical investigations, and the conduct of empirical work in light of social theory, are the best ways of engaging in theoretically informed historical studies and historically grounded social sciences.

Bibliography

Official Publications

Palestine/Israel

Anglo-American Committee of Inquiry. 1946. *Hearings in Jerusalem*. Palestine.
Colonial Office. 1921. *Report on Middle East Conference Held in Cairo and Jerusalem*. March 12–30, 1921. Printed for the Colonial Office. London.
Government of Palestine. 1930. *Report of a Committee on the Economic Condition of Agriculturalists in Palestine and the Fiscal Measures of Government in Relation Thereto. Official Gazette* no. 258. May (Johnson-Crosbie Report).
———. 1931. *Report on Agricultural Development and Land Settlement in Palestine*, by Lewish French. Jerusalem. (French Report).
———. 1937. *Memoranda Prepared by the Government of Palestine for the Palestine Royal Commission*. London.
———. 1946. *A Survey of Palestine*. 2 vols. Prepared for the Anglo-American Committee of Inquiry. Palestine: Government Printer.
His Brittanic Majesty's Government. 1947. *The Political History of Palestine under British Administration*. Jerusalem.
League of Nations. 1922. *Mandate for Palestine*. Cmd 1785. London.
Palestine. 1921. *Disturbances in May 1921*. Report of the Commission of Inquiry. Cmd. 1540. London. (Haycraft Commission Report).
———. 1922. *Correspondence with the Palestine Arab Delegation and the Zionist Organization*. Cmd. 1700. London. (Churchill White Paper).
———. 1923. *Proposed Formation of an Arab Agency, Correspondence with the High Commissioner for Palestine*. Cmd. 1989. London.
———. 1925. *Report of the High Commissioner on the Administration of Palestine, 1920–1925*. Colonial No. 15. London.
———. 1930a. *Palestine Commission on the Disturbances of August 1929*. Evidence Heard by the Commission in Open Sittings. Colonial No. 48. London.
———. 1930b. *Report of the Commission on the Palestine Disturbances of August 1929*. Cmd. 3530. London. (Shaw Commission Report).
———. 1930c. *Report on Immigration, Land Settlement and Development*. (Hope Simpson Report).

———. 1930d. *Statement of Policy by His Majesty's Government in the United Kingdom.* Presented by the Secretary of State for the Colonies to Parliament. Cmd. 3692. London. (Passfield White Paper).
———. 1939. *Statement of Policy.* Cmd. 6019. London.
Palestine Royal Commission. 1937a. *Minutes of Evidence Heard at Public Sessions.* Colonial No. 134. London.
———. 1937b. *Palestine Royal Commission Report.* Cmd. 5479. London. (Peel Commission Report).
United Nations. 1947. *Report to the General Assembly by the United Nations Special Committee on Palestine.* Geneva, Switzerland. August 31. London.

South Africa

Department of Native Affairs. 1942. *Report of the Inter-departmental Committee on the Social, Health and Economic Condition of Urban Natives.* Pretoria. (Smit Commission).
Province of Transvaal. 1922. *Report of the Local Government Commission.* T.P. 1-1922. Pretoria. (Stallard Commission).
South African Native Affairs Commission. 1905. Volume 1. *Report of the Commission with Annexures.* Cape Town. (SANAC Report).
Union of South Africa. 1916. *Report of the Natives Land Commission.* U.G. 19, 22, 25-1916. Cape Town. (Beaumont Commission).
———. 1922. *Report of the Inter-Departmental Committee on the Native Pass Laws.* U.G. 41-1922. Cape Town. (Godley Commission).
———. 1926. *Report of the Economic and Wage Commission.* U.G. 14-1926. Cape Town. (Mills Commission).
———. 1932. *Report of the Native Economic Commission.* U.G. 22-1932. Pretoria. (Holloway Commission).
———. 1936. *Joint Sitting of Both Houses of Parliament on Representation of Natives Bill.* Cape Town.
———. 1948. *Report of the Native Laws Commission.* U.G. 28-1948. Pretoria. (Fagan Commission).

Books and Articles

Aaronsohn, R. 1983. "Building the Land: Stages in the First Aliyah Colonization (1882–1904)." Pp 236–79 in *The Jerusalem Cathedra*, vol. 3, ed. L. Levine. Jerusalem: Yad Ben-Zvi.
Abboushi, W. F. 1977. "The Road to Rebellion: Arab Palestine in the 1930s." *Journal of Palestine Studies* 6(3): 23–46.
———. 1985. *The Unmaking of Palestine.* Cambridgeshire: Middle East and North African Studies Press.
Abcarius, M. F. 1946. *Palestine through the Fog of Propaganda.* London: Hutchinson.
Abramowitz, Z., and I. Guelfat. 1944. *The Arab Economy in Palestine and the Middle East* (in Hebrew). Tel Aviv: Hakibutz Hameuhad.
Abu-Ghazaleh, A. 1972. "Arab Cultural Nationalism in Palestine during the British Mandate." *Journal of Palestine Studies* 1(3): 37–63.
Abu-Lughod, J. 1989. *Before European Hegemony: The World System, A.D. 1250–1350.* New York: Oxford University Press.
Abu Manneh, B. 1978. "The Rise of the Sanjak of Jerusalem in the Late Nineteenth Century."

Pp. 21–32 in *The Palestinians and the Middle East Conflict*, ed. G. Ben Dor. Ramat Gan: Turtledove Publishing.

Adam, H. 1989–90. "Israel and South Africa: Conflict Resolution in Ethnic States." *Telos* 82: 27–46.

Adams, J. 1984. *The Unnatural Alliance: Israel and South Africa*. London: Quartet Books.

Agmon, I. 1986. "Foreign Trade as a Factor in the Transformation of the Arab Economy in Palestine (1879–1914)" (in Hebrew). *Kathedra*. 41 (Oct.): 107–32.

Ahad Ha-Am. 1930. *Standing at a Juncture* (in Hebrew). Berlin: Jüdischer Verlag.

Al-Hout, B. N. 1979. "The Palestinian Political Elite during the Mandatory Period." *Journal of Palestine Studies*. 9(1): 85–111.

Almog, S. 1987. *Zionism and History*. New York: St. Martin's Press.

Amikam, B. 1976. "The Expansion of the Jewish Community and Its Economic Infrastructure" (in Hebrew). Pp. 285–391 in *The Jewish National Home, from the Balfour Declaration to Independence*, ed. B. Eliav. Jerusalem: Keter.

Anderson, B. 1983. *Imagined Communities: Reflections on the Origins and Spread of Nationalism*. London: Verso.

Antonius, G. 1965 [1938]. *The Arab Awakening*. New York: Capricorn.

Arab Higher Committee. 1937. *A Memorandum Submitted to the Royal Commission*. Jerusalem.

Arab Office. 1947. *The Future of Palestine*. London.

Armstrong, J. 1982. *Nations before Nationalism*. Chapel Hill: University of North Carolina Press.

Armstrong, J., and N. Worden. 1989. "The Slaves, 1652–1834." Pp. 109–83 in Elphick and Giliomee 1989.

Arnon-Ohana, Y. 1981. *A Sword from Within* (in Hebrew). Tel Aviv: Hadar.

Asad, T. 1975. "Anthropological Texts and Ideological Problems." *Economy and Society* 4: 251–82.

Ashforth, A. 1990. *The Politics of Official Discourse in Twentieth Century South Africa*. Oxford: Clarendon.

Assaf, M. 1970. *The Relations between Arabs and Jews in Palestine (1860–1948)* (in Hebrew). Tel Aviv: Tarbut Vehinukh.

Atiash, M., ed. 1963. *Collection of Documents of the National Committee of the Jewish Community in Eretz Israel, 1918–1948* (in Hebrew). Jerusalem.

Atmore, A., and S. Marks. 1974. "The Imperial Factor in South Africa in the Nineteenth Century: Towards a Reassessment." *Journal of Imperial and Commonwealth History* 3(1): 105–39.

Atran, S. 1989. "The Surrogate Colonization of Palestine, 1917–1939." *American Ethnologist* 16(4): 719–44.

Avineri, S. 1981. *The Making of Modern Zionism: The Intellectual Origins of the Jewish State*. New York: Basic Books.

Avitsur, S. 1971. *Daily Life in Palestine in the Nineteenth Century* (in Hebrew). Tel Aviv: A. Rubenstein.

Baer, G. 1971. *Introduction to the History of Agrarian Relations in the Middle East, 1800–1970* (in Hebrew). Tel Aviv: Hakibutz Hameuhad.

———. 1983. "Landlord, Peasant, and the Government in the Arab Provinces of the Ottoman Empire in the Nineteenth and Early Twentieth Centuries." Pp. 261–74 in *Economie et sociétés dans l'Empire Ottoman*, ed. J. L. Bacque-Grammont and P. Dumont. Paris: Centre National de la Recherche Scientifique.

Bailey, C. 1980. "The Negev in the Nineteenth Century: Reconstructing History from Bedouin Oral Traditions." *Asian and African Studies* 14(1): 35–80.

Balandier, G. 1966 [1951]. "The Colonial Situation: A Theoretical Approach." Pp. 34–61 in *Social Change: The Colonial Situation*, ed. I. Wallerstein. New York: John Wiley.

Ballard, C. 1989. "Traders, Trekkers and Colonists." Pp. 116–45 in Duminy and Guest 1989.

Barbour, N. 1969 [1946]. *Nisi Dominus: A Survey of the Palestine Controversy*. Beirut: Institute for Palestine Studies.

Barnai, Y. 1973. "The 'Mughrabi' Community of Jerusalem in the Nineteenth Century" (in Hebrew). Pp. 129–40 in *Chapters in the History of the Jewish Community in Jerusalem*, vol. 1, ed. Y. Ben Porat et al. Jerusalem: Yad Ben-Zvi.

Bartal, I. 1976. "The 'Old' and the 'New' Yishuv: Images and Reality" (in Hebrew). *Kathedra* 2:3–19.

———. 1983. "The Crystallization of the Old Yishuv in Palestine." Pp. 194–257 in Ben-Arieh and Bartal 1983.

Be'eri, E. 1985. *The Beginning of the Israeli-Arab Conflict, 1882–1911* (in Hebrew). Tel Aviv: Sifrait Poalim.

Bein, A. 1954. *The History of Zionist Settlement* (in Hebrew). Ramat Gan: Masada.

Beinart, W. 1982. *The Political Economy of Pondoland, 1860–1930*. Cambridge: Cambridge University Press.

———. 1987a. "Women in Rural Politics: Herschel District in the 1920s and 1930s." Pp. 324–57 in *Class, Community and Conflict*, ed. B. Bozzoli. Johannesburg: Raven Press.

———. 1987b. "Worker Consciousness, Ethnic Particularism and Nationalism: The Experiences of a South African Migrant, 1930–1960." Pp. 286–309 in Marks and Trapido 1987.

Beinart, W., and C. Bundy. 1987. *Hidden Struggles in Rural South Africa*. Johannesburg: Ravan Press.

Beinart, W., and P. Delius. 1986. "Introduction." Pp. 1–55 in Beinart, Delius, and Trapido 1986.

Beinart, W., P. Delius, and S. Trapido, eds. 1986. *Putting a Plough to the Ground: Accumulation and Dispossession in Rural South Africa, 1850–1930*. Johannesburg: Ravan Press.

Beit Hallahmi, B. 1987. *The Israeli Connection: Who Israel Arms and Why?* New York: Pantheon.

Ben-Arieh, Y. 1970. *Palestine in the Nineteenth Century: Its Rediscovery* (in Hebrew). Jerusalem: Magnes Press.

———. 1976. "The Growth of the Jewish Community of Jerusalem in the Nineteenth Century" (in Hebrew). Pp. 80–113 in *Chapters in the History of the Jewish Community in Jerusalem*, vol. 2, ed. Y. Ben-Porat et al. Jerusalem: Yad Ben-Zvi.

Ben-Arieh, Y., and I. Bartal, eds. 1983. *The History of Eretz Israel: The Last Phase of Ottoman Rule (1799–1917)* (in Hebrew). Jerusalem: Keter.

Ben-Gurion, D. 1931. *We and Our Neighbors* (in Hebrew). Tel Aviv: Davar.

Ben-Porat, A. 1986. *Between Class and Nation*. Westport, Conn.: Greenwood Press.

Ben-Zvi, Y. 1962a. "National Defense and a Proletarian Perspective." Pp. 103–10 in Erez 1962.

———. 1962b. *Palestine and Its Jewish Settlement during Ottoman Rule* (in Hebrew). Jerusalem.

Bernstein, D. 1992. "Jews and Arabs in the Labor Market of Mandatory Haifa, 1920–1948." Report. Haifa.

Bickford-Smith, V. 1989. "A 'Special Tradition of Milti-racialism'? Segregation in Cape Town in the Late Nineteenth and Early Twentieth Centuries." Pp. 47–62 in James and Simons 1989.

Bonacich, E. 1979. "The Past, Present and Future of the Split Labor Market Theory." Pp.

17–64. in *Research in Race and Ethnic Relations*, ed. C. Marrett and C. Leggon. Greenwich, Conn.: JAI Press.

———. 1981. "Capitalism and Race Relations in South Africa: A Split Labor Market Analysis." Pp. 239–77 in *Political Power and Social Theory*, vol. 2, ed. M. Zeitlin. Greenwich, Conn.: JAI Press.

Bonne, A. 1955. *State and Economics in the Middle East*. London: Routledge and Kegan Paul.

Bonner, P. 1983. *Kings, Commoners and Concessionaires: The Evolution and Dissolution of the Nineteenth Century Swazi State*. Johannesburg: Ravan Press.

Bonner P., I. Hofmeyer, D. James, and T. Lodge, eds. 1989. *Holding Their Ground: Class, Locality and Culture in Nineteenth and Twentieth Century South Africa*. Johannesburg: Witwatersrand University Press.

Boustany, W. 1936. *The Palestine Mandate, Invalid and Impracticable*. Beirut: American Press.

Bowden, T. 1975. "The Politics of the Arab Rebellion in Palestine, 1936–39." *Middle Eastern Studies*, 11(2): 147–74.

Bozzoli, B. 1981. *The Political Nature of a Ruling Class: Capital and Ideology in South Africa, 1890–1930*. London: Routledge and Kegan Paul.

———. 1983a. "Marxism, Feminism and South African Studies." *Journal of Southern African Studies* 9(2): 139–71.

———. ed. 1983b. *Town and Countryside in the Transvaal: Capitalist Penetration and Popular Response*. Johannesburg: Ravan Press.

Bradford, H. 1987. *A Taste of Freedom: The ICU in Rural South Africa, 1924–1930*. Johannesburg: Ravan Press.

———. 1990. "Highways, Byways and Cul-de-Sacs: The Transition to Agrarian Capitalism in Revisionist South African History." *Radical History Review* 46/47: 59–88.

Brain, J. 1985. "Indentured and Free Indians in the Economy of Colonial Natal." Pp. 199–233 in Guest and Sellers 1985.

Braude, B. 1982. "Foundation Myths of the Millet System." Pp. 69–88 in *Christians and Jews in the Ottoman Empire: The Functioning of a Plural Society*, ed. B. Braude and B. Lewis. New York: Holmes and Meier.

Braudel, F. 1980. *On History*. Chicago: University of Chicago Press.

Brookes, E. 1934. *The Colour Problems of South Africa*. Phelps-Stokes Lectures 1933, delivered at the University of Cape Town. Lovedale: Lovedale Press.

Budeiri, M. 1979. *The Palestine Communist Party, 1919–1948: Arab and Jew in the Struggle for Internationalism*. London: Ithaca Press.

Buheiri, M. 1981. "The Agricultural Exports of Southern Palestine, 1885–1914." *Journal of Palestine Studies* 10(4): 61–81.

Bundy, C. 1979. *The Rise and Fall of the South African Peasantry*. Berkeley: University of California Press.

———. 1986. "Vagabond Hollanders and Runaway Englishmen: White Poverty in the Cape before Poor Whiteism." Pp. 101–28 in Beinart, Delius, and Trapido 1986.

———. 1987. "Land and Liberation: Popular Rural Protest and the National Liberation Movements in South Africa, 1920–1960." Pp. 254–85 in Marks and Trapido 1987.

———. 1990. "An Image of Its Own Past? Towards a Comparison of American and South African Historiography." *Radical History Review* 46/47: 117–43.

Burawoy, M. 1976. "The Functions and Reproduction of Migrant Labor: Comparative Materials from Southern Africa and the United States." *American Journal of Sociology* 81: 1050–87.

———. 1981. "The Capitalist State in South Africa: Marxist and Sociological Perspectives on Race and Class." Pp. 279–335 in *Political Power and Social Theory*, vol. 2, ed. M. Zeitlin. Greenwich, Conn.: JAI Press.

———. 1985. *The Politics of Production: Factory Regimes under Capitalism and Socialism*. London: Verso.
Caplan, N. 1978. *Palestine Jewry and the Arab Question, 1917–1925*. London: Frank Cass.
Carmel, A. 1973. *The German Settlement in Palestine in the Late Ottoman Period* (in Hebrew). Jerusalem: Ha-Hevrah ha-Mizrahit ha-Yisre'elit.
Cell, J. 1982. *The Highest Stage of White Supremacy: The Origins of Segregation in South Africa and the American South*. New York: Cambridge University Press.
Chazan, N. 1983. "The Fallacies of Pragmatism: Israeli Foreign Policy towards South Africa." *African Affairs* 82:169–99.
———. 1988. "Israel and South Africa: Some Preliminary Reflections." *New Outlook* 31(6): 8–11.
Cobbing, J. 1981. "The Ndebele State." Pp. 160–72 in Peires 1981a.
Cobley, A. 1990. *Class and Consciousness: The Black Petty Bourgeoisie in South Africa, 1924–1950*. Westport, Conn.: Greenwood Press.
Cohen, A. 1970. *Israel and the Arab World*. New York: Funk and Wagnalls.
Cohen, A. 1973. *Palestine in the Eighteenth Century*. Jerusalem: Magnes Press.
Cohen, P. 1988. "The Perversions of Inheritance." Pp. 9–118 in *Multi-Racist Britain*, ed. P. Cohen and H. Bain. Basingstoke: Macmillan.
Colenbrander, P. 1989. "The Zulu Kingdom, 1828–79." Pp. 83–115 in Duminy and Guest 1989.
Comaroff, J. 1989. "Images of Empire, Contests of Conscience: Models of Colonial Domination in South Africa." *American Ethnologist* 16:661–85.
Comaroff, J., and J. Comaroff. 1991. *Of Revelation and Revolution: Christianity, Colonialism, and Consciousness in South Africa*. Chicago: University of Chicago Press.
Cooper, F., and A. Stoler. 1989. "Tensions of Empire: Colonial Control and Visions of Rule." *American Ethnologist* 16 (4): 609–21.
Coplan, D. 1982. "The Emergence of an African Working Class Culture." Pp. 358–75 in Marks and Rathbone 1982.
———. 1985. *In Township Tonight! South Africa's Black City Music and Theatre*. Johannesburg: Ravan Press.
Couzens, T. 1982. "'Moralizing Leisure Time': The Transatlantic Connection and Black Johannesburg, 1918–1936." Pp. 314–37 in Marks and Rathbone 1982.
Crais, C. 1992. *The Making of the Colonial Order: White Supremacy and Black Resistance in the Eastern Cape, 1770–1865*. Johannesburg: Witwatersrand University Press.
Davies, R. 1979. *Capital, State and White Labour in South Africa, 1900–1960: An Historical Materialist Analysis of Class Formation and Class Relations*. Sussex: Harvester Press.
Davison, R. 1977. "Nationalism as an Ottoman Problem and the Ottoman Response." Pp. 25–56 in *Nationalism in a Non-National State*, ed. W. Haddad and W. Ochsenwald. Columbus: Ohio State University Press.
Dawn, E. 1973. *From Ottomanism to Arabism*. Urbana: University of Illinois Press.
Degler, C. 1971. *Neither Black nor White: Slavery and Race Relations in Brazil and the United States*. Madison: University of Wisconsin Press.
Delius, P. 1983. *The Land Belongs to Us: The Pedi Polity, the Boers, and the British in the Nineteenth Century Trarnsvaal*. Johannesburg: Ravan Press.
Delius, P., and S. Trapido. 1983. "Inboekselings and Oorlams: The Creation and Transformation of a Servile Class." In Bozzoli 1983b.
Department of Economics, Natal University College. 1949. "The National Income and the Non-European." Pp. 306–47 in Hellmann 1949.
Derrida, J. 1987. "The Laws of Reflection: Nelson Mandela, in Admiration." Pp. 13–42 in *For Nelson Mandela*, ed. J. Derrida and M. Tlili. New York: Seaver Books.

Doumani, B. 1992. "Rediscovering Ottoman Palestine: Writing Palestinians into History." *Journal of Palestine Studies* 21(2): 5–28.

Druyan, N. 1981. "Yemenite Immigrants in Jerusalem: A Historical Survey of the Community from 1881 to 1914." Pp. 212–26 in *The Jerusalem Cathedra*, vol. 1, ed. L. Levine. Jerusalem: Yad Ben-Zvi.

Dubow, S. 1989. *Racial Segregation and the Origins of Apartheid in South Africa, 1919–36.* New York: St. Martin's Press.

Duminy, A., and B. Guest, eds. 1989. *Natal and Zululand from Earliest Times to 1910: A New History.* Pietermaritzburg: University of Natal Press.

Du Toit, A., and H. Giliomee, eds. 1983. *Afrikaner Political Thought: Analysis and Documents. Vol. 1: 1780–1850.* Berkeley: University of California Press.

Edgar, R. 1988. *Because They Chose the Plan of God: The Story of the Bulhoek Massacre.* Johannesburg: Ravan Press.

Edwards, I. 1989. "Swing the Assegai Peacefully? 'New Africa,' Mkumbane, the Co-operative Movement and Attempts to Transform Durban's Society in the Late Nineteen-Forties." Pp. 59–103 in Bonner et al. 1989.

Ehret, C. 1982. "The First Spread of Food Production in Southern Africa." Pp. 158–81 in *The Archaeological and Linguistic Reconstruction of African History*, ed. C. Ehret and M. Posnansky. Berkeley: University of California Press.

Eliav, M. 1981. "The Jewish Community in Jerusalem in the Late Ottoman Period (1815–1914)." Pp. 132–73 in *Jerusalem in the Modern Period*, ed. E. Shaltiel. Jerusalem: Yad Ben-Zvi.

Elphick, R. 1977 [rev. ed. 1985]. *Kraal and Castle: Khoikhoi and the Founding of White South Africa.* New Haven: Yale University Press.

———. 1981. "Africans and the Christian Campaign in Southern Africa." Pp. 270–307 in Lamar and Thompson 1981.

———. 1983. "A Comparative History of White Supremacy." *Journal of Interdisciplinary History* 13(3): 503–13.

Elphick, R., and H. Giliomee, eds. 1989. *The Shaping of South African Society, 1652–1840.* Middletown, Conn.: Wesleyan University Press.

Elphick, R., and V. C. Malherbe. 1989. "The Koisan to 1828." Pp. 3–65 in Elphick and Giliomee 1989.

Elphick, R., and R. Shell. 1989. "Intergroup Relations: Khoikhoi, Settlers, Slaves and Free Blacks, 1652–1795." Pp. 184–242 in Elphick and Giliomee 1989.

Epstein, Y. 1907. "The Hidden Question" (in Hebrew). *Ha-Shiloah* 17: 193–206.

Erez, Y., ed. 1962. *"Ha-Ahdut": a Selection of the Periodical Literature of the Jewish Social Democratic Workers' Party in Palestine (Poalei Zion), 1907–1919* (in Hebrew). Tel Aviv: Am Oved.

Esco Foundation. 1947. *Palestine: A Study of Jewish, Arab, and British Policies.* New Haven: Yale University Press.

Etherington, N. 1985. "African Economic Experiments in Colonial Natal, 1845–1880." Pp. 265–85 in Guest and Sellers 1985.

———. 1989. "The 'Shepstone System'" in the Colony of Natal and beyond the Borders." Pp. 170–92 in Duminy and Guest 1989.

Ettinger, S., and I. Bartal. 1982. "The First Aliyah: Ideological Roots and Practical Accomplishments." Pp. 197–227 in *The Jerusalem Cathedra*, vol.2, ed. L. Levine. Jerusalem: Yad Ben-Zvi.

Eybers, G. W. 1918. *Select Constitutional Documents Illustrating South African History, 1795–1910.* London.

Fanon, F. 1963. *The Wretched of the Earth.* New York: Grove Press.

Farsoun, S. 1976. "Settler Colonialism and Herrenvolk Democracy." Pp. 13–21 in Stevens and Elmessiri 1976.
Fieldhouse, D. K. 1966. *The Colonial Empires*. London: Weidenfeld and Nicholson.
Finn, J. 1878. *Stirring Times or Records from Jerusalem Counsular Chronicles of 1853 to 1856*. 2 vols. London: C. Kegan Paul.
Firestone, Y. 1981. "Land Equalization and Factor Scarcities: Holding Size and the Burden of Impositions in Imperial Russia and the Late Ottoman Levant." *Journal of Economic History* 41 (4): 813–33.
———. 1982. "Crop-sharing Economics in Mandatory Palestine." Pp. 153–94 in *Palestine and Israel in the Nineteenth and Twentieth Centuries*, ed. E. Kedourie and S. Haim. London: Frank Cass.
Flapan, S. 1979. *Zionism and the Palestinians*. London: Croom Helm.
Foster-Carter, A. 1978. "The Modes of Production Controversy." *New Left Review* 107: 47–77.
Foucault, M. 1980. *Power/Knowledge*. Ed. C. Gordon, trans. C. Gordon et al. New York: Pantheon Books.
Fox-Genovese, E., and E. Genovese. 1983. *Fruits of Merchant Capital: Slavery and Bourgeois Property in the Rise and Expansion of Capitalism*. New York: Oxford University Press.
Frank, A. G. 1969. *Capitalism and Underdevelopment in Latin America*. New York: Monthly Review Press.
Fredrickson, G. 1981. *White Supremacy: A Comparative Study in American and South African History*. New York: Oxford University Press.
———. 1988. *The Arrogance of Race: Historical Perspectives on Slavery, Racism, and Social Inequality*. Middletown, Conn.: Wesleyan University Press.
Freund, B. 1989a. "The Cape under the Transitional Governments, 1795–1814." Pp. 324–57 in Elphick and Giliomee 1989.
———. 1989b. "The Social Character of Secondary Industry in South Africa, 1915–1945." Pp. 78–119 in *Organisation and Economic Change*, ed. A. Mabin. Johannesburg: Ravan Press.
Friedman, M. 1976. "On the Structure of Communal Leadership and the Rabbinate in the 'Old Ashkenazi Yishuv' towards the End of Ottoman Rule" (in Hebrew). Pp. 273–86 in *Chapters in the History of the Jewish Community in Jerusalem*, vol. 2, ed. Y. Ben Porat et al. Jerusalem: Yad Ben-Zvi.
———. 1978. *Society and Religion: The Non-Zionist Jewish Orthodoxy in Palestine, 1918–1936* (in Hebrew). Jerusalem: Yad Ben-Zvi.
Gat, B. 1974. *The Jewish Yishuv in Palestine, 1840–1881* (in Hebrew). Jerusalem: Yad Ben-Zvi.
Gellner, E. 1983. *Nations and Nationalism*. Ithaca, N.Y.: Cornell University Press.
Gerber, H. 1985. *Ottoman Rule in Jerusalem, 1890–1914*. Berlin: K. Schwarz.
———. 1987. *The Social Origins of the Modern Middle East*. Boulder, Colo.: Lynne Riener.
Giladi, D. 1983. "The Jewish Argicultural Settlements in Palestine, 1882–1917." Pp. 274–91 in Ben-Arieh and Bartal 1983.
Giladi, D., and Y. Shavit. 1983. "The Organization of the Yishuv: From Ethnic and Local to the Beginning of National Organization." Pp. 298–306 in Ben-Arieh and Bartal 1983.
Gilbar, G. 1986. "The Growing Economic Involvement of Palestine with the West, 1865–1914." Pp. 188–210 in *Palestine in the Late Ottoman Period*, ed. D. Kushner. Jerusalem: Yad Ben-Zvi.
Giliomee, H. 1981. "Processes in Development of the Southern African Frontier." Pp. 76–119 in Lamar and Thompson 1981.

———. 1983. "Eighteenth-Century Cape Society and Its Historiography: Culture, Race, and Class." *Social Dynamics* 9(1): 18–29.
———. 1989a. "The Eastern Frontier, 1770–1812." Pp. 421–71 in Elphick and Giliomee 1989.
———. 1989b. "The Beginnings of Afrikaner Ethnic Consciousness, 1850–1915." Pp. 21–54 in Vail 1989.
Giliomee, H., And J. Gagiano, eds. 1990. *The Elusive Search for Peace: South Africa, Israel and Northern Ireland*. Cape Town: Oxford University Press.
Godlo, R. H. 1933. "Urban Native Conditions." Pp. 100–107 in *Some Aspects of the Native Question: Selected Addresses Delivered at the Fifth National European-Bantu Conference in Bloemfontein*. Johannesburg: South African Institute of Race Relations.
Goldin, I. 1987. *Making Race: The Politics and Economics of Coloured Identity in South Africa*. Cape Town: Maskew Miller Longman.
Gorny, Y. 1985. *Zionism and the Arabs, 1882–1948: A Study of Ideology* (in Hebrew). Tel Aviv: Am Oved.
Gozansky, T. 1986. *The Formation of Capitalsim in Palestine* (in Hebrew). Haifa: University Publishing Projects.
Graham-Brown, S. 1982. "The Political Economy of Jabal Nablus, 1920–1948." Pp. 88–176 in Owen 1982.
Granott, A. 1952. *The Land System of Palestine*. London: Eyre and Spottiswoode.
Greenberg, S. 1980. *Race and the State in Capitalist Development: Comparative Perspectives*. New Haven: Yale University Press.
Greenstein, R. 1994. "The Study of South African Society: Towards a New Agenda for Comparative Historical Inquiry." *Journal of Southern African Studies* 20(4): 641–61.
Gross, N. 1976. "Economic Transformations in Palestine in the Late Ottoman Period" (in Hebrew). *Kathedra* 2: 109–25.
———. 1984. "The Economic Policy of the Mandatory Government in Palestine." *Research in Economic History* 9:143–85.
Guelke, L. 1989. "Freehold Farmers and Frontier Settlers, 1657–1780." Pp. 66–108 in Elphick and Giliomee 1989.
Guest, B. 1989. "The New Economy." Pp. 302–23 in Duminy and Guest 1989.
Guest, B., and J. Sellers, eds. 1985. *Enterprise and Exploitation in a Victorian Colony: Aspects of the Economic and Social History of Colonial Natal*. Pietermaritzburg: University of Natal Press.
Guy, G. 1979. *The Destruction of the Zulu Kingdom*. London: Longman.
———. 1982. "The Destruction and Reconstruction of Zulu Society." Pp. 167–94 in Marks and Rathbone 1982.
———. 1987. "Analysing Pre-Capitalist Societies in Southern Africa." *Journal of Southern African Studies* 14(1): 18–37.
Hadawi, S. 1988. *Palestinian Rights and Losses in 1948: A Comprehensive Study*. London: Saqi Books.
Halevi, S. 1976. "The Beginnings of the Hebrew Press in Palestine" (in Hebrew). Pp. 239–54 in *Chapters of the History of the Jewish Community in Jerusalem*, vol. 2, ed. Y. Ben-Porat et al. Jerusalem: Yad Ben-Zvi.
Hall, M. 1987. "Archaeology and Modes of Production in Pre-colonial Southern Africa." *Journal of Southern African Studies* 14(1): 1–17.
Halper, J. 1991. *Between Redemption and Revival: The Jewish Yishuv of Jerusalem in the Nineteenth Century*. Boulder, Colo.: Westview Press.
Hamilton, C. 1993. "Authoring Shaka: Models, Metaphors and Historiography." Ph.D. diss. Johns Hopkins University.

Hammond-Tooke, W. D. 1985. "Descent Groups, Chiefdoms and South African Historiography." *Journal of Southern African Studies* 11(2): 305–19.
Harries, P. 1982. "Kinship, Ideology and the Nature of Pre-colonial Labour Migration: Labour Migration from the Delagoa Bay Hinterland to South Africa, up to 1895." Pp. 142–66 in Marks and Rathbone 1982.
Harrinck, G. 1969. "Interaction between Xhosa and Khoi: Emphasis on the Period 1620–1750." Pp. 145–70 in *African Societies in Southern Africa,* ed. L. Thompson. New York: Praeger.
Hellmann, E., ed. 1949. *Handbook on Race Relations in South Africa.* Published for the South Africa Institute of Race Relations. Cape Town: Oxford University Press.
Hershlag, Z. 1964. *Introduction to the Modern Economic History of the Middle East.* Leiden: E. J. Brill.
Herzog, H. 1987. "The Terms 'Old Yishuv' and 'New Yishuv': A Sociological Approach " (in Hebrew). *Kathedra* 32: 99–108.
Hill, R., and G. Pirio. 1987. "'Africa for the Africans': The Garvey Movement in South Africa, 1920–1940." Pp. 209–53 in Marks and Trapido 1987.
Himadeh, S., ed. 1938. *Economic Organization of Palestine.* Beirut.
Hindson, D. 1987. *Pass Controls and the Urban African Proletariat.* Johannesburg: Ravan Press.
Hobsbawm, E., and T. Ranger, eds. 1983. *The Invention of Tradition.* Cambridge: Cambridge University Press.
Hoernlé, R. F. A. 1934. "Race-Mixture and Native Policy in South Africa." Pp. 263–81 in Schapera 1934.
Hoexter, M. 1973. "The Role of Qays and Yaman Factions in Local Political Divisions." *Asian and African Studies* 9(3): 279–311.
Hofman, Y. 1975. "The Administration of Syria and Palestine under Egyptian Rule (1831–1840)." Pp. 311–33 in Maoz 1975.
Hofmeyr, I. 1987. "Building a Nation from Words: Afrikaans Language, Literature and Ethnic Identity." Pp. 95–123 in Marks and Trapido 1987.
Hopewood, D. 1975. "The Resurrection of Our Eastern Brethren (Ignatev), Russia and Organized Arab Nationalism in Jerusalem." Pp. 394–407 in Maoz 1975.
Horowitz, D., and M. Lissak. 1978. *Origins of the Israeli Polity.* Chicago: University of Chicago Press.
Houbert, J. 1985. "Settlers and Seaways in a Decolonized World." *Journal of Modern African Studies* 23(1): 1–29.
Houghton, D. H., and J. Dagut, eds. 1972. *Source Material on the South African Economy.* 3 vols. Cape Town: Oxford University Press.
Hourani, A. 1962. *Arabic Thought in the Liberal Age, 1798–1939.* London: Oxford University Press.
Hunt, L. 1990. "History beyond Social Theory." Pp. 95–111 in *The States of "Theory,"* ed. D. Carrol. New York: Columbia University Press.
Hunter, J. 1987. *Israeli Foreign Policy: South Africa and Central America.* Boston: South End Press.
Ingrams, D. 1972. *Palestine Papers, 1917–1922: Seeds of Conflict.* London: John Murray.
Islamoglu-Inan, H., ed. 1987. *The Ottoman Empire and the World Economy.* Cambridge: Cambridge Universtiy Press.
Issawi, C. 1970. "Middle East Economic Development, 1815–1914: The General and the Specific." Pp. 395–411 in *Studies in the Economic History of the Middle East,* ed. M. Cook. London: Oxford University Press.

Itzkowitz, N. 1980. *Ottoman Empire and Islamic Tradition.* Chicago: University of Chicago Press.
Jabbour, G. 1970. *Settler Colonialism in Southern Africa and the Middle East.* Khartoum: University of Khartoum Press.
Jabotinsky, Z. 1969. "The Morality of the Iron Wall" (in Hebrew). *Ha-umah* 7(4): 469–75.
James, W., and M. Simons, eds. 1989. *The Angry Divide: Social and Economic History of the Western Cape.* Cape Town: David Philip.
Jbara, T. 1985. *Palestinian Leader Hajj Amin al-Husayni, Mufti of Jerusalem.* Princeton, N. J.: Kingston Press.
Jeeves, A. 1985. *Migrant Labour in South Africa's Mining Economy: The Struggle for the Gold Mines' Labour Supply, 1890–1920.* Johannesburg: Witwatersrand University Press.
John, R., and S. Hadawi. 1970. *The Palestine Diary.* New York: New World Press.
Johnson, N. 1982. *Islam and the Politics of Meaning in Palestinian Nationalism.* London: Kegan Paul International.
Johnstone, F. 1976. *Class, Race and Gold: A Study of Class Relations and Racial Discrimination in South Africa.* London: Routledge and Kegan Paul.
Jospeh, B. 1988. *Besieged Bedfellows: Israel and the Land of Apartheid.* New York: Greenwood Press.
Kallaway, P. 1981. "Tribesman, Trader, Peasant and Proletarian." Pp. 8–30 in *Working Papers in Southern African Studies,* vol. 2, ed. P. Bonner. Johannesburg: Ravan Press.
Kanafani, G. n.d. *The 1936–39 Revolt in Palestine.* California.
Kaniel, Y. 1973. "Cultural and Religious Cooperation between the Ashkenazis and Sephardis in the Nineteenth Century in Jerusalem" (in Hebrew). Pp. 289–300 in *Chapters in the History of the Jewish Community in Jerusalem,* vol. 1, ed. Y. Ben-Porat et al. Jerusalem: Yad Ben-Zvi.
———. 1976. "Organizational and Economic Contentions between Communities in Jerusalem in the Nineteenth Century" (in Hebrew). Pp. 97–126 in *Chapters in the History of the Jewish Community in Jerusalem,* vol. 2, ed. Y. Ben-Porat et al. Jerusalem: Yad Ben-Zvi.
Kaplan, J., ed. 1983. *The Zionist Movement: Documents.* Jerusalem: Hebrew University.
Karis, T., and G. Carter, eds. 1972–77. *From Protest to Challenge: A Documentary History of African Politics in South Africa, 1882–1964.* 4 vols. Stanford, Calif.: Hoover Institute Press.
Kark, R. 1983. "Jaffa—The Social and Cultural Center of the New Jewish Settlement." Pp. 212–35 in *The Jerusalem Cathedra,* vol. 3, ed. L. Levine. Jerusalem: Yad Ben-Zvi.
Karpat, K. 1972. "The Transformation of the Ottoman State, 1789–1908." *International Journal of Middle East Studies* 3:243–81.
———. 1985. *Ottoman Population, 1830–1914.* Madison: University of Wisconsin Press.
Kaye, H. 1984. *The British Marxist Historians.* London: Polity Press.
Kayyali, A. W. 1979. *Palestine: A Modern History.* London: Croom Helm.
Keddie, N. 1981. "Socioeconomic Change in the Middle East since 1800: A Comparative Analysis." Pp. 761–84 in *The Islamic Middle East, 700–1900: Studies in Economic and Social History.* Princeton, N. J.: Darwin Press.
Kedourie, E. 1958. "Religion and Politics: The Diaries of Khalil Sakakini." *St. Antony's Papers* 4:77–94.
Keegan, T. 1986a. *Rural Transformation in Industrialising South Africa: The Southern Highveld to 1914.* Johannesburg: Ravan Press.
———. 1986b. "White Settlement and Black Subjugation on the South African Highveld." Pp. 218–58 in Beinart, Delius, and Trapido 1986.
———. 1990. "The Making of the Rural Economy: Fron 1850 to the Present." Pp. 36–63

in *Studies in the Economic History of Southern Africa*, vol. 2, ed. Z. Konczacki et al. London: Frank Cass.
Khalaf, I. 1991. *Politics in Palestine: Arab Factionalism and Social Disintegration, 1939–1948.* Albany: State University of New York Press.
Khalidi, R. 1977. "Arab Nationalism in Syria: The Formative years, 1908–1914." Pp. 207–37 in *Nationalism in a Non-National State,* ed. W. Haddad and W. Ochsenwald. Columbus: Ohio State University Press.
———. 1988. "Palestinian Peasant Resistance to Zionism before World War I." Pp. 207–33 in *Blaming the Victims: Spurious Scholarship and the Palestine Question,* ed. E. Said and C. Hitchens. London: Verso.
———. 1991. "Ottomanism and Arabism in Syria before 1914: A Reassessment." Pp. 50–69 in *The Origins of Arab Nationalism,* ed. R. Khalidi, L. Anderson, M. Muslih, and R. Simon. New York: Columbia University Press.
Khalidi, T. 1981. "Palestinian Historiography, 1900–1948." *Journal of Palestine Studies* 10(3): 59–76.
Khoury, P. 1983. *Urban Notables and Arab Nationalism.* Cambridge: Cambridge University Press.
Kimble, J. 1982. "Labour Migration in Basutoland, c. 1870–1885." Pp. 119–41 in Marks and Rathbone 1982.
Kimmerling, B. 1983. *Zionism and Territory.* Berkeley, Calif.: Institute of International Studies.
Kirk, T. 1980. "The Cape Economy and the Expropriation of the Kat River Settlement, 1846–53." Pp. 226–46 in Marks and Atmore 1980.
Koch, E. 1983. "'Without Visible Means of Subsistence': Slumyard Culture in Johannesburg, 1918–1940." Pp. 151–75 in Bozzoli 1983b.
Kollat, I. 1975. "The Organization of the Jewish Population of Palestine and the Development of Its Political Consciousness before World War I." Pp. 211–45 in Maoz 1975.
Kubicek, R. 1990. "Mining: Patterns of Dependence and Development, 1870–1930." Pp. 64–86 in *Studies in the Economic History of Southern Africa*, vol. 2, ed. Z. Konczacki et al. London: Frank Cass.
Kuper, L. 1980. "The Theory of the Plural Society, Race and Conquest." Pp. 239–266 in *Sociological Theories: Race and Colonialism.* Paris: UNESCO.
Kupferschmidt, U. 1987. *The Supreme Muslim Council: Islam under the British Mandate for Palestine.* Leiden: E. J. Brill.
Kushner, D. 1977. *The Rise of Turkish Nationalism, 1876–1908.* London: Frank Cass.
———. 1984. "Intercommunal Strife in Palestine during the Late Ottoman Period." *Asian and African Studies* 18:187–204.
Lacey, M. 1981. *Working for Boroko: The Origins of a Coercive Labour System in South Africa.* Johannesburg: Ravan Press.
Lachman, S. 1982. "Arab Rebellion and Terrorism in Palestine, 1929–39: The Case of Sheikh Izz al-Din al-Qassam and His Movement." Pp. 52–99 in *Zionism and Arabism in Palestine and Israel*, ed. E. Kedourie and S. Haim. London: Frank Cass.
Laclau, E. 1990. *New Reflections on the Revolutions of Our Time.* London: Verso.
La Hausse, P. 1989. "The Message of the Warriors: The ICU, the Labouring Poor and the Making of a Popular Political Culture in Durban, 1925–1930." Pp. 19–57 in Bonner et al. 1989.
Lamar, H., and L. Thompson, eds. 1981. *The Frontier in History: North America and Southern Africa Compared.* New Haven: Yale University Press.
Lambert, J. 1989. "From Independence to Rebellion: African Society in Crisis, c. 1880–1910." Pp. 373–401 in Duminy and Guest 1989.

Legassick, M. 1969. "The Sotho-Tswana People before 1800." Pp. 86–125 in *African Societies in Southern Africa*, ed. L. Thompson. New York: Praeger.
———. 1974. "South Africa: Capital Accumulation and Violence." *Economy and Society* 3: 253–91.
———. 1980 [1970]. "The Frontier Tradition in South African Historiography." Pp. 44–79 in Marks and Atmore 1980.
Lerner, D. 1958. *The Passing of Traditional Society*. New York: Free Press.
Lesch, A. 1979. *Arab Politics in Palestine, 1917–1939*. Ithaca, N.Y.: Cornell University Press.
Lewis, B. 1968. *The Emergence of Modern Turkey*. London: Oxford University Press.
Lewis, G. 1987. *Between the Wire and the Wall: A History of South African "Coloured" Politics*. Cape Town: David Philip.
Lewsen, P., ed. 1988. *Voices of Protest: From Segregation to Apartheid, 1938–1948*. Johannesburg: Ad. Donker.
Macmillan, W. M. 1968 [1927]. *The Cape Colour Question*. Cape Town: A. A. Balkema.
Mandel, N. 1976. *The Arabs and Zionism before World War I*. Berkeley: University of California Press.
Maoz, M. 1968. *Ottoman Reform in Syria and Palestine, 1840–1861*. London: Oxford University Press.
———. ed. 1975. *Studies on Palestine during the Ottoman Period*. Jerusalem: Magnes Press.
———. 1982. "Communal Conflict in Ottoman Syria during the Reform Era." Pp. 91–105 in *Christian and Jews in the Ottoman Empire*, ed. B. Braude and B. Lewis. New York.
Marais, J. S. 1957 [1939]. *The Cape Coloured People, 1652–1937*. Johannesburg: Witwatersrand University Press.
Marks, S. 1972. "Khoisan Resistance to the Dutch in the Seventeenth and Eighteenth Centuries." *Journal of African History* 13:55–80.
———. 1986. *The Ambiguities of Dependence in South Africa: Class, Nationalism and the State in Twentieth Century Natal*. Baltimore: Johns Hopkins University Press.
Marks, S., and A. Atmore, eds. 1980. *Economy and Society in Pre-industrial South Africa*. London: Longman.
Marks, S., and R. Rathbone, eds. 1982. *Industrialization and Social Change in South Africa: African Class Formation, Culture and Consciousness, 1870–1930*. London: Longman.
Marks, S., and S. Trapido, eds. 1987. *The Politics of Race, Class and Nationalism in Twentieth-Century South Africa*. London: Longman.
Marx, K. 1977. *Karl Marx: Selected Writings*. Ed. D. Mclellan. Oxford: Oxford University Press.
Matsetela, T. 1982. "The Life Story of Nkgono Mma-Pooe: Aspects of Sharecropping and Proletarianisation in the Northern Orange Free State, 1890–1930." Pp. 212–37 in Marks and Rathbone 1982.
Mattar, P. 1988. *The Mufti of Jerusalem, al-Hajj Amin al-Husayni and the Palestinian National Movement*. New York: Columbia University Press.
May, H. J. 1949. *The South African Constitution*. 2d ed. Cape Town: Juta.
Maylam, P. 1986. *A History of the African People of South Africa: From the Early Iron Age to the 1970s*. Cape Town: David Philip.
Mda, E. 1929. "The Extension of the Council System into the Transkeian Territories." Pp. 86–95 in *Report of the National European-Bantu Conference*. Cape Town: Lovedale Press.
Memmi, A. 1967. *The Colonizer and the Colonized*. Boston: Beacon Press.
Miles, R. 1987. *Capitalism and Unfree Labour: Anomaly or Necessity?* London: Tavistock.
Miller, Y. 1985. *Government and Society in Rural Palestine, 1920–1948*. Austin: University of Texas Press.
Mogannam, M. 1937. *The Arab Woman and the Palestine Problem*. London: Herbert Joseph.

Mokitimi, S. M. 1949. "African Religion." Pp. 556–72 in Hellmann 1949.
Moodie, D. 1975. *The Rise of Afrikanerdom: Power, Apartheid and the Afrikaner Civil Religion.* Berkeley: University of California Press.
Morris, M. 1980. "The Development of Capitalism in South African Agriculture: Class Struggle in the Countryside." Pp. 202–53 in *The Articulation of Modes of Production*, ed. H. Wolpe. London: Routledge and Kegan Paul.
———. 1987. "Social History and the Transition to Capitalism in the South African Countryside." *Africa Perspective* 1(5–6): 7–24.
Moyer, R. 1974. "The Mfengu, Self Defence and the Cape Frontier Wars." Pp. 101–26 in *Beyond the Cape Frontier*, ed. C. Saunders and R. Derricourt. London: Longman.
Muslih, M. 1988. *The Origins of Palestinian Nationalism.* New York: Columbia University Press.
———. 1991. "The Rise of Local Nationalism in the Arab East." Pp. 167–85 in *The Origins of Arab Nationalism*, ed. R. Khalidi, L. Anderson, M. Muslih, and R. Simon. New York: Columbia University Press.
Nashif, T. 1979. *The Palestine Arab and Jewish Political Leadership: A Comparative Study.* Bombay: Asia Publishing House.
Neumark, S. D. 1957. *Economic Influences on the South African Frontier, 1652–1836.* Stanford: Stanford University Press.
Newton-King, S. 1980. "The Labour Market of the Cape Colony, 1807–28." Pp. 171–207 in Marks and Atmore 1980.
Nkadimeng, M., and G. Relly. 1983. "Kas Maine: The Story of a Black South African Agriculturalist." Pp. 89–107 in Bozzoli 1983b.
Odendaal, A. 1984. *Vukani Bantu! The Beginnings of Black Protest Politics in South Africa to 1912.* Cape Town: David Philip.
O'Meara, D. 1983. *Volkskapitalisme: Class, Capital and Ideology in the Development of Afrikaner Nationalism, 1934–1948.* Johannesburg: Ravan Press.
Omi, M., and H. Winant. 1986. *Racial Formation in the United States.* New York: Routledge.
Owen, R. 1981. *The Middle East in the World Economy, 1800–1914.* London: Methuen.
———. ed. 1982. *Studies in the Economic and Social History of Palestine in the Nineteenth and Twentieth Centuries.* Carbondale: Southern Illinois University Press.
———. 1988. "Economic Development in Mandatory Palestine, 1918–1948." Pp. 13–35 in *The Palestinian Economy: Studies in Development under Prolonged Occupation*, ed. G. Abed. London: Routledge.
Palestine Arab Delegation. 1922. *The Holy Land: The Moslem-Christian Case against Zionist Aggression.* London.
Pamuk, S. 1988. *The Ottoman Empire and European Capitalism, 1820–1913.* Cambridge: Cambridge University Press.
Parfitt, T. 1987. *The Jews in Palestine, 1800–1882.* Suffolk, England: Royal Historical Society.
Parsons, T. 1977. *The Evolution of Societies.* Englewood Cliffs, N.J.: Prentice-Hall.
Peires, J., ed. 1981a. *Before and after Shaka: Papers in Nguni History.* Grahamstown, South Africa: Rhodes University.
———. 1981b. *The House of Phalo: A History of the Xhosa People in the Days of Their Independence.* Johannesburg: Ravan Press.
———. 1989. "The British and the Cape, 1814–1834." Pp. 472–518 in Elphick and Giliomee 1989.
Peled, Y. 1989. *Class and Ethnicity in the Pale.* London: Macmillan.
Penn, N. 1989. "Land, Labour and Livestock in the Western Cape during the Eighteenth Century." Pp. 2–19 in James and Simons 1989.

Plaatje, S. 1982 [1916]. *Native Life in South Africa*. Johannesburg: Ravan Press.
Porath, Y. 1974. *The Emergence of the Palestinian Arab National Movement, 1918–1929*. London: Frank Cass.
———. 1977. *From Riots to Rebellion: The Palestinian Arab National Movement, 1929–1939*. London: Frank Cass.
Posel, D. 1991. *The Making of Apartheid, 1948–1961*. Oxford: Clarendon Press.
Proctor, A. 1979. "Class Struggle, Segregation and the City: A History of Sophiatown, 1905–1940." Pp. 49–89 in *Labour, Townships and Protest: Studies in the Social History of the Witwatersrand*, ed. B. Bozzoli. Johannesburg: Ravan Press.
———. 1987. "Capital, State, and the African Population of Johannesburg, 1921–1980." Pp. 255–68 in *African Population and Capitalism: Historical Perspectives*, ed. D. Cordell and J. Gregory. Boulder, Colo.: Westview Press.
Ranger, T. O. 1982. "Race and Tribe in Southern Africa: European Ideas and African Acceptance." Pp. 121–42 in *Racism and Colonialism*, ed. R. Ross. The Hague: Martinus Nijhoff.
Rayner, M. 1986. "Wine and Slaves: The Failure of an Export Economy and the Ending of Slavery in the Cape Colony." Ph.D. diss. Duke University.
Reilly, J. 1981. "The Peasantry of Late Ottoman Palestine." *Journal of Palestine Studies* 10(4): 82–97.
Rex, J., and D. Mason, eds. 1986. *Theories of Race and Ethnic Relations*. Cambridge: Cambridge University Press.
Richardson, P. 1985. "The Natal Sugar Industry, 1849–1905." Pp. 181–97 in Guest and Sellers 1985.
Richardson, P., and J. J. Van-Helten. 1982. "Labour in the South African Gold Mining Industry, 1886–1914." Pp. 77–98 in Marks and Rathbone 1982.
Robertson, H. M. 1934. "The Economic Condition of the Rural Native." Pp. 143–55 in Schapera 1934.
Robinson, R. 1972. "Non-European Foundations of European Imperialism: Sketch for a Theory of Collaboration." Pp. 117–40 in *Studies in the Theory of Imperialism*, ed. R. Owen and B. Sutcliffe. London: Longman.
Rogers, H. 1933. *Native Administration in the Union of South Africa*. Johannesburg: University of the Witwatersrand Press.
Ro'i, Y. 1968. "The Zionist Attitude to the Arabs, 1908–1914." *Middle Eastern Studies* 4(3): 198–242.
———. 1981. "Anti-Jewish Relations in the *Moshavot* of the First *Aliyah*" (in Hebrew). Pp. 245–68 in *The Book of the First Aliyah*, vol. 1, ed. M. Eliav. Jerusalem: Yad Ben-Zvi.
Ross, R. 1976. *Adam Kok's Griquas*. Cambridge: Cambridge University Press.
———. 1983. *Cape of Torments: Slavery and Resistance in South Africa*. London: Routledge and Kegan Paul.
———. 1986. "The Origins of Capitalist Agriculture in the Cape Colony: A Survey." Pp. 56–100 in Beinart, Delius, and Trapido 1986.
———. 1989a. "The Cape of Good Hope and the World Economy, 1652–1835." Pp. 243–80 in Elphick and Giliomee 1989.
———. 1989b. "Structure and Culture in Pre-industrial Cape Town: A Survey of Knowledge and Ignorance." Pp. 40–46 in James and Simons 1989.
Roth, M. 1986. "Domination by Consent: Elections under the Representation of Natives Act, 1937–1948." Pp. 144–67 in *Resistance and Ideology in Settler Societies*, ed. T. Lodge. Johannesburg: Ravan Press.
Roux, E. 1949. "Land and Agriculture in the Native Reserves." Pp. 171–90 in Hellmann 1949.
Rubinstein, E. 1976. "From Yishuv to State: Institutions and Parties" (in Hebrew). Pp.

129–284 in *The Jewish National Home: From the Balfour Declaration to Independence*, ed. B. Eliav. Jerusalem: Keter.
Ruppin, A. 1918. *Syria: An Economic Survey*. New York.
———. 1925. *The Agricultural Settlement of the Zionist Organization in Palestine* (in Hebrew). Tel Aviv.
———. 1971. *Memoirs, Diaries, Letters*. London: Weidenfeld and Nicholson.
Ryan, S., and D. Will. 1990. *Israel and South Africa: Legal Systems of Settler Dominance*. Trenton, N.J.: African World Press.
Sales, J. 1975. *Mission Stations and the Coloured Communities of the Eastern Cape, 1800–1852*. Cape Town: Balkema.
Sartre, J. P. 1976. *Critique of Dialectical Reason*. London: New Left Books.
Saunders, C. 1981. "Political Processes in the Southern African Frontier Zones." Pp. 149–71 in Lamar and Thompson 1981.
Schapera, I., ed. 1934. *Western Civilization and the Natives of South Africa*. London: George Routledge and Sons.
Schleifer, A. 1979. "The Life and Thought of 'Izz-id-din al-Qassam." *Islamic Quarterly* 23(1): 61–81.
Schölch, A. 1982. "European Penetration and the Economic Development of Palestine, 1856–1882." Pp. 10–87 in Owen 1982.
———. 1985. "The Demographic Development of Palestine, 1850–1882." *International Journal of Middle Eastern Studies* 17:485–505.
Schutte, G. 1989. "Company and Colonists at the Cape, 1652–1795." Pp. 283–323 in Elphick and Giliomee 1989.
Scott, J. 1976. *The Moral Economy of the Peasant*. New Haven: Yale University Press.
———. 1990. *Domination and the Arts of Resistance*. New Haven: Yale University Press.
Shafir, G. 1989. *Land, Labor and the Origins of the Israeli-Palestinian Conflict, 1882–1914*. Cambridge: Cambridge University Press.
Shalev, M. 1989. "Jewish Organized Labor and the Palestinians: A Study of State/Society Relations in Israel." Pp. 93–133 in *The Israeli State and Society: Boundaries and Frontiers*, ed. B. Kimmerling. Albany: State University of New York Press.
Shamir, S. 1986. "When Did the Modern Period in the History of Palestine Begin?" (in Hebrew). *Kathedra* 40: 139–58.
Shapira, A. 1977. *Futile Struggle: The Jewish Labor Controversy, 1929–1939* (in Hebrew). Tel Aviv: Tel Aviv University.
Sharabi, H. 1970. *Arab Intellectuals and the West: The Formative Years, 1875–1914*. Baltimore: Johns Hopkins University Press.
Shavit, Y. 1983. "Education and Culture in the New Yishuv: From Traditional Orthodoxy to Hebrew Nationalism." Pp. 306–16 in Ben-Arieh and Bartal 1983.
Shaw, S. 1976. *History of the Ottoman Empire and Modern Turkey*, vol. 1. Cambridge: Cambridge University Press.
Shell, R. 1989. "The Family and Slavery at the Cape, 1680–1808." Pp. 20–30 in James and Simons 1989.
Shillington, K. 1985. *The Colonisation of the Southern Tswana, 1870–1900*. Johannesburg: Ravan Press.
Skocpol, T. 1979. *States and Social Revolutions*. Cambridge: Harvard University Press.
———. 1984. "Emerging Agendas and Recurrent Strategies in Historical Sociology." Pp. 356–91 in *Vision and Method in Historical Sociology*, ed. T. Skocpol. Cambridge: Cambridge University Press.
Slater, H. 1980. "The Changing Pattern of Economic Relationship in Rural Natal, 1838–1914." Pp. 148–70 in Marks and Atmore 1980.
Smilianskaya, I. 1966. "The Disintegration of Feudal Relations in Syria and Lebanon in the

Middle of the Nineteenth Century." Pp. 227–47 in *The Economic History of the Middle East, 1800–1914*, ed. C. Issawi. Chicago: University of Chicago Press.

Smith, A. 1984. "National Identity and Myths of Ethnic Descent." *Research in Social Movements, Conflict and Change* 7:95–130.

Smith, K. W. 1976. *From Frontier to Midlands: A History of the Graaf-Reinet District*. Grahamstown, South Africa: Rhodes University.

Smith, P. 1984. *Palestine and the Palestinians, 1876–1983*. London: Croom Helm.

Smooha, S. 1988. "South Africa and Israel: Are They Really Similar?" Lecture at University of Wisconsin-Madison, October.

Solomos, J. 1986. "Varieties of Marxist Conceptions of 'Race,' Class and the State: A Critical Analysis." Pp. 84–109 in Rex and Mason 1986.

Stadler, A. 1979. "Birds in the Cornfields: Squatter Movements in Johannesburg, 1944–1947." Pp. 19–48 in *Labour, Townships and Protest: Studies in the Social History of the Witwatersrand*, ed. B. Bozzoli. Johannesburg: Ravan Press.

Stein, K. 1984. *The Land Question in Palestine, 1917–1939*. Chapel Hill: University of North Carolina Press.

Stern, S. 1988. "Feudalism, Capitalism, and the World-System in the Perspective of Latin America and the Caribbean." *American Historical Review* 92 (4): 829–72.

Stevens, R., and A. Elmessiri, eds. 1976. *Israel and South Africa: The Progression of a Relationship*. New York: New World Press.

Sussman, Z. 1974. *Wage Differentials and Equality within the Histadrut: The Impact of Egalitarian Ideology and Arab Labor on Jewish Wages in Palestine* (in Hebrew). Tel Aviv: Massada.

Swedenburg, T. 1988. "The Role of the Palestinian Peasantry in the Great Revolt (1936–1939)." Pp. 169–203 in *Islam, Politics and Social Movements*, ed. E. Burke and I. M. Lapidus. Berkeley: University of California Press.

Tabata, I. B. 1950. *The All African Convention: The Awakening of a People*. Johannesburg: People's Press.

Tamari, S. 1982. "Factionalism and Class Formation in Recent Palestinian History." Pp. 177–202 in Owen 1982.

Taqqu, R. 1980. "Peasants into Workmen: Internal Labor Migration and the Arab Village Community under the Mandate." Pp. 261–85 in *Palestinian Society and Politics*, ed. J. Migdal. Princeton: Princeton University Press.

Thompson, E. P. 1978. *The Poverty of Theory and Other Essays*. London: Merlin Press.

Thompson, L. M. 1985. *The Political Mythology of Apartheid*. New Haven: Yale University Press.

———. 1990. *A History of South Africa*. New Haven: Yale University Press.

Tilly, C. 1984. *Big Structures, Large Processes, Huge Comparisons*. New York: Russell Sage Foundation.

Trapido, S. 1980. "'The Friends of the Natives': Merchants, Peasants and the Political and Ideological Structure of Liberalism in the Cape, 1854–1910." Pp. 247–74 in Marks and Atmore 1980.

———. 1986. "Putting a Plough to the Ground: A History of Tenant Production on the Vereeniging Estates, 1896–1920." Pp. 336–72 in Beinart, Delius, and Trapido 1986.

Turrel, R. 1987. *Capital and Labour on the Kimberley Diamond Fields, 1871–1890*. Cambridge: Cambridge University Press.

Vail, L., ed. 1989. *The Creation of Tribalism in Southern Africa*. Berkeley: University of California Press.

Valkhoff, M. 1972. *New Light on Afrikaans and Malayo-Portuguese*. Louvain: Peeters.

Van den Berghe, P. 1990. "South Africa and Israel as Herrenvolk Democracies." Manuscript.

Van der Ross, R. E. 1986. *The Rise and Demise of Apartheid*. Cape Town: Tafelberg.

Van Onselen, C. 1982. *Studies in the Social and Economic History of the Witwatersrand, 1886–1914.* 2 vols. London: Longman.
———. 1990. "Race and Class in the South African Countryside: Cultural Osmosis and Social Relations in the Sharecropping Economy of the South-western Transvaal, 1900–1950." *American Historical Review* 95(1): 99–123.
Waines, D. 1971. "The Failure of the nationalist Resistance." Pp. 207–35 in *The Transformation of Palestine,* ed. I. Abu-Lughod. Evanston, Ill.: Northwestern University Press.
Walker, C. 1990. "Women and Gender in Southern Africa to 1945: An Overview." Pp. 1–32 in *Women and Gender in Southern Africa to 1945,* ed. C. Walker. Cape Town: David Philip.
Wallerstein, E. 1974. *The Modern World-System.* New York: Academic Press.
Walshe, P. 1970. *The Rise of African Nationalism in South Africa.* Johannesburg: Ad. Donker.
Warren, B. 1980. *Imperialism, the Pioneer of Capitalism.* London: New Left Books.
Waschitz, Y. 1987. "Peasant Migration into Haifa during the Mandate: A Process of Urbanization?" (in Hebrew). *Kathedra* 45:113–30.
Wasserstein, B. 1978.*The British in Palestine: The Mandatory Government and the Arab-Jewish Conflict, 1917–1929.* London: Royal Historical Society.
West, C. 1987. "Race and Social Theory: Towards a Genealogical Materialist Anaylsis." Pp. 74–90 in *The Year Left,* vol. 2, ed. M. Davis, M. Marable, F. Pfeil, and M. Sprinker. London: Verso.
Willan, B. 1984. *Sol Plaatje: South African Nationalist, 1876–1932.* London: Heinemann.
Wilmsen, E. 1989. *Land Filled with Flies: A Political Economy of the Kalahari.* Chicago: University of Chicago Press.
Wilson, M., and L. M. Thompson, eds. 1969. *The Oxford History of South Africa,* vol. 1. New York: Oxford University Press.
Wolf, E. 1982. *Europe and the People without History.* Berkeley: University of California Press.
Wolpe, H. 1972. "Capitalism and Cheap Labour-Power in South Africa: From Segregation to Apartheid." *Economy and Society* 1(4): 425–56.
———. 1986. "Class Concepts, Class Struggle and Racism." Pp. 110–30 in Rex and Mason 1986.
Worden, N. 1985. *Slavery in Early Dutch South Africa.* Cambridge: Cambridge University Press.
Worger, E. 1987. *South Africa's City of Diamonds: Mine Workers and Monopoly Capitalism in Kimberley, 1867–1895.* New Haven: Yale University Press.
Wright, E. 1982. "The Status of the Political in the Concept of Class Structure." *Politics and Society* 11(3): 321–41.
Wright, J. 1986. "Politics, Ideology and the Invention of the 'Nguni.'" Pp. 96–118 in *Resistance and Ideology in Settler Societies,* ed. T. Lodge. Johannesburg: Ravan Press.
Wright, J., and C. Hamilton. 1989. "Traditions and Transformations: The Phongolo-Mzimkhulu Region in the Late Eighteenth and Early Nineteenth Centuries." Pp. 49–82 in Duminy and Guest 1989.
Yaari, A. 1974. *Memoirs of Eretz Israel* (in Hebrew). Ramat Gan: Massada.
Yazbek, M. 1987. "Arab Migration into Haifa, 1933–1948: A Quantitative Analysis of Arab Sources" (in Hebrew). *Kathedra* 45: 131–46.
Younis, M. 1995. "Class, Resources and Resistance: A Comparative Study of National Liberation Movements in South Africa and Palestine, 1910–1993." Ph.D. diss. University of California, Berkeley.
Zeine, Z. 1966. *The Emergence of Arab Nationalism.* Beirut: Khayats.

Index

'Abduh, Muhammed, 75
Abdulhadi, Awni, 145
Abdülhamid II, Sultan, 74, 76
Abdülmecid, Sultan, 76
"aboriginal natives" (Africans), 233, 241
Acre, 30n, 78, 220, 221
African elites, 94, 112, 232, 237
African farmers, 57–58, 60–65, 163, 168–73, 176, 184–86
African identity and nationalism, 2, 110–11, 116–17, 175, 232, 241–42, 244, 247–50, 251–57, 260
African Methodist Episcopal (AME) church, 240
African National Congress (ANC; formerly South African Native National Congress), 2, 244, 249–50, 252–53; Youth League, 254–55
African People's Organization (APO), 237–38, 243, 255
African per capita income, 189
African population statistics, 182, 233–34
Africanism, 254, 260. See also African identity and nationalism
Afrikaans language, 95, 98, 107, 114–15, 232, 257, 266
Afrikaner Volksfront, vii, 2
Afrikaners: *bywoners*, 175–77; differentiation among, 108–10; and nationalism, 232–33, 257–59; *trekboers*, 53–54, 56; trekkers, 109–11
agriculture: agrarian elites, 41–42; agrarian relations, 37–38, 127; cattle farming, 41, 48–49, 50, 53–54; citrus orchards, 33, 40–41, 43, 44, 135, 136, 145–46, 154; commercialization, 28, 29, 33, 40, 41; fruit crops, 33, 40–41, 43, 44, 135, 136; grain and cereal cultivation (Palestine/Israel), 33, 40, 41, 139; intensive farming, 38, 40, 138–39; *kibbutzim*, 132–33; market crops, 41, 54–55, 136, 138–39; mixed vs. one-crop farming, 33, 40–41, 53, 132–33; *moshavim*, 132–33; *moshavot*, 30, 35–46, 89, 127, 131–35, 145–46; Palestine/Israel, 28–44 *passim*, 127–39 *passim*, 144, 155; peasant farming, 57–58, 60–65, 130, 131, 144, 168–73, 176, 184–86; sheep raising/wool production, 61, 62, 107–8; slave labor, 95–96; South Africa, 50–61 *passim*, 95–96, 98, 109, 163, 168–76 *passim*, 184–88 *passim*, 246, 248; subsistence farming, 28, 29, 36–37, 40, 41, 49, 50, 53, 57, 63, 132–33, 136, 160, 184–85, 187–88, 248; sugarcane plantations, 63; surplus extraction, 32, 50; wheat growing (South Africa), 53, 55, 61, 62, 98; wine production, 53, 55, 61, 62, 98
Ahad Ha-Am, 42–43
al-Aqsa mosque, 222, 223
Albany, 55
Aleppo, 29
al-Buraq (the Wailing Wall), 222
al-Haram al-Sharif (Temple Mount), 222
aliyah (immigration wave): first (1880s), 30, 38, 39, 43; second (1904–14), 43; third (1919–23), 147
Alkalai, Yehudah, 87
All African Convention (AAC), 251–53
al-Nadi al-'Arabi (Arab Club), 219
analytical factors, 16–18
Anatolia, 33, 73, 81
Anglo-Boer War (1899–1902), 168, 173, 231, 237, 240, 257
Anglo-Palestine Bank, 88

animism, 98
anti-Semitism, 36, 86, 87, 213–14
apartheid, 2, 9, 10, 168, 188, 258
Arab activists, 81–83, 144–45, 149–53, 202, 218, 219, 228
Arab Agency, 212
Arab Club (al-Nadi al-ʿArabi), 219
Arab Committee for the Defense of the Land, 143
Arab community, 27, 30–34, 142–43, 156–57, 213, 227
Arab Congress, first (Paris, 1913), 76–77. See also Third/Fifth/Seventh Palestine Arab Congress
Arab elites, 42, 72, 73, 220–21, 222
Arab Executive Committee (1921–34), 127, 211, 213, 214, 221 222, 225
Arab Higher Committee (AHC), 150, 152, 225–26, 229
Arab identity and nationalism, 72, 73, 74–77, 82, 202, 204, 215, 222, 224, 271
Arab-Jewish relations, 42, 46, 120, 124–25, 127, 135, 140–47 *passim*, 154–55, 156, 213, 215, 216; Arab Revolt (1936–39), 149–53; Wailing Wall conflict (1928–29), 140, 221, 222–24
Arab National Association (formerly Muslim-Christian Association), 214
Arab peasants (*fellahin*), 37, 43, 130; economic problems of, 136–40; and land tenure system, 32–33; and Land Transfer Ordinance (1920), 127–28; political protest of, 140–45
Arab Revolt (general strike, 1936–39), 144, 149–53, 219, 224, 225
Arab social stratification/internal inequality, 28, 29, 34, 47, 137–40, 155
Arab State of Palestine, 228, 230
Arabic language, 74, 75, 82, 85, 117, 206, 215, 266
Arabic press, 81–82, 147, 215
Arabism, 77, 204. See also Arab identity and nationalism
Arazi-i Mūqaddese (the Holy Land), 78
ʿArif, ʿArif al-, 82
Asefat ha-Nivharim (Delegates' Assembly), 206, 207
Ashkenazi ("German") Jews, 35, 83–86, 89
assimilationism, 234–35, 242, 250, 251
Atlantic Charter, 254
Austro-Hungarian empire, 86
autonomy: and incorporation, 260–61; indigenous cultural, 114, 117, 206, 261; Jewish, 41, 151, 206–7, 210, 226; model, 13–14; in Ottoman Empire, 74; political, 74, 151, 206–7, 210, 226, 231
Ayliff, John, 158

Balfour, Lord, 125, 208
Balfour Declaration (1917), 125, 192, 200–6 *passim*, 210, 212
Bambatha rebellion (Natal, 1906), 235
Bantu, 48, 49–50, 90, 91–92, 114, 115; and the Khoisan, 92, 117, 118
Bantustans, 11
barter, 49, 51
Basle Program (1897), 88
Basotho. See Basutoland
bastaards, 99, 102
Basutoland (Basotho, Lesotho, Sotho), 91–92, 93, 111, 114, 159, 169–70
Beaumont (Natives Land) Commission, 174–75
Bedford, 62
Bedouins, 42, 73, 79, 208
Beirut, 30n
Bengal, 96
Ben-Gurion, David, 45, 133–34, 151, 156, 210, 216, 227
bilad (country), 82
Bilad al-Sham, 27
Bilu society, 39, 88
blacks, 64, 158, 231, 241, 243, 258; black politics in the Cape, 236–38; black servants, 64, 110, 158, 173; free blacks, 97, 99; free people of color, 101, 106, 107
Bloemfontein Convention (1854), 111
Botswana, 90, 111
boundaries, internal/external, 23; Palestine/Israel, 200, 204, 205, 210–13, 214–15; South Africa, 91, 101–3, 236; the two compared, 11, 71, 115–20, 261–62, 271
bride-price (*lobola*), 160, 161
British Kaffraria, 108
"brown Afrikaners" (Cape coloreds), 107
Bulhoeck Massacre (1921), 247
Bushmen (San), 91
Buthelezi, Wellington, 248
bywoners (landless whites), 175–77

Caluza, Reuben, 173
Cape Colony (Cape Province after 1910): and the British, 58, 103–97; and the *bywoners*, 175; Cape liberalism and legal status of blacks, 58–60, 105, 106–7, 112–13, 171; color-blind franchise, 112, 236–37, 238, 243, 244, 251–52; and diamond industry, 163; and Dutch East India Company rule (1652–1795), 51–58, 94, 103; emancipation, 106–7, 112; frontier, 57–58, 98–99, 101–4, 105, 107–8; heterogeneous population growth, 94–96, 233–34; the Khoisan, 51–52, 56–58, 59, 99–100, 105; politics of incorporation, 235–39; settler differentiation, 108–10; slavery, 52–56, 94, 95–96; and the

South Africa Act (1909), 245; tenancy laws, 171; and the trekkers, 109, 110–11
Cape coloreds, 107, 232, 234
Cape Labour Commission, 236
Cape Malays, 107
Cape peninsulars, 48, 91
Cape Province (Cape Colony before 1910), 166, 251–52. *See also* Cape Colony
Cape Town, 53, 55, 90, 95, 97–98, 107, 169, 236
capitalism, 16, 20; Palestine/Israel, 28, 29, 31–32, 33, 34, 47, 155; South Africa, 157–67 *passim*, 170, 174, 177, 180; the two compared, 191
Capitulations Agreements, 84
Catholic church, 77
cattle farming, 41, 48–49, 50, 53–54
Ceylon, 96
Chancellor, John, 138, 141
cheap labor thesis, 20, 44, 68, 177–78, 270
chiefdoms, 91, 100, 106; "artificial" (appointed) chiefs, 113, 245–47; Council of Chiefs created by SANAC, 244; defeat and incorporation, 231, 235; and Frontier Wars treaty system, 107–8; and kinship-tribe relationship, 92–93
children, 57, 59, 64, 72, 182
Chinese labor, 52–53, 164–65
Christianity (*see also individual denominations by name*): and Arab nationalism, 74, 75, 76; and *bastaards*, 102; and civilizing colonialism, 61–62, 112, 242; conversion to, 63, 64, 103, 112; elites, 216, 232; millenarians, 87, 248, 249; missionaries, 59, 61, 62, 63, 103, 105; Muslim-Christian Associations, 203, 204, 213–14, 216; in the Ottoman Empire, 31, 72, 73, 74; and Palestinian-Arab identity, 77, 78, 80, 85, 117, 210, 222; and pan-Africanism, 247–48, 260; and religious separatism, 239–240; and the slaves, 98, 99; and the Xhosa, 108; and Zionism, 81, 82
Churchill, Winston, 127
Churchill White Paper (1922), 207
Ciskei, 62, 185, 245
citrus growing, 33, 40–41, 43, 44, 135, 136, 145–46, 154
clans, 91, 92, 244. *See also* tribalism; *individual clans by name*
class, identity, and state formation, 12–13, 14, 18–26, 268–70
class determinism, 13–14. *See also* Marxism; socialism
class factors vs. national factors, 45, 147–49, 152, 154–55, 156
class structure formation, 12–13, 14, 18–21, 268–70; Palestine/Israel, 45–46, 147–48, 152, 154–55; South Africa, 49–50, 106–7, 157, 167, 177–79, 195, 264, 265–66

classes, lower, 236
clientage, 49, 50, 102
collective farms (*kibbutzim*), 132–33
colonialism, 3–4; colonial expansion, 24–25; colonial strategies, 17 (*see also* settler strategies); indigenous resistance to, 25–26; models of, 4, 61–62; and racism, 13; state/settler/civilizing, 62
color bar (mandatory racial division of labor), 162, 166, 167, 178
colored people, 97, 114, 118, 232–41 *passim*, 254, 255, 258
Coloured Advisory Council, 255, 257
commando system, 101–2, 104
comparative historical research strategies, 6–7
conflict: external/internal (South Africa), 120; Palestine/Israel and South Africa compared, 2–3, 5–6
Conservative Party (South Africa), 2
Convention for a Democratic South Africa (CODESA; 1991), viii
cooperative settlements (*moshavim*), 132–33
cotton growing, 33
Council of Chiefs, 244
craft production, 29, 33–34, 35, 236
Crimean War (1853–56), 30, 78
Crown lands, 171, 172
cultural heterogeneity, 94–96; and national identity, 259–60
cultural interpenetration, 232
cultural syncreticism, 236, 256

Dajani, Kamil al-, 204
Damascus, 29, 77, 78, 202, 205, 221
Darwaza, Izzat, 142
De Beers Consolidated Mines, 159
De Beers Mining, 159
Delegates' Assembly (Asefat ha-Nivharim), 206, 207
democracy, 206, 209–10, 211–13, 226, 227, 228, 254, 258
demographic data sources, 195–98
demographic factors, 18, 78
demographic changes, 233–35
dependency theory, 20, 30, 138, 190
Devey (British consul in Damascus), 76
devşirme recruiting system, 72
diamond mining industry, 158–63, 168–73 *passim*
Diamond News, 159, 161–62
diplomatic protection, 39, 84, 85
division of labor: commercial, 28; by gender and age, 50; racial (color bar), 60, 162, 166, 167, 178
Drakenstein, 55
Druze, 38–39, 77
Durban, 169, 256

Dutch East India Company, 48, 51–58, 68–69; and the Khoisan, 51–52, 90–91, 94, 99–100, 122; political authority, 95–96, 100–1
Dutch East Indies, 96
Dutch language, 95, 96, 97, 98, 99, 102, 257
Dutch Reformed church, 107, 110, 236

East Africa, 52, 96
East Indies, 52, 54, 94, 116
Eastern and Western cultures, meeting of, 28–29
economic factors: and the British mandate in Palestine, 144, 145, 154, 156–57; and Cape liberalism, 58–60; and the Khoisan, 48–49, 50, 52; and the mining industry, 158, 160; and the Ottoman Empire, 28–36 passim, 47, 80; Palestine/Israel and South Africa compared, 30–31, 34, 62–63, 67, 68; "reserve" economy, 177; and underdevelopment, 20
effendi (landlord), 138
Effendi, Ahmed, 237
Egypt, 28, 30, 31, 33, 79, 200
elites: agrarian, 41–42; Christian, 216, 232; colored, 112, 237; indigenous intellectuals, 94, 232; Ottoman, 72, 73
emancipation, 98, 106–7
endogamy, 97, 110
English language, 114, 115, 206, 249, 260, 266
entrepreneurs, 31, 33, 35, 61, 105
epidemics, 52, 96
Eretz Israel (Land of Israel), 83, 133, 156, 206, 210
Ethiopian church movement, 239–40, 247, 249, 260
ethnicity, politicized, 232, 249–50
Eurafricans, 106
Eurasians, 96, 116
European consuls, 39, 84, 85
European expansionism, 18, 19, 20, 24–25
"European or white," 233–34
exclusionary dynamics: Palestine/Israel, 34, 46, 47, 86, 89–90, 119, 124–25, 127, 149, 230, 263–65; South Africa, 10, 99, 113–14, 167–68, 174, 236, 250; the two compared, 9–11, 15, 18, 24, 71, 123, 157, 193, 194, 195, 231–32, 259, 260

Fagan Commission (1948), 188, 265–66
Farah, Saleem, 195
fatwas (religious edicts), 143, 224
Faysal, Emir, 202, 205
fellahin/fellaheen. See Arab peasants
Fifth Palestine Arab Congress (1922), 127
Filastin (Palestine), 78, 210
Filastin (newspaper), 82
Fingoland, 166
Fort Beaufort, 171

France, 75, 202, 205
franchise, 112, 113, 114, 236–37, 238, 243, 250–53, 258
free blacks, 97, 99
freeburghers (independent settlers), 52, 95
Freedom Alliance, 11
Freeman, Rev. J. J., 61
French, Lewis, 131
French Huguenots, 95
French Report (1931), 138
"Frontier Tribes," 58, 59, 106
Frontier Wars, 235; third (1799–1802), 103; fourth (1811–12), 105; sixth (1834–35), 107; seventh (1840s), 108
fruit crops, 33, 40–41, 43, 44, 135, 136

Gagiano, J., 1
Garvey, Marcus, 249, 254
Garveyite pan-Africanism, 247, 248, 249
Gaza, 82
Gaza Strip, 1, 2, 10, 200
Gcalekland, 166
gender and age divisions, 49, 50, 160, 161
General Federation of Jewish Workers (Histadrut), 133, 156, 206
General Moslem Conference, 222–23
Georgian Jews, 84
German Templars, 39
Ghori, Emil, 142
Glenelg, Lord, 60
Godley Committee (1922), 182–83
gold mining industry, 158, 163–65; and indigenous rural population, 168–73 passim; and labor, 165–68
Gonaqua, 102
Graaf-Reinet, 55, 57, 58
Graetz, Heinrich, 87
Grahamstown, 236
grain and cereal cultivation: Palestine/Israel, 33, 40, 41, 139; South Africa, 53, 55, 61, 62, 98
Granott, A., 37–38, 129
Great Britain: Anglo-Boer War (1899–1902), 168, 173, 231, 237, 240, 257; Balfour Declaration (1917)/Mandate for Palestine (1922–48), 125–26, 156–57, 192, 195, 199–212; vs. communal land tenure, 138, 139, 171; and the Ottoman Empire, 75; and the radical al-Husayni, 219; role in Palestine/Israel and South Africa compared, 125–26, 201, 262; and South Africa, 58, 103–4, 163, 233–34, 235, 237, 243–44, 257; Sykes-Picot agreements (1916) with France, 202; and World War II, 154
Great Trek, 109, 110–11
Greek Orthodox church, 77, 80
Greek religious communities, 73
Griqua, 107, 110, 111, 160

Griqualand East and West, 114; East Griqualand, 166; Griqualand West, 159, 162
group identities, exclusive/inclusive, 199
Gulf crisis (1990–91), 204

Haderah, 135
haham bashi (chief rabbi), 83, 84
Haifa, 82, 143, 147, 150, 210, 214
Haifa *al-Karmil*, 81–82
Haining, Gen. Robert, 152
"half-castes," 114, 241
halukkah (money distribution) system, 35, 84
Hashemites, 204–5
Hasidim, 84
Hatt-i Hümayun (1856), 73
Hatt-i Şerif (1839), 73
Ha-Vaad ha-Leumi (the National Executive), 206
Haycraft Commission (1921), 127, 141, 214
Hebrew Boys School (Jaffa), 89
Hebrew language, 85, 87, 89, 206, 207, 210
Hebrew press, 85, 147, 207
Hebron, 34, 79, 83, 141, 222
Hertzog, Barry, 183, 187, 251, 257, 258
heterogeneity, 94–96; and national identity, 259–60
Hexter, Maurice, 140
Hibat Zion, 39
Highveld republics (Orange Free State and Transvaal), 235, 257
Hirsch, Shmuel, 38
Histadrut (General Federation of Jewish Workers), 133, 156, 206
history and theory, 267–68
historical outcomes, 9–10
historical processes, 12–13, 14, 18–26
historical research strategies, comparative, 6–7
Hofmeyr, J. H., 252
Holy Land, 78, 86–87, 203
homestead (communal landholding), 49, 50, 92
Hope Simpson, John, 131–32, 137
Hope Simpson report (1930), 131, 197
Hottentot Code (1809), 59
Hottentot Corps, 103
Hottentot Proclamation (1809), 105
"Hottentots" (Khoisan/Khoikhoi), 57, 91, 99, 102, 103, 104, 106
Husayni, Amin al-, 142–43, 152, 218–20, 222–24, 226, 227, 229
Husayni, Jamal al-, 196, 210, 228
Husayni, M. K. al-, 212, 213
hut tax, 170, 171

identity formation, 12–13, 14, 21–24; boundaries, internal/external, 11, 23, 71, 91, 101–3, 115, 117–18, 119, 200, 204, 205, 210–13, 214–15, 236, 261–62, 271; group identities, exclusive/inclusive, 199; Palestine/Israel, 74–75, 77–81, 89–90, 117–18, 119, 200, 201, 204, 210–13, 214–15, 224, 261; Palestine/Israel and South Africa compared, 11, 71–72, 115–20, 199, 205, 222, 225, 230, 261–62, 271, 273; and religion, 117, 272; South Africa, 91, 99, 101–3, 107, 115, 179, 180, 232–33, 236, 248–50, 253–57, 258, 264, 266; ideological imperatives, 193; ideology, and class interests, 269–70
ifraz (division of communal land into private plots), 140
Ikwan al-Qassam (Qassam movement), 144–45
iltizam (tax-farming) system, 32
Imvo Zabantsundu (Xhosa newspaper "Native Opinion"), 238
inboekselings (indentured African children), 64
inclusionary dynamics, 99, 112–13
incorporation, dynamics of, 2, 9–11, 15, 24, 26, 265–67; and assimilation, 96, 234–35, 242–43, 250, 251; and autonomy, 260–61; and exclusion, 157; and indigenous people, 112–13; and the Khoisan, 52, 56–57, 99–100; Palestine/Israel, 34, 157; Palestine/Israel and South Africa compared, 260–61; and segregation, 167–68, 174, 236, 250–53, 262; South Africa, 52, 56–57, 60–61, 72, 95–103 *passim*, 112–13, 120, 167–68, 174, 181–89, 194, 195, 231–43 *passim*, 247–62 *passim*
India, 230
Indians, 63, 96, 232, 234, 243, 254, 255
indigenous capacities (Palestine/Isreal and South Africa compared), 16–17, 66–68, 190, 217, 259–61, 274–75; for identity formation, 117–18, 205, 225, 235; for land and labor relations, 189, 191; for leadership, 260; for nationalism/national identity, 230, 255, 259–60; for political resistance, 20–21, 25–26, 46, 221, 222, 230, 235, 255; for state formation, 121–23, 189, 192, 213
indigenous elites, 25, 94, 232, 238–39, 260
indigenous languages, 114–15, 266
indigenous people: and cultural autonomy, 114, 117, 206, 261; incorporation of, 2, 9–11, 15, 24, 26, 52, 56–57, 60–61, 99–100, 112–13; legal status of (Palestine/Israel), 206, 209–13, 226, 227, 228; legal status of (South Africa), 95–102 *passim*, 106–7, 111, 112, 231, 232, 243, 251–62 *passim*; marginalization of, 209, 232, 255; moral economy of, 142, 247; racial identity among, 102–3, 110–11, 116–17; and settlers relationship, 3, 102, 110, 111, 205, 209, 260–61
indirect rule policy (Shepstone system), 113, 242, 245, 253

Indonesia, 230
Industrial and Commercial Union (ICU), 248, 249
industrial development: Palestine/Israel, 33, 41, 154, 155; South Africa, 157, 170, 181–86, 187, 250
intellectual elites, 216, 232
internal differentiation, 108–10, 191–92
internal inequalities, 28, 29, 34, 49–50
interpenetration: cultural, 232; political, 215–17
Intifadah (late 1980s), 204
Iraq, 210, 219
Iraqi activists, 202
Islam, 72, 73; in Cape Town, 97, 98, 107, 236, 237; Islamic modernism (reform), 75–76; Islamic nationalism, 212, 215, 222–25
Islamjilik (Islamism), 74
Israelite movement, 247
Istanbul, 27, 78
Istiqlal Party, 214
Izwi Labantu ("Voice of the People"; Xhosa newspaper), 238, 243

Jabal Nablus, 136
Jabavu, J. T., 238
Jabotinsky, Ze'ev, 209
Jaffa, 82, 85, 89, 147, 150, 152, 213
Jaffa *Filastin*, 82
Javanese convict labor, 52–53
Jenin, 152
Jerusalem, 30n, 34, 78–79, 82, 83, 85, 141, 147, 213, 219, 220–21
Jewish activists, 42, 45–46, 125, 134–35, 216, 228
Jewish Agency for Palestine, 128, 132, 140, 212
Jewish argricultural communities (*moshavot*), 30, 35–46, 89, 127, 131–35, 145–46; "Arabization" of, 41–42; collectives and cooperatives (*moshavim, kibbutzim*), 132–33; intra-Jewish protests, 145–46; and the Palestine Jewish Colonization Association, 131–32; Petah Tiqvah (1878), 35, 38, 41, 135; subsidization of, 35, 37, 40, 41; treatment of Arab workers, 42–43
Jewish-Arab relations. *See* Arab-Jewish relations
Jewish collective farms (*kibbutzim*), 132–33
Jewish Colonial Trust, 88
Jewish community, 34–36, 83–86, 88–89, 146, 206, 207, 209, 226; and Arab community, 88–89, 156–57, 213, 227; fragmentation of, 84; organizations (*kolelim*), 35, 84
Jewish cooperative settlements (*moshavim*), 132–33
Jewish employment of Arabs, 41–42, 135–36
Jewish financial institutions, 37, 88

Jewish identity, 85, 86, 88, 89, 204, 207, 223, 261, 271; and Palestinian-Arab identity, 118–19
Jewish immigration and settlement. *See* Zionist movement
Jewish labor, 39–40, 41, 43–47, 127, 132–35, 145–46, 147–49; and Arab labor, 44, 135, 145–47; and Histadrut (General Federation of Jewish Workers), 133, 156, 206; and socialism-nationalism tension, 45–46, 86, 147, 148
Jewish leaders and Palestinian-Arab leaders compared, 229
Jewish National Fund (JNF), 37, 38, 46, 88, 131, 132
Jewish National Home, 126–127, 133, 145, 200, 201, 203, 205, 206, 210, 212, 226
Jewish philanthropists, 35, 37, 40, 41
Jewish press, 85, 147, 207
Jews: Ashkenazi ("German"), 35, 83–86, 89; Hasidim/Prushim, 84; oriental, 207; Orthodox, 89, 207; under Ottoman rule, 30, 31, 34, 39, 73, 77, 78, 80–89; Sephardi ("Spanish"), 35, 83–86
jihad (holy war), 224
Johannesburg, 163, 165, 167, 177, 182, 236, 256
Johnson-Crosbie Commission (1930), 136, 137–38, 196–97
Jordan, 27, 200
Judaism, 83, 87, 203, 207
Judea, 42
Judeo-Spanish (Ladino), 35n

Kaffraria (Ciskei), 62
Kalischer, Zwi Hirsch, 87
Kalvaryski, Haim, 216
Kat River Settlement (1829), 61, 107
Kgatla, 111
Khoikhoi ("Hottentots"), 48, 91, 102
Khoisan ("Hottentots"), 48–61 *passim*, 91–108 *passim*; and the Bantu, 92, 117, 118; *bastaards*, 99, 102; divided into Khoikhoi and San, 48; and the Dutch East India Company, 51–52, 99–100; economic development, 48–49, 67, 68; and the Hottentot Code (1809), 59; and the Hottentot Proclamation (1809), 105; and the Kat River Settlement, 61; language, 96, 115; military service (Hottentot Corps), 102, 103; and the Xhosa, 103, 108
kholwa (African Christian converts), 63
kibbutzim (Jewish collective farms), 132–33
Kimberley, 158–63 *passim*, 169, 233, 236
Kimberley Central, 159
kinship principle, 91, 92, 160–61

Knesset Israel (the Jewish community): Asefat ha-Nivharim (Delegates' Assembly), 206, 207; Ha-Vaad ha-Leumi (National Executive), 206
kolelim (Jewish community organizations), 35, 84
Kora, 160
Koran (Qur'an), 75, 224
Korana, 91
Kūdūs-i Şerif, 78

labor: black and white, 177–80; "civilized"/"uncivilized," 187; compounds, 162, 166; "free," 58–60; indentured, 57, 59, 63, 105, 164–65; Jewish and Arab, 44, 135, 145–47; market, Palestine/Israel and South Africa compared, 15, 34, 49, 155; migrant, 63, 64, 143–44, 154, 159–61, 167–68, 181–86, 187, 249; relations, Palestine/Israel and South Africa compared, 146–47, 156–57, 162, 189; skilled, unskilled, 144, 177, 179, 236; slave, 52–56; tax, 171; wage-, 41–43, 44, 60, 64, 154, 173, 176–77, 185; wages, 52, 64, 162, 166; women's labor power, 49, 161
labor (Palestine/Israel), 39–47, 132–36, 143–49, 156; Arab employment in Jewish-owned economy, 135–36; Jewish and Arab in the 1930s, 145–47; Jewish, 43–47, 133–35, 147–49; the labor issue, 39–43; labor market, 34, 47, 144, 148; migrant Arab, 143–44; recruitment, 154; relations, 146–47, 154; self, 39–40, 41, 46, 132–33; unemployment, 134, 146; unions, 133, 156
labor (South Africa), 52–60, 159–68, 177–80; black and white, 167–68, 177–80, 184; black servants, 64, 158, 173; and Cape liberalism, 58–60; "civilized"/"uncivilized" labor policy, 187; coercion, 53, 54, 56, 59, 64, 158, 160; control, 161–63, 165–66, 181; and emancipation, 106–7; female, 49, 161; "free", 58–60; in gold- and diamond-mining industries compared, 163–64; indentured, 57, 59, 63, 105, 164–65; industrial, 181, 187; and the labor market, 58–60, 106, 173–75, 247; migrant, 63, 64, 159–61, 165–68, 181–86, 187, 249; recruitment of, 64, 165–66; skilled/unskilled, 177, 179, 236; slave, 52–56; and unemployment, 183; unions, 248; wage-, 60, 64, 173, 176–77, 185
Labor Zionist movement, 147
Ladino (Judeo-Spanish), 35n, 85
land: communal (*see* land tenure); "free," 53–54n, 268; speculation, 63, 109, 128, 138, 141, 172; untransferable (*waqf*), 143, 218
land, access to: Palestine/Israel and South Africa compared, 191; South Africa, 49, 50, 169, 170, 247, 248
land, dispossession of: Palestine/Israel, 38–39, 43, 46, 128–31, 141; Palestine/Israel and South Africa compared, 170; rural white dispossession, 175–177
Land, Group Areas, and Population Registration Acts, 10
land and labor relations: and class structure formation, 18–21; Palestine/Israel, 28, 37, 127, 149; South Africa, 64–65
Land of Israel. *See* Eretz Israel
land ownership, private: Palestine/Israel, 32, 40–41, 47; South Africa, 171, 172
land tenure: African homestead, 49, 50, 92; Arab *mushaʿ*, 28, 32–33, 47, 136, 138, 139
Land Transfer Ordinance (1920/1921), 127–28
land transfers: Palestine/Israel, 37–38, 43, 127–28, 130, 138, 141–42, 143, 150; Palestine/Israel and South Africa compared, 189
"landless," defined, 128–29
landlords, absentee: Palestine/Israel, 33, 37, 128, 138, 141–42; South Africa, 63, 169, 172, 173
languages, 266, 272; Afrikaans, 95, 98, 107, 114–15, 232, 257, 266; Arabic, 74, 75, 82, 85, 117, 206, 215, 266; Dutch, 95, 96, 97, 98, 99, 102, 257; English, 114, 115, 206, 249, 260, 266; Hebrew, 85, 87, 89, 206, 207, 210; indigenous, 91–92, 114, 115, 266; Ladino (Judeo-Spanish), 35n, 85; lingua franca/pidgin, 95, 96; official, 72, 114–15, 206; Persian, 72, 85; of slaves, 72, 115; Turkish, 72, 76, Yiddish, 35n, 84, 86
League of Nations, 125, 200, 201, 205
Lebanon, 27, 29, 33, 74, 77, 78, 81, 202
legal status (of indigenous people): Palestine/Israel, 206, 209–10, 211–13, 226, 227, 228; South Africa, 95–102 *passim*, 106–7, 111–12, 231, 232, 243, 251–58 *passim*, 262
Lembede, Anton, 254
Lesotho. *See* Basutoland
Levant, 86
Levantines, 31
liberalism, 58–60, 62, 105, 106, 183–84, 188, 231, 232, 262; and African political organizations, 250, 251–52, 258–59
lingua franca, 95
living standard, 40, 44
lobola (bride-price), 160
Low Grade Mines Commission, 179
Lower Galilee, 42, 79
Lowther (British ambassador to Instanbul), 76
Luthern church, 110
Lydenburg Republic, 111

Madagascar, 52, 96, 98
majlisiyyun (council supporters), 220–21
majority rule/democracy, 206, 209–10, 211–13, 226, 227, 228, 254, 258
Malagasy, 96
Malan, D. F., 252, 258
malaria, 40
Malawi, 166
Malay language, 95
Mandate for Palestine (1922–48), 125–26, 156–57, 199–200, 201, 205–6, 207, 209
Mansour, George, 147
manufactured goods, 29, 33, 34
marabi (urban poor) culture, 256
market relations: Palestine/Israel, 28–35 *passim*, 41, 47, 128, 136; South Africa, 49, 54–55
marriage: endogamous, 97, 110; mixed, 95, 99, 116–17, 236
Marxism, 13–14, 19
Masters and Servants laws, 106–7, 166, 186
material imperatives, 193–94
Matthews, Z. K., 253
Mejlis-i Idare (Administrative Council), 79
merchants and traders, 31, 33, 35, 61, 105, 109
Metulla settlement, 38–39
Mfecane Wars, 62, 104, 106, 113
Mfengu, 62, 106, 122
Middle East, 27–29
Middle East peace conference (Madrid, 1991), viii
Mikveh Israel agricultural school, 38
military, the: Palestine/Israel, 72, 153; South Africa, 101–2, 103, 104, 231, 235; the two compared, 122–23
Mill, J. S., 6
millenarians, 87, 248, 249
millet (religious minority communities) system, 73, 80, 83, 117, 206, 218
Mills Commission (1926), 184
Milner, Lord, 237
Mines and Works Act (1911), 167
mining industry, 157–72 *passim*, 176, 182, 233, 234, 249; diamonds, 158–59; gold, 163–65; labor control, 161–63, 165–66; labor recruitment, 165–66; migrant labor, 159–61, 166–68
miri (state-owned land), 32
mission lands, 171, 175
missionaries, 59, 61, 62, 63, 103, 105
mixed farming, 33, 40–41, 53, 132–33
modernization theory, 19–20, 28–29, 30, 62, 138, 190
moral economy concept, 142, 247
moshavim (Jewish cooperative settlements), 132–33
moshavot. *See* Jewish agricultural communities
Moshweshwe, 111

Mozambique, 96, 159, 160, 165, 166
Mpondo. *See* Pondoland
muʿaridun (oppositionists), 220–21
multazim (tax-farmer), 32
mushaʿ (communal Arab land), 32, 136, 138–40, 143
Muslim-Christian Associations, 203, 204, 213–14, 216
Muslim National Association (1921), 216
Muslims, 31, 72–85 *passim*, 152, 202–3; in Cape Town, 97, 98, 107, 236, 237; and Christians, 75–82 *passim*, 117, 210, 214; and *waqf* (untransferable) land, 143, 218
Muslumanlik (pan-Islam), 74

Nablus, 30n, 77, 78, 79, 82, 151, 152, 213, 214, 219, 220, 222
Nahdah movement, 75
Namaqua, 91
Namibia, 90
Nashashibi family, 221
Nassar, Najib, 46, 82
Natal, 60, 62, 63–65, 104, 111, 112, 171–72, 186, 232, 234, 235, 238, 243; demographics, 234; Mfecane Wars, 62, 106; Shepstone system of indirect rule, 113, 242, 245, 253
National Executive (Ha-Vaad ha-Leumi), 206
national factor vs. class factor, 45, 147–49, 152, 154–55, 156
national identity: vs. internal diversity, 259–60; Palestine/Israel and South Africa compared, 230, 255, 259–60; and religion, 117, 272. *See also* nationalism and national identity
National Liberation League (Palestine/Israel), 156
National Liberation League (South Africa), 255
National Party (South Africa), 188, 199, 252, 257, 258, 259
national "self-determination," 2, 175, 254
nationalism and national identity, 2, 16, 22–23; European, 80, 87, 116, 119; Palestine/Israel and South Africa compared, 255; Turkish, 73, 74. *See also* African identity and nationalism; Afrikaners, nationalism; Arab identity and nationalism; Jewish identity; national identity; Palestine/Israel; Palestinian-Arab identity and nationalism
Native Administration Act (1927), 245, 250
Native Bills, 250–53
Native Economic Commission (1932), 187
native locations, 170, 173
"Native Question," 25, 234–35, 240–42
native reserves, 160, 170, 173, 175, 181, 184, 187, 188, 231, 245, 247, 251
Native Service and Contract Act (1932), 186
Native Taxation and Development Act (1925), 186

"natives": defined, 168, 180, 186, 213, 241, 250; "de-tribalized," 108, 232, 251, 255
Natives Land Act (1913), 173–75, 186, 250
Natives Land and Trust Act (1936), 186
Natives Representative Council (NRC), 251, 252–53, 258
Natives Urban Areas Act (1923; amended 1927, 1937), 183, 250
Nazism, 145, 254
Ndebele, 111
Negev desert, 79
Netherlands, 94
newspapers: African, 232; Arabic, 81–82, 147, 215; *Diamond News*, 159, 161–62; Hebrew, 85, 147, 207; Xhosa, 238
Ngawane, 93
Nguni, 50, 91, 92, 93
Nimr, Ihsan al-, 221
nizami (civil) courts, 80
nomads, 42, 73, 79, 208; Khoikhoi, 48, 91, 102; *trekboers*, 53–54
Non-European Unity Movement, 255
North Africans, 84

Oays, 79
olive oil production, 33, 34
oorlams (African Christian servants), 64
Orange Free State, 60, 64, 104, 111, 169, 234, 245–53; anti-tenancy/sharecropping legislation, 170–71, 173–74, 186; incorporation and exclusion, 113–14, 235
Osmanli (Ottoman urban elite), 73
Osmanlilik (Ottomanism), 73
Ottoman Empire (1517–1917), 27–39 *passim*, 72–84 *passim*; Administrative Council and civil courts, 79–80; Arab community in Palestine, 30–34; and Arab Congress (Paris, 1913), 76–77; and Arab nationalism, 74–77, 116; elites, 72, 73; Egyptian rule (1831–40), 30, 79; and Europe, 28, 29, 31, 32, 33, 75, 84; and Islamic modernism (reform), 75–76; and Jerusalem, 78–79, 220–21; and the Jewish community in Palestine, 34–36, 83–86; land law (1858), 32, 47; and the Metullah settlement and Druze tenants, 38–39; *millet* system, 73, 206, 218; Osman dynasty, 72; and Palestine, 27, 30–34, 218, 220; and Sephardi Jews, 83, 84; Tanzimat reforms, 27–28, 30, 31, 73–74, 76, 77, 79, 120; and World War I, 200; and the Young Turks, 74, 76

Palestina/Palestina (EI), 210
Palestine: as the Holy Land, 78, 86–87, 203; and the Ottoman Empire, 27, 30–34; the State of Palestine, 2, 200; and Syria, 202–3, 204–5

Palestine Communist Party (PCP), 156
Palestine Foundation Fund, 132
Palestine/Israel (*see also* Palestine/Israel and South Africa compared): Arab community, 30–34; Arab labor, 135–36; Arab nationalism, 74–77; Arab rejection of Zionism, 81–83, 210-13; Arab Revolt (1936–39), 144, 149–53, 219, 224–27; Balfour Declaration/Mandate for Palestine, 125–26, 192, 199–212 *passim*; demographic data sources, 195–98; demographic factors, 18, 78; elections of 1923, 212; exclusionary dynamics, 263–65; "green line," 10; Israel-South Africa relations, 5; Jerusalem, 30n, 34, 78–79, 82, 83, 85, 141, 147, 213, 219, 220–21; Jewish and Arab labor in the 1930s, 145–47; Jewish community, 34–36, 83–86, 88–89; Jewish intevention in Palestinian-Arab politics, 215–17; Jewish labor, 43–47, 133–35, 147–49; June 1967 War, 204; labor issue, 39–43; land question, 38–39, 126–31, 136–40; languages, official, 206; mutual recognition agreement (1993), 1, 2; national identities, 117–18, 199, 200; and Ottoman Empire, 27–36, 72–74; Palestine, 27, 30–34, 202–5; Palestinian-Arab identity formation, 77–81, 210–13; Palestinian-Arab political institutions, 213–15; Palestinian inner conflict, 220–21; partition (1948), 2, 47, 199, 200, 227–30; political unrest in the 1930s, 140–45, 224–27; population statistics, 230; Public Works Department, 143; State of Israel established (1948), 9, 199; Supreme Muslim Council, 217–20; travel safety, 79, 85; Wailing Wall conflict (1928–29), 222–24; War of 1947–48, 18, 200; West Bank and Gaza Strip (occupied territories), 1, 2, 10, 200; World War I and aftermath, 46–47, 126, 199; World War II and aftermath, 10–11, 153–55; Zionist movement, 36–38, 86–88, 131–33

Palestine/Israel and South Africa compared: the British role, 125–26, 201, 262; conflict, 2–3, 5–6, 154–56; economic development, 30–31, 34, 62–63, 67, 68; group indentities, exclusive/inclusive, 199; identity formation, 72, 90, 115–20; ideological imperatives, 193; "inclusive expansion," 99; incorporation and assimilation, 96; incorporation and autonomy, 260–61; incorporationism, exclusive/inclusive, 157, 231–32; indigenous capacities, 66–68, 117–18, 121–23, 190–92, 259–61; indigenous elites and settler authority, 239; indigenous languages, 266; indigenous leadership, 260; indigenous people and settler relationship, 3, 102, 205, 209, 260–61; internal differentiation, 191–92;

labor market, 15, 34, 49, 155; labor relations, 146–47, 156–57, 162, 189; land and capital, access to, 191; land transfers, 189; material imperatives, 193–94; national identity, 230, 255, 259–60; nationalism, 255; separatist politics, 258; settler strategies, 68–70, 118–23, 193–95, 261–62; state, access to, 121–23, 189, 192, 213; state, role of, 192, 194–95, 201; state formation, 90, 94, 104, 120–23; world-historical context, 65–66, 116–17, 120–21
Palestine Jewish Colonization Association (PICA), 37, 41, 131–32, 216
Palestine Land Development Company, 37, 88, 132
Palestine Liberation Organization, 1, 204
Palestine National Council, 2
Palestine Royal Commission (1937), 151, 225–27, 230
Palestinian activists, 202, 203, 204, 218
Palestinian-Arab identity and nationalism, 46, 71–89 *passim*, 127, 210–17, 229; Arab nationalism under Ottoman rule, 72, 74–77; and the Balfour Declaration, 199–200, 201, 210, 212; and the elites, 221, 222; Palestinian-Arab identity under Ottoman rule, 77–81, 82–83, 85, 89, 117; and the Qassam movement, 144–45, 224; and Syria, 78, 202–3, 204–5, 210, 219, 224; and the Wailing Wall conflict, 222–24; and Zionism, 208–9
Palestinian-Arab leaders compared with Jewish leaders, 229
Palestinian-Arab refugee population, 200
Palestinian Arab Workers Association, 150
pan-Africanism, 244, 247–48, 249. *See also* African identity and nationalism
Paris Peace Conference (1919), 126
Pass Laws, 10, 56, 59, 105, 159, 162, 170, 171, 182, 238
Passfield White Paper (1930), 141, 197
pastoralism, 42, 73, 79, 208; Khoikhoi, 48, 91, 102; *trekboers*, 53–54
Pedi, 111
people of color, 97, 112, 114, 118, 232–41, 254, 255, 258; free, 97, 99, 101, 106, 107
periodization, 8–9
peripheralization process, 29, 33, 34
Persian language, 72, 85
Petah Tiqvah, 35, 38, 41
philanthropic organizations (Jewish), 35, 37, 40, 41
Philip, Rev. Dr. J., 59
Philips, Lionel, 180
pidgin, 96
pim, J. H., 167–68
Plaatje, Sol, 174, 185, 249

plantations, 63, 96
pluralist perspective, 13, 14
political autonomy: Ottoman Empire, 74; Palestine/Israel, 151, 210, 206–7, 226; South Africa, 231
political equality, 206, 235, 237–38, 253–55
political factionalism, 72, 93, 225, 226, 229
political goals, Arab and Jewish, 215–16
political interpenetration, 215–17
political legitimacy, 23, 72, 180
political mobilization, Arabs and Jews, 217, 224
political organizations: African, 232, 237, 253–55, 258–59; Palestinian-Arab, 213–15
political power and racial identity, 167–68
political separatism: Palestine/Israel, 156–57; South Africa, 246–47; the two compared, 258. *See also* religious separatism
politicized ethnicity, 232, 249–50
politics: and ideology, 148–49; national vs. local/regional, 253
Pondoland (Mpondo), 50, 114, 166, 171, 185, 235
precolonial society, 27n, 48–49
profit motive, 134
proletarianization, 64, 143, 154, 155, 176–77, 257–58
property ownership: livestock and clientage (the Khoisan), 49; land privatization (Ottoman Empire), 32, 47
Protection of Cultivators Ordinance (1929), 130
Protestants and the Holy Land, 86–87
Pro-Wailing Wall Committee, 223
Prushim, 84

Qassam, Sheikh 'Izz al-Din al-, 144, 152
Qassam movement (Ikwan al-Qassan), 144–45, 152, 224
qawmiyya (pan-Arab nationalism), 202
Qawuqji, Fawzi al-, 224

race, 13, 23–24; categories, 64, 91, 104, 106, 107, 114, 162, 233, 241; color-blind policy (Cape Colony), 106–7; division of labor by (color bars), 60, 162, 166, 167, 178; exclusionary policy (Orange Free State and Transvaal), 113–14; and legal status in South Africa, 95–102 *passim*, 106–7, 111–12, 231, 232, 243, 251–58 *passim*, 262; relations (South Africa), 95, 97–99
racial identity: not developed among Africans, 102–3, 110–11, 116–17; and political power, 167–68; and state formation, 272–73; of white workers and capitalists, 180
racial institutions and the role of capitalism, 162, 164, 166, 173–75
racial logic, 168, 177
racial politics, 261–62

"racial purity," 97, 99, 110
racial segregation, 98, 233; and incorporation, 181–83, 236, 250–53, 262; labor compounds, 162, 166–68; and liberals, 231, 258; native reserves, 173–75, 184, 186; "native villages," 182–83; total segregation impossible, 184, 259; and tribalism, 246, 251
racism, 59, 97, 98, 254; and colonialism, 13
Rand, the. *See* Witwatersrand
Rand Revolt (1922), 180, 193
Rehovot, 135
religion: African, 98, 239–40, 247, 249, 260; and identity, 117, 272; and incorporation, 266; and indigenous capacities, 259, 260, 261
religious conversion: to Christianity, 63, 64, 103; to Islam, 72, 97
religious separatism, 239–40, 247, 260. *See also* political separatism
representative government/democracy, 206, 209–10, 213, 226, 227, 228, 254, 258
Rhodes, Cecil, 243
Rida, Rashid, 75, 81, 219
rishon le-tzion (Sephardi rabbi), 84
Rishon le-Tzion settlement, 41, 42
Rothschild, Baron Edmund de, 40, 41
Rothschild, Lord James, 200
Rubusana, W., 238
Ruppin, A., 40, 41, 42, 69, 133, 196
rural political movements: Palestine/Israel, 144–45, 150–53; South Africa, 247–50
Russian Empire, 36, 40, 74, 86, 87

Safed, 34, 83, 222
Sakakini, Khalil al-, 80
Samuel, Herbert, 208, 214
San, 48, 90–91, 102
San Remo Conference (1920), 205
sanjaks (districts), 30n, 78, 82, 220
Sauer Report (1947), 188
Schreiner, W. P., 244
Sekwati, 111
"self-determination," 2, 175, 254
self-labor, 39–40, 41, 46, 132–33
Seme, Pixley, 244, 250
Separate Amenities Act abolished (1990), 10
separatist politics: Palestine/Israel, 156–57; South Africa, 246–47; the two compared, 258. *See also* religious separatism
Sephardi ("Spanish") Jews, 35, 83–86
"servants" (Africans), 162
service sector, 33, 42
settler strategies, 17, 25–26, 46, 62; and identity formation, 118–20; and ideological imperatives, 193; and material imperatives, 193–94; Palestine/Israel and South Africa compared, 68–70, 118–20, 123, 193–95, 261–62; and role of the state, 194–95; and state formation, 123
settlers (*see also* settler strategies): British, 109; Cape, 105; differentiation, 108–10; freeburghers, 52–53; on frontier, 57–58, 107–8; internal/external boundaries, 261–62; in Natal, 60, 63; origins of, 30, 86–88, 95; Palestine/Israel, 30, 42–43, 86–88; Palestine/Israel and South Africa compared, 102, 205, 209, 260–62; relationship with indigenous people, 42–43, 61, 63–64, 65, 101–3, 107–8, 110, 111, 205, 209, 260–61; sense of identity, 99, 109–10; South Africa, 52–53, 57–65 *passim*, 95, 99–111 *passim*; in Transvaal and Orange Free State, 60, 104; *trekboers*, 53–54; trekkers, 110–11; and Zulus, 63–64
Seventh Palestine Arab Congress (1928), 221
sharecropping: clientage, 40, 49; Palestine/Israel, 136–37; South Africa, 49, 50, 169, 173, 185–86
Shaw Commission, 130, 131, 141, 195, 196, 214, 223
sheep raising/wool production, 61, 62, 107–8
Shepstone, Theophilus, 113, 242
Shepstone system of indirect rule, 113, 242, 245, 253
Shukayri, As'ad al-, 221
Sidon, 78
silk production, 33
slave languages, 72, 115
slavery, 52–56, 60, 61, 94–100 *passim*, 105–12 *passim*; diversity of slaves, 52, 96, 97, 98; and the Dutch East India Company, 52–53, 95–96, 100; and emancipation, 55, 60, 98, 106–7, 112; "family mode of control" vs. plantation system, 55, 96
smallpox, 52, 96
Smilansky, Moshe, 38
Smit Commission of Inquiry, 187–88
Smith, Harry, 108
Smooha, S., 6
Smuts, Jan, 183, 188, 252, 257
soap manufacture, 33, 34
social differentiation, 34, 47, 137–40, 155
social stratification, 155, 191–92
socialism: and class determinism, 13–14; vs. nationalism, 45–46, 86, 147–48
Society for the Protection of Moslem Holy Places, 223
Somerset, 55
Sotho. *See* Basutoland
Sotho-Tswana, 92
sources, primary/secondary, 7–8
South Africa (*see also* Palestine/Israel and South Africa compared): African farmers, 57–58; African nationalism, 253–55; Afrikaner na-

Index | 305

tionalism, 257–59; Anglo-Boer War (1899–1902), 168, 173, 231, 237, 240, 257; black and white labor, 177–80; black politics, 236–38; British takeover, 103–4; Cape Colony, 104–6; Cape liberalism, 58–60; Cape politics, 236–39; Cape settlement, 51, 94; Cape Town, 97–98; constitution of 1983, 10; constitution (interim) of 1993, 1, 10; cultural heterogeneity, 94–96, 233–34; demographic changes, 233–35; diamond-mining industry, 159–63; Dutch East India Company, 100–1; (of 1948), 258; (of 1994), 1, 10; emancipation, 106–7; and European state system (17th–18th centuries), 120–21; frontier and Frontier Wars, 98–108 *passim*; gold-mining industry, 163–66; Great Trek, 110–11; and incorporationism, 99–100, 112–14, 181–89, 235, 250–53; indigenous peoples, 48–50, 51–52, 56–57, 90–94, 111; indigenous resistance, 247–48; and Israel, 5; land dispossession (blacks), 168–73, (whites), 175–77; languages, 114–15; migrant labor system, 159–63, 165–68; Natives Land Act (1913), 173–75; Parliament, 10, 243–44, 251, 252; post-1948 period, 10–11; religious separatism, 239–40; rural-urban relations, 248–50; segregation, 250–53; settlers, 60–65, 108–10, 111; slavery, 52–56; tribalism, 242–43, 245–47; Union (1910), 48, 157, 173, 199, 231, 235, 241, 243–44; and United States, 6, 95, 96, 97, 248, 256; urban life, 255–57
South Africa Act (1909), 245
South African Native Affairs Commission (SANAC), 240–46
South African Native Congress (1902), 238–39, 242
South African Native National Congress (1912; renamed African National Congress, 1925), 244
South India, 96
Southeast Asia, 94
split labor market theory, 44–45, 147–48, 177, 178–79, 270
"squatting" 169, 170, 171, 173, 175, 186, 188
Stanley, Lord, 113
state, access to (Palestine/Israel and South Africa compared), 121–23, 189, 192, 213
state, role of (Palestine/Israel and South Africa compared), 192, 194–95, 201, 262
state formation, 12–13, 14, 24–26; indigenous capacities (Palestine/Israel and South Africa compared), 94, 121–23; Palestine/Israel, 147–48, 206, 264–65; Palestine/Israel and South Africa compared, 71, 90, 120–23, 272–73; settler strategies (Palestine/Israel and South Africa compared), 123; South Africa, 99–100, 104, 110, 111, 167–68, 177–80, 232, 245–47, 250–53, 266–67; world historical context (Palestine/Israel and South Africa compared), 120–21, 273–74
Steenkamp, Anna, 109
Stellenbosch, 55
Stockenstrom, Andries, 58, 106, 107
subsidization, foreign, 35, 37, 40, 41
subsistence farming; Palestine/Israel, 28, 29, 40, 41, 136; South Africa, 49, 50, 57, 63, 132–33, 160, 184–85, 187–88, 248
sugarcane plantations, 63
Sunduq al- Umma (National Trust), 143
Supreme Muslim Council, 143, 214, 218–21, 222, 225
surplus extraction, 32, 50
Swazi/Swaziland, 50, 93, 111, 114
Swellendam, 55
Sykes-Picot agreements (1916), 202
symbols, use of, 224–25, 240, 247, 260–61
Syria, 27, 29, 33, 74–82 *passim*; and France, 202, 205; General Syrian Congress (1919), 202–3; and Lebanon, 77, 81; and Palestine, 202–5, 210, 219, 224

Tanzimat reforms, 27–28, 30, 31, 73–74, 76, 77, 79, 120
taxes: hut tax, 170, 171; tithe (ʿushr) tax, 136
Tel Aviv, 134
Temple Mount (al-Haram al-Sharif), 222
tenants: *bywoners*, 175–77; dispossession of, 38–39, 43, 46, 128–31, 141; Druze/Metullah settlement, 38–39; Jewish, 40–41; Palestine/Israel, 38–46 *passim*, 128–31, 141; and sharecropping, 49, 50, 136–37, 169, 173, 185–86; South Africa, 49, 50, 62, 64, 169–77 *passim*, 185–86, 246, 247, 248
textile production, 29, 34
Thembu/Thembuland, 102, 166
Third Palestine Arab Congress (Haifa, 1920), 210, 213
Tiberias, 34, 83
tithe tax (ʿushr), 136
Tlhaping, 160
trade relations, 28, 62, 136; the Khoisan, 49, 50, 51; Ottoman Palestine, 30–34 *passim*
trade routes, 28, 29, 34, 50
traditions (Eastern/Western), 28–29
Trans-Jordan, 210
Transkei, 62, 163, 171, 175, 184, 185, 232, 237, 245, 246, 248, 252, 253, 255
Transvaal, 60, 104, 111, 159–68 *passim*, 234, 235, 238, 245, 253; migrant labor from, 159, 160; racial exclusion by, 113–14; sharecropping in, 185–86; and the South African Native Affairs Commission (SANAC), 172, 173; Stallard Commission, 182, 183

trekboers, 53–54, 56
trekkers, 110–11
tribalism, 23, 91, 113, 171, 242–50 *passim*, 254, 258; "creation of," 232; and kinship, 92–93
Trichard, Louis, 110
Tsonga, 93
Tswana, 93, 102, 114, 163, 169
Turks/Turkey, 43, 72–77 *passim*, 108; Turkish language, 72, 73, 76; Young Turks, 74, 76, 81

Uitenhage, 55
underdeveloped countries, 20
unemployment, 134, 146, 183
Union Native Council, 251
United Nations, 156, 157, 230, 264
Universal Negro Improvement Association (UNIA), 249
Upper Galilee, 42
urbanization: and African identity, 232, 250, 255–57; of Arab migrants, 143–44, 155; demographics, 182, 233; elites, 32, 46, 73, 204, 220–21; living conditions, 187–88; *marabi* culture, 256; Palestine/Israel, 29, 32, 33, 35, 46, 73, 134, 143–44, 145, 146, 151, 155, 204, 216, 220–21; segregation of indigenous population, 167–68, 182–83; South Africa, 167–68, 176–77, 181, 182–83, 187–88, 232, 233, 248–50, 251, 255–57; urban-rural political movements, 248–50; of white migrants, 176–77, 233
ʿ*ushr* (tithe) tax, 136

vagrancy laws, 60, 172
Valley of Esdraelon, 129, 195, 196
van der Riet, R. J., 57
van Imhoff, Baron, 54
van Ryneveld, W. S., 54, 57
Venda, 114, 235
Verwoerd, H. F., 258
vezirs (highest Ottoman administrators), 72
Victoria, 108
Victoria East, 185
vilayet (province), 30n
voting rights, 112, 113, 114, 236–37, 238, 243, 250–53, 258

Wadi Hawarith, 131
Wadi Sarar, 153
wage-labor: Palestine/Israel, 41–43, 44, 154; South Africa, 52, 60, 64, 162, 166, 173, 176–77, 185
Wailing Wall conflict (1928–29), 140, 221, 222–24
waqf (untransferable) land, 143, 218
War of 1947–48, 18, 200
watan (patrimony), 82

wataniyya (patriotic nationalism), 202, 210
Watson, Major General H. D., 127
West Africa, 52
West Bank, 1, 2, 10, 200
west Jerusalem, 35
wheat growing, 53, 55, 61, 62, 98
white rule, 167–68, 181, 182–83, 189, 194, 231–43 *passim*; and Afrikaner nationalism, 257–59; and ethnic divisions among whites, 258; and the Native Bills, 250–53; and the South African Native Affairs Commission (SANAC), 242–43
wine industry, 33, 41, 53, 55, 98
Witwatersrand (the Rand), 158, 163–69 *passim*, 176, 233, 245, 256
Witwatersrand Native Labour Association (WNLA), 166
women, 49, 161, 182
workers' collectives (*kibbutzim*), 132–33
world-historical context, 16, 65–66, 273–74; and identity formation (Palestine/Israel and South Africa compared), 116–17; and state formation (Palestine/Israel and South Africa compared), 120–21
world-system perspective, 20, 29, 30, 34, 47, 62, 190
World War I, 33, 46, 126, 199
World War II, 144, 153–55, 227, 254
World Zionist Congress, 88
World Zionist Organization, 46, 88, 125, 200, 205, 206, 207–8, 216

Xhosa, 49–50, 61, 92, 112, 122; frontier treaties, 107–8; frontier wars, 103, 104; identity boundaries, 102–3; language, 92, 238; newspapers, 238
Xuma, Dr. Alfred, 255

Yaman, 79
Yazur, 38
Yellin, D., 80
Yemenites, 84
Yeniçeri corps, 72
Yiddish language, 35n, 84, 86
Young Turks (Committee of Union and Progress), 74, 76, 81
Youth League (of the African National Congress), 254–55

Zikhron Yaakov, 41, 42
Zimbabwe, 166
Zionist Christian church, 240
Zionist movement: *aliyah* (immigration waves), 30, 38, 39, 43, 147; and anti-Zionism, 29, 46, 127, 144, 152; Arab response to, 81–83, 145, 203, 210–13; Basle Program of first World Zionist Congress, 88; and the British,

125–26, 200–201; and diplomatic protection of Jews, 39, 84, 85; exclusionary dynamics of, 71, 89; founded in 1897, 86; and the Hashemite family, 204–5; and the Haycraft Commission, 127; intervention in Arab politics, 215–17; labor policy, 42, 45–46, 127, 132, 133–35, 147–48, 206; land policy, 128, 129, 138, 139; and the Metullah settlement and Druze tenants, 38–39; and the *moshavot*, 35–46; and representative government/majority rule, 227; and the rise of Zionism, 86–88; settlement strategies, 119, 131–33

Zionist Organization. *See* World Zionist Organization

Zionist Revisionist Organization, 223

Zulus/Zulu kingdom/Zululand, 50, 63–64, 93, 111, 112, 114, 172, 184, 232, 235, 246, 256

Zuurveld, 57, 102, 105

UNIVERSITY PRESS OF NEW ENGLAND

publishes books under its own imprint and is the publisher for Brandeis University Press, Dartmouth College, Middlebury College Press, University of New Hampshire, University of Rhode Island, Tufts University, University of Vermont, Wesleyan University Press, and Salzburg Seminar.

ABOUT THE AUTHOR

Ran Greenstein is the author of several articles on the politics of race, class, and ethnicity in South Africa and Israel/Palestine. He currently works in the Education Policy Unit at the University of Witwatersrand in Johannesburg.

LIBRARY OF CONGRESS CATALOGING-IN-PUBLICATION DATA

Greenstein, Ran.
    Genealogies of conflict : class, identity, and state in
Palestine/Israel and South Africa / Ran Greenstein.
    p.   cm.
Includes bibliographical references and index.
ISBN 0–8195–5288–7
1. Jewish-Arab relations. 2. Israel-Arab conflicts. 3. Zionism—
History. 4. Israel—Politics and government. 5. Social classes—
Israel. 6. South Africa—Race relations. 7. Apartheid. 8. South
Africa—Politics and government. 9. Social classes—South Africa.
I. Title.
DS119.7.G6595   1995
305.8′00968—dc20   95–13355

Genealogies of Conflict

**MARY AND JOHN GRAY LIBRARY
LAMAR UNIVERSITY**

Purchased

with the

Student Library Use Fee

DISCARDED